Communications in Computer and Information Science 2051

Rationale

The CCIS series is devoted to the publication of proceedings of computer science conferences. Its aim is to efficiently disseminate original research results in informatics in printed and electronic form. While the focus is on publication of peer-reviewed full papers presenting mature work, inclusion of reviewed short papers reporting on work in progress is welcome, too. Besides globally relevant meetings with internationally representative program committees guaranteeing a strict peer-reviewing and paper selection process, conferences run by societies or of high regional or national relevance are also considered for publication.

Topics

The topical scope of CCIS spans the entire spectrum of informatics ranging from foundational topics in the theory of computing to information and communications science and technology and a broad variety of interdisciplinary application fields.

Information for Volume Editors and Authors

Publication in CCIS is free of charge. No royalties are paid, however, we offer registered conference participants temporary free access to the online version of the conference proceedings on SpringerLink (http://link.springer.com) by means of an http referrer from the conference website and/or a number of complimentary printed copies, as specified in the official acceptance email of the event.

CCIS proceedings can be published in time for distribution at conferences or as post-proceedings, and delivered in the form of printed books and/or electronically as USBs and/or e-content licenses for accessing proceedings at SpringerLink. Furthermore, CCIS proceedings are included in the CCIS electronic book series hosted in the SpringerLink digital library at http://link.springer.com/bookseries/7899. Conferences publishing in CCIS are allowed to use Online Conference Service (OCS) for managing the whole proceedings lifecycle (from submission and reviewing to preparing for publication) free of charge.

Publication process

The language of publication is exclusively English. Authors publishing in CCIS have to sign the Springer CCIS copyright transfer form, however, they are free to use their material published in CCIS for substantially changed, more elaborate subsequent publications elsewhere. For the preparation of the camera-ready papers/files, authors have to strictly adhere to the Springer CCIS Authors' Instructions and are strongly encouraged to use the CCIS LaTeX style files or templates.

Abstracting/Indexing

CCIS is abstracted/indexed in DBLP, Google Scholar, EI-Compendex, Mathematical Reviews, SCImago, Scopus. CCIS volumes are also submitted for the inclusion in ISI Proceedings.

How to start

To start the evaluation of your proposal for inclusion in the CCIS series, please send an e-mail to ccis@springer.com.

Miguel Botto-Tobar ·
Marcelo Zambrano Vizuete ·
Sergio Montes León · Pablo Torres-Carrión ·
Benjamin Durakovic
Editors

International Conference on Applied Technologies

5th International Conference on Applied Technologies, ICAT 2023
Samborondon, Ecuador, November 22–24, 2023
Revised Selected Papers, Part III

Editors
Miguel Botto-Tobar
Eindhoven University of Technology
Eindhoven, The Netherlands

Marcelo Zambrano Vizuete
Universidad Técnica del Norte
Ibarra, Ecuador

Sergio Montes León
Universidad Rey Juan Carlos
Madrid, Spain

Pablo Torres-Carrión
Universidad Técnica Particular de Loja
Loja, Ecuador

Benjamin Durakovic ⓘD
International University of Sarajevo
Sarajevo, Bosnia and Herzegovina

ISSN 1865-0929   ISSN 1865-0937 (electronic)
Communications in Computer and Information Science
ISBN 978-3-031-58949-2   ISBN 978-3-031-58950-8 (eBook)
https://doi.org/10.1007/978-3-031-58950-8

This Springer imprint is published by the registered company Springer Nature Switzerland AG
The registered company address is: Gewerbestrasse 11, 6330 Cham, Switzerland

If disposing of this product, please recycle the paper.

Preface

The 5th International Conference on Applied Technologies (ICAT) was held on the main campus of the Universidad Espíritu Santo, in Samborondón, Ecuador during November 22 until 24, 2023, and it was organized jointly by Universidad Espíritu Santo in collaboration with GDEON. The ICAT series aims to bring together top researchers and practitioners working in different domains in the field of computer science to exchange their expertise and to discuss the perspectives of development and collaboration. The content of this volume is related to the following subjects:

- Intelligent Systems

ICAT 2023 received 250 submissions written in English by 435 authors coming from 12 different countries. All these papers were double-blind peer-reviewed by the ICAT 2023 Program Committee consisting of 183 high-quality researchers. To assure a high-quality and thoughtful review process, we assigned each paper at least three reviewers. Based on the peer reviews, 66 full papers were accepted, resulting in a 26% acceptance rate, which was within our goal of less than 40%.

We would like to express our sincere gratitude to the invited speakers for their inspirational talks, to the authors for submitting their work to this conference, and to the reviewers for sharing their experience during the selection process.

November 2023

Miguel Botto-Tobar
Marcelo Zambrano Vizuete
Sergio Montes León
Pablo Torres-Carrión
Benjamin Durakovic

Organization

General Chair

Miguel Botto-Tobar   Eindhoven University of Technology,
The Netherlands

Program Committee Chairs

Miguel Botto-Tobar   Eindhoven University of Technology,
The Netherlands
Marcelo Zambrano Vizuete   Universidad Técnica del Norte, Ecuador
Sergio Montes León   Universidad Rey Juan Carlos, Spain
Pablo Torres-Carrión   Universidad Técnica Particular de Loja, Ecuador
Benjamin Durakovic   International University of Sarajevo,
Bosnia and Herzegovina

Organizing Chairs

Miguel Botto-Tobar   Eindhoven University of Technology,
The Netherlands
Marcelo Zambrano Vizuete   Universidad Técnica del Norte, Ecuador
Sergio Montes León   Universidad Rey Juan Carlos, Spain
Pablo Torres-Carrión   Universidad Técnica Particular de Loja, Ecuador
Benjamin Durakovic   International University of Sarajevo,
Bosnia and Herzegovina

Steering Committee

Miguel Botto-Tobar   Eindhoven University of Technology,
The Netherlands
Angela Díaz Cadena   Universitat de València, Spain

Program Committee

A. Bonci	Marche Polytechnic University, Italy
Ahmed Lateef Khalaf	Al-Mamoun University College, Iraq
Aiko Yamashita	Oslo Metropolitan University, Norway
Alejandro Donaire	Queensland University of Technology, Australia
Alejandro Ramos Nolazco	Instituto Tecnólogico y de Estudios Superiores Monterrey, Mexico
Alex Cazañas	University of Queensland, Australia
Alex Santamaria Philco	Universitat Politècnica de València, Spain
Allan Avendaño Sudario	Escuela Superior Politécnica del Litoral, Ecuador
Alexandra González Eras	Universidad Politécnica de Madrid, Spain
Ana Núñez Ávila	Universitat Politècnica de València, Spain
Ana Zambrano	Escuela Politécnica Nacional, Ecuador
Andres Carrera Rivera	University of Melbourne, Australia
Andres Cueva Costales	University of Melbourne, Australia
Andrés Robles Durazno	Edinburgh Napier University, UK
Andrés Vargas Gonzalez	Syracuse University, USA
Angel Cuenca Ortega	Universitat Politècnica de València, Spain
Ángela Díaz Cadena	Universitat de València, Spain
Angelo Trotta	University of Bologna, Italy
Antonio Gómez Exposito	University of Sevilla, Spain
Aras Can Onal	TOBB University of Economics and Technology, Turkey
Arian Bahrami	University of Tehran, Iran
Benoît Macq	Université Catholique de Louvain, Belgium
Benjamin Durakovic	International University of Sarajevo, Bosnia and Herzegovina
Bernhard Hitpass	Universidad Federico Santa María, Chile
Bin Lin	Università della Svizzera italiana, Switzerland
Carlos Saavedra	Escuela Superior Politécnica del Litoral, Ecuador
Catriona Kennedy	University of Manchester, UK
César Ayabaca Sarria	Escuela Politécnica Nacional, Ecuador
Cesar Azurdia Meza	University of Chile, Chile
Christian León Paliz	Université de Neuchâtel, Switzerland
Chrysovalantou Ziogou	Chemical Process and Energy Resources Institute, Greece
Cristian Zambrano Vega	Universidad de Málaga, Spain/Universidad Técnica Estatal de Quevedo, Ecuador
Cristiano Premebida	University of Coimbra, Portugal
Daniel Magües Martinez	Universidad Autónoma de Madrid, Spain
Danilo Jaramillo Hurtado	Universidad Politécnica de Madrid, Spain

Darío Piccirilli	Universidad Nacional de La Plata, Argentina
Darsana Josyula	Bowie State University, USA
David Benavides Cuevas	Universidad de Sevilla, Spain
David Blanes	Universitat Politècnica de València, Spain
David Ojeda	Universidad Técnica del Norte, Ecuador
David Rivera Espín	University of Melbourne, Australia
Denis Efimov	Inria, France
Diego Barragán Guerrero	Universidad Técnica Particular de Loja, Ecuador
Dimitris Chrysostomou	Aalborg University, Denmark
Domingo Biel	Universitat Politècnica de Catalunya, Spain
Doris Macías Mendoza	Universitat Politècnica de València, Spain
Edwin Rivas	Universidad Distrital de Colombia, Colombia
Ehsan Arabi	University of Michigan, USA
Emanuele Frontoni	Università Politecnica delle Marche, Italy
Emil Pricop	Petroleum-Gas University of Ploiesti, Romania
Erick Cuenca	Université Catholique de Louvain, Belgium
Fabian Calero	University of Waterloo, Canada
Fan Yang	Tsinghua University, China
Fariza Nasaruddin	University of Malaya, Malaysia
Felipe Ebert	Universidade Federal de Pernambuco, Brazil
Fernanda Molina Miranda	Universidad Politécnica de Madrid, Spain
Fernando Almeida	University of Campinas, Brazil
Fernando Flores Pulgar	Université de Lyon, France
Firas Raheem	University of Technology, Iraq
Francisco Calvente	Universitat Rovira i Virgili, Spain
Francisco Obando	Universidad del Cauca, Colombia
Freddy Flores Bahamonde	Universidad Técnica Federico Santa María, Chile
Gabriel Barros Gavilanes	INP Toulouse, France
Gabriel López Fonseca	Sheffield Hallam University, UK
Gema Rodriguez-Perez	LibreSoft/Universidad Rey Juan Carlos, Spain
Ginger Saltos Bernal	Escuela Superior Politécnica del Litoral, Ecuador
Giovanni Pau	Kore University of Enna, Italy
Guilherme Avelino	Universidade Federal do Piauí, Brazil
Guilherme Pereira	Universidade Federal de Minas Gerais, Brazil
Guillermo Pizarro Vásquez	Universidad Politécnica de Madrid, Spain
Gustavo Andrade Miranda	Universidad Politécnica de Madrid, Spain
Hernán Montes León	Universidad Rey Juan Carlos, Spain
Ibraheem Kasim	University of Baghdad, Iraq
Ilya Afanasyev	Innopolis University, Russia
Israel Pineda Arias	Chonbuk National University, South Korea
Jaime Meza	Universiteit van Fribourg, Switzerland
Janneth Chicaiza Espinosa	Universidad Técnica Particular de Loja, Ecuador

Javier Gonzalez-Huerta	Blekinge Institute of Technology, Sweden
Javier Monroy	University of Malaga, Spain
Javier Sebastian	University of Oviedo, Spain
Jawad K. Ali	University of Technology, Iraq
Jefferson Ribadeneira Ramírez	Escuela Superior Politécnica de Chimborazo, Ecuador
Jerwin Prabu	BRS, India
Jong Hyuk Park	Korea Institute of Science and Technology, South Korea
Jorge Eterovic	Universidad Nacional de La Matanza, Argentina
Jorge Gómez Gómez	Universidad de Córdoba, Colombia
Juan Corrales	Institut Universitaire de France et SIGMA Clermont, France
Juan Romero Arguello	University of Manchester, UK
Julián Andrés Galindo	Université Grenoble Alpes, France
Julian Galindo	Inria, France
Julio Albuja Sánchez	James Cook University, Australia
Kelly Garces	Universidad de Los Andes, Colombia
Kester Quist-Aphetsi	Center for Research, Information, Technology and Advanced Computing, Ghana
Korkut Bekiroglu	SUNY Polytechnic Institute, USA
Kunde Yang	Northwestern Polytechnic University, China
Lina Ochoa	CWI, The Netherlands
Lohana Lema Moreta	Universidad de Espíritu Santo, Ecuador
Lorena Guachi Guachi	Yachay Tech, Ecuador
Lorena Montoya Freire	Aalto University, Finland
Luis Galárraga	Inria, France
Luis Martinez	Universitat Rovira i Virgili, Spain
Luis Urquiza-Aguiar	Escuela Politécnica Nacional, Ecuador
Manuel Sucunuta	Universidad Técnica Particular de Loja, Ecuador
Marcela Ruiz	Utrecht University, The Netherlands
Marcelo Zambrano Vizuete	Universidad Técnica del Norte, Ecuador
María José Escalante Guevara	University of Michigan, USA
María Reátegui Rojas	University of Quebec, Canada
Mariela Tapia-Leon	University of Guayaquil, Ecuador
Marija Seder	University of Zagreb, Croatia
Marisa Daniela Panizzi	Universidad Tecnológica Nacional – Regional Buenos Aires, Argentina
Marius Giergiel	KRiM AGH, Poland
Markus Schuckert	Hong Kong Polytechnic University, China
Matus Pleva	Technical University of Kosice, Slovakia
Mauricio Verano Merino	Technische Universiteit Eindhoven, The Netherlands

Miguel Botto-Tobar	Eindhoven University of Technology, The Netherlands
Miguel Gonzalez Cagigal	Universidad de Sevilla, Spain
Miguel Murillo	Universidad Autónoma de Baja California, Mexico
Miguel Zuñiga Prieto	Universidad de Cuenca, Ecuador
Mohamed Kamel	Military Technical College, Egypt
Mohammad Al-Mashhadani	Al-Maarif University College, Iraq
Mohammad Amin	Illinois Institute of Technology, USA
Muneeb Ul Hassan	Swinburne University of Technology, Australia
Nam Yang	Technische Universiteit Eindhoven, The Netherlands
Nathalie Mitton	Inria, France
Nayeth Solórzano Alcívar	Escuela Superior Politécnica del Litoral, Ecuador/Griffith University, Australia
Noor Zaman	King Faisal University, Saudi Arabia
Omar S. Gómez	Escuela Superior Politécnica del Chimborazo, Ecuador
Óscar León Granizo	Universidad de Guayaquil, Ecuador
Oswaldo Lopez Santos	Universidad de Ibagué, Colombia
Pablo Lupera	Escuela Politécnica Nacional, Ecuador
Pablo Ordoñez Ordoñez	Universidad Politécnica de Madrid, Spain
Pablo Palacios	Universidad de Chile, Chile
Pablo Torres-Carrión	Universidad Técnica Particular de Loja, Ecuador
Patricia Ludeña González	Universidad Técnica Particular de Loja, Ecuador
Paulo Chiliguano	Queen Mary University of London, UK
Pedro Neto	University of Coimbra, Portugal
Praveen Damacharla	Purdue University Northwest, USA
Priscila Cedillo	Universidad de Cuenca, Ecuador
Radu-Emil Precup	Politehnica University of Timisoara, Romania
Ramin Yousefi	Islamic Azad University, Iran
René Guamán Quinche	Universidad de los Paises Vascos, Spain
Ricardo Martins	University of Coimbra, Portugal
Richard Ramirez Anormaliza	Universitat Politècnica de Catalunya, Spain
Richard Rivera	IMDEA Software Institute, Spain
Richard Stern	Carnegie Mellon University, USA
Rijo Jackson Tom	SRM University, India
Roberto Murphy	University of Colorado Denver, USA
Roberto Sabatini	RMIT University, Australia
Rodolfo Alfredo Bertone	Universidad Nacional de La Plata, Argentina
Rodrigo Barba	Universidad Técnica Particular de Loja, Ecuador
Rodrigo Saraguro Bravo	Universitat Politècnica de València, Spain

Ronnie Guerra	Pontificia Universidad Católica del Perú, Peru
Ruben Rumipamba-Zambrano	Universitat Politècnica de Catalanya, Spain
Saeed Rafee Nekoo	Universidad de Sevilla, Spain
Saleh Mobayen	University of Zanjan, Iran
Samiha Fadloun	Université de Montpellier, France
Sergio Montes León	Universidad Rey Juan Carlos, Spain
Stefanos Gritzalis	University of the Aegean, Greece
Syed Manzoor Qasim	King Abdulaziz City for Science and Technology, Saudi Arabia
Tenreiro Machado	Polytechnic of Porto, Portugal
Thomas Sjögren	Swedish Defence Research Agency (FOI), Sweden
Tiago Curi	Federal University of Santa Catarina, Brazil
Tony T. Luo	A*STAR, Singapore
Trung Duong	Queen's University Belfast, UK
Vanessa Jurado Vite	Universidad Politécnica Salesiana, Ecuador
Waldo Orellana	Universitat de València, Spain
Washington Velasquez Vargas	Universidad Politécnica de Madrid, Spain
Wayne Staats	Sandia National Labs, USA
Willian Zamora	Universidad Laíca Eloy Alfaro de Manabí, Ecuador
Yessenia Cabrera Maldonado	University of Cuenca, Ecuador
Yerferson Torres Berru	Universidad de Salamanca, Spain/Instituto Tecnológico Loja, Ecuador
Zhanyu Ma	Beijing University of Posts and Telecommunications, China

Organizing Institutions

Sponsoring Institutions

Collaborators

Contents – Part III

Z AT for Engineering Applications

Communications

Analysis of the Influence of Driving Style on Energy Consumption of a Hybrid Vehicle in High-Altitude Environments During Standardized Driving Cycles

Juan Molina Campoverde$^{(\boxtimes)}$, Néstor Rivera, Andrés Juarez, and Pedro Mendoza

Automotive Mechanical Engineering: GIIT Transport Engineering Research Group,
Salesian Polytechnic University, Cuenca, Ecuador
jmolinac@ups.edu.ec

Abstract. This article analyzes the influence of driving maneuvers on a hybrid vehicle's energy consumption and emission rates. Employing data collected through OBD II and GPS technologies, route variables are meticulously documented following the EURO 6 standard, primarily for assessing pollutant levels within a Real Driving Emissions (RDE) cycle, facilitated by the use of a Portable Emissions Measurement System (PEMS). Throughout the study, we identify key variables that exhibit the strongest correlation with fuel consumption, including Longitudinal acceleration (Ax), Torque, Accelerator pedal open position (APS), and engine speed (RPM). These variables enable us to discern the Internal Combustion Engine's (ICE) operational conditions and devise a model that accurately estimates the rate of fuel consumption change concerning vehicle acceleration. Furthermore, we classify driving modes as ecological, RDE, or aggressive based on the State of Charge (SOC) of the vehicle. Our findings reveal that the type of driving conducted on the road and city altitude directly influence fuel consumption and emission factors (CO_2, CO, HC, and NO_x). Notably, we observe a remarkable 31.36% reduction in fuel consumption during ecological driving compared to aggressive driving.

Keywords: driving modes · emission factors · GPS · OBD · PEMS · RDE

1 Introduction

The increase in environmental pollution, generated by motor vehicles, is due to the growing number of cars that circulate in cities, which shows an air quality decrease [1]. From the implementation of the OBD protocol, the variables of the vehicle sensors are acquired [2]. The pollutant emissions obtained by tests carried out on chassis dynamometers reveal considerable differences concerning those carried out on the road [3–5]. Hybrid car models show greater acceptance in the market due to the exchange of energy sources used for their operation, they show a reduction in gasoline consumption as well as a reduction in polluting emissions compared to combustion vehicles [6]. Hybrid

M. Botto-Tobar et al. (Eds.): ICAT 2023, CCIS 2051, pp. 3–14, 2024.
https://doi.org/10.1007/978-3-031-58950-8_1

vehicle demand and the growing interest by users in low-consumption cars, evidences the increase in this type of car in the Ecuadorian vehicle fleet according to AEADE, having sold 5,827 hybrid cars in Ecuador from January to October of 2022 [7]. Variables such as the driver's decision regarding maneuvers or driving routes directly influence the performance and fuel economy of vehicles [8]. The Regulation Commission of the European Union implements approval requirements through the RDE (Real Driving Emissions) method for the evaluation of pollutants in real driving conditions. The quantification of vehicle emissions obtained on the road collects information from driving maneuvers in addition to the emission factors emitted on the route such as CO, HC, CO_2, and NO_x [9]. The pollutants obtained in the tests carried out in real conditions apply the PEMS (Portable Emissions Measurement Systems) method from portable devices for the measurement of absolute emissions (mass per unit of distance) on the road [10]. A methodology to determine driving techniques through the implementation of driving modes such as sport, eco, and normal driving modes [11].

Driving cycles allow real driving patterns to be represented on the road by applying car dynamics equations to obtain the behavior of emissions on the road [12]. The behavior of the thermodynamic cycle of combustion engines is influenced by the effect of altitude as observed in cities such as Cuenca, Ecuador located at an altitude of 2550 m above sea level (m.a.s.l) [13], showing a reduction in engine power, an increase in fuel consumption and polluting emissions [14].

2   Materials and Methods

2.1   Experimental Overwiev

Driving maneuver data from vehicle sensors can be acquired through the OBD II port [15], Real driving data collection is done by portable devices (PEMS) without increasing the mass of the vehicle [16]. A methodology based on fuzzy logic characterizes the efficient driving behavior from input and output variables, where the output is estimated between a range of 0 to 1 based on the driving efficiency through data acquired by telemetry [17]. [18] presents a mobile application based on fuzzy logic capable of estimating driving efficiency in order to obtain the specific fuel consumption in the model with an accuracy of 85%. [19] presents a driving mode estimation model based on machine learning using PID signals obtained by OBD-II, the model is capable of providing information on engine performance, and fuel efficiency to classify driving mode into three categories: economical, normal, and sporty. [20] performs an estimate of NO_x and CO emissions through the recording of OBD-II data and Machine Learning architectures based on regression models in real driving conditions. [21] implements a low computational cost model for calculating CO_2 emissions in hybrid vehicles by applying several artificial intelligence algorithms (robust regression, vector support machines, neural networks) with the data from the sensors acquired in the vehicle such as MAP, APS, VSS, and IAT.

This study exposes real numbers of the energy consumption of a sedan-type hybrid vehicle under specific conditions in Cuenca-Ecuador, located at an altitude of 2550 m.a.s.l [22], The objective is based on evaluating the acquired data on energy consumption based on the type of driving, in urban, rural and highway roads with the application of standardized driving cycles, in addition to the implementation of eco-logical, normal, and aggressive driving modes, in order to obtain data in real-time and create a model to analyze energy consumption in the hybrid vehicle. After reviewing the state of the art proposed by several authors, the following methodological process is proposed for this study (Fig. 1).

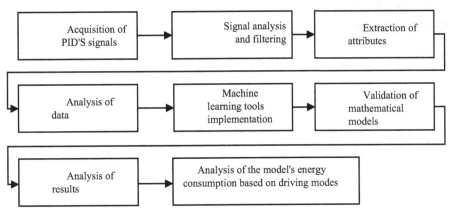

Fig. 1. Methodology

2.2 Acquisition of Real Driving Data

Vehicle data for the sedan-type Toyota Corolla HV XEI 1.8 hybrid vehicle was obtained using the "Freematics ONE+" device through the OBD II connector, allowing real-time storage of ECU (Electronic Control Unit) sensor variables on a micro-SD. The variables recorded during the journey are detailed in Table 1. Furthermore, the Freematics ONE+ data logger, equipped with GPS capabilities and a sampling rate of 15.15 Hz, efficiently captured and stored the relevant road data on a micro-SD card. These tests were conducted in Cuenca, Ecuador, at an altitude of 2550 m, with an average ambient temperature of 17 °C and no rainfall during the tests.

2.3 Portable Emission Measurement System (PEMS)

Pollutant emissions are obtained using the portable gas analyzer (Kane Exhaust Gas Analyzer EGA4/5). The analyzer operates using the method of non-dispersive infrared measurement of gases (NDRI), which is based on infrared spectroscopy. This method allows for the identification of the concentrations of carbon dioxide exhaust emissions (CO_2 [%]), carbon monoxide (CO [%]), unburned hydrocarbons (HC [ppm]), and nitrous oxides (NOx [ppm]) in real driving conditions of the vehicle, as shown in Fig. 2. The portable gas analyzer provides accurate measurements of these pollutants, enabling a comprehensive analysis of the vehicle's emissions during the test cycle.

To analyze vehicle handling maneuvers in real driving conditions, the Real Driving Emission (RDE) method [5] is applied through routes that comply with the aforementioned protocol. Data was obtained from the route in Cuenca, Ecuador, encompassing

Table 1. On route variables registration

Variables	Nomenclature	Units	Range
Vehicle Speed Sensor	VSS	km/h	0–109
Engine Speed	RPM	rpm	0–4383
Engine Coolant Temperature	ECT	°C	0–92
Intake Air Temperature	IAT	°C	0–40
Mass Air Flow	MAF	g/s	0–49.73
Accelerator Pedal Sensor	APS	%	0–100

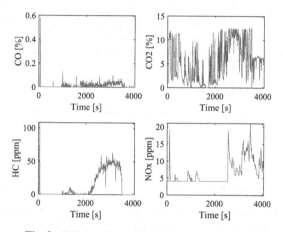

Fig. 2. Tailpipe CO, CO2, HC & NOX emissions

urban, rural, and highway areas. Figure 3 displays the sections traveled, as well as the altitude recorded during the journey. It is noteworthy that Cuenca is a high-altitude city, situated approximately 2500 m above sea level. This elevated altitude can potentially impact vehicle performance and emissions. To ensure the validity of the test cycle, strict adherence to the restrictions outlined by the Euro 6 regulations is crucial. These regulations encompass various aspects, including speed limits on different road segments, required stopping times, and prescribed distances to be traveled. It is important to emphasize that certain parameters, such as road speed, are subject to limitations imposed by legal regulations that prohibit exceeding 90 km/h within Ecuadorian territory.

2.4 On-Route Emission Rates Estimation

The emission factor calculates the number of pollutants by mass that are emitted into the atmosphere by vehicles for each kilometer traveled. (g/km). [20] determine emission factors from exhaust mass flow:

$$\dot{m}_{ex} = \dot{m}_{in} + \dot{m}_f \tag{1}$$

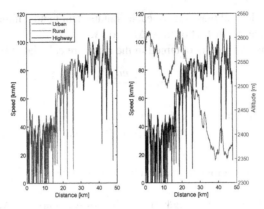

Fig. 3. RDE cycle

$\dot{m}_{in}$ = mass air flow via OBD
$\dot{m}_f$ = measured fuel flow

Measured emissions on a dry basis are corrected from the following equations.

$$C_{wet,j} = k_{w,j} C_{dry,j} \tag{2}$$

$$k_w = \frac{1.008}{1 + 0.005\alpha(C_{CO_2} + C_{CO})} \tag{3}$$

where:
$C_{wet,j}$ = concentration on a wet basis of pollutant j by volume
k_w = dry to wet base correction factor
α = hydrogen mole ratio
C_{CO_2} = CO2 concentrations on a dry basis
C_{CO} = CO concentrations on a dry basis.

Next, the instantaneous mass emissions for each pollutant are obtained $\dot{m}_{j,i}$ [g/s].

$$\dot{m}_{j,i} = c_{j,i} \mu_{j,i} \dot{m}_{ex,i} 10^{-3} \tag{4}$$

where:
c_j = instantaneous concentration of the component
μ_j = ratio of the density of each element and the total exhaust density.
$\mu_{CO2} = 0.001518$; $\mu_{NOx} = 0.001587$; $\mu_{CO} = 0.000966$; $\mu_{HC} = 0.000499$

The pollutant amount $\dot{m}_j$ (g) emitted during the driving cycle is equivalent to the accumulation of instantaneous emissions of the same pollutant as a function of time, expressed in the following equation:

$$m_j = \sum_{i=1}^{n} \dot{m}_{j,i} \Delta t \tag{5}$$

where $\dot{m}$ represents the real mass rate of each contaminant j and n indicates the value of samples carried out at the instant of time $\Delta t = 0.1s$.

Finally, the emission factors obtained in the route are calculated from:

$$F_{j,k} = \frac{m_{j,k}}{s_k} \tag{6}$$

where $m_{j,k}$ indicates the mass of each pollutant, j, and s represent the route in section k of the route carried out in each section (Urban, Rural, and Motorway) (Table 2).

Table 2. Emission factors in RDE tests

EF	Urban (g/km)	Rural (g/km)	Motorway (g/km)	Average (g/km)
CO2	36.1127	67.9343	39.9838	48.0103
CO	0.0734	0.1001	0.0586	0.0773
NOX	0.0029	0.0070	0.0073	0.0057
HC	0.2492	0.0095	0.0027	0.0871

3   Results and Discussions

This section may be divided by subheadings. It should provide a concise and precise description of the experimental results, their interpretation, as well as the experimental conclusions that can be drawn.

3.1   Performance Study Based on the Longitudinal Dynamics of the Car

From the dynamics of the car, the forces that interact in the behavior of the vehicle are calculated and allow the estimation of energy consumption. The traction force F_T is related to the aerodynamic and rolling resistance F_{res}, the longitudinal acceleration a_x, the braking force F_{brk}, and the force on slopes F_{slope} [23].

$$ma_x = F_T - F_{res} - F_{slope} - F_{brk} \tag{7}$$

where the longitudinal acceleration a_x is calculated using GPS speed as:

$$a_x i = \frac{V_{GPSi+1} - V_{GPSi}}{t_{i+1} - t_i} \tag{8}$$

Rolling resistance is represented as $f_r = f + f_0 \left(\frac{V}{100}\right)^{2.5}$ where the static and dynamic rolling indices are $f = 0.015$ and $f_0 = 0.01$, an aerodynamic coefficient is considered $C_X = 0.3$ and a front area $A_f = 2.2\,\text{m}^2$, the slope resistance is obtained from:

$$F_{res} = mg\left(f + f_0 V_{GPSi}{}^{2.5}\right) + \frac{1}{2}\rho C_X A_f V_{GPSi}{}^2 \tag{9}$$

The force to the slope is expressed as the opposition that occurs in a slope ascent.

$$F_{slope} = mg\sin\left(\frac{Alt_{i+1} - Alt_i}{S_{i+1} - S_i}\right) \tag{10}$$

Finally, the driving force is presented, which is determined through on route obtained data by the data logger.

$$F_T - F_{brk} = ma_x + F_{res} + F_{slope} \tag{11}$$

Force F_i is the result of the forces sum required to overcome the movement of the vehicle, the torque T_r of the wheel depends directly on the dynamic radius of the wheel r_d and is determined through the:

$$T_r = F_i r_d \tag{12}$$

Once the automobile dynamics are applied, the variables with the greatest dependence on fuel consumption are determined, based on a correlation matrix with ranges from -1 to 1, being of greater influence, the variables that are closest to 1 or -1, obtaining the following variables with the greatest influence regarding consumption: torque with 0.47, acceleration 0.58 and APS 0.67 (Fig. 4).

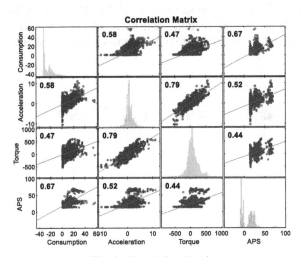

Fig. 4. Correlation Matrix

3.2   SOC Influence on RDE Route

The hybrid system of the vehicle monitors the internal combustion engine (ICE) and the battery state of charge (SOC) depending on the requirements on the demand for speed and power required to overcome the movement. Through the battery discharge over a period of time, the state of charge (SOC) in the carried-out route is calculated using the Eq. (13).

$$SOC = SOC_0 - \frac{1}{c_n} \int t_0^t I \cdot dt \tag{13}$$

where:
SOC = State of charge
c_n = capacity nominal of the battery
I = current flowing in and out of the battery
t = time

With the variables obtained from the analysis of the correlation matrix, a model is generated based on the rates of change in consumption concerning each variable (Ax, Torque, APS, RPM, and VSS), the model indicates when the consumption rate increases considerably respect to the acceleration an aggressive driving is identified. As the rate of consumption of this parameter tends to decrease about acceleration, normal driving is taken as a reference; if the rate of change tends to zero, consumption does not change significantly, and ecological driving is assumed. In Fig. 5 the route profile carried out is presented where it is possible to identify when the internal combustion engine (ICE) is in operation to the SOC since while the thermal engine is active the batteries are re-charging with the algorithm, it is possible to determine when ICE is on (100) and off (90) denoted by the black line. It is determined that ICE works 69.6229% during the urban section, 14.175% in the rural section, and 16.2029% on the highway, that is, ICE works continuously in the urban section due to the acceleration maneuvers and frequent stops produced by traffic, in addition to traffic signals and traffic signals.

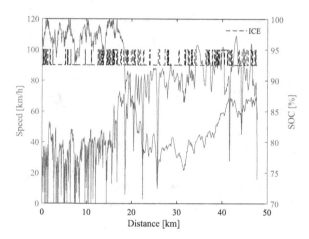

Fig. 5. Route profile in relation to SOC

3.3 Driving Modes Characterization

Based on the gasoline consumption factor of each route concerning time, the driving modes used on each route are estimated considering the area under the acceleration curve in random sections of the taken routes. Using the RMS (Root Mean Square) the mean square value of the acceleration is estimated [23] in three routes where ecological, RDE, and aggressive accelerations are identified from the PID's obtained through:

$$RMS = \sqrt{\frac{1}{n} \sum_{i=1}^{n} ax_i^2} \tag{14}$$

Ecological driving stands out for carrying out maneuvers with low acceleration and speeds while aggressive driving is distinguished by abrupt maneuvers in terms of speeds, accelerations, and progressive use of the brake, this directly affects fuel consumption (Fig. 6) where the RMS of the acceleration is indicated as a function of consumption in different routes, this is corroborated from the distribution of the density over the accelerations. In the case of eco mode, a high concentration of density is observed at low accelerations, therefore, low fuel consumption while the aggressive mode presents a high accumulation of density throughout high accelerations as a result of a notable increase in fuel consumption on the journey.

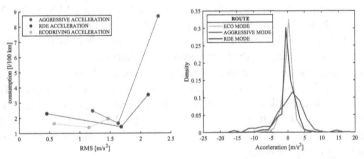

Fig. 6. Acceleration distribution based on Eco, RDE and Aggressive driving modes: (**a**) RMS; (**b**) Acceleration

The polluting emissions obtained in the different routes are characterized by the emission rates (CO_2, CO, NO_x, and HC) for the indicated driving modes concerning the average speed. The influence of speed for emissions is indicated in Fig. 7, generally, increasing the speed on the different routes shows an increase in the emission factors.

In the analysis of the consumption factors of each driving mode, it is observed that an ecological driving mode presents a consumption reduction of 31.36% compared to aggressive driving, when going from ecological mode to RDE mode it increases by 9.06%, and from RDE mode to Aggressive mode shows an increase of 22.31%.

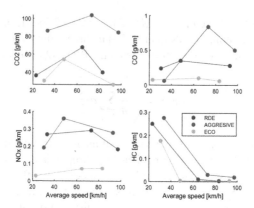

Fig. 7. Emission factors based on average speed

4 Conclusions

In the present investigation, the effect of driving style on energy expenditure and pollu-tants was analyzed. The study identified acceleration Ax, Torque, APS, and RPM as the influential variables, showing the strongest correlation with energy and fuel consump-tion. From these variables, a model was developed to detect when the ICE is operational and responsible for recharging the hybrid system's batteries.

By examining the rate of change of fuel consumption about acceleration, driving modes (ecological, RDE, and aggressive) were determined for the routes. This was reflected in the density distribution obtained from random sections along the route. Emission rates (CO, CO_2, HC, and NOx) were found to be directly influenced by driv-ing maneuvers. Ecological driving exhibited a 31.36% reduction in fuel consumption compared to aggressive driving.

The study demonstrates that driving technique significantly impacts energy con-sumption and pollutant emissions, with acceleration being the main factor for efficient driving. It is important to note that this study was conducted in a high-altitude city.

To ensure the validity of the test cycle, strict adherence to the restrictions outlined by the Euro 6 regulations is crucial. These regulations encompass various aspects, includ-ing speed limits on different road segments, required stopping times, and prescribed distances to be traveled. It is important to emphasize that certain parameters, such as road speed, are subject to limitations imposed by legal regulations that prohibit exceeding 90 km/h within Ecuadorian territory.

For future work, it would be beneficial to investigate the impact of driving vari-ables in cities with different altitudes or at sea level. This would provide insights into how geographical conditions influence energy consumption and emissions. Additional-ly, exploring other factors such as deceleration and gear-shifting patterns could further enhance our understanding of efficient driving techniques in different environments.

References

1. Meseguer, J.E., Calafate, C.T., Cano, J.C., Manzoni, P.: Assessing the impact of driving behavior on instantaneous fuel consumption. In: 2015 12th Annual IEEE Consumer Communications and Networking Conference (CCNC), pp. 443–448. IEEE (2015). https://doi.org/10.1109/CCNC.2015.7158016
2. ISO: ISO 14230–4:2000 - Road vehicles—Diagnostic systems—Keyword Protocol 2000—Part 4: Requirements for emission-related systems. https://www.iso.org/standard/28826.html. Accessed 31 Mar 2023
3. European Union: Commission Regulation (EU) 2017/1151 of 1 June 2017 supplementing Regulation (EC) No 715/2007 of the European Parliament and of the Council on type-approval of motor vehicles with respect to emissions from light passenger and commercial vehicles (Euro 5 and Euro 6) and on access to vehicle repair and maintenance information, amending Directive 2007/46/EC of the European Parliament and of the Council, Commission Regulation (EC) No 692/2008 and Commission Regulation (EU) No 1230/2012 and repealin… https://eur-lex.europa.eu/eli/reg/2017/1151/oj. Accessed 02 Mar 2023
4. European Union: Commission Regulation (EU) 2016/646 of 20 April 2016 amending Regulation (EC) No 692/2008 as regards emissions from light passenger and commercial vehicles (Euro 6). https://eur-lex.europa.eu/eli/reg/2016/646/oj. Accessed 02 Mar 2023
5. European Union: Commission Regulation (EU) 2016/427 of 10 March 2016 amending Regulation (EC) No 692/2008 as regards emissions from light passenger and commercial vehicles (Euro 6). https://eur-lex.europa.eu/eli/reg/2016/427/oj. Accessed 02 Mar 2023
6. Ehrenberger, S.I., Konrad, M., Philipps, F.: Pollutant emissions analysis of three plug-in hybrid electric vehicles using different modes of operation and driving conditions. Atmos. Environ. **234**, 117612 (2020). https://doi.org/10.1016/j.atmosenv.2020.117612
7. AEADE: Asociación de Empresas Automotrices del Ecuador: Boletín de ventas - Octubre 2022 (2022)
8. Sivak, M., Schoettle, B.: Eco-driving: strategic, tactical, and operational decisions of the driver that influence vehicle fuel economy. Transp Policy (Oxf). **22**, 96–99 (2012). https://doi.org/10.1016/J.TRANPOL.2012.05.010
9. Mahesh, S., et al.: On-road remote sensing of vehicles in Dublin: measurement and emission factor estimation. Transp Res D Transp Environ. **117**, 103620 (2023). https://doi.org/10.1016/J.TRD.2023.103620
10. Bernard, Y., Dornoff, J., Carslaw, D.C.: Can accurate distance-specific emissions of nitrogen oxide emissions from cars be determined using remote sensing without measuring exhaust flowrate? (2021). https://doi.org/10.1016/j.scitotenv.2021.151500
11. Lv, C., et al.: Cyber-physical system based optimization framework for intelligent powertrain control. SAE Int. J. Commer. Veh. **10**, 254–264 (2017). https://doi.org/10.4271/2017-01-0426
12. Lee, T.K., Filipi, Z.S.: Synthesis of real-world driving cycles using stochastic process and statistical methodology. Int. J. Veh. Des. **57**, 17–36 (2011). https://doi.org/10.1504/IJVD.2011.043590
13. Zambrano, O.I., Rivera, N.D., Chica, J.F., García, C.L.G.: Estudio del comportamiento de un motor ciclo otto de inyección electrónica respecto de la estequiometría de la mezcla y del adelanto al encendido para la ciudad de cuenca. Revista Politécnica **40**, 59–67 (2017)
14. Magín, L., Armas, O., John, A., Sánchez, C.: Study of the altitude effect on internal combustion engine operation. Part 1: performance. In: Technological Information, vol. 17, no. 5-2006, pp. 21–30 (2006)
15. Ericsson, E.: Independent driving pattern factors and their influence on fuel-use and exhaust emission factors. Transp Res D Transp Environ. **6**, 325–345 (2001). https://doi.org/10.1016/S1361-9209(01)00003-7

16. Yeh, C.-F., Lin, L.-T., Wu, P.-J., Huang, C.-C.: Using on-board diagnostics data to analyze driving behavior and fuel consumption. In: Zhao, Y., Wu, T.-Y., Chang, T.-H., Pan, J.-S., Jain, L.C. (eds.) VTCA 2018. SIST, vol. 128, pp. 343–351. Springer, Cham (2019). https://doi.org/10.1007/978-3-030-04585-2_42

17. Corcoba Magaña, V., Muñoz Organero, M.: Eco-driving: energy saving based on driver behavior (2015)

18. Pereira, A., Alves, M., Macedo, H.: Vehicle driving analysis in regards to fuel consumption using Fuzzy Logic and OBD-II devices. In: 2016 8th Euro American Conference on Telematics and Information Systems, EATIS 2016 (2016). https://doi.org/10.1109/EATIS.2016.7520160

19. Molina Campoverde, J.J.: Driving mode estimation model based in machine learning through PID's signals analysis obtained from OBD II. In: Botto-Tobar, M., Zambrano Vizuete, M., Torres-Carrión, P., Montes León, S., Pizarro Vásquez, G., Durakovic, B. (eds.) ICAT 2019. CCIS, vol. 1194, pp. 80–91. Springer, Cham (2020). https://doi.org/10.1007/978-3-030-425 20-3_7

20. Rivera-Campoverde, N.D., Muñoz-Sanz, J.L., Arenas-Ramirez, B.D.V.: Estimation of pollutant emissions in real driving conditions based on data from OBD and machine learning. Sensors 21, 6344 (2021). https://doi.org/10.3390/S21196344

21. Mądziel, M., Jaworski, A., Kuszewski, H., Woś, P., Campisi, T., Lew, K.: The development of CO2 instantaneous emission model of full hybrid vehicle with the use of machine learning techniques. Energies 15, 142 (2021). https://doi.org/10.3390/EN15010142

22. Molina Campoverde, P., Molina Campoverde, J., Bermeo Naula, K., Novillo, G.: Efficiency increase of supercharged engines, pp. 346–356 (2023). https://doi.org/10.1007/978-3-031-24327-1_30/FIGURES/6

23. Rivera Campoverde, N., Muñoz Sanz, J., Arenas Ramírez, B.: Modelo de bajo costo para la estimación de emisiones contaminantes basado en GPS y aprendizaje automático (2022). https://doi.org/10.5944/BICIM2022.179

e-Commerce

Adoption of Online Grocery Shopping: A Systematic Review of the Literature

Kirti Prashar[1,2]([✉]) [iD] and Anil Kalotra[1]

[1] University School of Business, Chandigarh University, Ajitgarh, Punjab, India
kirtipra96@gmail.com
[2] Sharda University, Greater Noida, U.P, India

Abstract. This article provides an SLR, or systematic review of the field of study known as "e-grocery adoption." It suggests using grocery apps or online buying groceries to enhance marketing research. The purpose of this study is to critically revise and produce an essay about the adoption of grocery applications. 38 studies were produced by the SLR and presented concurrently to the adoption of grocery apps. Results from ahead descriptive analytics show the most important research questions around the adoption of grocery applications as well as diverse strategies that link researchers and participants in various research methods. The essay looks into the factors that led to the acceptance of grocery applications. The writers emphasized how the subject has evolved over time and noted the prospective potential future research topics. The study eventually provides references for further research on adoption of grocery applications.

Keywords: Adoption of e-applications · E-grocery · systematic literature review (SLR)

1 Introduction

From its modest beginnings, online groceries is rapidly growing. According to Business Insider Intelligence collected from www.businessinsider.com, its market value grew between 2016 and 2018. This suggests that customers are beginning to ask more satisfactory questions about basic concepts and some meals online. Consumers are seeking better, more creative experiences in today's competitive marketplace, from check-out-free shopping to curbside pickup, feast packs, and home delivery. Anticipating what shops should think about for the future is intriguing. However, it is obvious that progress is being made quickly, and a few trends, such as the movement toward self-checkout and cashierless businesses, cannot be ignored. In a highly competitive industry, retailers are scrambling to take advantage of this potential. Both established supermarket players and local startups are expanding their doorstep pickup and conveyance options, the two key components of crucial online required to increase market share. Retailers need to improve omni systems to ensure that they are not just developing consumer preferences but also differentiating themselves from competitors while creating efficiencies to boost sales and profitability. Retailers should develop a channel to effectively manage their online grocery offers, taking into account customer adoption barriers.

© The Author(s), under exclusive license to Springer Nature Switzerland AG 2024
M. Botto-Tobar et al. (Eds.): ICAT 2023, CCIS 2051, pp. 17–25, 2024.
https://doi.org/10.1007/978-3-031-58950-8_2

According to data retrieved from www.statista.com there were 33.4 million adult supermarket app customers in the United States in 2019. The number of adult groceries app users in the U.S. is anticipated to increase to 41.5 million by 2025. Because Indonesia has such a large market potential, these global tendencies will soon affect how Indonesian grocery stores behave while making purchases. The retail sales of grocery stores in Indonesia were approximately 6.3 billion US dollars in 2019; the Food & Drinks segment will generate US$4603 million in revenue in 2025; and Platform-to-Consumer Delivery will account for the largest portion of the Indonesian market in 2025 with a market value of US$1878 million. This data shows that there are numerous opportunities for the online grocery market to expand.

Recent years have seen an increase in the number of research papers related to e-tailing [1, 2]. The study areas related to the acceptance of the development of online fulfilment are important to note [2]. The realisation of the study and the explanations in identifying the study issue areas were nevertheless compiled in a series of studies that detailed an unrelated methodical study. In this situation, several interesting reports pertaining to the subject of the adoption study of grocery applications are eventually gathered from research publications. With a different set of data depending on the SLR organisation, the article's main goal in this context is to demonstrate the causes of the adoption of grocery applications in the subject of inquiry. The structure of the essay includes four sections, including an introduction, the systematic inquiry method's methodology, the results of the SLR arrangement, and a conclusion.

2 Methodology

The study followed D. Tranfield, (2003) [3], B. Kitchenham and S. Charters (2003) [4], and B. Kitchenham and S. Charters (2007) [5] in using the SLR approach. The results show that SLR includes a number of projects, such as preparation (identifying the study questions), administration (examine paper, research choice, and data synthesis), and documentation (report writing) [4, 5]. The authors discuss the research topics in the preparatory projects using the outlined structure. This research's first focus was on identifying the causes of the adoption of grocery applications. Second, managerial activities include the search process, selecting a study topic, and integrating data. The keywords, paper sources, and search strategy are all part of the search strategy activity. "Online grocery," "grocery application," "e-grocery," and "adoption" were among the search terms. Additionally, the fusion of operators like AND and OR starts the terms associated to looking up publications while answering research inquiries. These terms—online groceries OR e-grocery—combined pair orders.

The study cites three online database sources from 2017 to 2022 to get the data based on the exact headline as well as abstract, including Science Direct, IEEE Explore, Emerald, & Sage Journals. The search terms are typed into the appropriate publishers, and then publications related to broad topics are shown. That pointed to the pertinent articles that were gathered in the project selection directory management tools. The subject selection was divided into three phases, as shown in Table 1.

The chosen articles are filled with information from 610 relevant research that will be analysed and afterwards categorised as topics. The next phase involves evaluating each

Table 1. Steps for selecting journals

	The procedure for searching phrases. Journal title selections	Abstracts match with research questions	Study results to answer research questions
Sources	Discovered Studies	Nominee Studies	Elected Studies
Sage	121	17	8
Science Direct	289	39	18
Emerald	115	24	9
IEEE	85	5	3
Total	610	85	38

Source: Author's compilation

relevant publication's overview in light of both research concerns. In the aforementioned instance, redundant and pointless publications were eliminated, resulting in an overall of 85 papers that fall within the category of nominated studies. At the third stage, the publication filtering is once again applied. To address both research needs, relevant papers are retrieved and scanned. They are all categorised as elective subjects. After communicating the removal procedures and screening of the particular outlines and complete manuscripts, 38 articles are then recognised for the creation of the data findings.

The review findings of collecting data are presented in this study report to highlight the primary inquiry areas of grocery app adoption. Based on the 38 items that were purchased, there are two different forms of analysis—respectively, retailers and consumers. The analysis of study topics of grocery app acceptance would be focused on such two different perspectives in order to address the research question, which is to uncover significant antecedents of grocery app adoption.

3   Retailers Point of View

In online grocery scenarios, switching behaviour is significantly influenced by customer service, problems with other delivered products, technological difficulties, and pricey pricing perception [6]. The store chain is the first distribution network available for the internet grocery retailers offering a variety of goods, perishable or not, to a large, dispersed society, while also satisfying their basic needs for a more prompt, such as on shipment, that also transforms into the a long-term competitive edge [7].

Cagliano, Anna Corinna, et al. (2017) found that every portable usage of the e-grocery has the features of product traceability, accessible setup, and time-based distribution monitoring. Research on overcoming the obstacles to assimilation, affiliation, and enhanced distinctness in digital food supply chain management is also encouraged by this study [8]. Kureshi, Sonal, and Sujo Thomas (2019) provided in-depth interviews and a technique for analysing how local retailers' control and normative attitudes toward online grocery purchasing may eventually convert into behaviour [10]. They used the theory of planned behaviour (TPB) [9].

Saskia, Seidel, and Corinne Blanquart (2016) try comparing the structure and rate of growth of the internet-based grocery in Germany and France where it was established about the same time and yet developed at a different rate, in order to examine cutting-edge online food concepts that retain out of varied meal online supplies. Three sorts of changes have been noted in online supply chains that have been attributed to comparatively easy impacts on supply, including youthful entrants connecting, new agreements among players occurring, and additional stock agreements [11]. The most difficult component of online groceries is undoubtedly the logistics and conveyor problems.

Saskia, Seidel, and Corinne Blanquart (2016) try comparing the structure and rate of growth of the internet-based grocery in Germany and France where it was established about the same time and yet developed at a different rate, in order to examine cutting-edge online food concepts that retain out of varied meal online supplies. Three sorts of changes have been noted in online supply chains that have been attributed to comparatively easy impacts on supply, including youthful entrants connecting, new agreements among players occurring, and additional stock agreements [11]. The most difficult component of online groceries is undoubtedly the logistics and conveyor problems. Matthias Ulrich et al. and colleagues (2019) used distributional stasis for trade forecasting in online groceries. In order to decrease the environmental impact of a conveyance agreement in a town and to increase consumers' knowledge of buying through applications, two steps of the epistemological procedure can be used. The competition, the distance among stores and customers' homes, and shop character traits in the age of e-commerce imply that all incremental innovation to take into account for various challenges associated with Omni-commerce dynamics, even though these based spatial interaction models (SIM) are still useful [15]. Additionally, the definition of touch of a button in Omni-commerce frameworks uses workshop features with trades regions, production volume, and demographic data obtained for latent catchments less often [15].

4 Consumers Point of View

Price of the goods, expiration date, and Service quality indications, together with tailored recommendations depending on the items, prompted the logistics and reduced currents while examining the E Apps [16]. They provided a variety of explanations for why people choose to buy groceries online, including the difficulty of doing so with children, the weariness and time waste associated with carrying around large shopping bags, the capacity for increased preparedness with reference to consumption patterns and the capacity for healthier consumption.. In order to better understand how Internet of Things (IoT) can benefit local grocery selection, Fagerstrm, Eriksson, and Siguresson (2017) examined the influence of Internet - of - things data on consumer decision-making in a purchase context. They discovered, in particular, that of the real-time allures, feature ratings from different consumers yielded one that stuck out the most and was associated by a cost.

Brya, Pawe (2018) found that factors such as age, income, desire to pay more for fresh foods, the meaning given to product demonstration, and quality indicators were statistically significant predictors of online buying behavior for foods in Poland [19]. Osman, Faustina (2017) concentrated their studies on how older individuals operate inside an internet grocery buying website regardless of the obstacles experienced [20] in order to assist retailers in developing E- Sites.

By analysing linked activities, providing information, and investigating the attitudes of SNAP recipients, qualitative study by Rogus, Stephanie, et al. (2019) examined the reasons for e-grocery purchase in addition to the benefits of the Supplemental Nutrition Assistance Program (SNAP) [21]. In 2016, Muhammad, and Rahman, Sofiah Abd evaluated how situational factors like predecessor nations, temporal viewpoint, and lifestyle changes affected the appropriation of online grocery shopping as well as electronic service quality factors [23]. The effects of response rate, fee, and service criticality on customer post-recovery compensation, as well as behavioural goals like feel euphoric (PWOM) and patronage, were examined by Crisafulli, and Singh, Jaywant (2017). The idea that slower progress is often ineffective is challenged by the possibility of slowed implement preventive setup crashes in online shopping [24]. The adoption of online grocery shopping did not change as a result of the time required to travel to offline grocery markets.

When Shukla, Anuja, and Sharma, Shiv Kumar (2018) and Mukerjee, Hory Sankar, Deshmukh, and TAM (TAM) [26] were used to test to wherever The findings shown that consumers in India recognise the use of technology in the acquisition of grocery shop using mobile applications, and that value and ease of use have a specific and significant impact on global on intention. [27, 28]. Using the technological acceptance (TAM) models [26] and the notion of reasoned action put forward by Ajzen (1991) [9], D. Chakraborty (2020) built on earlier research. Subjective norms showed no discernible impact on particular intent across Indian grocery store purchasing applications, despite the fact that attitude, perceived behaviour control, utility, and convenience of use all generate a genuine and obvious influence on intention [29]. In order to determine the variables that affect whether people throughout Thailand accept or oppose online grocery shopping, Driediger, Gomez (2019) used a growth of the model of technology acceptance that took into account perceived behaviour, distinctness, risk perception, as well as perceived enjoyment [30]. By combining a variety of forebears of e-supermarket purchase behaviour, including such conventional exertion, period restraint, enjoyment worth, merchandise variety, economic advantages, and web design aesthetic appeal, Sreeram, Anusha, and Desai, Sneha were also able to observe how those who develop the user's well-being and purchase dedication behaviour [31]. Kim, Eunhye, and Lee (2017) investigated how perceived risks as well as ignored development factors like correlating advantage, suitability, and complexity, influence consumers' choice to accept Purchase & Pickup in-Store (BOPS). Situational factors (area convenience) and advertising elements (association) considerably alter these connections [32].

Applying Bayesian analysis, Chen, Hong et al. (2017) explained that the use of free sampling is inextricably linked to Amazon WOM in persuading Amazon software traffic [33]. In order to determine whether retailing practises, which are frequently used within traditional departments within online commerce, are capable of promoting specific Sustainable Development, Sigurdsson, Valdimar (2019) used a signalling theory model. The outcomes boosted the influence of indicating on customer decisions related to other notable qualities [34]. González, Xulia (2017) asserts that above the repetition by charges are adjusted, pricing tactics at the successor level instead of the particular market level) have a big influence. Larger accessible commodities have more price swings when helpful factors Poisson design is taken into account and rivals' pricing changes provide a distinctive and notable influence [35].

A critical evaluation was published by Jain, Nikunj Kumar, et al. (2017) to look into the relationship between e-commerce and customer satisfaction with regards to product quality, price, availability, occasion, and convenience of return [1]. Similar recommendations were made in a literature analysis by Melacini, The three areas of shipping software architecture, inventory control, and function managerial staff, as well as distributing planning and achievement, were the subject of Marco et al. (2018) study.

According to study by Monica Faraoni et al. (2019) [36], connection investments, web layout, security, and also privacy had a positive impact on online trust, emotional engagement, and customer loyalty. Inman, (2017) proposed an architecture that centralises consumers by examining how they perceive the technology that is available and the behavioural responses that follow. They also discussed how specific consumer responses are significant to retailers by boosting sales by luring potential subscribers, increasing the volume of current customers, producing more renowned consumer surplus, or reducing costs [37]. Elke Huyghe (2017) showed that purchasing channel influence happens because e-channels perform goods symbolically, whereas traditional stores do so in a traditional way. These findings highlight a variety of understudied differences between online and offline buying, in addition to having substantial implications for consumers, decision-makers, and merchants [38, 39].

As Adrian Mackenzie (2018) shows, the creation of personalised projections does certainly strengthen agnostic relationships with others. It also important if the social system is made up of diverse professional backgrounds since interaction requires the capacity to correlate. A more extensive change includes the personalization of recommender systems for online grocery shopping inside models that use enormous amounts of data. The linkages in tendency patterns are operationalized by big data conversion scenarios [40]. Advanced modeling for internet grocery distribution progress was provided by Alzubairi, (2017) [41] and may be used to predict and simulate e-grocery purchase transactions prior to employment. A decision-support system was created by Christian Fikar in 2019 using data from the Product Basket Life Reports, customer preferences, and the effects of food quality on customer happiness and logistical success [42]. Bjrgen, (2019) examined the relevance of logistic service aid in order to better understand how city areas of the city can integrate trends of urban development and digitisation into trying to frame for a practical and environmentally friendly municipal delivery mover[43].

Ten of the 38 publications that were gathered looked at grocery stores as a unit of study, while 28 papers looked at customers. There is still little study that takes into account the perspectives of both customers and retailers. A total of 38 papers were gathered, with 74% of them mathematically expressing the viewpoint of the customer. Factory to house logistic, warehouse-t -house logistics, drive-through the shop, and online click collect option are the four programmes that online food grocers typically use to distribute grocery orders to customers. Future study may clearly characterise their unit analysis by characterising the types of commercial models used by e-retailers.

A cross-sectional temporal study is also used in every single publication. Investigating actual behaviour or the method of putting a goal into action could make the process take longer. (TAM) by Davis (1989) [26] and (TRA) by Fishbein & Ajzen (1975) [44] or (TPB) Ajzen (1991) [9] are the most widely used models to examine how portable technology affects consumer purchases of grocery items. Cross-cultural topics were not covered, and the entire evaluation was presented in a single social and national context. The research can also be explored in other countries [45]. The study looked at how EWOM affected consumers' intentions to shop for groceries online. Future studies may discuss other aspects of the marketing process, as well as issues with promotions and publicity aimed at attracting different consumers. As a result, we would have a better understanding of why consumers choose to shop for groceries online and what obstacles they face. Future study should concentrate on practical application rather than agent or customer approval, in contrast to studies that depend on the technological acceptance paradigm [26, 46, 47].

5 Conclusion

By using the SLR approach, the inquiry presents a summary of the causes of adoption issues for online grocery shopping. This research focuses more on the factors that influence the adoption of grocery apps, as opposed to other comparable SLR studies like that carried out by Melacini et al. in 2018 [2], which highlights the primary issues related to e-fulfillment and distribution in retailing. Each selected linked study has 610 articles. The section has the label "subjects acquired" on it. Following that, 85 articles were sifted over the blueprint and designated as nominee investigations. The whole text of the original article was ultimately reduced to 38 pieces, which were then labelled as chosen studies. Although it provides a starting point, The significant concern noted above is not resolved by this study. As a result, we strongly encourage other scholars to make contributions to advancing the evaluation, implementation, and specific enhancement of cutting-edge technologies that result in particular outcomes for both merchants and customers.

References

1. Jain, N.K., Gajjar, H., Shah, B.J., Sadh, A.: E-fulfillment dimensions and its influence on customers in e-tailing: a critical review. Asia Pacific J. Mark. Logist. **29**(2), 347–369 (2017)
2. Melacini, M., Perotti, S., Rasini, M., Tappia, E.: E-fulfilment and distribution in omni-channel retailing: a systematic literature review. Int. J. Phys. Distrib. Logist. Manag. **48**(4), 391–414 (2018)
3. Tranfield, D., Denyer, D., Smart, P.: Towards a methodology for developing evidenceinformed management knowledge by means of systematic review. Br. J. Manag. **14**(3), 207–222 (2003)
4. Kitchenham, B., Charters, S.: Guidelines for performing systematic literature reviews in software engineering (2007)
5. Okoli, C., Schabram, K.: A guide to conducting a systematic literature review of information systems research (2010)
6. Singh, R., Rosengren, S.: Why do online grocery shoppers switch? an empirical investigation of drivers of switching in online grocery. J. Retail. Consum. Serv. **53**, 101962 (2020)
7. Mkansi, M., Nsakanda, A.L.: Leveraging the physical network of stores in e-grocery order fulfilment for sustainable competitive advantage. Res. Transp. Econ. **87**, 100786 (2019)

8. Cagliano, A.C., De Marco, A., Rafele, C.: E-grocery supply chain management enabled by mobile tools. Bus. Process. Manag. J. **23**(1), 47–70 (2017)

9. Ajzen, I.: Theory of planned behavior. Acad. Press. Inc. All **50**, 179–211 (1991)

10. Kureshi, S., Thomas, S.: Online grocery retailing – exploring local grocers beliefs. Int. J. Retail Distrib. Manag. **47**(2), 157–185 (2019)

11. Saskia, S., Mareï, N., Blanquart, C.: Innovations in e-grocery and logistics solutions for cities. Transp. Res. Procedia **12**, 825–835 (2016)

12. Wollenburg, J., Hübner, A., Kuhn, H., Trautrims, A.: From bricksand-mortar to bricks-and-clicks: logistics networks in omni-channel grocery retailing. Int. J. Phys. Distrib. Logist. Manag. **48**(4), 415–438 (2018)

13. Ulrich, M., Jahnke, H., Langrock, R., Pesch, R., Senge, R.: Distributional regression for demand forecasting in e-grocery. Eur. J. Oper. Res. 294, 831–842 (2019)

14. Pan, S., Giannikas, V., Han, Y., Grover-Silva, E., Qiao, B.: Using customer-related data to enhance e-grocery home delivery. Ind. Manag. Data Syst. **117**(9), 1917–1933 (2017)

15. Davies, A., Dolega, L., Arribas-Bel, D.: Buy online collect in-store: exploring grocery click&collect using a national case study. Int. J. Retail Distrib. Manag. **47**(3), 278–291 (2019)

16. Fagerstrøm, A., Eriksson, N., Sigurdsson, V.: Investigating the impact of Internet of Things services from a smartphone app on grocery shopping. J. Retail. Consum. Serv. 52, 101927 (2020)

17. Berg, J., Henriksson, M.: In search of the 'good life': Understanding online grocery shopping and everyday mobility as social practices. J. Transp. Geogr. **83**, 102633 (2020)

18. Fagerstrøm, A., Eriksson, N., Siguresson, V.: What's the 'thing' in Internet of Things in grocery shopping? a customer approach. Procedia Comput. Sci. **121**, 384–388 (2017)

19. Bryła, P.: Organic food online shopping in Poland. Br. Food J. **120**(5), 1015–1027 (2018)

20. Osman, R., Hwang, F.: A method to study how older adults navigate in an online grocery shopping site. In: 2016 4th International Conference on User Science and Engineering (i-USEr), pp. 247–252 (2016)

21. Rogus, S., Guthrie, J.F., Niculescu, M., Mancino, L.: Online grocery shopping knowledge, attitudes, and behaviors among SNAP participants. J. Nutr. Educ. Behav. **52**(5), 539–545 (2020)

22. Martinez, O., Tagliaferro, B., Rodriguez, N., Athens, J., Abrams, C., Elbel, B.: EBT payment for online grocery orders: a mixed-methods study to understand its uptake among SNAP recipients and the barriers to and motivators for its use. J. Nutr. Educ. Behav. **50**(4), 396-402.e1 (2018)

23. Muhammad, N.S., Sujak, H., Rahman, S.A.: Buying groceries online: the influences of electronic service quality (eServQual) and situational factors. Procedia Econ. Finan. **37**(16), 379–385 (2016)

24. Crisafulli, B., Singh, J.: Service failures in e-retailing: examining the effects of response time, compensation, and service criticality. Comput. Human Behav. **77**, 413–424 (2017)

25. Kang, C., Moon, J., Kim, T., Choe, Y.: Why consumers go to online grocery: Comparing vegetables with grains. In: Proceedings of the Annual Hawaii International Conference on System Sciences, vol. 2016-March, pp. 3604–3613 (2016)

26. Davis, F.D.: Perceived usefulness, perceived ease of use, and user acceptance of information technology. MIS Q. 319–340 (1989)

27. Shukla, A., Sharma, S.K.: Evaluating consumers' adoption of mobile technology for grocery shopping: an application of technology acceptance model. J. Bus. Perspect. **22**(2), 185–198 (2018)

28. Mukerjee, H.S., Deshmukh, G.K., Prasad, U.D.: Technology readiness and likelihood to use self-checkout services using smartphone in retail grocery stores: empirical evidences from Hyderabad, India. Bus. Perspect. Res. **7**(1), 1–15 (2019)

29. Chakraborty, D.: Indian shoppers' attitude towards grocery shopping apps: a survey conducted on smartphone users. Metamorph. A J. Manag. Res. **18**(2), 83–91 (2019)
30. Driediger, F., Bhatiasevi, V.: Online grocery shopping in Thailand: consumer acceptance and usage behavior. J. Retail. Consum. Serv. **48**, 224–237 (2019)
31. Sreeram, A., Kesharwani, A., Desai, S.: Factors affecting satisfaction and loyalty in online grocery shopping: an integrated model. J. Indian Bus. Res. **9**(2), 107–132 (2017)
32. Kim, E., Park, M.-C., Lee, J.: Determinants of the intention to use Buy-Online, Pickup In-Store (BOPS): the moderating effects of situational factors and product type. Telemat. Inf. **34**(8), 1721–1735 (2017)
33. Chen, H., Duan, W., Zhou, W.: The interplay between free sampling and word of mouth in the online software market. Decis. Support. Syst. **95**, 82–90 (2017)
34. Sigurdsson, V., Larsen, N.M., Alemu, M.H., Gallogly, J.K., Menon, R.G.V., Fagerstrøm, A.: Assisting sustainable food consumption: the effects of quality signals stemming from consumers and stores in online and physical grocery retailing. J. Bus. Res. **112**, 458–471 (2019)
35. González, X.: Chain heterogeneity and price-setting behavior: evidence from e-grocery retailers. Electron. Commer. Res. Appl. **26**(September), 62–72 (2017)
36. Faraoni, M., Rialti, R., Zollo, L., Pellicelli, A.C.: Exploring eLoyalty antecedents in B2C e-Commerce: empirical results from Italian grocery retailers. Br. Food J. **121**(2), 574–589 (2019)
37. Inman, J.J., Nikolova, H.: Shopper-facing retail technology: a retailer adoption decision framework incorporating shopper attitudes and privacy concerns. J. Retail. **93**(1), 7–28 (2017)
38. Huyghe, E., Verstraeten, J., Geuens, M., Van Kerckhove, A.: Clicks as a healthy alternative to bricks: how online grocery shopping reduces vice purchases. J. Mark. Res. **54**(1), 61–74 (2017)
39. Prashar, K., Kalotra, A.: Modelling the effect of E service quality on consumer satisfaction towards E grocery. Webology **18**(4) (2021). ISSN: 1735–188X
40. Mackenzie, A.: Personalization and probabilities: impersonal propensities in online grocery shopping. Big Data Soc. **5**(1), 1–15 (2018)
41. Alzubairi, A., Alrabghi, A.: Assessing the profitable conditions of online grocery using simulation store to home click-and-collect home drive-through. In: Proceedings of the 2017, pp. 1838–1842. IEEE IEEM (2017)
42. C. Fikar, A. Mild, and M. Waitz, "Facilitating consumer preferences and product shelf life data in the design of e-grocery deliveries," Eur. J. Oper. Res., vol. 239, no. 3, (2019)
43. Bjørgen, A., Bjerkan, K.Y., Hjelkrem, O.A.: E-groceries: sustainable last mile distribution in city planning. Res. Transp. Econ. **87**, 100805 (2019)
44. Ajzen, I., Fishbein, M.: Attitude-behavior relations: a theoretical analysis and review of empirical research. Psychol. Bull. **84**(5), 888 (1977)
45. Hofstede, G.: Dimensionalizing cultures: the hofstede model in context. Online Read. Psychol. Cult. **2**(1), 1092–1096 (2011)
46. Venkatesh, V.: Determinants of perceived ease of use: Integrating control, intrinsic motivation, and emotion into the technology acceptance model. Inf. Syst. Res. **11**(4), 342–365 (2000)
47. Venkatesh, V., Morris, M.G., Davis, G.B., Davis, F.D.: User acceptance of information technology: toward a unified view. MIS Q. 425–478 (2003)

Significance and Effect of Green Logistics on Buying Behaviors' of Consumer Towards E-Grocery

Kirti Prashar[1,2](✉) ⓘ and Anil Kalotra[1]

[1] University School of Business, Chandigarh University, Ajitgarh, Punjab, India
kirtipra96@gmail.com
[2] Sharda University, Greater Noida, U.P, India

Abstract. The impact of green logistics in e-grocery on customer purchase behaviour is investigated in this study. Businesses that have implemented green logistics are seen as being successful in influencing customer product choices. Businesses are sensitive to shifting customer preferences and environmental conditions, and a factor that may have an impact on consumer purchasing behaviour is whether or not they embrace green logistics in line with their growth objectives. As a result, "acceptance of the green principle" develops into an international and societal phenomenon. Consumers consider the product's environmental effect in addition to its performance and quality when assessing a good or service. Businesses adopted the green idea as a result of realizing this, their duties regarding environmental impact, their quest of competitive edge, and their goal to enhance the marketability of their brands. The importance of R&D research has been acknowledged in this respect, and related efforts have increased. Overall, these actions improved living circumstances while lowering lifetime expenses. Consumer awareness of green brands has risen. Technology's usage in grocery delivery has increased e-grocery and integrated into everyday life. In this regard, it is important to ascertain if consumer environmental consciousness in e-grocery has an impact on channel choice. The adoption of green logistics is greatly influenced by consumer environmental awareness and needs, and green logistics practices in e-grocery have an impact on consumer purchasing behaviour, according to study findings on the impact of green logistics practices on the buying behaviour of enterprises. At this stage, a green strategy to domestic or global business activity has been demonstrated and must also be put into practice.

Keywords: E-Commerce · Green logistics · Purchase behavior · Consumer · Service network

1 Introduction

Consumption has existed throughout history for as long as there have been people [1]. The environment is polluted by all forms of consumerism. Resources have been heavily utilised for both monetary gain and the satisfaction of fundamental necessities. On the

M. Botto-Tobar et al. (Eds.): ICAT 2023, CCIS 2051, pp. 26–34, 2024.
https://doi.org/10.1007/978-3-031-58950-8_3

other hand, nature has continually replenished and put its resources at the disposal of people [2]. Since it has been devoured for so long, nature is no longer able to stop consumption during the self-renewal process. Green products and strategies are thus required for environmental conservation. Everyone needs to be more aware of the environment. The goal of green logistics is to minimise environmental harm by using limited natural resources over the long run. Along with being environmentally friendly, this objective is a consideration for customers when making purchases. If environmental issues are tied to consumption rather than production, the answer is said to be an increase in consumer education and awareness, preference for green products in products and applications, and company investment in this field [3, 4]. How much customers consume, what they choose to buy, and their post-purchase behaviours have all grown in importance [5]. In this regard, it is important to investigate how green logistics affects customer brand preferences in e-commerce.

1.1 Meaning of Green Logistics

In the middle of the 1990s, "green logistics" emerged as a unique concept. There isn't a common definition as of now. According to H.J. Wu and S. Dunn, "green logistics" refers to a logistics system that is concerned with the environment [6]. It covers the reverse logistics operations, which deals with trash recycling and disposal, in addition to the forward logistics system, which deals with the raw materials acquisition through manufacture, packing, transportation, and storage to distribution to end users. Jean-Paul Rodrigue and Brian Slack Green infrastructure is an effective and environmentally sustainable logistics solution [7]. Green logistics is ecologically responsible and attempts to reduce resource consumption and pollutants in order to promote sustainable development, as can be observed from the many definitions.

Regarding e-adherence commerce's to green ideals, the selling of things via the internet is insufficient. Companies must recover their logistical operations from the conventional framework and adapt them to the green principles for profitable and sustainable e-commerce activities [8]. Many buyers base their purchasing decisions on how environmentally friendly a product is [3]. The environmental concern is the most significant aspect in this decision. In this situation, people have modified their purchasing and product preferences to favour goods that are environmentally friendly or do the least amount of harm to the environment [9].

2 Background

Many academics have proposed numerous standards and measures to evaluate the value of e-services. Delivery Speed, User-Friendliness, Reliability, Satisfaction, and Control were listed by Dabholkar (1996) as the five primary characteristics of high-quality e-services in an early study on e-service quality. He also looked at how customers make assumptions about the quality of self-service innovation. According to the study's findings, control and pleasure were key factors in determining service excellence, whereas ease of use and delivery speed had minimal impact on service quality (save for the long waiting time and control groups) [10]. This model is still being used in a number of recent studies [11–13]. SERVQUAL was evolved into a number of models by several researchers for application in online commerce. WebQualTM assesses factors such as informational task fit, interaction, trust, trustworthiness, reaction time, understanding simplicity, intuitive operation, originality, flow (emotional appeal), image consistency, online completeness, and superiority over rival channels. The study provides a reliable, well-established website quality metric for use by researchers. It also broadens our understanding of TAM by emphasising the factors that influence usability and simplicity of use. With an emphasis on the value of user-friendly websites, later in 2002, the WebQual e-service quality rating system was also developed. The WebQual assessment is comprised of five factors: design, knowledge, confidence, and empathy. The measurement underwent several changes before WebQual.

Wolfinbarger and Gilly (2003) used focus groups to develop the four categories of attributes that make up the e-service quality model: customer service, web design, confidentiality and security, and delivery and reliability [14].

Parasuraman et al. (2002) acquired the most recent data on websites' fulfilment and reliability, accessibility, privacy and security, product arts, and availability of information and its content. In a study by Parasuraman et al., the e-service quality level (E-S-QUAL) and the e-service qualitative recovery scale were used to categorise e-service excellence (E-RecS-QUAL). Reactivity, compensation, and contact are the components of E-RecS-QUAL, whereas confidentiality, reliability, satisfaction, efficacy, and personalised attention are the components of E-S-QUAL. The findings of the study demonstrate how important consumers' higher-order judgements of websites are to privacy [15].

In the context of online buying, Gounaris et al. (2010) investigated the impact of word-of-mouth (WOM), site redesigns, and purchase intent on client satisfaction and service quality [16]. In 2005, Lee and Lin added two more requirements: aesthetics and post-purchase support. These criteria—along with the WebQual scale developed by Barnes and Vidgen in 2002—were utilised by these authors to evaluate the calibre of e-services. The study also showed that the quality of an e-service affects user behaviour intentions, using 240 randomly selected individual surveys from a Greek supplier of internet services [17].

Determining the impact of user care on female word-of-mouth and future purchase intent as well as the impact of the service quality factor on patient satisfaction. In their 2014 study, Kitapci et al. sought a strong link between word-of-mouth marketing and repeat business. The SERVQUAL model, created in 1984 by Parasuraman et al., was utilised in the framework to evaluate service quality. The study's findings showed a significant correlation between customer satisfaction and both repurchase intention and word-of-mouth advertising (WOM). The method e-service quality is now assessed in online commerce has certain problems. According to Blut (2016), E-S-Qual and eTailQ measures lack criteria for judging online firms, making it challenging for them to effectively account for consumer dissatisfaction and their choice to buy at alternative online merchants. The other problem is the inability to predict client behaviour. eTailQ performs poorly when evaluating service to customers and security while meeting 13 of the 16 criteria for e-service quality. It also scores ninth in terms of its predictive skills (Blut et al., 2015). WebQual may be the greatest at anticipating client behaviour, but its functionality is constrained [18].

Blut et al. (2015) used meta-analysis to create a hierarchical model after examining the flaws in the structure of the present e-service quality ratings. The hierarchical architecture provides a more detailed way of logging online store characteristics. The findings indicate that web page, customer service, protection, and fulfilment are the four pillars of excellence in e-services. Additionally, the hierarchical model is more effective in forecasting customer behaviour than other measures now in use. This approach makes a link between opinions about the value of online services and specific, implementable elements like site design, delivery, customer assistance, and protection [18].

3 Consumer Behaviour and Sensitivity to Environment

According to Guner (2016), a customer is a real person who purchases marketing collateral (i.e., products, price promotion, and distribution) to fulfil his or her own and/or family's requirements, wants, and desires. According to Wikipedia, consumption is the use of manufactured commodities and services by individuals to satisfy their wants and requirements [19]. Our society, according to Bauman (2012), is a consumer society. Consumption occurs via the acquisition and consumption of a wide range of goods, from necessities to desirables. The assumption that civilizations are in a "consumer society" is supported by the growing economy, new goods, steadily rising consumption, and consumerist way of life [20]. Our shopping habits are influenced by a variety of circumstances [19]. Psychological elements can be seen as the primary influencers of behaviour among the internal variables that have an impact on a person's purchasing decisions. They cover topics including education, inspiration, cognition, perception, and personality and attitude. Sociocultural factors are determined by external factors. Family, socioeconomic status, culture, subculture, and personal effects are a few of the subjects covered. Age, income, education, and geography are all considered demographic factors. Marketing initiatives also have an impact on consumer behaviour. It is the collection of tactics used by marketers. This collection of factors includes product attributes, pricing, distribution, and advertising. Examples of situational consequences include the physical surroundings, timing, motive for buying, emotional state, and financial circumstance [21]. Consumers' decisions to purchase new technologies are no longer just influenced by price; convenience, personalization, community, information collecting, etc. have also begun to play a role [22]. Consumers' green purchasing habits are significantly correlated with their gender, marital status, age, level of education, and income. According to Ekinciet al. (2007), green product buyers tend to be female, married, young, well-educated, and of high household income [23]. According to Yilmaz and Arslan (2011), gender, the location of the household, and the educational level of the parents all affect how environmentally conscious the pupils are and how responsive they are to environmental protection pledges [24].

Green customers are commonly understood to be those who are environmentally conscious, uphold high standards of living, and purchase green goods. Individual consumption, in the opinion of green consumers, is a practical means of preserving the environment [13]. With thoughtful purchase habits, green customers may support sustainable development [25]. According to Gerçek(2011), students lack sufficient knowledge of the green network activities and are hesitant to purchase environmentally friendly items

[26]. The attitudes and behaviours of students who attended environmentally friendly enterprises were examined [27]. It has been discovered that tourism students exhibit positive views and behaviours toward green items. According to Kükrer(2012) research, customers care about environmental awareness and the use of ecologically friendly products. Institutions and organisations must fulfil their environmental obligations and responsibilities in order to recognise people as environmentally conscious consumers [28]. They must also actively encourage people to pick environmentally friendly options for their purchases. The goal of the network managers should be to increase customer trust in the brand and position it among other consumers' top choices when making a purchase [29]. Consumers now choose goods that contribute the least to environmental harm.

4   Strategic Significance of Green Logistics

The need for sustainable economic growth and environmental preservation in logistics is known as green logistics. The different features of contemporary logistics operations will have detrimental effects on the environment, which will worsen as the economy develops and ultimately have a detrimental influence on sustainable development. Making great efforts to achieve the as a whole optimization for the logistics system and get the least amount of environmental damage by constructing and trying to perfect the policy as well as theoretical framework on green logistics, trying to improve and adjusting this same logistics facilities, technology, and logistics system organisation will be beneficial to enhancing logistics management, safeguarding the environment, and promoting economic development [30].

Creating green logistics is a crucial step in ensuring that resources are used effectively. Natural resources include things like crude, land, and people. The three resources are required to operate the logistics system. Resource waste will result from an increase in the volume of logistics or an irrational logistics plan. The complete circulation of products from the supplier to the client is viewed as one unit in modern logistics. The growth of the logistics industry has brought the supply chain's relationships between businesses and customers closer together. Creating green logistics will help the supply chain as a whole become "green" and utilise all of its resources [30].

Green logistics is a must-have option for sustainable growth. The idea behind sustainable development is to prevent present-day production, circulation, and consumption from having an adverse impact on the planet's resources and environment in the future. To put this principle into practise, contemporary logistics management operations must first develop the idea of a symbiotic logistics system with the environment by analysing modern logistics systems from the perspective of environmental protection. A contemporary logistics system that can support the growth of the economy and consumer spending is also being developed [31].

5   Preventive Strategies for the Growth of Green Logistics

Today, the sustainable growth of the social economy and the enhancement of human life depend greatly on the content of the economy, and one such content is green logistics. We need to design relevant policies from the perspectives of the government, business, and customer in order to accomplish "green" development for logistics.

1) Government: rules and laws sharpen the propaganda for public opinion, and alter the ideology. Government should actively promote environmental protection, including it in all socioeconomic processes as a key management strategy, and not just focus on economic development while disregarding environmental protection in logistics' production and consumption processes. The government should place a high priority on green logistics in the beginning and provide comprehensive instructions to ensure a smooth transition. Enact legislation, create administrative rules, and improve environmental management [32]. The government should create and finalize a set of regulations on green logistics in order to give the logistics industry a sound legal foundation and to promote a supportive environment for logistics companies. The experiences in industrialized nations show that government laws on the environment primarily encompass three aspects: restrictions on the sources of pollution, restrictions on the amount of traffic, and restrictions on traffic flow. Incentives and monetary recompense. The government should provide tax breaks or other financial incentives to businesses who use reverse logistics and garbage recycling to make up for the higher cost of doing so [33].
2) Green supply chain management for businesses in the end, business must implement green logistics in a tangible way. Therefore, it is essential to run logistics with the idea of environmental preservation and sustainable growth, regardless of whether they are company or logistical firms. Green supply chain management is simply a viable option. By implementing green supply chain management, businesses may reduce resource waste and pollution discharge at every stage.
3) Green consumer spending Green needs are driven by consumers. The term "green need" refers to a demand that naturally develops in human physiological processes as a result of the species' reliance on ecology and the natural world. In the real world, the economical need for sustainability translates into a demand for sustainability, which serves as the impetus for consumer-controlled sustainability logistics [34]. As a result of this motivation, customers are crucial to the management of green logistics. First, consumers support businesses that are embracing green logistics management through green consumption habits. Second, the customer drives businesses to adopt self-restraint when it comes to managing their green logistics. The public's perception of green consumption is another way in which the consumer demands that the government regulate green logistics management.

6   Result Suggestions

The impact of green logistics in e-commerce on customer purchasing behaviour is examined in this study. E-commerce is becoming a common practise. E-commerce has an impact on a variety of operations, including customer buying patterns, business production, storage, marketing, distribution, and service networks. Consumers consider the product's environmental effect in addition to its performance and quality when assessing a good or service [35]. Businesses adopted the green concept as a result of realising this, their obligations regarding environmental effect, ideas for gaining a competitive advantage, and a desire to improve their brand's reputation in the marketplace. In this regard, the significance of R&D studies has been recognised, and associated activities have grown [36]. Overall, these actions improved living circumstances while lowering lifetime expenses. Consumer awareness of green brands has risen. The study's findings indicate that the businesses' influence on consumers' decisions to buy green logistics software is as follows. It has been shown that customer expectations and environmental awareness have a significant impact on the adoption of green logistics, and that green logistics practises in e-commerce have an impact on consumer purchasing behaviour [37]. In this framework, national or worldwide business activity must demonstrate and implement a greener strategy.

Numerous elements influence our shopping decisions. The purchase behaviour is influenced by both internal aspects as well as external influences. Because of this, a factor influencing customer preferences for items is their knowledge of green consumption [38]. It is effective among the customer preferences' demographic characteristics. Another aspect that affects how customers locate, recognise, and buy green products is the marketing strategies and tactics used by the businesses.

On the contrary hand, it may be noteworthy that now the green credentials are offered online from the sale sites with the company logo. These manufacturers are distinct from other green producers in that they want customers to focus their own brands. Customer purchasing behaviour may be impacted by the fact that businesses are responsive to changing environmental circumstances and consumer behaviour and embrace green supply chain management in line with their growth objectives. Because of this, adopting the green philosophy has become a societal and international requirement [39]. The brand's image needs to be consistent in order for consumers to remember it and to find it more appealing.

The enterprises must fulfil the facilities and duties that will enable them to expand their competitiveness given that customers choose items with the least environmental impact. To enhance the preference for green products, businesses should first adhere to the investments and regulations necessary for e-commerce. In this sense, it is possible to argue that the government ought to support and facilitate taxation of e-commerce apps. Additionally, it is possible to guarantee that the user may access the internet quickly and affordably from any location by expanding the accessibility of internet networks [40]. The demand for the product can increase if the buyer thinks that there is an ecological difference associated to the sensitivity of the product. Businesses that plan to engage in e-commerce must digitalize operations like product follow-up, supply chain management, and storage, and update them to meet industry standards [41]. Another reason why the popularity of environmentally friendly businesses is not higher is that customers do not find the businesses' environmentalist efforts to be very convincing and authentic. The businesses ought to work more on ecological initiatives.

References

1. Durand, B., Gonzalez-Feliu, J.: Urban logistics and e-grocery: have proximity delivery services a positive impact on shopping trips? Procedia Soc. Behav. Sci. **39**, 510–520 (2012)
2. Güner, S., Coşkun, E.: Environmental perceptions of small and medium-sized enterprises and effect of supplier relations on environmental practices. Aegean Acad. Perspect. **12**(2), 151–167 (2013)
3. Vahrenkamp, R., Kotzab, H.: Logistics – Management und strategien. München: Oldenbourg Wissenschaftsverlag; Auflage **7**, 54–282 (2012)
4. Sadowski, P. Grüne Logistik – Grundlagen, Ansätze und Hintergründe zur Optimierung der Energieeffizienz in der Logistik, pp. pp. 4–53. VDM Verl, Müller, Saarbrücken (2010)
5. Akdeniz, A.A.: Green Marketing: Examples from Textile Industry. Beta Publishing, Istanbul (2011)
6. Allen, C., Clouth, S.: A guide book to the green economy; issue 1: Green economy, green growth, and low-carbon development – History, definitions and a guide to recent publications. UN Division for Sustainable Development, UNDESA, New York (2012)
7. Chen, Y.-S.: The drivers of green brand equity: green brand image, green satisfaction, and green trust. J. Bus. Ethics **93**(2), 307–319 (2010)
8. Kantarcı, Ö., Özalp, M., Sezginsoy, C., Özaşkınlı, O., Cavlak, C.: The driving force of the economy in the digitalized world: E-commerce, TÜSİAD-T/2017, 04-587 (2017)
9. Uydaci, M.: Green marketing, 2nd edn. Turkmen Bookstore, Istanbul (2011)
10. Aslan, F., Çınar, R.: A study on determining the trends of using the environment-sensitive products of the Caucasus University students in the context of green marketing activities. KAU J. Bus. Adm. **6**(9), 169–184 (2015)
11. Kansra, P., Jha, A.K.: Measuring service quality in Indian hospitals: an analysis of SERVQUAL model. Int. J. Serv. Oper. Manag. **24**(1), 1–17 (2016)
12. Bolat, H.B., Bayraktar, D., Ozturk, M., Turan, N.: A model proposal for the vehicle routing problem in the green logistics chain. In: XI Within the Production Research Symposium, pp. 536–548 (2011)
13. Boztepe, A.: Green marketing and economic developments. Eur. J. Econ. Polit. Stud. **5**(1), 5–21 (2012)
14. Wolfinbarger, M., Gilly, M.C.: ETailQ: dimensionalizing, measuring and predicting etail quality. J. Retail. **79**(3), 183–198 (2003)
15. Parasuraman, A., Berry, L., Zeithaml, V.: Refinement and reassessment of the SERVQUAL scale. J. Retail. **67**(4), 114 (2002)
16. Gounaris, S., Dimitriadis, S., Stathakopoulos, V.: An examination of the effects of service quality and satisfaction on customers' behavioral intentions in e-shopping. J. Serv. Mark. **24**(2), 142–156 (2010)
17. Marimon, F., Vidgen, R., Barnes, S., Cristóbal, E.: Purchasing behaviour in an online supermarket: the applicability of ES-QUAL. Int. J. Mark. Res. **52**(1), 111–129 (2010)
18. Blut, M.: E-service quality: development of a hierarchical model. J. Retail. **92**(4), 500–517 (2016)
19. Güner, M.: Development of internet and special shopping websites. J. Soc. Sci. **3**(6), 594–606 (2016)
20. Cakir, M., Cakir, F., Master, G.: Determining the factors affecting consumption preferences of university students. J. Organ. Manag. Sci. **2**(2), 87–94 (2010)
21. Çabuk, S., Nakıboğlu, B., Keleş, C. Investigation of consumers' green (product) purchasing behaviors in terms of socio-demographic variables. Ç.Ü. J. Inst. Soc. Sci. **17**(1), 85–102 (2018)

22. Karaca, Ş: Elik investigation of consumers' attitudes towards green products incel. Ege Acad. Rev. **13**(1), 99–111 (2013)
23. Ekinci, B.T.: Problems in green marketing applications and a case study. M.Sc. thesis, Marmara University, Institute of Social Sciences, Istanbul (2007)
24. Yılmaz, V., Arslan, T.: Environmental protection promises of the university students and investigation of environmental friendly consumption behaviors. Anadolu Univ. J. Soc. Sci. **11**(3), 1–10 (2011)
25. Gök, A., Türk, M.: A research on the consciousness of protecting the environment in Parakendeci enterprises. J. Econ. Adm. Sci. **16**(2), 125–152 (2011)
26. Gerçek, H., Zeren Gülersoy, N., Cılız, N., Altan Ocakverdi, H.: Vision 2050 Turkey, TUSIAD, 09/518 (2011)
27. Yildiz, S.B., Kilic, S.N.: The attitudes and behaviors of the students taking bachelor's degree tourism education about eco-friendly products. Int. J. Hum. Sci. **13**(1), 1304–1323 (2016)
28. Kükrer, Ö.: The effects of consumers' environmental responsibilities towards attitudes of the green advertising: a sample in Eskişehir. J. Yasar Univ. **26**(7), 4505–4525 (2012)
29. Gerlevik, D. Effect of shopping through internet on consumer behavior. Master thesis, Atılım University Institute of Social Sciences (2012)
30. Handfield, R.B.: Green supply chain: best practices from the furniture industry. Proc.-Ann. Meet. Decis. Sci. Inst. USA **3**, 1295–1297 (1996)
31. Hoek, R.I.V.: From reversed logistics to green supply chains. Supply Chain Manag. **4**(3), 129–134 (1999)
32. Prashar, K., Kalotra, A.: Modelling the effect of e service quality on consumer satisfaction towards E grocery. Webology **18**(4) (2021)
33. Prashar, K., Singhal, S.: Study of consumer perception towards online grocery shopping. J. Xi'an Univ. Arch. Technol. **12**, 5629–5644 (2020)
34. Sheu, J.B., et al.: An integrated logistics operational model for green-supply chain management. Transport. Res. Part E: Logist. Transport. Rev. **41**(2), 287–313 (2005)
35. Tirkeş, Ç.: Green marketing: Strategies for increasing the use of organic food products in Turkey. Ph.D. thesis, Marmara University Institute of Social Sciences, Istanbul (2008)
36. Tiwari, S., Tripathi, D., Srivastava, U., Yadav, P.K.: Green marketing – emerging dimensions. J. Bus. Excell. **2**(1), 18–23 (2011)
37. Türkoğlu, A.: Examining the effects of green market on the product law and behaviours of consumers in socio-demographic aspects. Master's thesis, Bahas In Untirer (2016)
38. Wang, C.Q.: Study on green logistics management based on sustained development. Sci. Technol. Prog. Policy **1**(2), 12–13 (2002)
39. Wu, H.J., Dunn, S.: Environmentally responsible logistics systems. Int. J. Phys. Distrib. Logist. Manag. **25**(2), 20–38 (1995)
40. Yaraş, E., Akın, E., Şakacı, B.K.: A research on determining environmental consciousness levels of consumers. Suggest. J. **9**(35), 117–126 (2011)
41. Yesilbilgi. Consumption habits and environment (2011). http://www.yesilbilgi.org/tuketim-aliskanliklari-ve-cevre.aspx

e-Government

A New Model of Trust in e-Participation: An Empirical Research in Germany and Spain

Alex Santamaría-Philco[✉], Doris Macías-Mendoza, Luis Vargas Parraga, and Patricia Quiroz Palma

Universidad Laica Eloy Alfaro de Manabí, Manta, Ecuador
{alex.santamaria,doris.macias,luis.vargas,
patricia.quiroz}@uleam.edu.ec

Abstract. E-Participation provides a means to involve citizens in e-government decision-making. The ease of access to e-Participation processes has raised the issue of trustworthiness of both the institutions promoting processes and the citizens participating in these processes. Trust is an important factor influencing all human decisions consciously or unconsciously. This also applies to decisions to engage in e-Participation activities. Trust is perceived as a complex construct and is influenced by various factors. Consequently, different factors have to be taken into account in an e-Participation activity. While trust in ICT applications, such as e-commerce and social media networks, has been widely studied, trust in e-Participation has not been studied in depth. Since it is necessary to create a trusted environment so that citizens choose to participate in e-Participation processes, this paper analyzes the factors that directly influence trust in e-Participation initiatives through an empirical research. Based on the model of trust for e-Participation by [1] the influence of "Technology" and "Participatory Processes" on trust and the decision to engage in an e-Participation is investigated by means of a systematic literature study together with an empirical study. The online survey was conducted in cooperation with the cities of Bonn (Germany) and Valencia (Spain). The study analyzes predominantly the factors that influence the procedure, the technology, and the perceived risk and/or the benefits of the electronic participation. The analysis of the variables and their effects is carried out by the use of the "Structural Equation Modeling" and "Partial Least Squares" method. The result of this study reveals an influence of the investigated variables related to trust in technology and participatory processes of an e-Participation which leads to corresponding design recommendations for optimization of trust in e-Participation regarding technology and participatory process.

Keywords: E-participation · trust · model · empirical research

1 Introduction

1.1 A Subsection Sample

With the rise of e-Participation, traditional participation processes are combined with the use of Information and Communication Technologies (ICT) as a fundamental support to the different stages in the policy lifecycle (i.e. agenda setting, policy formulation, decision making, policy implementation and policy evaluation - see [2] denominating e-Participation [3].

The further development of information and communication technology (ICT) allows ever better, global communication. The rapid exchange of information via digital media has a high priority today. In 2013, as many as 76.8% of Germans already had the opportunity to participate in these communications, as the technical requirements are cheap, available and therefore available [4]. Politicians are also picking up the possibilities of better communication. Not only subsequent evaluations on political decisions, political barometer or popularity scale of politicians are in the focus but participation and co-decision. According to [5]), 44% of respondents in 2013 wished to be directly involved in political decisions. In 2014, this figure was already 50% [5]. This can be achieved through e-participation initiatives. E-participation is referred to in the literature as the use of ITC to support democratic decision-making processes involving citizens [3, 6].

Several efforts have been made to find success factors for the design of better e-Participation initiatives [7] aimed at improving the ICT tools used. When planning new public participation processes, especially with large numbers of potential participants, the problem of trust arises naturally.

Trust is a concept of great importance and has been extensively studied in recent decades. Its diversity of application has raised interest from a variety of research fields, like psychology, sociology, organizational behavior scientists, anthropologists and political scientists [8]. Over the past few years, trust emerged also as an important factor in ICT driven domains such as in information systems, e-commerce [9], social networks [10] e-government [11], e-voting systems [12], multi-agent systems. In e-Participation, trust is particularly relevant in helping citizens to decide whether to join public participation processes or not. In the same way, decision-makers need to trust that the participations obtained correspond to the opinions of citizens and not to the influences of, for example, organized groups. There are a variety of trustworthiness perception factors that influence the action of creating trust in participation. These factors must be carefully analyzed to be able to make more reliable and trustworthy e-Participation processes. Hence, modern e-Participation environments should support trust on technology, trust in the process, trust in the use of information and trust in how the results of the process are being used [13].

Scherer and Wimmer have developed a trust model for e-Participation through a combination of the 'Integrative model for trust in organizational settings' (Mayer & Davis, 1995) and 'The interdisciplinary model of trust' [14]. The authors argue that empirical research is needed to evaluate the e-Participation model proposed.

In particular, this work examines the relationship between trust in e-Participation and willingness to participate. The influence of "trust in technology" and "in the participation process" is analyzed for a willingness to participate. Since trust is an influencing factor that consciously or unconsciously influences every decision of a person, a person's trust in an e-Participation must be considered. The study builds on Scherer and Wimmer's model of trust (2014a), which outlines various aspects that must be trusted in e-Participation participation. Among other things, the trust model considers factors that influence the perceived trustworthiness of stakeholders and e-Participation tools involved. Stakeholders in this model can be individuals, groups or institutions, such as decision-makers, moderators or even the public institution that implements e-participation. E-participation tools include weblogs and web portals, consultation platforms, e-petition systems, and virtual churches. The sum of the perceived trustworthiness of the individual entities in their entirety in turn influences the trust in a specific e-participation.

The study is based on the empirical cycle of design science methodology [15] (research problem analysis, research design, validation of research design, execution and data analysis), making out an adaptation of the trust model for e-Participation [16].

This paper is structured as follows: Sect. 2 provides a summary of relevant general trust literature by specifying its various definitions and models, factors and characteristics. In Sect. 3, the interplay between trust and e-Participation is shown through a description of the trust model for e-Participation and the relevant findings of the influence of trust on the participation process and technology. In Sect. 4, the empirical research is described along the three stages: research problem analysis, research design, and data collection. Section 5 presents the findings, including a validation of trust factors, a description of the results models and the discussion thereof. Finally, the conclusions and roadmap for further research are presented in Sect. 6.

2   Trust in e-Participation

Citizen participation is an area that has been studied very extensively during the last decades. We can highlight various aspects such as the various stakeholders (decision-makers and citizens or participants), the importance of citizen participation in a decision-making collaborative environment [17], and the bi-directionality of the process [18]. The use of ICT tools within the public participation context led to the term e-participation (electronic participation). In Macintosh's words, e-Participation means "ICT-supported participation in processes involved in government and governance. Processes may concern administration, service delivery, decision-making, and policy making" [3].

In the specific context of e-Participation, trust has not been widely studied yet. There are also various risks involved in e-Participation, such as trust influence e-Participation. Few authors designed specific models with the aim of identifying the relationships between trust and e-Participation. Kim and Lee proposed a model of e-Participation and trust in government [19]. The model focuses on five transparency-oriented dimensions: (i) satisfaction with e-Participation applications, related with the development and assessment of government transparency; (ii) satisfaction with government responsiveness to online participants, associated to perceptions of influencing government decision making; (iii) participants' development through the participation; (iv) perceived influence on decision making; and (v) assessment of government transparency related to trust in the local government providing e-participation.

Trust is investigated to a particular aspect that might influence in the possible participation of a citizen and, and trust in the specific context of participation. The trust model for e-Participation results from a combination of the integrative model for trust in organizational settings [20] and the interdisciplinary model of trust with a marked influence of the first one; and adding the e-participation projects component. The roles trustor (participant) and trustee are defined based on the work of [20]. As visualized in Fig. 1, the model expands the view of Mayer et al. Since the factors of perceived trustworthiness are classified according to the stakeholders (ability, benevolence and integrity) and along the functionality of e-Participation tools (functionality, helpfulness and reliability). These factors influence the decision of trust in e-Participation regarding "1) the trustees' perceived ability, benevolence, and integrity; 2) the trustor's propensity to trust; 3) trustor's trust in situation and structures, and 4) tools and processes perceived as functional, helpful and reliable. Trust in e-Participation causes the trustor to partici- pate (RTR) in the action as a result of trust, considering the perceived risk and benefits (the concept of benefits was added by the authors, too). The result of this action is the positive outcomes that directly influence that the trustor increases its level of trust and, in the case of being negative, the opposite. Finally, the e-Participation project interventions are aimed at positively influencing trust through designing trustful e-Participations.

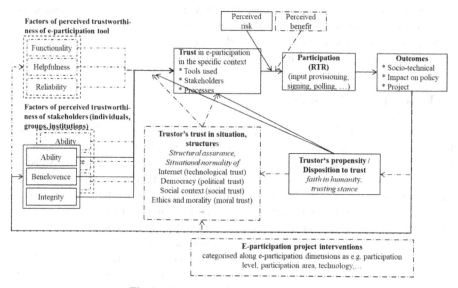

Fig. 1. Trust model for e-Participation [1]

Alharbi et al. examine a number of "factors" (trust in internet, family influence, friends influence, media influence, subjective norms and intention to engage in) that may influence the intentions of citizens to engage in e-Participation activities on governments' websites. They conclude that "factors of trust and subjective norms have a significant impact on citizens' intentions to engage in e-Participation activities" [21].

After having reviewed the literature on trust and its diffusion in e-government and e-Participation, the next section presents the empirical research, where the trust model for e-Participation serves as the basis. In the literature on trust, authors often use different labels (e.g., factors, variables, dimensions, and attributes) for trust-influencing factors. In this paper, in order to better distinguish the influences on trust in e-Participation, the terms "trust in technology" and "trust in the participation process" are referred to as "factors" and the expressions that influence them in turn. Referred to as "variables".

3 Empirical Work - Trust in e-Participation

The empirical study investigates the influence of various factors on trust in e-Participation using the design science methodology of Wieringa, which is specified in an empirical cycle [15]. Of the trust model for e-Participation [1] in particular, this work examines the relationship between trust in e-Participation and willingness to participate. We investigate aspects related to trust in technology and e-Participation procedures. Since trust is an influencing factor that consciously or unconsciously influences every decision of a person, a person's trust in an e-Participation must be considered. In this work, the listed variables of perceived trustworthiness of the technology are examined in more detail and possibly extended by additional variables. Also, the perceived trustworthiness of e-Participation processes is examined. This was not considered in the model of [1] and is intended to expand the model. Also, the empirical study will contribute to validate part of the trust model for e-Participation. In this study, the following research objectives emerge:

- To validate the factors and variables in the reference model and make an extension with respect to the "technology" and "process" factors.
- To identify the technical and procedural factors that influence the trust of a trustor towards an e-Participation initiative.
- To identify which means are necessary to achieve a trustworthy e-Participation.

3.1 Analysis of the Research Problem

The procedure (tasks, artifacts) is one of the main components of the e-Participation; therefore, its correct definition and execution are predominant factors of the success of a new initiative regardless of its area of application. We believe that the procedure should be incorporated into the trust model of e-Participation, as one of the factors that have a direct influence on the trustor and his or her decision to trust. In the current context, where ICTs are indispensable to use as the medium where e-Participation initiatives are implemented, it is necessary to have more robust and reliable e-Participation systems that provide a high degree of technological trust to the participants. A proposal may be to incorporate into this domain, techniques usually used in e-commerce applications. Furthermore, in the search for more reliable processes, the potential risks and benefits that make a trustor decide to participate in an initiative must be analyzed. The study is driven by the following research questions (RQs) aimed at responding to the problems raised in this work:

- RQ1: What are the factors that determine the fair and transparent procedures in e-Participation projects?
- RQ2: What are the factors that influence the trust in the e-Participation system?
- RQ3: What are the perceived risks/benefits in participating in an e-Participation initiative?

3.2 Research Design

The research design is based on the realization of an adaptation of the trust model for e-Participation (abstract view) of Scherer and Wimmer [1]. As shown in Fig. 2, dotted lines represent the incorporations to the model. The original model represents the e-participation project interventions that are related to several trust influence factors like technical aspects (tools) and other factors: "trustor's trust in situation and trustor's disposition of trust".

In this study three sub-objectives are established to answer the research questions. A first sub-objective is oriented to analyze the procedural factors from influencing the trustor's trust, we believe that the main factors among others are transparency and impact/influence on decision making represented by dotted red lines. RQ1 attempts to determine the relationship between these factors and the e-participation process. In addition, in the analysis of the RQ1 a series of sub-questions of research emerge, oriented to know the influence that diverse variables found perform on the e-Participation process: RQ1-1: Which factors along the participation process influence trust in e-participation and what influence does process transparency, information provision and information quality have on trust? RQ1-2: Does the previous participation in e-Participation initiatives have an impact on trust in e-Participation? RQ1-3: How does the quality of the contributions affect trust in e-participation?

The second sub-objective is to identify the primordial technical factors of trustworthiness in the e-participation tools. RQ2, represented by green lines, identifies the relationship between trustworthiness of tools and the trust in participation factors. Trust in systems is usually determined by the level of satisfaction achieved based on properties such as: functionality, reliability, helpfulness, data security and protection (dotted blue lines). In the same way as in the previous research question, in RQ2 we set out the following research sub-questions: RQ2-1: How does information on data security and privacy affect trust? And RQ2-2: Which variables of the design of an online participation portal have an influence on the trust in an e-Participation?

Finally, in order to analyze the behavior of the trustor in terms of the potential risks and benefits of participating in an initiative, a third sub-objective is developed. Participation in a new e-Participation project originates primarily after of a comparison, made by the trustor, between risks and benefits to be obtained. The RQ3 aims to identify these diverse characteristics among citizens who have participated in e-participation initiatives in a local context.

3.3   Data Collection

In order to obtain a broad view of the European context, the empirical study is carried out with citizens of two municipalities (Bonn in Germany and Valencia in Spain). In order to obtain a broad view of the European context, the empirical study is carried out with citizens of two municipalities (Bonn in Germany and Valencia in Spain). As a subject of the survey, the e-participation offers of the two cities were selected. The city of Bonn offers citizens the opportunity to get involved in their city through the participation portal *"Bonn macht mit den"* and to participate in decisions at the municipal level. The same function fulfills the portal of participation "Decidimvlc" of the city council of Valencia. Citizens interested in e-participation were invited to participate.

For the empirical investigation, an online survey was designed and implemented with LimeSurvey tool (https://www.limesurvey.org). The survey consisted of two parts: the first part asked aspects of demographic information; the second one consisted of

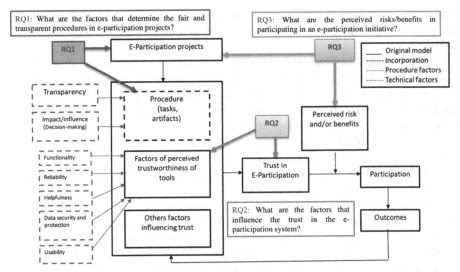

Fig. 2. Research model for the empirical study

four sections of questions, including (i) previous experience with e-Participation, (ii) technical factors, (iii) e-Participation process and (iv) general e-Participation aspects. The survey has been active for four weeks in each city (from February 15, 2016, to March 20, 2016 for Bonn and from May 12, 2017, to June 12, 2017, for Valencia). The online survey has been promoted among citizens via e-mail, meetings and social media platforms. In addition, participants of previous e-Participations were addressed by e-mail. The answers obtained by the survey and the analysis procedure to determine the influence of the identified variables and factors are described in the following chapter. It also allows filtering respondents into users and non-users of e-Participation.

In Bonn, 152 citizens participated in the survey, 119 of which completed the questionnaire in full. Of these 119 persons, 48 participants stated that they had already participated in an e-Participation. For Valencia city in total, 101 usable results have been obtained, corresponding to 54 non-users of e-Participation and 47 participants with previous experiences in e-Participation processes.

For the sake of clarity, the PLS-SEM models use abbreviations for the respective latent variables, which are listed in Table 2 with their meanings. In addition, Table 3 shows the relationship between the research questions posed and the various variables that involve them. It is proposed to model the results based on five base variables: Influence on decision making, Trust in e-Participation process transparency, Trust in process, Trust in technology and Trust in contributions. Further, a series of related variables correspond to each base variable. Finally, the various questions posed to the participants are shown.

4 Validation of Trust Factors

For the validation of the empirical study, five models have been carried out to verify the relationships between the factors represented in the research model. To respond to RQ1, the behavior of the responses on the *influence on decision making, trust in e-Participation process transparency* and *trust in process* variables are analyzed. The RQ2 question is analyzed by the variable *trust in technology,* and the variable *trust in contributions* for RQ3.

In each model, various components are depicted. The blue circles represent the variables, the yellow boxes belong to the questions (codes), the numerical results in the relationship dates between variables correspond to the *path coefficient* (β), the numerical result within the central circle corresponds to *Pearson coefficient* (R^2) and the numerical results between the variables and questions belong to the *significance* (p).

To answer the RQ1, Fig. 3 shows the '*influence on decision making*' model. First the results of the city of Bonn are shown. IQZI (β = 0.385), IQE '' (β = 0.343), MO '' (β = 0.233), and IQA '' (β = 0.194) have a positive effect on EE and together account for 84.2% of its variance. Accordingly, this model has a very good quality. This shows that the perceived impact on decision-making (EE) is reflected in the perceived quality of the information on the goals (IQZI), the process (IQA) and outcome of participation (IQE) as well as the perceived quality of the moderation (MO) is positively influenced.

Of the Valencia data, the model is of good quality proven by R2 of 34.40%. The behavior of four variables (results, moderation, process flow and other contributions) on the '*decision making*' variable is analyzed. The model's highest values correspond to the '*information regarding to the results*' (β = 0.337) and '*quality of information with regard to the process flow*' (β = 0.321) variables. This indicates that the results publication contributes to transparency of the process and gives to the participant a trust feeling that their contributions are important for decision making. In the same way, the '*quality of information with regard to the process flow*' positively influences the feeling of perceived trust in decision making. Moreover, the process moderation obtains a slightly lower value below the required mean (β = 0.152), because several responses are oriented to the low moderation level in the studied e-Participation initiative. Finally, the lowest value of the model corresponds to '*information regarding to the other contributions*' (β = -0.270), due to the lack of visualization of other participations in the e-Participation tool used. In relation to significance values, very good results are observed throughout the model except for the question P6SQ001 (p = 0.000) related to the limited help found in previous participations.

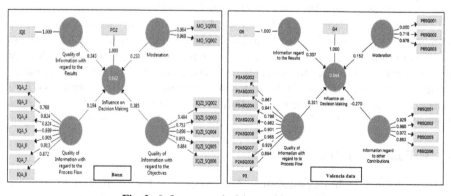

Fig. 3. Influence on decision making model

Figure 4 shows the significant model for trust in the participation process. The model made from the Bonn data shows the latent variables IQA, VIT, VIB, and VTB result a significant impact on VIP. It displays 53.20% of the variance of VIP and thus also has a good quality. The most positive influence in this submodel is IQA ($\beta = 0.360$), followed by VIT ($\beta = 0.276$), VTB ($\beta = 0.271$) and VIB ($\beta = 0.266$). For the Valencia data, the model analyzes the behavior of the variables 'Quality of information with regard to the process flow', 'Trust in technology', 'Trust in contributions' and 'Trust in conditions of participation' in function on the 'trust in the process'. The model is of good quality proven by R^2 of 27.60%. The highest path coefficient is obtained by 'Trust in contributions' variable ($\beta = 0.250$), confirming the importance of contributions in an e-Participation process.

Also, the model shows that the variable 'Trust in conditions of participation' ($\beta = 0.245$) affects the trust feeling on the decision to participate or not in an initiative. Values slightly below the average have been received for the 'Trust in Technology' ($\beta = 0.186$) and 'Quality of information regarding to the process flow' ($\beta = 0.151$) variables. Finally, in relation to the significance values (p), high and very high values are observed, increasing the validation quality of the model. The models represented in Fig. 3, Fig. 4 and Fig. 5 provide answers to the RQ1 and RQ3.

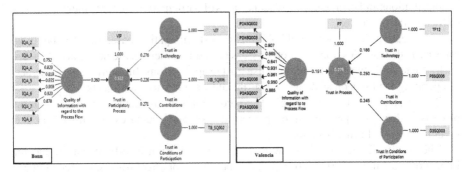

Fig. 4. Trust in process model

5   Conclusions

The advances in ICT have brought public participation to a new era. Nowadays, a vast majority of citizens, not only in western countries, have Internet access from their desktop or mobile devices. This means that they can be involved in political decision processes in a way (known as e-Participation) much easier than usual. However, an area barely studied until now is the interference of trust in e-Participation initiatives, which is given by various factors such as technology, process, sociological and/or psychological aspects, among others.

In this paper, we have presented an empirical study of the influence of trust on e-Participation processes, specifically our research is based on the e-Participation trust model of Scherer and Wimmer [16]. We have analyzed the behavior of the trustor on the influence factors in relation to the e-Participation procedure, technical factors and the perceived risk/benefits of participating.

The results of the survey and the PLS analysis carried out confirm that the examined variables of the factors "technology" and "participation process" influence the trust in e-participation. The technical variables "functionality" listed in [1] and the variable "data security" could be identified as influencing trust and also confirmed. Both variables have a comparable influence on the trust in the technology.

Trust in the participation process is most positively influenced by the variable "information quality of the process", followed by the variables "trust in the contributions" and "trust in the participation condition". However, the biggest influence on trust in e-Participation is the process variable "influencing the finding of results". This alone has a significant and strong influence ($\beta = 0.689$) on the change in trust due to a previous participation and explains 47.50% of its variance (R2).

We have found that transparency and impact in decision-making are two factors of direct influence on the trustor's trust in the e-Participation initiatives. The quality of information with regard to the process flow contributes to transparency and achieves a sensation of impact of the participations on decision making. The quality and transparency of the results of the participation initiatives influence trust on the processes and they increment the interest in future participations. For a trustor, trust in the transparency of contributions and in processes with conditions of participation are fundamental aspects of trust in the processes.

The creation of technological solutions for e-Participation based on trust-building aspects, as they are developed for other areas (e.g. e-commerce), are necessary. Aspects such as data security and information raise trust in applications. In addition, the existence of operating facilities on systems such as the aids, are key to the projects.

The creation of better technological and procedures infrastructures in e-Participation projects reduce the perception of perceived risk and increases the trust that the participations will bring benefits.

The results of this survey show that prior participation in e-Participation has an impact on trust in the participation process, but does not affect trust in the technology. Furthermore, when designing trustworthy e-Participation initiatives, a special value has to be placed on the perceived influence of the citizen on the decision making as well as on the clarity of the web pages. It should also take into account the transparency of the results and their justifications, as well as the grouping function of the contributions. Finally, it should be pointed out that, due to the low number of participants, further investigations should be carried out in order to re-examine the findings and confirm their relevance. These surveys should combine various survey tools such as online survey, paper-based interviewing and interviews to reach different audiences and achieve representative results.

Future research should be concerned with the study of the influencing factor stakeholder. The results of this paper suggest that trust in decision-makers, moderators or in the administration also influences trust in e-Participation. Furthermore, the influence of the perceived risks and the perceived benefits of e-participation should be examined more closely. As future work, we propose the incorporation of trust into an e-Participation framework in order to support the development of future e-Participation solutions.

References

1. Scherer, S., Wimmer, M.A.: Conceptualising trust in E-participation contexts. In: 6th International Conference on eParticipation (ePart 2014), vol. 8654 (2014)
2. Howlett, M., Ramesh, M., Perl, A.: Studying public policy: Policy cycles and policy subsystems, 3er, 163rd edn. Don Mills (1995)
3. Macintosh, A.: Characterizing e-participation in policy-making, vol. 00, no. C, pp. 1–10 (2004)
4. Santamaria-Philco, A., Canós, J.H., Penadés, M.C.: Advances in e-participation: a perspective of last years. IEEE Access 7, 155894–155916 (2019)
5. Forsa. Meinungen zum Thema E-Participation Umfrage im Rahmen des Wissenschaftsjahres 2014 – Die digitale Gesellschaft (2014)
6. Rose, J., Sanford, C.: Mapping eParticipation research: four central challenges. Cais 20, 909–943 (2007)
7. Panopoulou, E., Tambouris, E., Tarabanis, K.: Success factors in designing eParticipation initiatives. Inf. Organ. 24(4), 195–213 (2014)
8. Bannister, F., Connolly, R.: Trust and transformational government: a proposed framework for research. Gov. Inf. Q. 28(2), 137–147 (2011)
9. Beatty, P., Reay, I., Dick, S., Miller, J.: Consumer trust in e-commerce web sites. ACM Comput. Surv. 43(3), 1–46 (2011)
10. Sherchan, S.N., Paris, C.: A survey of trust in social networks. ACM Comput. Surv. 45(4), 1–33 (2013)
11. Papadopoulou, P., Nikolaidou, M.: What Is Trust in E- Government?. In: 43rd IEEE Hawaii International Confernce System Science, pp. 1–10 (2010)
12. Antoniou, A., et al.: A trust-centered approach for building e-Voting systems. Electron. Gov. Proc. 4656, 366–377 (2007)
13. Mayer, R., Davis, J.: An integrative model of organizational trust. Acad. Manag. Rev. 20(3), 709–734 (1995)
14. Harrison McKnight, D., Chervany, N.L.: Trust and distrust definitions: one bite at a time. In: Falcone, R., Singh, M., Tan, Y.-H. (eds.) Trust in Cyber-societies. LNCS (LNAI), vol. 2246, pp. 27–54. Springer, Heidelberg (2001). https://doi.org/10.1007/3-540-45547-7_3
15. Wieringa, R.: Design Science Methodology for Information Systems and Software Engineering. Springer, Heidelberg (2014). https://doi.org/10.1007/978-3-662-43839-8
16. Wimmer, M., Scherer, S., Appel, M.: The role of trust in E-participation: predictors, consequences, and design. In: Electronic Goverment and Electronic Participation: Joint Proceedings of Ongoing Research Project, IFIP WG 8.5 EGOV ePart 2015, pp. 3–10 (2015)
17. Creighton, J.L.: Public Participation Handbook, 1st edn. Jossey Bass, San Francisco (2005)
18. Canadian Environmental Assessment Agency. Public Participation Guide. Ottawa (2008)
19. Kim, S., Lee, J.: E-Participation, transparency, and trust in local government. Public Adm. Rev. 72(6), 819–828 (2012)
20. Mayer, R.C., Davis, J.H., Schoorman, D.: An integrative model of organizational trust. Acad. Manag. Rev. 20(3), 709–734 (1995)
21. Napitupulu, D., Adiyarta, K., Albar.: Public participation readiness toward e-GOv 2.0: lessons from two countries. In: ACM International Conference on Proceeding Series, vol. Part F1481, pp. 240–243 (2019)

e-Learning

Mapping for Quality Analysis of the Instructional Model for MOOCs. Case Study: Open Campus Initiative

Elizabeth Cadme-Samaniego[1]([✉]) , Veronica Segarra-Faggioni[2] ,
Audrey Romero-Peláez[1] , Juan Carlos Morocho[1] , Diana Torres-Guarnizo[1] ,
and Nelson Piedra[1]

[1] Universidad Técnica Particular de Loja, Loja, Ecuador
iecadme@utpl.edu.ec
[2] Ecole De Technologie Superieure, Montreal, Canadá

Abstract. The objective of this study was to determine the agreement with the quality parameters of MOOC courses offered by the Open Campus initiative. It begins with an analysis of related literature that allows us to gather a Ten-Dimensional Model that presents quality and pedagogical guidelines for the design of this type of course and the 7Cs Learning Design Framework. In addition, the extent to which the participants evaluated the courses they had taken was analyzed by responding to a satisfaction survey. Quality criteria and compliance mapping were performed for a selected group of courses. Likewise, data from the satisfaction survey were analyzed to consider the opinions of the participants who took the courses. The results were analyzed based on the selected models. Finally, the level of compliance and the aspects to be improved that should be addressed by those who integrate the development teams of massive open online courses were determined.

Keywords: MOOC · Instructional Design · Open Campus · Quality Criteria

1 Introduction

Massive Open Online Courses (MOOC) emerge from innovation in the field of Open Knowledge and follow the principles of content massive and open dissemination mediated by online spaces [1]. The First MOOC course was held in 2008 and was called "Connectivism and Connective Knowledge (CK08)", it was designed by George Siemens, Stephen Downes, and Dave Cormier. Since then, MOOCs have transcended geographical boundaries, achieving a great impact on Higher Education, both in training jobs and in autonomous and lifelong learning. To date, there are numerous initiatives developed by prestigious universities, including Coursera[1], edX[2], Udemy[3], and others. The Universidad Técnica Particular de Loja[4] (UTPL), Ecuador, has the Open Campus Initiative.

---

[1] https://www.coursera.org.
[2] https://www.edx.org.
[3] https://www.udemy.com.
[4] https://www.utpl.edu.ec/.

M. Botto-Tobar et al. (Eds.): ICAT 2023, CCIS 2051, pp. 51–64, 2024.
https://doi.org/10.1007/978-3-031-58950-8_5

Under this initiative, it has offered approximately 325 MOOC courses in different knowledge and training areas in the Spanish language, which were developed between 2017 and 2023 and have been carried out for 18 academic offerings so far. Open Campus[5] aims to provide a space for educators and trainers who propose new learning strategies and, at the same time, offer a training path for participants/students from anywhere in the world. Additionally, technology experts participate in this initiative in the construction of learning components to integrate innovative solutions that benefit the actors in the teaching and learning process.

MOOCs in principle are free, massive, and ubiquitous, and to take advantage of the benefits promoted, considerations must be made, both in the course hosting platform and the educational design of the content. Since a vast number of people learn from a variety of MOOCs offered by universities and other organizations around the world, it has become a great opportunity to access knowledge; however, there is a high dropout rate in MOOC courses available, and little work has been dedicated to reducing this situation. On the other hand, in some studies highlight the need to study the quality of the instructional design of courses [2, 3]. Likewise, according to [2], Higher Education Institutions have begun to explore and experiment with hybrid initiatives, in which, using MOOCs (their own or from third parties), they apply flipped classroom models to mitigate the high dropout rate in courses and improve student learning.

According to [2], instructional design is an influential factor in the motivation of the participant, and consequently in the results. In addition, other factors involved are material organization, content quality, interaction established, and methodology applied. Likewise, [3] maintains that instructional designers play an essential role in ensuring the quality of online courses through the effective use of technology, robust pedagogical design of learning materials, and management of the course design process. These characteristics make the courses more attractive to students and at the same time allow them to better understand the content, achieving greater retention of information and satisfaction.

In [4] maintains that, despite the advantages that are present in MOOCs, the number of users of MOOC platforms has been increasing rapidly, although so has the dropout rate of these courses. Many registered participants did not complete the course. Course they had chosen. Only about 10% of all registered MOOC participants successfully completed their course. One of the causes of the high dropout rate in MOOCs is their instructional design. At Open Campus during the COVID-19 pandemic, this situation was no different, as the number of participants increased exponentially; however, approval rates remained low. One way to solve this situation is to work on the instructional design of MOOC courses and another option is to incorporate them into active learning strategies as observed in the work of [5].

In [6] a Ten-dimensional model for quality MOOC design is proposed that provides a comprehensive understanding of the essential elements of course design. These dimensions must be present in a MOOC: resources, general structure, vision, student background, and intention, pedagogy, communication, evaluation, technology, learning analytical data, and help. The four guidelines they analyzed correspond to the nine quality reference criteria taken from literature review and one more identified the interaction

---

[5] Open Campus Initiative http://opencampus.utpl.edu.ec/.

with the previous ones. The guidelines taken of reference in this work are: *OpenupEd Quality Benchmarks for MOOCs, MOOC Scan Questionnaire, Guidelines for Quality Assurance and Accreditation of MOOCs*, and *Quality Reference Framework (QRF) for MOOCs from the European Alliance for the Quality of MOOC*. The authors examined and identified how each dimension of their model is addressed in the quality standards of these guidelines.

In [4] six categories of MOOCs were defined based on the instructional design of the 7Cs learning design framework which refers to Conceptualize, Capture, Communicate, Collaborate, Consider, Combine, and Consolidate. Elements have been mapped in each of the categories: mission, resources, social, activity, additional features, and results. With this mapping, it is expected that the instructor/developer will focus on the design of the MOOC which will allow him to propose solutions to increase student retention and reduce dropout.

Furthermore, in [7] ideas are proposed for the educational design of Massive Open Online Courses (MOOCs), focused on their educational scalability. In most of the MOOCs in the sample, which are 50 MOOC courses, it is found that there is inter-action between the student and the content during the knowledge transfer activities ("knowledge"). Although the study shows examples of scalable design options in online (open) education, it also indicates the need for more elaborate interactions and feedback in MOOCs to improve their educational value and quality.

For their part, [8] suggest five principles: 1) meaningful, 2) attractive, 3) measurable, 4) accessible, and 5) scalable that can apply to future MOOC development projects without leaving aside the analysis of the possible implications of these principles. This work highlights the importance of integrating pedagogical theory with information systems for the design of MOOCs.

Table 1 shows a summary of the works related to the quality of instructional design in MOOCs.

These related works were analyzed to obtain the criteria that are necessary to evaluate the instructional design of open online courses that allow identifying aspects to improve and maximize the learning experience of the participants. The evaluation was applied to 13 courses of the Open Campus Initiative.

Next, Sect. 2 presents the methodology applied for the evaluation of the selected courses. In Sect. 3, the mapping of the instructional design elements is carried out using the 10-Dimensional Model of [6] and the 7Cs Learning Design Framework of [5]. Section 4 details the results obtained and, finally, Sect. 5 presents the conclusions of this work.

Table 1. Summary of works related to quality of instructional design in MOOCs.

Work	Study Case	Advantages/Limitations
Aguaded & Medina-Salguero, (2015)	Identifies the key elements that ensure the quality and management indexes of MOOCs	The lack of regulations to guarantee quality learning in MOOCs is mentioned. In addition, it is emphasized that a pedagogical model should be standardized to assess the quality of MOOC courses
Ramírez-Montoya & Beltrán-Hernández (2019)	Analyzes how innovation in instructional design can contribute to the development of entrepreneurial skills in the context of energy sustainability	Only two MOOC courses related to energy sustainability are selected, which may not be representative of generalizing an instructional design model
Ichimura et al. (2020)	It proposes a 10-dimensional model for the design of quality MOOCs, which involves improvements in instructional design and thus improvements in the learning experience	It highlights the need for instructional design for a quality learning experience through MOOCs
Kasch & Kalz (2021)	Identifies key points about educational design of MOOCs, mainly educational scalability. Apply a design analysis tool developed for large-scale online courses to analyze fifty MOOCs qualitatively	The study shows examples of scalable design options in online education, it also indicates the need for more elaborate interactions and feedback in MOOCs to improve their educational value and quality
Sabjan et al. (2021)	Identifies quality design criteria for MOOC development for both programmers and non-programmers	The results indicate that four criteria need to be prioritized: Video Content, Instructional Design, Culture and Digital Assessment
Fatich et al. (2022)	Analyzes dropout rates by highlighting the importance of instructional design as a means of student retention. It is based on the 7C's Learning Design Framework	The number of participants and MOOCs used to map their elements into categories related to instructional design is omitted

2 Methodology

This work has integrated a systematic literature review, the planning and development of a quality criteria mapping, and an analysis of a survey to determine the degree of compliance with quality criteria and the level of satisfaction of participants of massive open online courses (MOOCs). The Open Campus initiative, which aims to provide a space for educators and trainers who propose new strategies for learning and at the same time offers a training path for participants from anywhere in the world, has been taken as a case study.

The literature review and analysis allowed us to determine that several of the studies consulted coincide with the Ten-Dimensions Model by [6], which develops a design guide, supported by instructional design principles and tools; and the 7Cs Learning Design Framework by [5], which maps six elements of instructional design to improve the quality of MOOC courses. These elements were taken as a basis for mapping with a selection of Open Campus courses.

To map the elements of instructional design and the level of compliance, a sample of 13 courses that have been offered Open Campus from 2017 to October 2022. For the selection of these courses, we considered the number of interactions by students, the number of interactions by teachers registered during the course execution, and the degree of compliance in terms of updates prior to the course offering. A matrix of quality criteria and 7Cs principles was previously elaborated and a mapping was made with each of the selected courses. The criteria were adjusted to aspects such as organizational and presentation information, instruction on the work methodology, schedule of activities, information on the teaching team, communication strategies with the participants, and spaces for forming learning communities, mainly. The researchers registered as participants in the courses and coded the presence of criteria by examining the content, resources, and strategies used for the design of the courses.

Likewise, a grouping of criteria was made to conduct a satisfaction survey of online courses. Data was collected on the organization and presentation of contents, the evaluation of resources used, the teaching staff's instructions, and student adaptation to this online course modality. The survey was administered at the end of each course, it was not mandatory and was completed by 2,580 participants, 63.8% corresponded to the female opinion and 36.2% to the male opinion. A qualitative approach was used for the analysis, using a Likert scale. It was considered important to know the opinion of the participants regarding the quality and relevance of the contents and whether they are appropriate. Questions were also included to obtain the opinion on the way in which the teacher has presented his course and finally an opinion on the acceptance of the course in general. Table 2 shows the aspects considered for the satisfaction survey.

The data were worked on a Power BI panel as a tool that allowed obtaining the results described in the analysis and discussion section of this document.

The results obtained from the mapping of the course design and the opinions collected in the satisfaction survey made it possible to determine the level of compliance with quality criteria and the perception of the participants who took these courses.

Table 2. Aspects to evaluate in the satisfaction survey for Open Campus courses.

Aspects to evaluate	Item
Contents	Degree of relevance
	Distribution of subjects
	Integrity in the treatment of the proposed topics
	Methodological adequacy
Resources	Presentation and design of resources and activities
	Adaptation of reused resources
	Frequency of publication is adequate
	The videos presented are in line with the explanation of the subject matter
Teacher's instructions	Clearly states directions
	Uses several means of message dissemination
	Motivates and awakens the interest and participation of course members
	The videos presented are in line with the explanation of the subject matter
Participants rating	Adaptation to working environment (platform)
	It allows me to expand my network of contacts and interact with professionals from different fields
	I will use this modality to further enrich my curriculum
	The course is a key and interesting experience for continuing education
	General evaluation of the course

3 Mapping of Instructional Design Elements

In this study, two studies on guidelines for MOOCs were considered: the 10 Dimensions Model for quality MOOC [6] and the 7Cs Learning design framework [5].

The 10 Dimensions Model provides quality and pedagogy guidelines for MOOC course design and examines and identifies how each dimension is addressed in quality standards. Additionally, this work presents quality guidelines and measures that were analyzed, indicating the focus and elements covered by each of the [6]. On the other hand, the 7Cs Learning design framework is defined as a proposal to facilitate effective learning and to develop courses and materials consistently and reliably. This work focuses on mapping the available MOOC elements to group them into categories related to MOOC instructional design [5].

Once the relationship between instructional design and the elements available in a MOOC was established, the elements of Open Campus MOOCs were mapped to the categories and critical elements proposed in the studies. The elements that align with those in the two models were identified, as well as the elements that were missing and can be considered as instructional design approaches for MOOCs.

Figure 1 presents the results of mapping the elements associated with the categories of the 7Cs Learning design framework and the 10 Dimensions model for quality MOOC design.

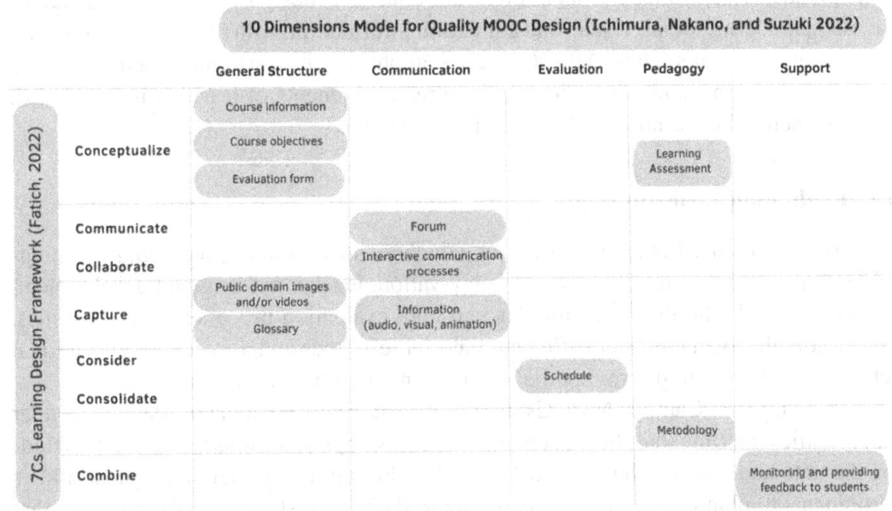

Fig. 1. Mapping MOOC - Open Campus course elements to the 10 Dimensions Model and the 7Cs Learning Design Framework.

3.1 General Structure Elements

The general structure of a MOOC aims to facilitate effective learning, achieve participant engagement, and intuitive navigation through course content and interactions. Detailed information about the course, objectives, and evaluation method is provided in UTPL Open Campus MOOCs. In addition, public domain images and/or videos relevant to the topic covered are included, thus enriching the learning experience. In addition, a glossary is incorporated that functions as a list of definitions (dictionary type), so that participants can consult and clarify key terms used throughout the course.

3.2 Communication Elements

According to [5], it is important to include communication and collaboration as an integral part of the learning process in the MOOC course, because this encourages interaction between course participants.

In UTPL Open Campus MOOCs, there is a welcome forum that enables students to get in touch with the instructor or the designated contact person on the forum page. The discussion forum is the most used tool by instructors to establish a learning community, facilitating the initiation of discussion threads and thereby promoting interactive communication processes.

In addition, MOOC courses have a space for communication with the site administrator, offering a direct contact channel for inquiries or doubts.

Furthermore, the presentation of information on MOOC design is synchronized with elements such as text, images, fonts, colors, and consistent designs. Multimedia resources are used, including sound, visual, and animation information, with the goal of motivating and engaging students. These MOOC courses emphasize the use of multimedia features, images, animations, and simulations as integral components of learning materials [9], thus enhancing the learning experience of participants.

3.3 Evaluation Elements

Numerous and varied elements influence educational innovation, including meaningful learning, effective teaching, student motivation, teacher training and development, attitudes toward learning, academic background, evaluation processes, and outcomes. In addition, the availability of sufficient material resources and a variety of educational activities contribute to improving the teaching and learning processes [10].

In UTPL Open Campus MOOCs, participants have access to an academic calendar that specifies the time that the student must spend studying the course material, including the date and time of challenge closures. In addition, the academic calendar allows participants to plan their activities according to their interests and needs, ensuring that the selected class is relevant to their learning. In this way, a structured and organized learning experience is offered, enabling participants to efficiently manage their study time and actively engage in the educational process.

3.4 Pedagogy Elements

In Open Campus MOOCs, the roles and functions of those responsible for the educational process have been assigned, ensuring an appropriate distribution of tasks. Additionally, the working method has been precisely socialized, establishing communication channels and interaction strategies among participants. The methodological proposal presented guarantees a solid pedagogical approach focused on achieving learning objectives.

Similarly, a learning assessment proposal was designed to measure student progress and performance fairly and objectively. The introduction of 'challenge' activities incorporates peer review (co-evaluation) tasks designed to foster innovative learning. The course content was carefully selected to ensure its relevance and pertinence for the development of skills and knowledge necessary in the current context. All of this combines to provide participants with an enriching and meaningful learning experience that enhances their academic and professional growth.

3.5 Support Elements

According to [5], the support or guidance elements used in MOOC course, not only impact the design but also enhances participant satisfaction when used. The support elements include search bars, help systems, themes, and personalized or avatars. The search bar function enables users to find courses or materials they want to learn from the list of available courses. It is important to emphasize that Open Campus MOOCs offer effective methods for tracking and providing feedback to participants, both on a massive and individual scale. Regardless of the proposed activity, meaningful feedback is generated for the student, allowing them to learn and reinforce concepts properly. According to [11], feedback plays a fundamental role in the learning process, promoting understanding and student progress in the course.

3.6 Technology Elements

In the study [6], the integration of technological tools is proposed with the aim of promoting interaction, communication, and support for participants. Similarly, there is an emphasis on social learning, collaboration, and knowledge communities through the use of elements such as online documents, video conferencing, discussion forums, and chat. With the same perspective, Open Campus MOOCs have leveraged technology as a fundamental resource to enrich the learning experience. Although the platform used, Open EdX, has some limitations, some components have been implemented, especially to collect information from assessment activities, which have been proposed and developed by teacher-researchers. This has allowed for the design of more elaborate activities that enable the development of skills through activities involving more complex processes.

4   Results and Discussion

The Open Campus platform offers a wide range of courses on various topics for participants. To evaluate the elements, present in the MOOC courses, an analysis was carried out using a set of items of aspects to evaluate with which each researcher made a checklist, this allowed identifying the fields and elements present in each MOOC course of the Open Campus platform. In our study, in Table 3, information was collected from the following courses:

After mapping the elements linked to instructional design, we proceed to the evaluation of the elements present in the selected MOOCs. As can be seen in Fig. 3, most of the MOOC courses have elements associated with instructional design. Regarding the General Structure (Sect. 3.1), the MOOC courses achieve 79% compliance. However, it was identified that the course "Prácticas sostenibles para zonas urbanas (Edition 3)" lacks the inclusion of the evaluation form and a glossary, which needs to be incorporated.

When evaluating the Communication element (Sect. 3.2), it was found that the MOOC courses achieved 43% compliance. It was identified that the courses "Prácticas sostenibles para zonas urbanas (Edition 3)", "Conocimiento ancestral de plantas medicinales" and "Fundamentos Informáticos" do not have welcome content, a welcome forum, or a space for communication with the site administrator.

Figure 3 shows that the evaluation elements are absent in most of the courses, reaching only 14% compliance. In relation to the Pedagogy elements (Sect. 3.4), in general, the MOOC courses achieve 87% compliance. However, the courses "Salud bucal, prevención y cuidado" and "Cuidados bucodentales en pacientes con enfermedades crónicas" should

Table 3. Open Campus - UTPL initiative course selection

MOOC	Course name	#Edition
1	Manejo del recurso suelo	17
2	Prácticas sostenibles para zonas urbanas	2
3	Salud bucal, prevención y cuidados	2
4	Cuidados bucodentales en pacientes con enfermedades crónicas	2
5	Huertos familiares	17
6	Bebidas alcohólicas fermentadas	15
7	Educación para una alimentación saludable	17
8	Emprendimiento y generación de ideas	10
9	Bases de la legislación ambiental ecuatoriana	2
10	Conocimiento ancestral de plantas medicinales	17
11	Fundamentos Informáticos	7
12	Psicología social	7
13	Matemáticas para la vida diaria	2

include a methodology proposal and present a proposal for learning assessment, in addition to specifying the way of working.

On the other hand, some MOOC courses need to consider the elements of Support (Sect. 3.5) and Technology (Sect. 3.6) to improve their structure and provide greater support to participants in their learning process. It is evident the need to work on these aspects to achieve a more complete and enriching educational experience in Open Campus MOOC courses (Fig. 2).

The analysis of the results of the Open Campus MOOC courses satisfaction survey shows promise. The parameters evaluated in terms of quality of content and resources, teacher expertise, student gain, and adequate course planning are of great importance to measure the effectiveness and educational value of online courses.

The scale used was from 1 to 4, with 1 being insufficient and 4 being satisfactory. The average rating is close to 4, indicating that the courses have achieved a generally high level of quality from the participants' point of view, as shown in Fig. 3.

In the Content parameter, the participants gave an overall rating of 3.74 out of 4. This score indicates that in general, the content of the courses was considered satisfactory by the participants. It is encouraging to note that the specific aspects of the content parameter were also evaluated positively.; among which we can highlight: the degree of relevance obtained a score of 3.73, which means that the participants considered that the content was relevant and applicable to their learning needs; the order of the subject matter received a score of 3.77; This score suggests that the structure and sequence of the content were considered adequate and logical for an effective learning progression. Likewise, the integrity in the treatment of the proposed topics obtained a score of 3.75,

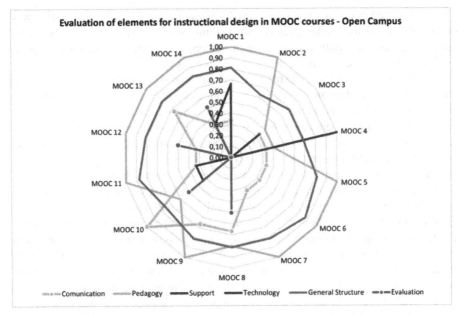

Fig. 2. Evaluation of elements for instructional design in MOOC courses - Open Campus

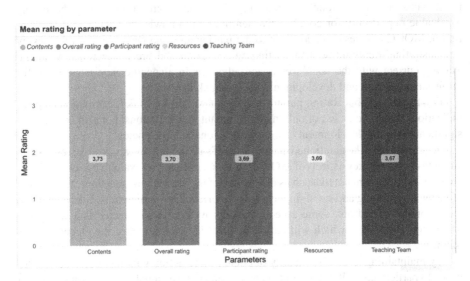

Fig. 3. Overall average of participant satisfaction indicators (PowerBI Panel)

which indicates that the courses address the developed topics in a complete and adequate manner. Regarding the methodology used, with a score of 3.75, the participants recognized that the teaching approach and methods used were appropriate and effective for their learning.

In the second evaluation parameter which corresponds to the Teaching Team, it was evaluated whether the teacher presents instructions clearly, uses various means of disseminating messages, motivates and awakens interest and the participation of the course members; the average evaluation is 3.7; It is important to recognize the strengths identified in the analysis to expose the mastery and ability of the teachers. These aspects are fundamental to providing an effective and engaging educational experience. In addition, the analysis highlights one area of potential improvement is in the quality of the assessment questions; assessments are a crucial part of the learning process, and the use of high-quality, meaningful questions can improve participants' understanding and provide them with opportunities to reflect and apply what they learned. It is positive that this area has been identified to make improvements and alternative solutions.

The analysis of the Resources parameter corresponds to the assessment of resources used, shows an overall rating of 3.70; this result indicates that, in general terms, the resources presented in the MOOC courses have been well received by the participants. The fact that the quality of the videos was highly rated and that participants found them useful, and motivating is a good indicator that the work in the course is going in the right direction. This recognition should serve as additional motivation to continue to strive to maintain and improve the quality of resources and activities in future MOOCs.

The analysis of the Valuing as a participant parameter is positive, with a score of 3.7, which indicates that the participants had a satisfactory experience in the MOOC courses; It is motivating for the team to see that the MOOC courses have provided a platform for participants to establish connections with professionals from different areas, becoming a valuable opportunity for collaborative learning and knowledge exchange. Participation in MOOC courses can add value to the participants and professionals resumes by demonstrating a commitment to continuing education and professional development. Staying current with the latest trends and advances in a specific field is essential for professional growth and development of relevant skills.

Finally, the Global Rating parameter, with a weighting of 3.72, provides us clear indications that the course not only met participant's expectations, but also contributed significantly to the development of their professional competencies.

In general, it can be mentioned that the level of satisfaction reveals positive results and strengths in several key aspects of MOOC courses. However, it is valuable to consider the areas of improvement noted, such as the quality of the assessment questions, to continue offering an enriching and satisfying learning experience for participants. Likewise, from the mapping carried out, some aspects for improvement are collected that will serve to develop guidelines, which will enrich the instructional model of the Open Campus initiative.

By maintaining a focus on quality of content, interaction with instructors, and relevance to participants, MOOC courses can continue to be a valuable option for education and professional development.

5 Conclusions

This paper aims to determine the extent to which the courses offered by the Open Campus initiative comply with the principles of the 10 Dimensions Model presents quality and pedagogy guidelines for MOOC course design by [6], and the 7Cs Learning Design

Framework by [5], as well as the extent to which participants rate the courses, they have taken by responding to a satisfaction survey.

Strengths have been identified, with Open Campus MOOC courses demonstrating strengths in areas such as overall structure (79%) and pedagogy (87%). The resources, in general, have been well-rated, especially the videos, indicating that they are useful and motivating. The overall rating of 3.72 indicates that the courses not only met expectations but also contributed significantly to the development of the professional competencies of the participants. This indicates that the experience is satisfactory, although this is due to the opinion of those who filled out the voluntary surveys and could be biased toward those who participated more actively, leaving out important observations of those who did not participate.

Communication and evaluation elements need attention, with lower ratings (43% and 14% respectively). This reflects that improvements need to be made in the design of the next editions of the courses. Specifically, the course "Sustainable Practices for Urban Areas (Edition 3)" requires improvements in the inclusion of evaluation ways and a glossary. Other courses need to work on the inclusion of support elements and technology to enhance the learning experience. Areas for improvement, such as the quality of questions in the assessments, should also be considered to continue to provide an enriching and satisfying learning experience. This reaffirms that constant updating is necessary, especially in courses that are offered several times due to their demand.

It also highlights an added value gained by participants, as MOOC courses have provided a mechanism for participants to establish connections with professionals from different areas, fostering collaborative learning and knowledge sharing. Participation in these courses can add value to the curriculum of participants and professionals, demonstrating their commitment to continuing education and professional development.

Regarding the resources used, recognition of the quality of the resources, especially the videos, should motivate the team to maintain and improve the quality of the resources in the future offers, especially in those courses that have been running for more than 2 editions. The assessment given in general should serve as additional motivation to continue to strive to maintain and improve the quality of the resources and activities.

While the results are positive, it is valuable to consider the areas of improvement noted, such as the quality of the questions in the assessments, to continue to provide an enriching and satisfying learning experience.

Maintaining a constant focus on content quality, effective interaction with teachers, and relevance to participants is crucial to the continued success of MOOC courses. The mapping performed enriches the instructional model, contributes to more complete experiences, and leads us to conclude that it should be performed periodically. Remarkable successes have been distinguished and areas for improvement have also been identified that determine the quality of this type of course, which motivates us to continue studying ways to improve the courses offered by the Open Campus initiative.

References

1. Aguaded, I., Medina-Salguero, R.: Criterios de calidad para la valoración y gestión de MOOC. RIED Revista iberoamericana de educación a distancia **18**, 119–143 (2015)

2. Maldonado, J.J., Pérez-Sanagustin, M., Bermeo, J.L., Muñoz, L., Pacheco, G., Espinoza, I.: Flipping the classroom with MOOCs: a pilot study exploring differences between self-regulated learners. In: 2017 Twelfth Latin American Conference on Learning Technologies (LACLO), pp. 1–8 (2017)
3. Ramírez-Montoya, M.S., de Beltran-Hernandez, M.J.: Innovation in the instructional design of open Mass Courses (MOOCs) to develop entrepreneurship competencies in energy sustainability. Educ. Knowl. Soc. **20**, 1–15 (2019)
4. Chen, Y., Carliner, S.: A special SME: an integrative literature review of the relationship between instructional designers and faculty in the design of online courses for higher education. Perform. Improv. Q. **33**, 471–495 (2021)
5. Fatich, E., Santosa, P., Ferdiana, R.: Mapping of instructional design of MOOC's elements. JATISI (Journal Teknik Informatika dan Sistem Informasi). **9**, 1762–1770 (2022)
6. Ichimura, Y., Nakano, H., Suzuki, K.: 10 dimensions model for quality MOOC design (2020)
7. Kasch, J., Kalz, M.: Educational scalability in MOOCs: analysing instructional designs to find best practices. Comput. Educ. **161**, 104054 (2021)
8. Drake, J.R., O'Hara, M.T., Seeman, E.: Five principles for MOOC design: with a case study. J. Inf. Technol. Educ. Innov. Pract. **14**, 125 (2015)
9. Sabjan, A., Wahab, A.A., Ahmad, A., Ahmad, R., Hassan, S., Wahid, J.: MOOC quality design criteria for programming and non-programming students. Asian J. Univ. Educ. **16**, 61–70 (2021)
10. Gazca-Herrera, L.A., Velazco-Ramírez, M.L., Culebro-Castillo, K., Zabala-Arriola, O.: Propuesta metodológica para el diseño instruccional y evaluación de un MOOC (2017)
11. Olivos, T.M.: La retroalimentación: un proceso clave para la enseñanza y la evaluación formativa (2021)

Using Gamification with Affective Computing for Second Language Learning

Astrid Avilés Mujica[(⊠)] and Marco Sotomayor Sánchez

Faculty of Engineering, Universidad Espíritu Santo, Samborondón, Ecuador
{astridam,mvinicio}@uees.edu.ec

Abstract. Existing educational games for second language learning often lack consideration for a crucial aspect of the learning process: emotions, since these can influence the motivation and comprehension of the student. This study explores the application of affective computing as a complement to a gamified educational application, aiming to provide tailored feedback aligned with the student's current emotional state. The implemented emotion detection model classifies users into four categories: satisfied, engaged, bored, and confused, then feedback is given according to the result of this model, which may include a comment on the content, an emotional one to re-integrate the student, or both to provide additional assistance, depending on the given scenario. To test this system, an experiment was conducted in a classroom, the results of which showed an effectiveness of the emotions model of 81.25%; moreover, with the use of a usability metric for gamified applications, it was obtained that in terms of the system Usability, there is an 84.87% efficiency, in Educational Usability there is an 85.71% effectiveness, in User Experience, there is a 75.24% of user satisfaction.

Keywords: Affective computing · Education · Feedback · Gamification · Second Language Learning

1 Introduction

Teaching English as a second language aims to establish a robust foundation for future development by focusing on essential language skills such as speaking, listening, reading, and writing in English. Using books as primary tools, educators and students engage with key teaching principles [1], including content and language-integrated learning, communicative English teaching, and language instruction customized to students' age and context [2].

In the English learning process, approximately 70 pedagogical modules for primary and secondary school courses incorporate multimedia content and digital activities. Complementary online resources, such as Easy World of English, All Things Grammar, and BBC Learning English [3], enhance classroom knowledge. The integration of educational games within the curriculum, structured around gamification principles [4], introduces a dynamic and interactive element. Badges and rewards, administered

M. Botto-Tobar et al. (Eds.): ICAT 2023, CCIS 2051, pp. 65–79, 2024.
https://doi.org/10.1007/978-3-031-58950-8_6

through a ranking system, acknowledge students' achievements, proving more effective for language acquisition compared to non-game learning environments [5].

Educational games serve as a strategic approach to adapt classroom strategies and resources to individual student needs [6]. However, their efficacy relies on the synergy between teacher explanations, the learning environment, and students' emotional engagement. To optimize second language acquisition, students must be physically, mentally, and emotionally immersed [7], fostering motivation for active participation. Prolonged confusion negatively impacts student success in class activities, underscoring the importance of a holistic and engaging language learning experience [8].

While the impact of the affective factor on second language learning is well-recognized, educational games predominantly concentrate on task completion, rewards, and progress without addressing the emotional dimension of students during the learning process, which can cause motivation to decrease and make it more difficult to give concrete and useful feedback to each of the students.

This study seeks to assess the effectiveness of gamification with affective computing in teaching English as a second language. The focus is on an educational game designed to generate adaptive feedback for each student. The objectives include analyzing the learning skills of A2-level English students, identifying key emotions affecting the learning process, designing a model to distinguish students' current emotional states for tailored feedback, selecting game elements to enhance motivation, and evaluating the application's impact on skill development according to each student's proficiency level.

2   Theoretical Framework

This section is going to be divided into two categories; related studies will present research on the use of gamification in an educational environment, as well as studies that have applied affective computing in computer systems, while the relevant concepts section will delve into the definition and relevant aspects of these two topics.

2.1   Related Studies

Gamification in education enhances interpersonal and intrapersonal skills [9], fostering decision-making and problem-solving abilities. Effective educational games include diverse modalities, engaging activities, and constructive feedback [10], contributing to motivation, confidence, and satisfaction in collaborative learning [11].

For optimal learning outcomes, game experiences should be of high quality [12], considering both behavioral and emotional aspects. Recognizing the impact of emotions on learning, and identifying common emotional traits guides the selection of feedback strategies [13], enabling students to evolve and respond effectively to future challenges. A computational model of emotions, validated for diverse pedagogical content, helps tailor feedback to individual student competencies [14], preventing random learning strategies.

Gamification, aiming to boost motivation and engagement, integrates intrinsic and extrinsic motivation for enhanced productivity [15]. Numerous experiments demonstrate improved learning outcomes, sustained student attention, and motivation [16]. Leveraging models like the GBL Design Model and the ARCS Model facilitates the adoption of behaviors that expedite tasks while keeping quality and proactivity [17].

GamiCAD, an educational game for AutoCAD beginners [18], incorporates reward systems, task repetition stimulation, and immediate feedback, reinforcing user motivation and learning experience [19, 20]. Affective computing, recognizing students' emotions in second language learning, allows for adaptive teaching approaches, mitigating negative impacts, and boosting motivation [21, 22]. Clear objectives and customized feedback enhance the learning experience [23], and the relationship between affect-based feedback and engagement supports personalized instructional decision-making [24]. Various gamification elements, including point systems, rewards, progress bars, user levels, and leaderboards, are employed in second-language learning. The integration of affective computing in educational game development provides automatic responses to user emotions, enhancing design and activity flow [25, 26].

Despite the recognized importance of the affective factor in second language studies, its significance is often overlooked in educational game development. Integrating affective computing can provide automatic responses to user emotions, enhancing design and activity flow [27]. Challenges arise from neglecting the five personality traits in the widely used academic psychology model, potentially leading to attention loss, decreased performance, and demotivation [28]. Consideration of these traits is essential for the effective development of language-learning games [29].

An example of the application of affective computing in a gamified application is observed in a study that combined both concepts to influence user behavior [30]. Recognizing that users react to events and mood changes [31], rewards are granted based on behavior. Another study integrated gamification into an intelligent tutoring system, resulting in improved exercise-solving times and increased learning levels compared to a control group following a traditional learning process.

Research conducted in the field of second language learning includes elements of gamification to reinforce knowledge and improve student motivation; however, affective computing has not been widely used as a complement to the gamified application to support the learning process to monitor student behavior, so a personalized follow-up can be provided using the emotions recorded and generating useful and adaptive feedback to what the user needs. For this reason, this study proposes the combination of affective computing with gamification to monitor and support the process of learning English as a second language.

2.2 Relevant Concepts

Gamification

Gamification uses game elements in a non-ludic context, taking advantage of the effect it has on people to compete and gain status [23]. Gamification accepts the MDA framework in the basic elements that comprise it [17], which is based on game design theory. This framework is made up of the concepts of game mechanics, dynamics, and aesthetics. Mechanics comprise the components, controls, and courses found in the system, indicating the rules, actions, algorithms, and structures that support the dynamics of the game; Dynamics describes the context, behavior, and consequences that act on the player, basing its operation on user inputs and other outputs over time; Aesthetics is described as the emotional responses of the players during their interaction with the game, as it relates to challenge, creativity, compliance, and contribution during the game [32].

To achieve player stimulation, several components are used to maximize the gaming experience and learning motivation, which can be grouped and classified according to their use as shown in Table 1 [8, 12].

Table 1. Game elements used in gamified applications.

Game element	Usability	Examples
Achievement (Performance)	Motivates and recognizes players' efforts and provides information to the student	Points, badges, leaderboards, certificates
Reward	Recognizes time, effort, dedication, and the skills acquired during the process	Bonuses, collectibles, and in-game resources
History	Narrative scenario that uses an argument to arouse interest in the player	Quests, narrative arcs
Time	Creates a sense of urgency and demand in the activity	Stopwatch, calendar of events

These elements are adjusted according to the game experience and difficulty levels to enhance students' enjoyment; to control the current difficulty level of each player, a difficulty curve model is used to measure the point difference in the system [8].

In educational games, several types of players can be found, among them are philanthropists, sociable, achievers, free-spirited, gamers, and disruptors [28]. Each of them has a different behavior, so it is necessary to include in the game design features that are attractive to all players.

GBL Design Model

Game-based learning (GBL) is an instructional approach where students learn through cycles of repetition, failure, and goal attainment within a game environment. The effectiveness of this model depends on several key aspects, including the design of the game environment and its application in the learning context.

Within the GBL model, the game objectives play a crucial role, and they are influenced by three interconnected factors: Mechanism (the methods employed by players to achieve the game objectives), Game Value (the game must attract and engage players from the outset), and Game Fantasy (this involves the environment and background of the game, encompassing the narrative and sensations perceived by players). The successful integration of these factors enhances the learning experience, making GBL an effective method for achieving educational objectives through engaging and interactive gameplay.

ARCS Model

It is a teaching model focused on student motivation and ensuring that it does not diminish during instruction. The ARCS model analyzes the different motivational categories to design strategies that help both teachers and students lead a successful learning process [35].

This model has four categories: attention, relevance, confidence, and satisfaction. Attention refers to how the student responds to the educational stimuli that have been provided and this must be stimulated and maintained during the process as it is related to curiosity and sensation seeking; relevance is helpful for students to relate the experience to the instructions given, showing the usefulness of the content in real situations; confidence focuses on developing positive expectations of success in students in their performance so that they can control their learning processes; and satisfaction occurs when students put into practice their acquired knowledge throughout the learning process [17].

Affective Computing

Emotions play a crucial role in the learning process, reflecting an individual's response to their environment [31]. Various studies have explored basic emotions like curiosity, interest, pleasure, and anxiety, which are integral, binary, and interconnected. Emotions serve as representations of a person's state and behavioral tendencies [13], encompassing both visible behaviors and subtler aspects related to attention, perception, and cognition. Motivation, whether positive or negative, relies on the interplay between emotions and internal/external factors, with students in a classroom influenced not only by their emotions but also by the behaviors of peers and teachers [20].

The value of emotions in learning, including their impact on entertainment, user experience, training, and evaluation, has been emphasized through educational emotion studies. Affective computing, involving the detection of a user's emotional state, plays a crucial role in technology-based learning techniques [30]. It contributes to decision-making and perception, ultimately enhancing comprehension performance [22]. Affective computing has been effectively utilized to represent emotional responses, influencing student behavior and fostering long-term use of educational technologies. The ability to detect emotions and provide emotional feedback contributes to improved user productivity, usability, and interaction throughout the learning journey [22].

3 Methodology

This research is exploratory, aiming to assess the impact of emotions on students with an A2 level of English during language learning. It employs a qualitative approach, incorporating gamification elements from prior ESL studies and applying affective computing as a complementary tool. Data collection will involve student surveys, open questionnaires, and literature reviews to gain insights into the emotional dynamics and the effectiveness of the educational game in language acquisition.

This project will leverage the React Native framework for mobile application development, serving as the foundation for the game. The facial recognition component will be implemented using Firebase's MLKit cognitive service. The project will utilize Firebase Firestore, a NoSQL database known for its flexibility and scalability in data handling. For efficient prototyping, the Figma tool will be employed, offering a quick and user-friendly interface for editing and refining results.

This study follows a four-stage research design: collection, preparation, development, and evaluation. Initial data gathering focuses on identifying students' language skills, knowledge, and emotions in the classroom. Subsequently, a Girard and Johnson-based emotion detection model [14] will be designed, integrating gamification elements for motivation, progress assessment, and feedback. The development stage employs the Scrum methodology for iterative and incremental cycles, ensuring quick solutions and high-quality standards. The evaluation stage involves a final test and usability surveys, utilizing metrics for Usability (U), Educational Usability (EU), and User Experience (UX) to comprehensively assess the effectiveness and user-friendliness of the educational game.

4   Implementation

This section will explain the application development procedure, which includes the four stages of the methodological process explained above.

4.1   Stage 1: Data Collection

A survey involving 15 eighth-grade students (ages 11–13) with a majority (66%) being male was conducted to gauge their language knowledge and assess their learning process. The survey, encompassing 10 questions, focused on the affective factor in the classroom, addressing subject content, tutor feedback, and student satisfaction.

To evaluate language proficiency, a 15-min EFSET proficiency test was administered, providing scores corresponding to Common European Framework of Reference (CEFR) levels: A1 Beginner, A2 Elementary, B1 Intermediate, B2 Upper Intermediate, C1 Advanced, and C2 Proficient. Approximately 45% of students demonstrated A2 proficiency, indicating basic language knowledge, while others scored at A1 (20%), B1 (20%), and B2 (15%) levels. The survey results provide a reliable approximation for estimating scores in alternative proficiency systems.

Survey findings indicate that students overestimate their English proficiency, and there's limited practice of English outside the classroom, obstructing consistent skill reinforcement. Common emotions experienced during activities and teacher explanations include boredom, confusion, satisfaction, and interest. Differences exist in how students perceive activity feedback and their connection to the language within the class.

4.2   Stage 2: Preparation

At this stage, the previously collected data was used to start planning the components that are going to be used in the system, which involves the model for emotion detection, the elements that will be included in the gamified application, and, finally, the creation of the prototype of the application.

Emotion Model

According to Girard and Johnson's work, the response model of the application prioritizes user practices and interactions, with a focus on skill acquisition [14]. It aims to motivate students with unsatisfactory results, fostering continued learning and praises high achievers to maintain their dedication. The selection of emotions for this model is based on stimuli, creating an emotion model tied to different skill levels. These emotions, recognized by students, influence their interaction with the learning process, ensuring sustained commitment to progress.

The Emotion Detection model, shaped by survey results and literature review, centers on the classroom environment. Extracting traits from users, it classifies emotions into engagement, boredom, confusion, and satisfaction—critical in educational contexts [23]. If classified as satisfaction or engagement, it signifies positive states, suggesting a lack of emotional challenges. Conversely, if boredom or confusion is identified, the system responds to enhance understanding and prevent subsequent negative affective states impacting topic comprehension.

Gamification Elements

The system will apply gamification techniques to motivate students to continue their voluntary learning. For this reason, considering the literature review, three elements of progression will be used: points, progress bar and leaderboard, in-app rewards, and the time factor, that the student can be rewarded for their effort and encourage their competitiveness and sense of self-improvement when using the app. These elements were selected due to their usefulness in educational aspects and their function of giving the student a form of recognition of their work, which is complemented by the feedback that will be given; specifically, the progression elements, which are a complement of additional information that the student receives for their performance within the application.

The topics will be divided into chapters, each of which will have activities and a final test with which the student will obtain a certain number of accumulative points; the points, which will be managed as stars, will depend on the time it takes the user to answer the correct alternative. There will also be a system of attempts, represented as lives, in which one is lost every time the user does not complete the activity in the established time; if it reaches zero, the points obtained can be exchanged to get more attempts and keep practicing with the activities of the chapters.

The topics will be organized into chapters, each featuring activities and a final test. Students earn accumulative points, represented as stars, based on the time taken to provide correct answers. A system of attempts, portrayed as lives, deducts one for each incomplete activity within the set time. If attempts reach zero, users can exchange accumulated points to acquire additional attempts and continue practicing with chapter activities.

Design Prototypes

The design of the application should be friendly, entertaining, easy to understand, and easy to use, to keep the student's attention during its use. These prototypes were made in

Figma, to visually establish the user's needs and have a clear vision of what is expected in the product. This tool was also used to establish the flow of interactivity that the application would have.

The application will be divided into several screens: the login and user registration screen; the main page; the current lesson the student is viewing; the activities screen, which will give users a space to practice the topic in question; and the final test, which will be a cumulative evaluation of the lessons viewed in each chapter it will have approximately 15 statements with a duration of 30 s for each exercise.

4.3 Stage 3: Development

During this phase, the system requirements were analyzed, and each was defined before listing corresponding functionalities in the project's Product Backlog. Tasks were then organized, prioritizing application development to establish a foundational structure for working with feedback content based on the results from implementing the emotion model. This approach ensures better organization when implementing the emotion detection code and integrating it into the mobile application.

Sprint 1
The objective of this sprint was to implement the first three screens, login, account creation, and the home page, as well as establish the connection with the database. For this, the React Native framework was used, and, based on the designs made in the previous stage, JavaScript was used as the code base for its implementation and development of the methods to be used. The project was also created in Firebase to have access to its functionalities, with which the database was created in Firestore and the user login system with Firebase Authentication.

Sprint 2
During this sprint, the focus was on developing the remaining screens of the application and implementing navigation between them. With the front-end completed, a meeting with the Product Owner (PO) was held to review the design and determine the content of the chapters.

The PO suggested changes to the home screen and the current lesson screen to align with the first category of the ARCS model (Fig. 1), emphasizing the stimulation of students' attention to prevent a decrease in motivation. Additionally, the content structure for the system was defined and categorized based on student progress. The content includes three general topics, each with five sub-topics covering theory, examples, important notes, and related activities. Subsequently, screens were corrected, and information on the topics was organized into a JSON file, detailing subtopic descriptions, example lists with explanations, and related activities.

Sprint 3
In this iteration, the emotion recognition module was integrated into the app using Firebase MLKit and the Mobile Vision Face Detection API. The face detection process identifies the person's face and reports its position, considering various angles to determine face orientation through Euler Y and Euler Z measurements. Then, reference

Fig. 1. Changes in the indicated screens.

points (eyes, nose, and mouth) are located. The Face API recognizes the entire face before pinpointing reference points, providing a JSON response with face information.

Once this information is gathered, the face image is classified into four emotions within the established model. Unlike most studies using Plutchik's emotion theory with eight primary emotions, this model focuses on emotions related to attention and perception during activities and topic explanations, making it more personalized to the study's objectives.

Tests were conducted to assess the accuracy of the emotion module (Fig. 2). The model exhibited high effectiveness in recognizing two positive emotions –satisfaction and engagement (or neutral), but lower efficiency in detecting confusion and boredom.

Fig. 2. Emotion detection of the established model.

Moreover, a feature was integrated to monitor the duration of a student's emotional state. This functionality is particularly valuable for managing negative emotions, allowing the execution of specific actions to prevent or assist the student during prolonged periods of confusion.

Sprint 4

Once the emotion detection module was integrated into the mobile application, the feedback that the student would receive according to their emotion was created.

As there are two positive and two negative values in the established emotion model, three types of feedback were implemented to provide help to students during the development of the activities: emotional feedback, content feedback, and emotional + content feedback. If a student has a satisfactory performance, emotional feedback will be given to maintain the student's motivation; However, if the student manages to answer several questions satisfactorily in a row, then the feedback will be reduced so that it is not invasive during the lesson. On the other hand, if the student presents a negative affective state, the first-emotional + content feedback will be provided, to re-integrate and re-engage the student to the lesson; if the confusion continues, content feedback will be given that is helpful to understand a topic and can continue with the flow of activities, and once they complete that question, emotional feedback will be shown.

4.4   Stage 4: Evaluation

Some tests were performed to evaluate the functionality and usability of the application, which evaluated the two main modules, emotion detection, and feedback, to verify their effectiveness in different scenarios.

For the tests, Expo Go was used, a platform that allows React applications to run on a mobile device.

Unit Testing

The initial testing focused on the core function of the emotion detection module, ensuring accurate identification of the current affective state. Effectiveness was verified by assessing a sample of 25 representative faces for each emotion in the model. The results aligned with expectations, reflecting the intended outcomes for various presented scenarios.

Following this, tests were conducted on the feedback module, employing random numbers to simulate different emotions. The results were satisfactory, demonstrating accurate execution of various types of feedback, with a particular emphasis on the content related to the activities.

Integration Tests

During the tests, the detection and feedback modules were collectively evaluated. Time tracking was incorporated to assess specific functions within the feedback module, such as providing comments that adjust according to the progression of a negative affective state. The integration of both modules works properly: the given feedback is in line with the current needs of the student and is kept within a limit to keep the student's motivation and encourage them to continue practicing even if they have an unsatisfactory result while taking care not to get a counterproductive result by displaying these comments continuously.

Usability Measurement
Usability metrics for game-based courses [36] were employed to measure the usability of the application, involving a 29-question questionnaire with three evaluation criteria: usability (U), educational usability (EU), and user experience (UX). These metrics assess efficiency, effectiveness, and user satisfaction. The experiment involved two groups—one using the gamified application and the other following traditional learning methods. The one-week experiment, lasting 40 min per day, concluded with a final test evaluating reading, comprehension, and writing skills. The group using the application then assessed its usability using the designated metric.

5 Results Analysis

To evaluate the effectiveness of the emotion detection model, the detector was set to a 100-ms interval between two emotion detection events and run with a set of 100 images to be analyzed and classified according to emotion.

Table 2. Results of tests performed in the emotion detection module.

Excitement	Efficiency (%)
Commitment/Neutral	93%
Satisfaction	88%
Confusion	76%
Boredom	68%

The lower efficiency in detecting negative emotions is attributed to their subtler expressions linked to attention and perception (Table 2). The feedback module is seamlessly integrated with the emotion module output, providing timely responses based on user engagement. However, in cases of 3-min inactivity or prolonged negative emotion recording, a series of comments is activated, alternating between content and emotional feedback based on the event.

Results from the experiment indicate an enhancement in student performance. Correct answers from the final test were categorized into three groups: low performance (7 or fewer correct answers), medium performance (8–15 correct answers), and high performance (more than 15 correct answers). Notably, 27% of students relying solely on tutoring and textbooks achieved low performance. In contrast, the group using the gamified application demonstrated medium or high performance, highlighting the positive impact of the application on learning outcomes (Fig. 3).

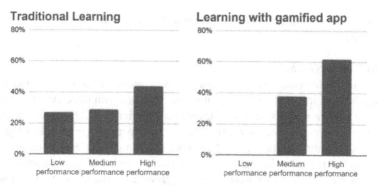

Fig. 3. Percentage of correct responses obtained with (a) traditional learning and (b) gamified application.

On the other hand, for the usability evaluation, the students were surveyed with the metric of application usability, with which the following results were obtained:

5.1 Usability

In this section, students expressed their perception that the gamification elements in the application aligned with their needs and the flow of content activities. This alignment positively influenced motivation and performance in classroom activities, leading to increased active participation and satisfaction. The survey results showed variations in the impact of the application on different criteria, with the lowest being the impact on the course (0.60), and the highest being the improvement in the comprehension of class content (0.94). Overall, the average usability score for the system was 0.804.

Task completion times were taken to calculate the relative overall efficiency, where N is the total number of tasks, R is the total number of users, and N_{ij} is the result of task i per user j; if the user completes the task, then N_{ij} has a value of 1; otherwise, its value is 0; and t_{ij} is the time taken by the user to complete the task.

$$RelativeOverallefficiency = \frac{\sum_{j=1}^{R}\sum_{i=1}^{R}\frac{n_{ij}}{t_{ij}}}{NR} \tag{1}$$

The relative overall efficiency formula, which calculates the ratio of time spent by students who completed the tests in each module to the total time spent by all students, yields the following efficiency results: Task 1 (100%), Task 2 (84.55%), and Task 3 (70.05%).

5.2 Educational Usability

In terms of educational usability, the results show alignment between the application's content and class topics, maintaining expected progress for students. However, the set objectives within the application received a lower score (0.65). Conversely, students appreciated the structure and division of activities (0.94). Overall, this section, encompassing student feedback, achieved a satisfaction score of 0.824.

This module was analyzed by calculating the completion rate of a task, where it will be assigned a value of 1 if the user has completed the task or a value of 0 if the opposite is the case.

$$Efficiency = \frac{\#Taskssuccessfullycompleted}{Totaltakscompleted} \tag{2}$$

Tasks within the system are considered incomplete if the test cannot be completed within the designated 10 min; resulting in Task 1 having high efficiency (100%) and Task 3 having the lowest efficiency (71.42%).

5.3 User Experience

The results of the User Experience section indicate that, for the most part, students had a good impact during its use, with an average of 0.752, considering that the use of a gamified application is an interesting and enjoyable way to learn a second language (0.94) but that it would have been ideal to be able to cooperate and integrate with their peers within the system (0.54).

6 Conclusions, Limitations, and Future Work

This study introduces and assesses a gamified application incorporating affective computing to aid second language learners in acquiring English. The proposed objectives were successfully achieved, including the implementation of an emotion detection module with 81.25% effectiveness. This module identifies four fundamental emotions in the classroom—two positive and two negative emotions. The study also developed an adaptable feedback model tailored to each student's unique scenario. These modules were seamlessly integrated with gamification elements aligned with student progress, resulting in improved subject performance. The system's metrics indicate strong performance: 84.87% efficiency in usability, 85.71% effectiveness in educational usability, and a 75.24% user satisfaction rate in the User Experience module.

Several limitations impact the scope of this research. The focus on a single proficiency level, particularly aiding students with unsatisfactory results, may potentially demotivate those already performing well, lacking challenges for their skill level. Additionally, the study couldn't be implemented in a broader sample environment. Despite this, it introduces a unique approach to gamification in education, emphasizing the importance of the affective factor for application effectiveness.

Recommendations for future research include refining the emotion detection model for an improved user experience and incorporating a difficulty model to motivate ongoing student progress. These enhancements would contribute to a more comprehensive understanding and implementation of gamification in educational settings.

References

1. Sevy-Biloon, J., Recino, U., Munoz, C.: Factors affecting English language teaching in public schools in Ecuador. Int. J. Learn. Teach. Educ. Res. **19**(3), 276–294 (2020)
2. Torres, P., Llerena, C.: Percepciones de los maestros de inglés sobre el uso de los módulos pedagógicos en Ecuador: Una entrevista de grupo focal. (English teachers' perceptions of the use of pedagogical modules in Ecuador: A focus group interview.) (2021)
3. Macancela, J.: Sitios Web como herramientas de apoyo para el aprendizaje del idioma Inglés (Websites as support tools for learning the English language) (2019)
4. Silva, R., Rodrigues, R., Leal, C.: Gamification in management education: a systematic literature review. BAR- Braz. Adm. Rev. **16**(2), e180103 (2019)
5. Dehganzadeh, H., Dehganzadeh, H.: Investigating effects of digital gamification-based language learning: a systematic review. J. Engl. Lang. Teach. Learn. **12**(25), 53–93 (2020)
6. Chamba-Leiva, K., Paladines-Costa, M., Torres-Carrión, P.: Strategies and gamified teaching tools to reduce English learning difficulties in children with down syndrome: comparative study between digital and traditional resources in regular education environments. In: Proceedings of the 5th Workshop on ICTs for improving Patients Rehabilitation Research Techniques, pp. 131–135 (2019)
7. Dehghanzadeh, H., Fardanesh, H., Hatami, J., et al.: Using gamification to support learning English as a second language: a systematic review. Comput. Assist. Lang. Learn. **37**, 1–24 (2019)
8. Zatarain, R., Barrón, M., Ríos, J., Alor, G.: A virtual environment for learning computer coding using gamification and emotion recognition. Interact. Learn. Environ. **28**(8), 1048–1106 (2020)
9. Pivec, M.: Play and learn: potentials of game-based learning (2007)
10. Tan, P., Ling, S., Ting, C.: Adaptive digital game-based learning framework. In: Proceedings of the 2nd International Conference on Digital Interactive Media in Entertainment and Arts, pp. 142–146 (2007). https://doi.org/10.1145/1306813.1306844
11. Liu, T., Chu, Y.: Using ubiquitous games in an English listening and speaking course: Impact on learning outcomes and motivation. Comput. Educ. **55**(2), 630–643 (2010)
12. Deterding, S., Dixon, D., Khaled, R., Nacke, L.: From game design elements to gamefulness: defining "gamification". In: Proceedings of the 15th International Academic MindTrek Conference: Envisioning Future Media Environments, pp. 9–15 (2011). https://doi.org/10.1145/2181037.2181040
13. Hudlicka, E.: Affective computing for game design. In: Proceedings of the 4th International North American Conference on Intelligent Games and Simulation, pp. 5–12. McGill University Montreal, Canada (2008)
14. Girard, S., Johnson, H.: Designing affective computing learning companions with teachers as design partners. In: Proceedings of the 3rd International Workshop on Affective Interaction in Natural Environments, pp. 49–54 (2010). https://doi.org/10.1145/1877826.1877840
15. Bouça, M.: Mobile communication, gamification and ludification. In: MindTrek, pp. 295–301 (2012)
16. Barata, G., Gama, S., Jorge, J., et al.: Improving participation and learning with gamification. In: Proceedings of the First International Conference on Gameful Design, Research, and Applications, pp. 10–17 (2013). https://doi.org/10.1145/2583008.2583010
17. Kim, J.T., Lee, W.-H.: Dynamical model for gamification: optimization of four primary factors of learning games for educational effectiveness. In: Kim, T., Cho, H., Gervasi, O., Yau, S.S. (eds.) FGIT 2012. CCIS, vol. 351, pp. 24–32. Springer, Heidelberg (2012). https://doi.org/10.1007/978-3-642-35600-1_4

18. Li, W., Grossman, T., Fitzmaurice, G.: GamiCAD: a gamified tutorial system for first time AutoCAD users. In: Proceedings of the 25th Annual ACM Symposium on User Interface Software and Technology, pp. 103–112 (2012). https://doi.org/10.1145/2380116.2380131

19. Mekler, E., Brühlmann, F., Opwis, K., Tuch, A.: Disassembling gamification: the effects of points and meaning on user motivation and performance. In: CHI'13 Extended Abstracts on Human Factors in Computing Systems, pp. 1137–1142 (2013). https://doi.org/10.1145/2468356.2468559

20. Méndez, M., Peña, A.: Emotions as learning enhancers of foreign language learning motivation. Prof. Issues Teach. Prof. Dev. **15**(1), 109–124 (2013)

21. Flores, J.: Using gamification to enhance second language learning. Dig. Educ. Rev. **27**, 32–54 (2015)

22. Wu, C., Huang, Y., Hwag, J.: Review of affective computing in education/learning: trends and challenges. Br. J. Edu. Technol. **47**(6), 1304–1323 (2016)

23. Boyinbode, O.: Development of a gamification based English vocabulary mobile learning system. Int. J. Comput. Sci. Mob. Comput. **7**(8), 183–191 (2018)

24. Cabestrero, R., Quirós, P., Santos, O., et al.: Some insights into the impact of affective information when delivering feedback to students. Behav. Inf. Technol. **37**(12), 1252–1263 (2018). https://doi.org/10.1080/0144929X.2018.1499803

25. Aslan, S., Alyuz, N., Okur, E., et al.: Effect of emotion-aware interventions on students' behavioral and emotional states. Educ. Tech. Res. Dev. **66**(6), 1399–1413 (2018)

26. Udjaja, Y.: Gamification assisted language learning for Japanese language using expert point cloud recognizer. Int. J. Comput. Games Technol. **2018**, 1–11 (2018)

27. Hakak, S., Noor, N., Ayub, M., et al.: Cloud-assisted gamification for education and learning - recent advances and challenges. Comput. Electr. Eng. **74**, 22–34 (2019)

28. El-Shorbagy, S., Sherief, N., Abdelmoez, W.: Unexplored gamification elements in learning environments. In: Proceedings of the 2020 9th International Conference on Software and Information Engineering, pp. 102–107 (2020). https://doi.org/10.1145/3436829.3436852

29. Tamtama, G., Suryanto, P., Suyoto, S.: Design of English vocabulary mobile apps using gamification: an Indonesian case study for kindergarten. iJEP **10**(1), 150–162 (2020)

30. Silva, F., Analide, C.: Gamification and affective computing for the improvement of driving assessments. In: AfCAI (2018)

31. Fu, J., Ge, T., Li, M., Hu, X.: Affective computation of students' behaviors under classroom scenes. In: NeuroManagement and Intelligent Computing Method on Multimodal Interaction, pp. 1–6 (2019)

32. Kusuma, G., Wigati, E., Utomo, Y., et al.: Analysis of gamification models in education using MDA framework. Procedia Comput. Sci. **135**, 385–392 (2018)

33. Vandercruysse, S., Elen, J.: Towards a game-based learning instructional design model focusing on integration. In: Wouters, P., van Oostendorp, H. (eds.) Instructional techniques to facilitate learning and motivation of serious games. AGL, pp. 17–35. Springer, Cham (2017). https://doi.org/10.1007/978-3-319-39298-1_2

34. Shi, Y., Shih, J.: Game factors and game-based learning design model. Int. J. Comput. Games Technol. **2015**, 11 (2015)

35. Molaee, Z., Dortaj, F.: Improving L2 learning: an ARCS instructional-motivational approach. Procedia Soc. Behav. Sci. **171**, 1214–1222 (2015)

36. Sobodić, A., Balaban, I., Kermek, D.: Usability metrics for gamified e-learning course: a multilevel approach. Int. J. Emerg. Technol. Learn. **13**(5), 1–15 (2018)

Student Perceptions of the Gamification Process in Virtual Learning Environments at University Level

Soratna Navas Gotopo[1]([✉]) [iD], Eduardo Jesús Garces Rosendo[2] [iD],
Inés del Carmen Flores Perozo[3] [iD], Carmen Soto Ramírez Sáenz[4] [iD],
and Haymin Teresa Raez Martínez[1,2,3,4] [iD]

[1] Universidad Tecnológica del Perú, Lima 15836, Perú
C19491@utp.edu.pe
[2] Universidad Científica del Sur, Lima 15841, Perú
[3] Universidad Autónoma del Perú, Lima 15307, Perú
[4] Universidad Cesar Vallejo, Lima 15836, Perú

Abstract. Gamification strategies are proved to motivate students while helping them develop the key skills related to a particular subject, especially when
work- ing in virtual environments. During gamification students move forward,
and go up levels while the learn new concepts. This research, is bases on the
application of gamification strategies in the subject of Digital Thinking at the
Universidad Autónoma de Perú. This was done through a quasi- experimental
methodology. Among the main results there can be mentioned that the students
felt more motivated, getting a more meaningful learning process.

Keywords: Gamification · Learning · Motivation · Teaching Experience

1 Introduction

Making an initial review of the most current studies on the subject of gamification, it can
be seen that a large part of them have been approached from a theoretical perspective,
making an extensive definition of its key concepts. This, on the one hand, is positive,
since it forms a firm theoretical basis, but on the other hand, it exposes everything that is
lacking in documentation on the implementation and actual operation of these concepts
in reality.

In this sense, the existing documentation refers more frequently to specific aspects
of gamification, justifying its validity and stating indications to carry it out correctly,
but fails to report how these indications are adapted to real contexts and participants,
which leaves aside the value of experience, since without a doubt all learning is more
significant once it is applied and practiced [1].

In this way, since gamification is, in effect, a teaching and learning technique, it is
important not to limit itself to knowing it in a purely theoretical way, as this would limit
its domain and the acquisition of data on its advantages, limitations and challenge in the

M. Botto-Tobar et al. (Eds.): ICAT 2023, CCIS 2051, pp. 80–90, 2024.
https://doi.org/10.1007/978-3-031-58950-8_7

educational environment [2]. The study of gamification from practice in school allows actions and strategies to be adapted to the contextualized needs of students, through personalization to theirtastes and interests, which would not happen when only.generic indications based on data are described in theory, which, many times, only take into account ideal situations or scenarios [1].

It is undeniable that the students' point of view in relation to teaching strategies and techniques offer the possibility of assessing the positive and negative contributions in the development of their learning. This conveys a real experience, beyond the explanation of the teacher who has carried out this technique, which also offers other professionals an example by which they can be guided, appreciating the facilit ies or obstacles that may arise.

In this sense, the work will revolve around the answer to the following questions: How

do students perceive the benefits and challenges of this method with respect to the virtual learning environments? What benefits do students report with the use of gamification strategies? Such questions will outline the research objectives which will be developed in the present study in two parts; Firstly, a theoretical review of the most important concepts about gamification and secondly, a report of the benefits and challenges perceived by the students if the Digital Thinking subject, at the Universidad Autónoma of Perú themselves, as the best way to perceive the real effects of gamification as a teaching and learning strategy.

1.1 ICT in Education

Information and Communication Technologies (ICT) in schools can be used as communication tools to improve the teaching and learning process. With the advancement of technology in education, schools use technological means to diversify the educational process to make it more attractive and even to expand the boundaries of the class room [3].

Technology adds value to teaching and learning, improving its effectiveness, by adding a dimension that was not available before, this is the dimension of versatility and customization, bringing a series of benefits that can be mentioned below (Acosta et al., 2020):

_Improves engagement in learning: When technology is integrated into lesson s, students are expected to be more interested in the subjects they are studying. Technology offers different opportunities to make learning more fun and enjoyable in terms of teaching the same things in new ways [3].

_Improves knowledge retention: When students are engaged and interested in things they are studying, it is expected that they can have better knowledge retention. As previously mentioned, technology can help foster active participation in the classroom, which is also a very important factor for greater knowledge retention [4].

_Fosters personalized learning: It is well known that no one learns in the same way, as each person has different learning styles and different abilit ies. Technology provides a great opportunity to make learning more effective for all people with different needs [3].

_Fosters collaboration: Students can practice collaborative learning strategies by engaging in different online activities. For example, working on different projects by collaborating with others in forums or sharing documents in their virtual learning environments.

With all this in mind, technology can encourage collaboration between students at the classroom, institution level or even establishing links with other institutions, in other cities or countries [1]. Currently, learning is about collaborating with others, to solve complex problems, develop crit ical thinking, and establish different forms of communication and leadership skills and improve motivation and productivity [5], so the inclusion of ICT in the classroom is not only presented as a valuable option, but, in truth, as a necessity.

1.2 Motivati on from the Point of View of Gamification

Motivation in the conte xt of teaching and learning is a psychological aspect related to the development of the human being and their performance in school activities [1]. It is not simply a personal trait, but is based on the interaction between specific factors, under certain situations, and arises from the stimulus and feeling of satisfaction with their environment, for the achievement of objectives that contribute energy and gratification for an effort [2].

Thus, motivation includes everything that drives the human being to do certain activities out of necessity, or the impulse of a stimulus, therefore it is considered a mechanism that promotes action, whose origin can be of a psychological or physiological nature [2]. It is then, what affects the level of energy and directionality of the individual's acts, responding to a motivational cycle [3]:

At the beginning of the motivational cycle, the individual is normally in a state of internal balance, that is, calm. When a stimulus is presented, a tension is generated from which a need arises, a mechanism aimed at satisfying that need, which encourages the person to take action to respond to the requirement that arises from the stimulus, whether it is of physiological or psychological origin [2].

When a need arises, it breaks the state of balance of the organism and produces a state of tension, dissatisfaction and non-conformity and leads the individual to develop a behavior oraction capable of releasing tension. Once the need is satisfied, the organis m returns to its initial equilibrium state [1].

If this is contextualized within the framework of this study, a student can feel motivated in the school context as long as there is a stimulus capable of generating interest in learning. When this stimulus ceases, the student returns to his state of internal balance, as part of his daily life.

There are various theories about the nature of motivation, including Maslow's pyramid ofneeds, which states that human beings can stay motivated while satisfying their basic needs, described in the so-called Maslow Pyramid. In this pyramid, the first four levels are conservation or survival needs (food, shelter, clothing and security). The higher level is called growth motivation or need of being. Indeed, as long as the individual handles his lower needs satisfactorily, he will be able to fill the higher ones [1].

In the specific case of gamification, studies verify its potential influence on people's behavior, illustrating its relationship with people's actions to achieve objectives [2].

This is how various theories have emerged to understand the motives that generate certain actions in individuals, which can be applied to gamification strategies and resources oriented to each student profile and/or theme, associated with their specific enjoyment and greater status. of participation within the developed activity; Therefore, the ultimate purpose of gamification is to induce states of the games, which maintain the player's interest by providing a new stimulus at each advance or level [4].

However, when implementing a gamification process, it is important to take into account the typ eof infor mation trans mitted byvide ogames, which is mainly of a practical and non-theoretical nature [2]. Therefore, since the video game is the basis of gamification, it shows the nature of the information preferred by the mind, how it likes to receive it and what must be done to produce more and better learning, mainly at a practical level [1]. In this way, the principles of video games can contribute to achieving an effective and innovative didactic model, capable of particularly enhancing the motivation of students and the mechanis ms to measure real progress in learning; in other words, a true continuous and formative evaluation [2].

In this way, when talking about school motivation in the context of gamification, it can be understood as that internal and positive attitude expressed by a student towards the new learning due to the desire to achieve an objective that will make them advance in their skill level. on a specific theme. Likewise, motivation is capable of awakening in the student the need to acquire new knowledge, therefore it plays a fundamental role in any learning process [3].

1.3 Gamification as a Teaching -Learning Strategies

The development of new technologies and the evolution of the video game industry have favorably impacted the sector, leveraging a marked increase in various game mechanics in non-game contexts, such as the educational [3]. The result is seen in the clear popularization and adoption of video games among people of any age and regardless of gender in recent years; largely supported by its high motivational potential [4]. The rapid rise of the phenomenon of this growing industry has aroused the interest of many professionals who understand the potential of gamification in different areas and encourage the search for those intrinsic factors associated with the success and wide-spread use of video games, while increasing the interest in the concepts that are taught [5].

However, the concept of gamification as it is understood today, emerged from 2003 when the importance of the playful e xperience began to be highlighted as the need to transfer concentration, fun and emotions e xperienced through the game to the real world. In this way, "gamification is conceived from the perspective of th e use of playful thinking and game mechanics to solve problems and encourage team participation" [6]; emphasizing the use of game elements in non-game contexts.

Gamification thus corresponds to a teaching-learning method aimed at promoting the mechanics of games in the educational area with the purpose ofachieving better results generally related to the student's academic performance, as well as their motivation and attention, improving skills or rewarding specific actions [7]. Likewise, the importance of gamification lies in its potential to stimulate learning in students, being considered one of the best methods to learn in the classroom.

In this sense, gamification in the classroom is considered a key factor to increase student motivation, therefore it is necessary to study the motivating factors to design the right game capable of arousing interest in the different types of players [8]. In this way, gamification techniques are considered innovative in the area of education by fostering student motivation and commitment and including not only the learning process in specific topics or subjects, but also the development of healthy learning habits, as Valderrama [9] states:

_Dynamics: concept and implicit structure of the game.

_Mechanics: processes that cause the development of the game.

_Components: specific implementations of the dynamics and mechanics: points, avatars, badges, rankings, levels or teams.

_Aesthetics: motivating design of the emotions, e xperiences, fantasies and experience of each player. They are the elements that allow us to understand the rules of the game and generate the dynamics of each of these.

On the other hand, regarding the types of players (students) and according to the taxonomy of Bartle [10], there are 4 types depending on the motivation of each one:

_Achievers: They are related to the game and its action; they focus on meeting objectives and overcoming specific achievements. They seek status within the team.

_Exp lorer: They focus on the interaction of the game itself; their goal is to go where no one else has, they are focused on continuous improvement and learning and tend to be more individualistic.

_Socializers: They enjoy the interaction with the other members of the game and not so much the game itself, they are good at working as a team.

_Assassins: they are focused solely on the competition; they can make their opponents lose in order to win.

In the educational context, gamification goes beyond the application of teaching-learning tools in various subjects and enables its application for the development of attitudes, certain collaborative behaviors and autonomous study [9]. Although the process of applying playful methodologies in a subject should not be seen as an institutionalprocess, but rather relate it to a didactic project within a specific context and with a specific meaning [11].

Although certainly, it is important to highlight the start of gamification from a didactic content and is generated from elements or thoughts of the game [12]. In addition, this method must be based on bottom-up experiences to keep the player entertained and motivated during their learning process. Apprenticeship Likewise, when developing a strategy for recreational activities, it is advisable to carry out a preliminary study to identify possible overstimulation in the current technological environment; which would imply an additional challenge in the learning area.

It is important to take into account the main differences between traditional teaching and gamification, as can be seen in table 2. First of all, the abuse of the rote mechanism of traditional education should be highlighted. This fact demotivates and bores most of the students, which is reflected in the evaluation, which is carried out at the end of the period and generally with drastic consequences. Additionally, the process does not promote feedback, it encourages individual work and students do not receive personalized treatment [13].

Traditional education abuses memory, when applying the video game model, many elements will be found that are precisely the opposite and therefore can be incorporated into teaching to increase its affinity for students [14]. To understand the reasons for the lack of interest of traditional educational methodologies for current students, the antagonistic differences between the characteristics of the video game and those of traditional education are shown. A teaching-learning strategy such as gamification, within the framework described so far, generates a series of positive impacts on all the actors involved in the process.

Now, it is important to highlight gamification as a process aimed at modifying specific behaviors in the student; however, it is not a behavior modifier. The dynamic focuses on generating changes in the learning process, accompanied by a motivation process [15]. Thus, to consider a game as part of gamification, it must meet requirements: questions, challenges, levels, competition and collaboration. Therefore, before establishing a playful learning method, it is necessary to observe the types of users and the role to be fulfilled in the classroom, so that an ideal activity for everyone can be achieved. In this sense, among the necessary elements to make gamification a successful process and pro vide a strate gy capable of working in th e long term and helping to achiev e learning objectives, are the following [16]:

_Give players the motivation to do something, be it through receiving rewards, wining, or gaining recognition.

_Provide the player with the facility to carry out a task, usually divided into parts in a way that increases the perceived ability of the student.

_Give the player a start marker and a finish marker. In this framework, when implementing a gamification process, its final objective must be clearly considered, which in no case should correspond to entertainment; on the contrary, its goal is definitely academic-educational. Therefore, if it is not applied assertively, it will result in nonsense [17]. It is equally important to have an attractive narrative to arouse student motivation. Under this conception, the use of gamification as a learning tool pursues a series of eminently academic objectives orapproaches.

This set of objectives can be summed up in designing a game or academic activity that is entertaining, authentic, regulated, fundamentally motivating and pleasurable. These objectives ultimately seek to immerse students in an inclusive and unique reality where the rules, although they represent the rigor of learning, are indirectly stimulating their creativity and innovation to achieve success.

2. Materials and Methods

The method applied was quasi-experimental. Researchers worked with a control group and an experimental group of the Digital Thinking subject in the Universidad Autónoma del Perú. In this way, teaching strategies based on gamification were applied to the experimental group, while the control group continued with traditional teaching strategies, during the course of a semester of the aforementioned subject. After the application of the gamified strategies, a survey was applied to assess the students' perceptions about the role the gamified strategies played in their process in the context of the virtual learning. The results of this survey are discussed below.

3. Results

The total number of participants in the experimental group reached 241, who participated in the survey by providing their answers. Thus, the function of gamification can be approached from different angles, either as a complement to traditional teaching processes or by totally replacing the teaching process. In both cases, it is necessary to establish the learning objectives and direct the game components towards them. Similarly, when defining a game, it is important to consider the specific area of knowledge, the complexity of the discipline and the profiles of the players in order to obtain a positive effect and not distort its initial objective [18].

On the other hand, it is important to differentiate gamification from a serious game. This is a very common confusion due to the purpose of learning in a specific topic of the serious game; however, it does not include the fun factor in the process; that is, it does not seek to motivate the student or his attention [19]. In this sense, gamification is not just about a system of rewards or score tables, these are game elements necessary to create the process of developing a playful dynamic for the classroom.

Regarding this, it can be seen that the majority of students report a positive experience with the gamification strategies. In more detail, 58, 1% of the consulted students, expressed that the gamification strategies made more meaningful their learning process and 57.3% say that it helped them comprehend better the concepts, as it can be seen in the previous figure (Fig. 1). This shows that in each aspect, less than half of the consulted students reported a negative experience with the gamification strategies, which reflects an overall positive appreciation of the gamification strategies.

Fig. 1. Type of experience with the gamification process

In this same order of ideas, 45.7% of students have reported that gamification strategies make the learning process more interactive, 16.3% said it was funnier, 17.4% said it was more motivating and 14.2 expressed it was more practical, while only 3.8% of the students reported feeling that the gamification made the learning process more complicated and 2.6% saw it as an obstacle for learning (Fig. 2). This has a lot to do with the advantages and disadvantages of gamification in the educational field, mainly when it must be kept in mind that the relevance of gamification today does not rest on its condition of fashion or novelty in the academic field, on the contrary, this e merges as a logical response aimed at satisfying the growing trends and concerns of the group of young generations, who demand to reconcile their technological expectations with their most immediate training needs in the educational context [20].

This brings with it the responsibility of both teachers and institutions to innovate in emerging methodologies through which strategies aimed at increasing commitment and

Fig. 2. Advantages and Disadvantages of the gamification Process

motivation are incorporated into classes, providing all possible tools and resources to promote autonomous learning that is significant of their students; even more so when the expectations of these students are focused on perceiving that their opinions are valued, following their own passions and interests, creating new things using all available tools, working through group projects, making decisions and sharing control, cooperating and competing. Students need to feel that the education they receive is real, that it has value.

This impacts the learning process in the same way that a gamer goes forward in the development of his skills, as it can be seen in the following figure (Fig. 3). The students reported that the gamification strategies helped them develop their competence in the subject with each challenge completed. 88.8% of them felt that they were getting better in the subject as they advanced in the gamification challenges, while only 11.2% felt that it didn't help them at all.

Fig. 3. Perception of Gamification Helping the Learning Process

2   Discussion and Conclusions.

After analyzing the results, it can be said that there are many differences between the traditional methodology of teaching and the gamification approach, that ultimately have an undeniable effect in the learning process of students, especially when using ICT learning environments. In the following table (Table 1) they can be appreciated.

Table 1. Differences between gamification approach and traditional teaching.

Traditional Teaching	Gamification Approach
Tedious	**Fun**
Generally, for the majority of students.	Generally, for the majority of students.
Final evaluation	**Continuous assessment**
The lack of motivation and interest is reflected in an evaluation at the end of the educational process, with few opportunities to repair the damage.	The evaluation is of a formative type, promotes learning, with multiple opportunities to correct errors.
Indivi dual experience	**Collective experience**
Teamwork is not encouraged.	Social and team interaction is encouraged.
Mass attention	**Individualized attention**
A single speech for the entire group of students.	Each action is individual and is personally attended.
Narrative	**Narrative**
Learn this to pass the subject	You are going to achieve something successful
Monocognition	**Multi-cognition**
Only memory works	The whole brain is worked on: critical reasoning, psychomotor skills and social relationships.

Source [20]

Traditional education abuses memory, when applying the model of video games, many elements will be found that are precisely the opposite and therefore they can be incorporated into teaching to increase its affinity for students [21]. In order to understand the reasons for the lack of interest traditional educational methodologies have for current students, the antagonistic differences between the characteristics of the video game and those of traditional education are shown. A teaching-learning strategy such as gamification, within the framework described so far, generates a series of positive impacts on all the actors involved in the process. Among these, benefits reported by students regarding the gamification process there are the following [21]:

_Students
Reward the effort.
Warns and penalizes lack of interest.
Indicates the exact moment when the student enters a danger zone.
Reward extra work.
It provides a clear measure of the performance of each student.
Proposes ways to improve the grade in the subject and their learning curriculum.
_Teacher:
Encourages work in the classroom.
It makes it easier to reward those who really deserve it.
It allows automatic control of the status of each student, reducing curricular management tasks.
_Institution
Provide a measure of student performance to their parents.
It is a new and effective system.

2.1 Conclusions

Having reviewed the results and based on the literature review, it can be said that a good gamification strategy must meet certain conditions to be accepted by a group of students. Also, it must meet all the elements associated with the academic requirements outlined.

Indeed, it is important to be clear about the ultimate goal of gamification: to achieve a desired behavior, in this case, to model better students, with greater.

communication skills. Therefore, gamification uses aspects of the human brain to generate motivation and autonomous work in order to manipulate and achieve that desired behavior. By way of closing, it is important to highlight gamification as a train ing pro cess option with a high level of challenge: the teacher must have the ability to propose activities that are sufficiently attractive to promote the use of the game and develop critical thinking, scientific thinking in students, search for alternative solutions, perseverance, recognition of the other, self-knowledge, self-control, autonomy, work skills, collaborative work and decision-making. These characteristics make gamification in education a complex framework that teachers must face through their creativity and knowledge of it.

This situation complements the role of the teacher as a mediator between student knowledge, and transforms him into a teacher interested in promoting in his students the knowledge of the other and the knowledge of themselves. The higher education teacher is, then, for gamification, a promoter of comprehensive training who is interested in generating educational.

References

1. García, N., Muñoz, S.: Experiencias Reales De Gamificación En Educación. En P. Rivera, P. Neut, P.Luchini (2019)
2. Pascual, S., Prunera, P.: Pedagogías Emergentes en la Sociedad Digital, Liber-Libro, pp. 7–21.
3. Gil, J., Prieto, E.: La realidad de la gamificación en educación primaria. Estudio multicaso de centros educativos españoles. Perfiles Educativos **42**(168), 107–134 (2020)
4. Borrás, O.: Fundamentos de la gamificación. Universidad Politécnica de Madrid, Vicerrectorado de Planificación Académica y Doctorado. Madrid: Creative Commons (2015)
5. Williams, D., Consalvo, M., Caplan, S., Yee, N.: Lookingfor gender: Gender roles and behaviors among online gamers. J. Commun. **59**(4), 700–725 (2009)
6. Hamari, J., Lehdonvirta, V.: Game design as marketing: how game mechanics create demand for virtual goods. Inter. J. Bus. Sci. Appli. Manag. **5**(1), 14–29 (2010)
7. Gómez, A., Vergara, D.: Origen de la gamificación educativa. Expertos: http://espacioen iac.com/origen-de-la-gamificacion- educativa-por-diego-vergara-rodri- guez-y-ana-isabel-gomez-vallecillo (junio de 2017)
8. Gaitán, V.: Gamificación: el aprendizaje divertido. Recuperado el 18dejuliode2021,deBlog:educativa: https://d1wqtxts1xzle7.cloudfront.net/619226 01/gamificacion_juegos20200128–124256-ewbquk.pdf?1580252831=&response-content- disposition=inline%3B+filename%3DGa-mificacion_e=I4pyjyPoZEWlq dT8cc~WVrxCmdxP7 (15 de octubre de 2013)
9. Ortiz, A., Jordán, J., Agredal, M.: Gamificación en educación: una panorámica sobre el estado de la cuestión. Educacao e Pesquisa **44**, 1–17 (2018). https://doi.org/10.1590/S1678-463420 1844173773

10. Valderrama, B.: Los secretos de la gamificación: 10 motivos para jugar. Capital Hu-mano, pp. 73–78 (2015)
11. Bartle, R.: Virtual worlds: Why people play. University of Essex (2005)
12. Contreras, R., Eguia, J.: Gamificación en aulas universitarias. Universitat Autònoma de Barcelona, Institut de la Comunicació (2016)
13. Quiroga, G.: La gamificación en educación y su trasfondo pedagógico. Universidad Complutense de Madrid. Recuperado el 19 de julio de 2021 (2018). de https://docpla-yer.es/844 78682-La-gamificacion-en-educacion-y-su-trasfondo-pedagogico.html
14. Prieto, A., Díaz, D., Monserrat, J., Reyes, E.: Experiencias de aplicación de estra-tegias de gamificación a entornos de aprendizaje universitario. ReVisión 7(2), 328–355 (2014)
15. Fernández, I.: Juego serio: gamificación y aprendizaje. Centro de Comunicación y Pedagogía (24 de mayo de 2018). http://www.centrocp.com/juego-serio-gamificacion-aprendizaje/
16. Fuerte, K.: ¿Qué son los serious games?. Observatorio (28 de septiembre de 2018). https://observatorio.tec.mx/edu-news/que-son-los-serious-games
17. Arévalo, J., Ventura, Y.: Una Experiencia Docente Basada En Eluso Del Instagram Para El Fortalecimiento De Las Destrezas Orales En Ile. Educare 2021(2), 1–15 (2021)
18. Markzewski, A.: Thin Layer vs Deep Level Gamification. International Society for Technology in Education (2014)
19. Marne, B., Wisdow, J., Huynk, B., Labat, J.: The sixfacets of serious gamedesign: a methodology enhanced by our design pattern library. In: European Conference on Technology Enhanced Learning, pp. 208–221 (2012)
20. Ayre, R.: Elementos de la gamificación que mejoran el compromiso de losalumnos. docebo (19 de julio de 2018). https://www.docebo.com/es/learning-network/blog/elementos-de-gamificacion-para-mejorar-el-desempeno-de-empleado
21. Lobo, D., Lobo, M.: El Inversor: un ejercicio gamificado para mercados de valores. I+D Revista de Investigaciones 16(1), 75–86 (2021). https://doi.org/10.33304/revinv.v16n1-202 1007

Mixed Method Research Approach. Defining and Enhancing the Level of Digital Competence Development of University Faculty

Andrés Cisneros-Barahona[1,2(✉)] ⓘ, Luis Marqués Molías[2] ⓘ,
Gonzalo Samaniego Erazo[1] ⓘ, Catalina Mejía-Granizo[3] ⓘ, Pablo Rosas-Chávez[1] ⓘ,
and Patricia Avalos-Espinoza[1] ⓘ

[1] Universidad Nacional de Chimborazo, Riobamba 060150, Ecuador
ascisneros@unach.edu.ec
[2] Universitat Rovira I Virgili, 43007 Tarragona, Spain
[3] Banco Guayaquil, Riobamba 060150, Ecuador

Abstract. The necessity to integrate training processes related to the development of Digital Competence (DC) levels has received widespread support in the field of education. However, it is important to emphasize that the definition of these levels may vary depending on the context and the tools employed. The design of initiatives to enhance these skills is influenced by the depth of the study, the approach taken, and the research methods utilized. This research aims to underscore the advantages of a mixed methodological approach, demonstrating how methodological and data triangulation enhances studies in this domain. A mixed methodological approach based on the Explanatory Sequential Design (ESD) was selected for conducting this study. This approach has allowed for a more profound and rigorous comprehension of the phenomenon, thus yielding a comprehensive perspective on it. Methodological and data triangulation has enriched the research by considering diverse viewpoints and approaches, offering a coherent, holistic, and thorough understanding of the subject matter. In the future, we propose the incorporation of data triangulation as an integrated methodology within the technological research ecosystem.

Keywords: Dexplis · Triangulation · E-Research · Training · Explanatory Sequential Design

1 Introduction

Numerous studies in this field have substantiated the connection between the development of Digital Competence (DC) levels and the necessity for both initial and ongoing training processes in educational institutions [1–10].

Nonetheless, the comprehension of the definition of DC development levels varies significantly depending on the context and the assessment criteria employed [11].

The design of actions to strengthen these skills depends on both the depth of the study and the researcher's expertise, the applied approach, as well as the research

M. Botto-Tobar et al. (Eds.): ICAT 2023, CCIS 2051, pp. 91–101, 2024.
https://doi.org/10.1007/978-3-031-58950-8_8

methods, tools, and techniques employed for this purpose. The combination of different approaches and sources of information enriches the understanding of the studied phenomenon and provides a more comprehensive and detailed perspective of it.

The formulation of strategies to enhance these competencies is contingent on several factors, including the extent of the study, the researcher's proficiency, the chosen approach, and the research methods, tools, and techniques utilized. The amalgamation of diverse approaches and information sources enhances the comprehension of the examined phenomenon, yielding a more comprehensive and in-depth perspective [12].

Mixed methods represent an approach that harnesses evidence from various data types, including numerical, verbal, textual, visual, symbolic, and others, to tackle issues in the sciences [13]. In the realm of Digital Competence (DC) development, a multitude of studies have showcased the efficacy of this methodology. [10, 14–20]. The integration of these diverse approaches and information sources enables a more profound and rigorous comprehension of the examined phenomenon.

Mixed methods are founded on the principle of triangulation, which extends beyond the mere comparison and integration of quantitative and qualitative data [21, 22]. Triangulation affords a holistic, diverse, and highly enriching perspective. By applying various methods in sequence and amalgamating multiple data sources, it allows for rigorous and efficient data collection and analysis, thereby conferring confidence and validity to the obtained results [21].Moreover, triangulation contributes to achieving a more comprehensive and robust understanding of the examined phenomenon by taking into account diverse viewpoints and methodological approaches (Fig. 1).

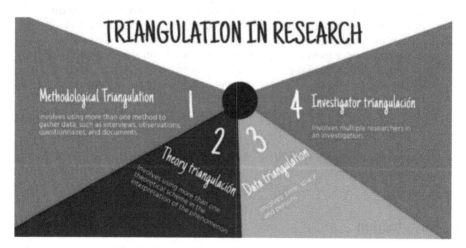

Fig. 1. Types of triangulations in research [21, 22]

The primary objective of this research is to underscore the strengths and advantages of the mixed methodological approach, particularly within the realm of educational technology. The intention is to illustrate how methodological and data triangulation enhances studies in this domain, encompassing various phases of the research process. These phases involve a thorough examination of pertinent documents, the validation and utilization of both quantitative and qualitative tools, an evaluation of DC, and the development and validation of training initiatives aimed at enhancing DC levels, among other facets. By employing this comprehensive approach, the goal is to attain a more comprehensive and robust comprehension of the examined phenomena, leveraging the synergy of diverse methods and information sources. The research aims to contribute to the advancement of knowledge in the field of educational technology and promote more effective and tailored practices in response to current demands.

The Universidad Nacional de Chimborazo (Unach) is a Ecuadorian institution accredited by the Consejo de Aseguramiento de la Calidad de la Educación Superior (CACES). It is situated in the heart of the country and is composed of four faculties, providing 31 undergraduate degree programs. The university is supported by two centers and four campuses. Furthermore, it offers 41 master's degree programs and has an enrollment of over 13,000 students. The institution employs approximately 700 professors who play a pivotal role in the university's performance [23].

This research aims to emphasize the benefits of using a mixed methodological approach, illustrating how the combination of methodological and data triangulation enhances studies in this field. A mixed methodological approach, specifically the ESD, was selected for this study. This approach has allowed for a more profound and rigorous understanding of the phenomenon, resulting in a comprehensive perspective. Methodological and data triangulation has enriched the research by considering diverse viewpoints and approaches, offering a coherent, holistic, and comprehensive understanding of the subject matter.

2 Methods

The research journey commenced with the initiation of a Systematic Literature Review (SLR) in adherence to the Preferred Reporting Items for Systematic Reviews and Meta-Analyses (PRISMA) guidelines [24, 25]. A comprehensive analysis of the scientific output pertaining to Digital Competence (DC) was conducted using the Web of Science (WoS) and Scopus databases. To refine the scope of the research, key concepts were employed, incorporating a controlled vocabulary of descriptors such as "digital competencies," "higher education," "university teachers," and "teaching," linked with the operator "and." The results of this exploration encompassed research published from 2012 to July 2023.

Subsequently, a mixed-methods approach founded on the Explanatory Sequential Design (ESD) [12, 13, 21, 26–28] was adopted. This approach enabled the study to be divided into two sequentially developed stages: a quantitative stage and a qualitative stage.

In the quantitative phase, a descriptive-correlational approach was embraced to characterize and elucidate Teaching Digital Competence (TDC) in a group of participants, as well as to establish associations with personal variables. Additionally, a non-experimental cross-sectional design was selected, given that no interventions were carried out on the analyzed variables, and data were collected at a single time point [21, 29–34].

A validated questionnaire [35, 36] for measuring the level of DC development, was administered to a representative sample of teachers from the Unach in Ecuador. The collected data were analyzed using descriptive and inferential statistical techniques to identify patterns, trends, and relationships among the variables.

Once the SLR and the quantitative phase were concluded, the obtained results were transitioned to the qualitative stage of the study. In this phase, a training proposal was formulated and validated to enhance the previously established levels of DC development.

The validation of the proposal was conducted through a combination of techniques, employing expert judgment implemented via the Delphi method and conducting two rounds of iterations [37–40].

Documentation Availability

Zenodo: Underlying data for 'La Competencia Digital Docente. Diseño y validación de una propuesta formativa. Teaching Digital Competence. A training proposal desing and validation [41]. https://doi.org/https://doi.org/10.5281/zenodo.8316175.

3 Results

Throughout the research process, multiple publications were generated, employing the PRISMA protocol, meta-analysis, and bibliometric analysis [42–46].

The potency of the applied mixed design, ESD, becomes evident when the initial quantitative findings are subsequently integrated into the qualitative stage, facilitating a continuous and rich research process with outcomes that are both valid and reliable [47–51]. Figure 2 illustrates the resultant framework of the mixed-methods design. In the initial stage, the quantitative phase, quantitative data were gathered and analyzed to assess the level of DC development among the professors at Unach during the first academic period of 2022. To achieve this, the COMDID A instrument designed for practicing teachers was utilized [52, 53].

To ascertain the reliability of the COMDID A instrument, the Cronbach's alpha statistic was applied [54]. The results obtained were as follows: for Dimension 1, a coefficient α of 0.836; for Dimension 2, a coefficient α of 0.871; for Dimension 3, a coefficient α of 0.857; and for Dimension 4, a coefficient α of 0.891. Concerning the overall instrument, a coefficient α of 0.956 was achieved [55, 56].

To validate the dimensional structure of the instrument, a confirmatory factor analysis was conducted. A Kaiser-Meyer-Olkin (KMO) sample adequacy value of 0.974 was obtained. Bartlett's test of sphericity yielded a statistic value of 7025.987, with a significance value of 0. Using the principal component extraction method and a fixed value criterion of 4, an explained variance of 65.31% was achieved [41, 55].

The quantitative phase revealed that over 60% of the academic staff at Unach do not attain the intermediate level of DC development, as per the COMDID A framework.

The results from the quantitative phase informed the second (qualitative) stage, where a training course proposal was designed and validated through an expert judgment using a Delphi study. This process involved experts in the educational technology field with the aim of enhancing the level of DC development among Unach teachers.

In the first iteration, experts evaluated the training proposal in terms of its "relevance," "clarity," "coherence," "sufficiency," and "appropriateness" using a Likert scale of 1 to 4. The objective was to obtain a revised version of the proposal and generate a report with the

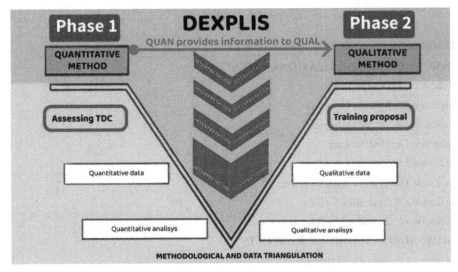

Fig. 2. Explanatory Sequential Design (ESD) scheme used.

results obtained. In the second iteration, another round of evaluation was conducted with the selected experts to assess their "degree of satisfaction" regarding the improvements made in the proposal, using a Likert scale of 1 to 4, based on the results report obtained in the first iteration. This allowed for the definitive version of the training course plan to be obtained. Finally, the Delphi study concluded with the submission of the definitive version and a new results report to the experts [39, 41].

The training plan proposal adheres to the dimensional structure depicted in Table 1.

Table 1. Dimensions and Indicators of the Training Proposal.

DIMENSION 1: INFORMATIONAL ASPECTS
Indicator 1.1: Name
Indicator 1.2: Knowledge Area
Indicator 1.3: Schedule and Total Duration
Indicator 1.4: Required Location
Indicator 1.5: Profile of facilitators/mentors
DIMENSION 2: PREPARATORY ASPECTS
Indicator 2.1: Introduction
Indicator 2.2: Presentation
Indicator 2.3: Justification
Indicator 2.4: Legal Basis

(continued)

Table 1. (*continued*)

DIMENSION 1: INFORMATIONAL ASPECTS
DIMENSION 3: ORGANIZATIONAL ASPECTS
Indicator 3.1: General Objective
Indicator 3.2: Specific Objectives
Indicator 3.3: Target Audience
Indicator 3.4: Methodology
Indicator 3.5: Materials
Indicator 3.6: Content Administration
Indicator 3.7: Evaluation Criteria
Indicator 3.8: Teaching-Learning Activities
DIMENSION 4: ACHIEVABLE ASPECTS
Indicator 4.1: Strategic Planning
Indicator 4.2: Academic Criteria
Indicator 4.3: Impact
Indicator 4.4: Number of Participants
Indicator 4.5: Mentoring
Indicator 4.6: Training proposal evaluation and adjustments

4   Discussion and Conclusions

The ESD, allows for the quantitative phase's collected and analyzed results to inform the qualitative phase [12, 13]. In this context, based on the Systematic Literature Review (SLR) and the diagnosis of Unach TDC levels, an initial training course plan proposal was developed. This proposal was subsequently validated by a group of experts in the field of educational technology in the Ecuadorian context through a two-iteration Delphi study.

The qualitative data has furnished in-depth and enriching insights into the participants' perceptions, experiences, and practices concerning the suggested training plan aimed at enhancing the level of DC. Conversely, the quantitative data has provided objective and quantifiable information regarding the definition of competency levels, ensuring the validity and reliability of the instruments employed. Through the amalgamation of these two approaches, more comprehensive and validated results are achieved, thereby bolstering confidence in the drawn conclusions [12, 13].

Upon analyzing the level of DC development among the teachers at Unach, it becomes evident that most of them fall within the "Medium" level, as per the COMDIA A framework [52, 53]. These findings underscore the pressing need to implement training initiatives aimed at enhancing these digital skills. Concrete measures must be taken to elevate the level of DC by equipping teachers with the requisite tools and resources to tackle the challenges of the digital educational landscape [57].

The utilization of a mixed-method approach in this research has facilitated a deeper comprehension of the digital skills possessed by Unach teachers [26]. Beyond merely defining DC levels, it has yielded a clear perspective on how to enhance these skills to promote more effective and context-adapted teaching within the current digital landscape. The mixed-method research design has contributed to a more comprehensive understanding of the issue, addressed its intricacies, and provided practical insights [28]. Moreover, the combination of quantitative and qualitative validation techniques has enriched the scientific process by enhancing the overall consistency of the research [27].

In the future, it is proposed to incorporate data triangulation as a comprehensive approach to gathering and analyzing information in the field of educational technology. Additionally, the utilization of educational data mining [58–63] is suggested to extract valuable insights from studies employing mixed methodologies. These approaches will allow for the assessment of not only the level of DC development in students but also other pertinent aspects within the context of the Higher Education System.

Funds

The present research has been developed as part of the Doctoral thesis entitled "Fortaecimiento de la Competencia Digital Docente: Definición del nivel y diseño de una propuesta de plan de curso de capacitación en la Universidad Nacional de Chimborazo" at the Rovira i Virgili University in Tarragona, Spain. It received support from the Doctoral Program in Educational Technologies, led by the research group Applied Research in Education and Technology (ARGET 2021SGR00707). Additionally, it was funded by the Fundación Carolina, Universitat Rovira i Virgili and the Universidad Nacional de Chimborazo.

References

1. Esteve-Mon, F.M., Llopis-Nebot, M.A., Adell-Segura, J.: Digital Teaching competence of university teachers: a systematic review of the literature. IEEE Revista Iberoamericana de Tecnologias del Aprendizaje. **15**, 399–406 (2020). https://doi.org/10.1109/RITA.2020.3033225

2. Biel, L.A., Ramos, E.Á.: Digital teaching competence of the university professor 3.0. Caracteres **8**, 205–236 (2019)

3. Martín Cuadrado, A., Pérez Sánchez, L., Jordano de laTorre, M.: Las competencias digitales docentes en entornos universitarios basados en el Digcomp. Educar em Revista **36** (2020). https://doi.org/10.1590/0104-4060.75866

4. Galindo-Domínguez, H., Bezanilla, M.J.: Digital competence in the training of pre-service teachers: Perceptions of students in the degrees of early childhood education and primary education. J. Digital Learn. Teacher Educ., 1–16 (2021). https://doi.org/10.1080/21532974.2021.1934757

5. Pérez-Calderón, E., Prieto-Ballester, J.M., Miguel-Barrado, V.: Analysis of digital competence for spanish teachers at pre-university educational key stages during COVID-19. Int. J. Environ. Res. Public Health **18**, 8093 (2021). https://doi.org/10.3390/ijerph18158093

6. Silva Quiroz, J., Miranda Arredondo, P.: Presencia de la competencia digital docente en los programas de formación inicial en universidades públicas chilenas. Revista de Estudios y Experiencias en Educación **19**, 149–165 (2020). https://doi.org/10.21703/rexe.20201941silva9

7. Cabero-Almenara, J., Barroso-Osuna, J., Palacios-Rodríguez, A.: Digital competences of educators in Health Sciences: Their relationship with some variables | Estudio de la competencia digital docente en Ciencias de la Salud. Su relación con algunas variables. Educacion Medica **22**, 94–98 (2021). https://doi.org/10.1016/j.edumed.2020.11.014

8. Cabero-Almenara, J., Barroso-Osuna, J., Gutiérrez-Castillo, J.-J., Palacios-Rodríguez, A.: The teaching digital competence of health sciences teachers. a study at Andalusian universities (Spain). Int. J. Environ. Res. Public Health **18**, 2552 (2021). https://doi.org/10.3390/ijerph 18052552

9. Silva, J., Morales, M.-J., Lázaro-Cantabrana, J.-L., Gisbert, M., Miranda, P., Rivoir, A., Onetto, A.: Digital teaching competence in initial training: case studies from Chile and Uruguay. Educ. Policy Anal. Arch. **27**, 93 (2019). https://doi.org/10.14507/epaa.27.3822

10. Cateriano-Chávez, T.J., Rodríguez-Rios, M.L., Patiño-Abrego, E.L., Araujo-Castillo, R.L., Villalba-Condori, K.O.: Digital skills, methodology and evaluation in teacher trainers | Competencias digitales, metodología y evaluación en formadores de docentes. Campus Virtuales. **10**, 153–162 (2021)

11. Sánchez-Caballé, A., Gisbert-Cervera, M., Esteve-Mon, F.: The digital competence of university students: a systematic literature review. Aloma: Revista de Psicologia, Ciències de l'Educació i de l'Esport. **38**, 63–74 (2020). https://doi.org/10.51698/aloma.2020.38.1.63-74

12. Cohen, L., Manion, L., Morrison, K.: Research Methods in Education (2018)

13. Creswell, J.W.: Research-Design_Qualitative-Quantitative-and-Mixed-Methods-Approaches (2014)

14. Alonso-Ferreiro, A.: Project-based learning to foster preservice teachers' digital competence. Revista Latinoamericana De Tecnologia Educativa-Relatec. **17**, 9–24 (2018). https://doi.org/10.17398/1695-288X.17.1.9

15. Lázaro-Cantabrana, J.L., Usart-Rodríguez, M., Gisbert-Cervera, M.: Assessing teacher digital competence: the construction of an instrument for measuring the knowledge of pre-service teachers. J. New Approach. Educ. Res. **8**, 73–78 (2019). https://doi.org/10.7821/naer.2019.1.370

16. Silva, J., Usart, M., Lázaro-Cantabrana, J.-L.: Teacher's digital competence among final year Pedagogy students in Chile and Uruguay. Comunicar. **27**, 33–43 (2019). https://doi.org/10.3916/C61-2019-03

17. González, M.J.M., Rivoir, A., Lázaro-Cantabrana, J.L., Gisbert-Cervera, M.: How does the digital teaching competence matter? an analysis of initial teacher training programs in Uruguay. Innoeduca. Inter. J. Technol. Educ. Innovat. **6**, 128–240 (2020). https://doi.org/10.24310/innoeduca.2020.v6i2.5601

18. Laurente-Cárdenas, C., Rengifo-Lozano, R., Asmat-Vega, N., Neyra-Huamani, L.: Development of digital skills in university professors through virtual environments: experiences of university professors in Lima. Eleuthera **22**, 71–87 (2020). https://doi.org/10.17151/eleu.2020.22.2.5

19. Domingo-Coscollola, M., Bosco, A., Segovia, S.C., Valero, J.A.S.: Fostering teacher's digital competence at university: The perception of students and teachers. Revista de Investigacion Educativa. **38**, 167–182 (2020). https://doi.org/10.6018/rie.340551

20. Gómez Trigueros, I.M.: La interdisciplinariedad y las tecnologías como nuevas estrategias para el aprendizaje del paisaje. Cuadernos Geográficos **57**, 77–96 (2018). https://doi.org/10.30827/cuadgeo.v57i3.5898

21. Hernández Sampieri, R., Fernández Collado, C., Baptista Lucio, P.: Metodología de la investigación, México (2014)

22. Denzin, N.K.: Sociological Methods. Routledge (2017). https://doi.org/10.4324/978131512 9945

23. Universidad Nacional de Chimborazo: Rendición de Cuentas de la Gestión 2022. , Riobamba (2022)

24. Hutton, B., Catalá-López, F., Moher, D.: La extensión de la declaración PRISMA para revisiones sistemáticas que incorporan metaanálisis en red: PRISMA-NMA. Med. Clin. (Barc.) **147**, 262–266 (2016). https://doi.org/10.1016/j.medcli.2016.02.025
25. Urrutia, G., Bonfill, X.: PRISMA declaration: A proposal to improve the publication oy systematic reviews and meta-analyses (2010). http://es.cochrane.org/sites/es.cochrane.org/files/public/uploads/PRISMA_Spanish.pdf,
26. Collins, K.: Handbook of Mixed Methods in Social & Behavioral Research. SAGE Publications, Inc., 2455 Teller Road, Thousand Oaks California 91320 United States (2010). https://doi.org/10.4135/9781506335193
27. Venkatesh, V., Brown, S.A., Sullivan, Y.W.: Guidelines for conducting mixed-methods research: an extension and illustration. J. Assoc. Inf. Syst. **17**, 435–495 (2016). https://doi.org/10.17705/1jais.00433
28. Plano-Clark, V., Huddleston-Casas, C.A., Churchill, S.L., Neil, G.O., D., Garrett, A.L.: Mixed methods approaches in family science research. J. Fam. Issues **29**, 1543–1566 (2008). https://doi.org/10.1177/0192513X08318251
29. Arias, F.: El Proyecto De Investigación: Guía para su elaboración, Caracas (1999)
30. Arias, F.: El Proyecto De Investigación: Introducción a la metodología científica, Caracas (2012)
31. Ramos-Galarza, C.A.: Alcances de una investigación. CienciAmérica **9**, 1–6 (2020). https://doi.org/10.33210/ca.v9i3.336
32. Arnal, J., Del Rincón, D., Latorre, A.: Investigación Educativa: Fundamentos y metodologías, Barcelona (1992)
33. Bisquerra, R.: Métodos de investigación educativa: Guía práctica, pp. 55–69 (1989)
34. Bisquerra, R., Alzina, B., Tejedor, J., Alonso, G.: Metodología de la Investigación Educativa, Madrid (2009)
35. Usart Rodríguez, M., Lázaro Cantabrana, J.L., Gisbert Cervera, M.: Validation of a tool for self-evaluating teacher digital competence. Educación XX1 **24**, 353–373 (2020). https://doi.org/10.5944/educxx1.27080
36. Lázaro, L., Gisbert, M.: Elaboración de una rúbrica para evaluar la competencia digital del docente. UT. Revista de Ciències de l'Educació (2015)
37. Burguet Lago, I., Burguet Lago, N.: Empleo del excel para el procesamiento de los criterios de expertos mediante el método de evaluación de comparación por pares. 3C TIC: Cuadernos de desarrollo aplicados a las TIC **9**, 17–43 (2020). https://doi.org/10.17993/3ctic.2020.94.17-43
38. García Martínez, V., Aquino Zúñiga, S.P., Guzmán Sala, A., Medina Meléndez, A.: Using the delphi method as a strategy for the assesment of quality indicators in distance education programs. Revista Calidad en la Educación Superior **3**, 200–222 (2012)
39. Molero-Aranda, T., Lázaro-Cantabrana, J.L., Cervera, M.G.: A Technological Solution for People with Intellectual Disabilities in Emergency Situations. REICE. Revista Iberoamericana Sobre Calidad, Eficacia y Cambio en Educacion **20**, 65–83 (2022). https://doi.org/10.15366/reice2022.20.2.004
40. Cabero Almenara, J.: Formación del profesorado universitario en TIC. aplicación del método Delphi para la selección de los contenidos formativos. Educacion XX1 **17**, 111–131 (2013). https://doi.org/10.5944/educxx1.17.1.10707
41. Cisneros Barahona, A.S., Marqués Molías, L., Samaniego Erazo, N., Mercedes, C.: La Competencia Digital Docente. Diseño y validación de una propuesta formativa. Pixel-Bit, Revista de Medios y Educación, 7–41 (2023). https://doi.org/10.12795/pixelbit.100524
42. Cisneros-Barahona, A., Marqués Molías, L., Samaniego Erazo, G., Uvidia-Fassler, M.I., de la Cruz-Fernández, G.: Bibliometric Mapping of Scientific Literature Located in Scopus on Teaching Digital Competence in Higher Education. In: Botto-Tobar, M., Gómez, O.S., Rosero

Miranda, R., Díaz Cadena, A., Luna-Encalada, W. (ed.) Trends in Artificial Intelligence and Computer Engineering. pp. 167–180. Springer Nature Switzerland, Cham (2023). https://doi.org/10.1007/978-3-031-25942-5_14

43. Cisneros-Barahona, A., Marqués Molías, L., Samaniego-Erazo, N., Uvidia-Fassler, M.I., Castro-Ortiz, W., Villa-Yánez, H.: Digital competence, faculty and higher education: Bibliometrics from the Web of Science (2023). https://doi.org/10.37467/revhuman.v12.4680

44. Cisneros-Barahona, A., Marqués-Molías, L., Samaniego-Erazo, N., Uvidia-Fassler, M., Castro-Ortiz, W., Rosas-Chávez, P.: Digital competence of university teachers. An overview of the state of the art (2022). https://journals.eagora.org/revHUMAN/article/view/4355, https://doi.org/10.37467/revhuman.v11.4355

45. Cisneros-Barahona, A., Marqués-Molías, L., Samaniego-Erazo, G., Uvidia-Fassler, M., De la Cruz-Fernández, G., Castro-Ortiz, W.: Teaching Digital Competence in Higher Education. A Comprehensive Scientific Mapping Analysis with Rstudio In: Abad, K., Berrezueta, S. (eds) DSICT 2022, CCIS, vol.1647, pp. 14–31. Springer, Cham (2022). https://doi.org/10.1007/978-3-031-18347-8_2

46. Cisneros-Barahona, A., Marqués Molías, L., Samaniego Erazo, G., Uvidia-Fassler, M.I., De la Cruz-Fernández, G., Castro-Ortiz, W.: Teaching digital competences in university professors: a meta-analysis and systematic literature review in web of science. In: Botto-Tobar, M., Zambrano Vizuete, M., Montes León, S., Torres-Carrión, P., Durakovic, B. (ed.) ICAT 2022. CCIS, vol 1755, pp. 61–74. Springer Nature Switzerland, Cham (2023). https://doi.org/10.1007/978-3-031-24985-3_5

47. Dalla, R.L., Gamble, W.C.: Exploring Factors Related to Parenting Competence among Navajo Teenage Mothers: Dual Techniques of Inquiry. Fam. Relat. **46**, 113–121 (1997)

48. Javo, C., Alapack, R., Heyerdahl, S., Rønning, J.A.: Parental values and ethnic identity in indigenous sami families: A qualitative study. Fam. Process. **42**, 151–164 (2003). https://doi.org/10.1111/j.1545-5300.2003.00151.x

49. Marshall, T., Solomon, P.: Provider Contact with Families of Adults with Severe Mental Illness: Taking a Closer Look. Fam Process. 43, (2004)

50. Weine, S., et al.: A mixed methods study of refugee families engaging in multiple-family groups*. Fam Relat. 54 (2005)

51. Ivankova, N.V., Stick, S.L.: Students' persistence in a distributed doctoral program in educational leadership in higher education: a mixed methods study. Res. High. Educ. **48**, 93–135 (2007). https://doi.org/10.1007/s11162-006-9025-4

52. Lázaro-Cantabrana, J.L., Gisbert-Cervera, M., Silva-Quiroz, J.E.: Una rúbrica para evaluar la competencia digital del profesor universitario en el contexto latinoamericano. Edutec. Revista Electrónica de Tecnología Educativa (2018). https://doi.org/10.21556/edutec.2018.63.1091

53. Lázaro-Cantabrana, J.L., Gisbert-Cervera, M.: Elaboración de una rúbrica para evaluar la competencia digital del docente. UT. Revista de Ciències de l'Educació (2015). https://doi.org/10.17345/ute.2015.1

54. Cronbach, L.J.: Coefficient alpha and the internal structure of tests. Springer-Verlag (1951). https://doi.org/10.1007/BF02310555

55. Cisneros-Barahona, A., Marqués Molías, L., Samaniego Erazo, Ni., Mejía Granizo, C., De la Cruz Fernández, G.: Data availability. Multivariate data analysis. validation of an instrument for the evaluation of teaching digital competence (2023). https://doi.org/10.5281/ZENODO.8005514

56. Cisneros-Barahona, A.S., Marqués-Molías, L., Samaniego-Erazo, N., Mejía-Granizo, C., De la Cruz-Fernández, G.: Multivariate data analysis: validation of an instrument for the evaluation of teaching digital competence. F1000Res **12**, 866 (2023). https://doi.org/10.12688/f1000research.135194.1

57. Motz, R., et al.: Aspectos a considerar en el diseño de acciones formativas virtuales y accesibles. In: Moreira Teixeira, A., Bengochea, L., Hilera, J.R. (eds.) Para uma Formação Virtual Acessível e de Qualidade, Liboa, pp. 57–64 (2013)
58. Uvidia-Fassler, M., Cisneros-Barahona, A., Viñan-Carrera, J.: Minería de Datos de la Evaluación Integral del Desempeño Académico de la Unidad de Nivelación. Descubre, 44–54 (2017)
59. Uvidia Fassler, M.I., Cisneros Barahona, A.S., Ávila-Pesántez, D.F., Rodríguez Flores, I.E.: Moving towards a methodology employing knowledge discovery in databases to assist in decision making regarding academic placement and student admissions for universities. In: Botto-Tobar, M., Esparza-Cruz, N., León-Acurio, J., Crespo-Torres, N., Beltrán-Mora, M. (eds.) CITT 2017. CCIS, vol. 798, pp. 215–229. Springer, Cham (2018). https://doi.org/10.1007/978-3-319-72727-1_16
60. Uvidia Fassler, M.I., Cisneros Barahona, A.S., Dumancela Nina, G.J., Samaniego Erazo, G.N., Villacrés Cevallos, E.P.: Application of knowledge discovery in data bases analysis to predict the academic performance of university students based on their admissions test. In: Botto-Tobar, M., León-Acurio, J., Díaz Cadena, A., Montiel Díaz, P. (eds.) ICAETT 2019. AISC, vol. 1066, pp. 485–497. Springer, Cham (2020). https://doi.org/10.1007/978-3-030-32022-5_45
61. Cisneros-Barahona, A., Uvidia-Fassler, M., Samaniego-Erazo, G., Dumancela-Nina, G., Casignia-Vásconez, B.: Complementary admission processes implemented by ecuadorian public universities promote equal opportunities in access: an analysis through knowledge discovery in databases. In: Botto-Tobar, M., Zamora, W., Larrea Plúa, J., Bazurto Roldan, J., Santamaría Philco, A. (eds.) ICCIS 2020. AISC, vol 1273, pp. 208–222. Springer, Cham (2021). https://doi.org/10.1007/978-3-030-59194-6_18
62. Uvidia, M., Cisneros Barahona, A.: Análisis de data mining para la toma de decisiones en la unidad de nivelación y admisión a nivel universitario (2017)
63. Uvidia Fassler, M.I., Cisneros Barahona, A.S., Méndez Naranjo, P.M., Villa Yánez, H.M.: Minería de datos para la toma de decisiones en la unidad de nivelación y admisión universitaria ecuatoriana. Cumbres **4**, 55–67 (2019). https://doi.org/10.48190/cumbres.v4n2a5

Electronics

SparksAIR: A Low-Cost IoT Solution to Manage Air Pollution in Urban Areas

Willian Zamora[1,3]([✉]) [ID], Jorge Luis Zambrano-Martinez[2,3] [ID],
Carlos T. Calafate[3] [ID], Marcos Ponce-Jara[1] [ID], and Mike Machuca[1]

[1] Universidad Laica Eloy Alfaro Manabi, Via San Mateo, SN, Ecuador
{willian.zamora,marcos.ponce,mike.machuca}@uleam.edu.ec
[2] Universidad del Azuay, Cuenca, Ecuador
jorge.zambrano@uazuay.edu.ec
[3] Universitat Politècnica de València, Valencia, Spain
calafate@disca.upv.es

Abstract. The combustion of polluting materials in industrial processes and motor vehicles, among other factors, causes atmospheric pollution that gradually degrades human health. Thus, air pollution monitoring has become an essential requirement for cities worldwide. However, traditional fixed monitoring stations present challenges in terms of cost and installation difficulty. In this context, monitoring solutions based on emerging technologies such as the Internet of Things and embedded systems have shown increasing interest. In this article, SPARKS-AIR, a low-cost fixed solution for air pollution monitoring, is described. SPARKS-AIR combines the design of an electronic board with a Raspberry Pi. The board allows connecting of up to six electrochemical gas sensors manufactured by Alphasense. The collected data is stored in a local database and sent directly to the cloud. The solution has been deployed in Manta, Ecuador, to validate our proposal. Our purpose is to analyse the behaviour of the solution in two areas of high vehicular traffic. In particular, we monitor and analyze the levels of Carbon monoxide (CO), Sulfur dioxide (SO_2), and Nitrogen dioxide (NO_2). Experimental results show that, in the two target locations, the hour associated with the highest pollution levels is 10 am. In addition, we observed that the values obtained for NO_2 exceed the permitted thresholds by 200%, according to the World Health Organization (WHO).

Keywords: IoT · Alphasense · air pollution · testbed measurements

1 Introduction

Air pollution is one of the most pressing environmental problems. The emission of air pollutants has increased due to increased demand for energy and industrialisation. In fact, industrial activities, power generation, transportation, and burning fossil fuels are some of the primary sources of pollution. These pollutants include Carbon dioxide (CO_2), Carbon monoxide (CO), Nitric oxide (NO),

© The Author(s), under exclusive license to Springer Nature Switzerland AG 2024
M. Botto-Tobar et al. (Eds.): ICAT 2023, CCIS 2051, pp. 105–116, 2024.
https://doi.org/10.1007/978-3-031-58950-8_9

Nitrogen dioxides (NO_2), Ozone (O_3), Sulfur dioxide (SO_2), Volatile Organic Compounds (VOCs), Particulate Matter 2.5 ($PM_{2.5}$), and Particulate Matter 10 (PM_{10}). These pollutants, including toxic gases and suspended particles, have severe consequences for humans and the environment according to the World Health Organization (WHO) [7]. In particular, respiratory, cardiovascular and neurological diseases are caused by prolonged exposure to high levels of pollutants [11].

Nowadays, different cities with nearly unbreathable air indicate the magnitude of the air pollution problem. Consequently, governments, international organisations and communities recognise the importance of tackling this problem [18]. Therefore, it is important to consult local environmental legislation and regulations, along with those of international organisations, to obtain precise information on allowable rates of air pollutants. In addition, government air quality agencies often provide recent information on applicable standards and permissible limits.

In this context, Manta City, located on Ecuadors' southern Pacific coast, is not exempt from air pollution issues. Yet, the city still misses official studies or local reports on air quality monitoring. With a population of approximately 250,000 inhabitants, this city has an urban area with a high concentration of vehicles. So, conducting an exhaustive analysis of the concentration levels of atmospheric pollutants in this area is essential.

In response to this growing concern, solutions based on emerging technologies, such as the Internet of Things (IoT), represent an innovative and promising response to address these challenges [17]. Thus, embedded systems of compact and low-consumption electronic devices play a fundamental role in developing air quality monitoring solutions. These systems allow custom sensors to be integrated into portable and easy-to-deploy devices. By combining these sensors, intelligent devices, and wireless connectivity, IoT enables the real-time collection of related data, such as pollutant concentrations.

In this article, we propose developing a system that allows environmental monitoring of air based on IoT called SPARKS-AIR. Our solution combines the design of an electronic board that combines Raspberry Pi and Alphasense brand sensors. The solution enables storing and displaying data in real-time through CO_2, CO, NO_2, SO_2, O_3, $PM_{2.5}$ and PM_{10} sensors. To evaluate our proposal, the values collected by three sensors have been analysed in two locations in Manta, Ecuador.

This document is organised as follows: Sect. 2 presents related works. Section 3 describes the proposed architecture for air quality monitoring using low-cost sensors. In addition, the sensors analysed for this study are described. Section 4 shows the evaluation and validation of the proposal, highlighting the results obtained through statistical graphs in two locations. Finally, Sect. 5 presents the conclusions, and discusses future work.

2   Related Work

Low-cost air quality monitoring solutions have gained popularity. Consequently, there are numerous research papers related to this topic.

Recently, systematic reviews have been performed that evaluate low-cost air quality sensors, and where aspects such as architecture, sensor selection, and calibration, among others, are studied [9,10,13]. Some related solutions are described below.

Mead et al. [12] implement a network of autonomous sensor nodes in Cambridge, United Kingdom. The authors use electrochemical sensors with sensitivity at the parts per billion (ppb) level, and analyse NO, NO_2 and CO in high-density areas. Their results show the potential of these approaches, obtaining air quality values with high granularity.

Alvear et al. [3] present a solution that allows the collection of air pollution using mobile sensors. This solution combines an architecture using a commercial device from the Libelium brand, Raspberry Pi, smartphones and a web server. The impact of O_3 gas and its best sampling strategy in Valencia, Spain, was analysed. In particular, it was sought to determine a promising approach for estimating the distribution of the O_3 contaminant in a specific area. To this end, kriging statistical interpolation techniques were used.

Sharma et al. [16] present a low-cost wireless sensor device for real-time air quality monitoring. These authors use low-power electrochemical NO_2 and O_3 sensors, and add sensors to obtain the values of $PM_{2.5}$ Their solution uses a Raspberry Pi to collect, store, and upload the data to a web server.

Instead, Johnston et al. [8] deployed six IoT devices to monitor air quality at two locations in Southampton, United Kingdom. Each device has four low-cost PM sensors and LoRaWAN wireless network transceivers to test city-scale coverage. Their results show that not all PM sensors are equal, and that a reasonable correlation with reference stations is possible. Also, Parri et al. [15] presented a solution to monitor air quality in a foundry plant where a furnace operates. The design allows the use of low-cost commercial sensors. Its architecture uses non-proprietary hardware and software, and the sensor nodes transmit the data collected via LoRa to a remote LoRaWAN server.

Regarding the brand of gas sensors used, in [1] authors evaluated low-cost electrochemical sensors from Alphasense Ltd. for real-time monitoring of CO, NO_2 and O_3 gases. Sensor responses were highly linear concerning gas concentrations measured with reference instruments. Furthermore, Cross et al. [6] indicate the potential of air pollution measurements using this brand, and focus on validating measurements obtained from CO, NO, NO_2 and O_3 gases.

Compared with previous works, our proposal integrates up to six gas sensors, particulate matter, temperature, humidity and pressure sensors on the same board. In addition, our solution focuses on collecting atmospheric data in urban areas of Manta, Ecuador, with low-energy consumption and at low-cost.

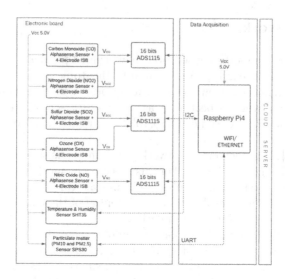

Fig. 1. Proposed Architecture for SPARKS-AIR.

3   Research Method

This section describes the proposed solution that was developed, and details the gases that were evaluated, while keeping in mind the current local and international regulations.

3.1   Proposed Architecture

Our proposed monitoring system has an architecture based on three main components. The first corresponds to the electronic board connecting the different low-cost sensors. The second corresponds to the device that captures and stores the sensors' data; the third component is the web server. Figure 1 shows the architecture of the air quality measurement system in more detail.

Electronic Board. Our electronic board allows you to connect up to six Alphasense electrochemical gas sensors. In particular, with SPARKS-AIR, we have used the sensors to measure CO, NO_2, SO_2, O_2, and NO [2], each with a signal adapter circuit of the same brand (4-Electrode ISB). The use of the Alphasense ISB circuit allows for further noise reduction. In addition, it has a temperature and humidity sensor (SHT35) and a particulate matter sensor (SPS30) that measures PM_{10} and $PM_{2.5}$. To convert the analogue signals from the electrochemical sensors, a 16-bit analogue-to-digital converter (ADS115) is used. All sensors (except the particle sensor) use the Universal Asynchronous Receiver/Transmitter (UART) serial protocol. This component communicates with the data acquisition component through the Inter-Integrated Circuit (I2C) serial communication protocol. The entire system is powered by 5V. In Fig. 2 we can see the architecture of the connected electronic board.

(a) Electronic gas boards and PM.

(b) SPARKS-AIR Box.

Fig. 2. SPARKS-AIR box electronic board.

Data Collection. A Raspberry Pi 4 has been used for the data acquisition process. The device is connected using the I2C communication protocol, allowing data to be obtained from the sensors connected to the electronic card. The Raspberry Pi 4 also processes and stores data in the internal microSD memory. For local storage, SQLite was used, and through a service, it allowed sending the data to the cloud and transmitting the captured information in real time. The communication has been done through both WiFi and Ethernet networks.

Cloud Server. The Cloud server allows visualising the data in real-time. To this end, the data is first stored in a database on the server. In this case, PostgreSQL v12 has been used. They can then be accessed with a web interface based on Grafana v9.2.18. This allows us to observe the data obtained from the dashboard offered by this open-source platform.

3.2 Method Proposed

Once the SPARKS-AIR proposal has been described, the gases analysed for our tests are described below, along with regulations for maximum permitted values of some air pollutants. The objective was to compare the values obtained from our proposal with reference values defined by both national and international organisations.

Gases Analyzed. In this article, we refer to the analysis of 3 of the five gases considered in our proposal. In particular, CO, NO_2, and SO_2, which are mainly formed as a result of the combustion of fossil fuels, are analysed. In addition, these gases, being in continuous exposure, can cause diseases, especially in the respiratory tract. In general, SPARKS-AIR measures these gases' values in ppb

Table 1. Maximum values allowed in 1 h and 24 h according to the control organisms.

Gases	A.M97 (1 hr.) ($\mu g/m^3$)	AQG Level (24 hr.) ($\mu g/m^3$)
CO	30000	4000
SO_2	500	40
NO_2	200	25

and obtains them in micrograms per cubic meter ($\mu g/m^3$) for their subsequent analysis, as we can observe in Eq. 1 [14].

$$Concentration(mg/m^3) = 0.0409 \cdot ppm \cdot mw \qquad (1)$$

where mw is the molecular weight of each of the gases studied [5], and ppb is the value obtained by the gas sensor.

Allowable Values Guidelines. Environmental regulations and standards have been established for the different pollutants in each country or region, where the maximum permissible limits for each of these polluting gases are indicated. Knowing this indicator allows us to compare the values obtained by our proposal. To this end, the global air quality guidelines of the WHO [7] and, at the national level, the ministerial agreement related to the environmental quality standard [4], have been taken as reference. Table 1 shows the allowed average limit values for gases in $\mu g/m^3$ for time periods of 1 h and 24 h, respectively.

4   Result Report

In this section, the results obtained are described. In particular, two locations have been taken as a reference, one facing the sea, and the other distant from it, as shown in Fig. 3. Both locations are places of high vehicular traffic flow levels, and data was taken for seven consecutive days, from Monday to Sunday, for each location. The evaluations performed were i) Analysis of CO, NO_2, and SO_2 behaviour per week, in each location. ii) Evaluation of the day and time of the highest concentration, and iii) the results obtained from the analysis were compared with the limits established by the corresponding regulations. This allows determining whether the gas concentrations are within the permitted thresholds, or exceed the recommended limits.

(a) Location A.   (b) Location B.

Fig. 3. SPARKS-AIR analysis locations in Manta, Ecuador.

4.1 Weekly Analysis of Gas Sensor Data

This section analyses the data obtained from the gas sensors used. In particular, CO, SO_2, and NO_2 gases have been evaluated in the two locations previously indicated. The objective was to determine the impact of each of these gases in the analysed sites for seven consecutive days. The established sampling frequency was of one sample every five minutes. In general, approximately 2020 records per location were obtained.

Figures 4a and 4b show the values obtained in ppb for each gas sensor analysed. In general, it is observed that in locations A and B, CO presents higher ppb concentration levels compared to SO_2 and NO_2 gases, respectively. On the contrary, low ppb concentration levels on both locations are observed for SO_2. Figure 4b shows a more uniform concentration values for NO_2 gas during the seven days analysed.

Table 2 shows the statistical values obtained for this first analysis in the two locations. In particular, it can be seen that the standard deviation values for each of the sensors at location B are lower than at location A. Additionally, it can be seen that the mean temperature for location B is higher than location A because the information processed is from the month of November, and location A is from the month of October, both from the year 2022.

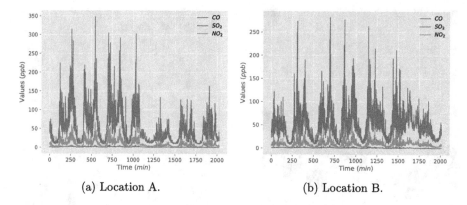

(a) Location A.   (b) Location B.

Fig. 4. Gas sensors analysis per location.

Table 2. Gas analysis per location in 7 d.

Loc.	Gas sensor	Avg.(ppb)	Max.(ppb)	Min.(ppb)	Std.(ppb)
A	CO	52.19	347.79	8.30	46.46
	NO_2	9.89	65.90	1.57	8.80
	SO_2	0.97	61.11	0.06	0.83
B	CO	50.06	281.55	7.81	34.15
	NO_2	9.48	53.35	1.48	6.47
	SO_2	1.05	6.13	0.14	0.67

4.2 Gas Sensor Analysis by Day and Hour

In the previous section, a general analysis of the behaviour of gases in two different locations (A-B) was performed. In this section, we seek to identify the day and time of the week with the highest average ppb concentration. For this purpose, the information has been processed to classify each record, specifying the day and time of the week corresponding to it. Then, the SO_2 gas sensor was selected because it presents the lowest standard deviation at both locations, A and B, in Table 2. Finally, a box plot was grouped per day and another per hour to represent the information obtained. The number of records processed is the same as in the first scan.

Figure 5 shows the results obtained for SO_2 gas classified by day of the week. In general, it is observed that location B has a uniform mean concentration of particulate matter during business days (Monday to Friday), while location A shows similar mean values during the first three days of the week in operation, slightly decreasing between Thursday and Friday. In addition, it is observed that, on Sunday, the values decrease for both locations; this is because Sunday is a day with less labour-related activities. In particular, and taking only business days as a reference, it is observed that, for Wednesday, the maximum values obtained are 15.99 ppb and 16.05 ppb for locations A and B, respectively.

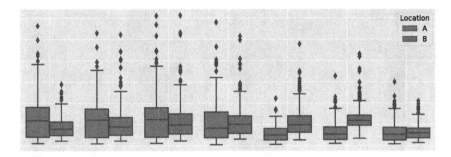

Fig. 5. SO$_2$ gas analysis per day at both locations.

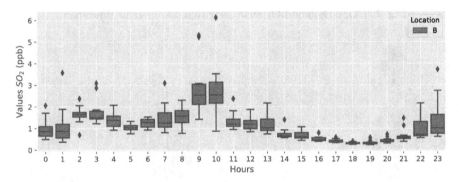

Fig. 6. SO$_2$ gas Analysis per hour at location B.

Once the day of the week with the highest ppb concentration was established, the information was classified by time slots. This purpose aims to identify the hour range of the greatest concentration gases. Thus, the gas evaluated SO$_2$ was taken as a reference. Figure 6 shows the per-hour behaviour of SO$_2$ gas. We find that, at 10 in the morning, the highest concentration of SO$_2$ gas is produced in that location. In addition, a non-linear behaviour is evidenced as sunset falls, with the lowest point of ppb concentration being at 6:00 pm.

4.3   Gas Analysis According to Regulations

Once the day of the week and the hour of the highest ppb concentration were identified, these values were compared with the Ecuadorian regulations and the WHO global air quality guidelines. For this purpose, we first converted the values obtained into $\mu g/m^3$ standard units of measurement according to the evaluated regulations. Next, 10 am was the reference time to compare the values obtained against the threshold values defined by Ecuadorian laws. Regarding the global air quality guidelines, the day with the highest ppb concentration (Wednesday)

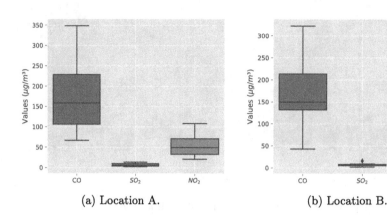

(a) Location A.   (b) Location B.

Fig. 7. CO, NO$_2$, and SO$_2$ analysis within an one-hour time span.

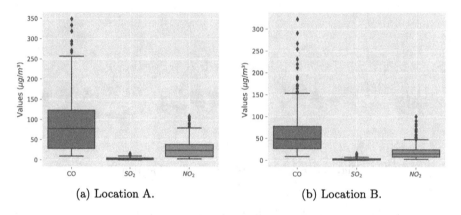

(a) Location A.   (b) Location B.

Fig. 8. CO, NO$_2$, y SO$_2$ analysis in 24 h.

was established as a reference. In this context, the data obtained is from the 24 h of said day. In both cases, the calculated values are the average limit values.

Figures 8 and 7 show the values obtained in $\mu g/m^3$ of CO, NO$_2$, and SO$_2$ gases in 1 h and 24 h. Those Figures show that the values with the highest concentration of particles are found for CO, while the one with the lowest concentration is for SO$_2$.

Table 3 shows the average limit values obtained from the case study gases in 1 and 24 h, respectively. These values make it possible to compare the concentrations of gases in each location with the limits established by Ecuadorian regulations and the WHO (see Table 1). In general, in Table 3 it is observed that, on both locations A and B, the average limit values of the gases in 24 h are lower than those obtained in 1 h. On the contrary, according to the WHO regulations, the percentage values of the gases studied are higher than the Ecuadorian regulations.

Table 3. Maximum percentage for the average concentration according to regulations in periods of 1 h and 24 h, by location.

Loc.	Gas	Average maximum value		Regulations	
		1 h ($\mu g/m^3$)	24 h ($\mu g/m^3$)	Decree 97 [4] (1 h)	AQG (24 h)
A	CO	339.3	218.18	1.13%	5.45%
	SO_2	13.82	8.7	6.91%	21.75%
	NO_2	105.6	67.91	52.80%	271.64%
B	CO	312.33	162.3	1.04%	4.06%
	SO_2	13.9	7.46	6.95%	18.65%
	NO_2	97.21	50.51	48.61%	202.04%

In particular, according to Ecuadorian regulations, values for the NO_2 gas for the two locations remain between 48% and 53% of what is considered as acceptable concentration limits. As for the same gas, based on the WHO recommendations, the levels found within 24 h exceeded the regulatory limits by 271.64% for location A, and 202.04% for location B.

These findings highlight the need to address air quality at both locations to protect public health and apply appropriate air pollution control and mitigation measures.

5 Conclusions

SPARKS-AIR has been described in this article as a solution that enables air quality monitoring using low-cost sensors. The proposed architecture combines i) an electronic board interconnecting sensor, ii) the data acquisition component formed by a Raspberry Pi 4, and iii) the cloud server. Analysing data obtained through the weekly gas sensors is an excellent referential practice to measure the impact of the readings obtained in different areas in consecutive periods. Results obtained show that there are high concentration levels in the studied locations. In particular, it was evidenced that the NO_2 gas exceeds the limit values allowed according to the WHO regulation. In the short term, we plan to analyse other gases, and seek also to implement an intelligent calibration system.

Acknowledgements. Please place your acknowledgments at the end of the paper, preceded by an unnumbered run-in heading (i.e. 3rd-level heading).

References

1. Afshar-Mohajer, N., et al.: Evaluation of low-cost electro-chemical sensors for environmental monitoring of ozone, nitrogen dioxide, and carbon monoxide. J. Occup. Environ. Hyg. **15**(2), 87–98 (2018)
2. Alphasense, A.: Products by target gas. https://www.alphasense.com/product_type/target-gas/
3. Alvear, O., Zamora, W., Calafate, C.T., Cano, J.C., Manzoni, P.: Ecosensor: monitoring environmental pollution using mobile sensors. In: 2016 IEEE 17th International Symposium on a World of Wireless, Mobile and Multimedia Networks (WoWMoM), pp. 1–6. IEEE (2016)
4. Ambiental, C.: Reforma texto unificado legislación secundaria. Medio ambiente, Libro VI, Decreto Ejecutivo 3516, Registro Oficial Suplemento 2, 31/03/2003 (2003)
5. Cooper, C.D., Alley, F.C.: Air pollution control: A design approach. Waveland press (2010)
6. Cross, E.S., et al.: Use of electrochemical sensors for measurement of air pollution: correcting interference response and validating measurements. Atmospheric Measurem. Tech. **10**(9), 3575–3588 (2017). https://doi.org/10.5194/amt-10-3575-2017
7. Hoffmann, B., et al.: Who air quality guidelines 2021–aiming for healthier air for all: a joint statement by medical, public health, scientific societies and patient representative organisations. Inter. J. Public Health, 88 (2021)
8. Johnston, S.J., et al.: City scale particulate matter monitoring using lorawan based air quality iot devices. Sensors **19**(1), 209 (2019)
9. Kang, Y., Aye, L., Ngo, T.D., Zhou, J.: Performance evaluation of low-cost air quality sensors: a review. Sci. Total Environ. **818**, 151769 (2022)
10. Kumar, P., et al.: The rise of low-cost sensing for managing air pollution in cities. Environ. Int. **75**, 199–205 (2015)
11. Manisalidis, I., Stavropoulou, E., Stavropoulos, A., Bezirtzoglou, E.: Environmental and health impacts of air pollution: a review. Front. Public Health, 14 (2020)
12. Mead, M., et al.: The use of electrochemical sensors for monitoring urban air quality in low-cost, high-density networks. Atmos. Environ. **70**, 186–203 (2013)
13. Narayana, M.V., Jalihal, D., Nagendra, S.: Establishing a sustainable low-cost air quality monitoring setup: a survey of the State-of-the-art. Sensors **22**(1), 394 (2022)
14. Orona, C., Carter, V., Kindall, H.: Understanding standard units of measure. Teach. Child. Math. **23**(8), 500–503 (2017)
15. Parri, L.: A distributed iot air quality measurement system for high-risk workplace safety enhancement. Sensors **23**(11), 5060 (2023)
16. Sharma, A., Mishra, B., Sutaria, R., Zele, R.: Design and development of low-cost wireless sensor device for air quality networks. In: TENCON 2019 - 2019 IEEE Region 10 Conference (TENCON), pp. 2345–2350 (2019).https://doi.org/10.1109/TENCON.2019.8929304
17. Toma, C., Alexandru, A., Popa, M., Zamfiroiu, A.: Iot solution for smart cities' pollution monitoring and the security challenges. Sensors **19**(15), 3401 (2019)
18. Walker, G., Booker, D., J Young, P.: Breathing in the polyrhythmic city: a spatiotemporal, rhythmanalytic account of urban air pollution and its inequalities. Environ. Planning C: Politics Space **40**(3), 572–591 (2022)

Machine Vision

A Model to Support the Music Streaming Service Using Blockchain-Based Smart Contracts

Julio C. Mendoza-Tello$^{(\boxtimes)}$ (iD), Jonathan J. Sánchez-Lucas, and Juan G. Orosco-Pantoja

Facultad de Ingeniería y Ciencias Aplicadas, Universidad Central del Ecuador, Quito, Ecuador
{jcmendoza,jjsanchez11,jgorosco}@uce.edu.ec

Abstract. There is a pattern that prevails in the music business for a long time. An artist writes, records, produces, and distributes a song so that the public can listen to it, and thus acquire financial compensation. This marketing and distribution effort is done collaboratively with record labels and companies that know the music business, because the artist alone cannot achieve a large audience. Because the actors involved in this process are too many, the main author gets the smallest percentage of the benefits. For this reason, this research proposes a model to support the music streaming service using blockchain-based smart contracts. For this, a prototype based on smart contracts is developed so that the author exhibits his musical works and gets an economic benefit. Using a web interface, a user can listen to a song by recording a monetary transaction within the blockchain. Consequently, this proposal allows a direct relationship between creators and consumers of musical content. Thus, blockchain was used to eliminate intermediation and directly reward the profits to the author of the melody. Conclusions and future work were presented at the end of the paper.

Keywords: blockchain · smart contracts · music · innovation

1 Introduction

The new trends in the consumption of digital services achieve a great worldwide impact in the musical environment. Recently, live content streaming services are the main channels for advertising, distribution, and playback of musical creations. These services are constantly evolving due to the changing demand for audiovisual entertainment. In addition, collaborative marketing and distribution efforts are necessary for the promotion of the songs. In this way, the music can be heard by fans and promoted in a niche market. In this context, for an artist to receive financial compensation (for playing music), it is necessary to comply with the rules of use. However, this research identifies a big problem: intermediation.

Currently, there is an incredible amount of consumers; however, these services are run by intermediary platforms that earn most of the profits, as opposed to the content authors. Faced with this inconvenience, the author cannot control its content and assigns the copyright to other advertising companies. Faced with these challenges, blockchain proposes to replace the current intermediation with a decentralized platform based on smart contracts that allows the automation of the streaming process, which includes user authentication and registration, content management and consumption, as well as fees and payments for the service. Therefore, this research proposes a model to support the music streaming service using blockchain-based smart contracts.

With these considerations, the sections of this paper are structured as follows. Section 2 describes the methodology used for this research. Section 3 explains the following: an overview of blockchain and smart contracts, related research, and materials used for this research. In Sect. 4, a model was designed using three layers, namely: storage, business-logic, and user. Finally, contributions, conclusions and future research were described in Sect. 5.

2 Methodology

Three consecutive phases were addressed during this research, namely: theory, practice, and conclusions. Regarding the theoretical phase. A brief description of the theoretical framework that supports this proposal. In this context, the way in which a smart contract interacts with a chain of blocks is described, as well as a review of the related works. In addition, hardware and software were identified to develop our proposal.

Regarding the practical phase. A layered model was designed according to the following functional requirements, namely: authentication, authorization, management, and consumption of musical content. Consequently, several software components were developed, namely: Ethereum smart contracts (using Solidity), and web interfaces (using CSS and HTML).

Regarding the conclusions phase. Contributions and future research were proposed to advance blockchain research for media streaming services.

3 Theoretical Background

This section explains core concepts (such as blockchain and smart contract), related works, and the materials (hardware and software) used to design the model.

3.1 Core Concepts: Blockchain and Smart Contract

Blockchain gains relevance because it is the underlying technology of cryptocurrencies. It was developed by an entity under the pseudonym Satoshi Nakamoto. Basically, blockchain is a set of blocks generated chronologically and stored in a P2P distributed network. Through the use of encryption algorithms and a decentralized consensus mechanism, the trust of the scheme is guaranteed without the need for third-party supervision [1]. From this perspective, the blockchain provides four essential features.

First, decentralization. There is no centralized and intermediary entity that controls and certifies operations. Transactions carried out at the same instant of time are compiled within a block; then these are propagated by the network for verification and each transaction gets a cryptographic hash. In turn, each block is added to the chain and propagated throughout the network. In this context, those responsible for verifying and storing the transactions are the same participants (or nodes) of the network.

Second, immutability. It's almost impossible to modify a block of transactions that was added to the chain. To alter the integrity of the blockchain, a high computational cost is necessary. This is because each block has a cryptographic hash that represents all transactions; This same hash is found in the header of the next block. Consequently, if a change is made, the previous header hash of all previous blocks must be recomputed. The greater the number of blocks generated, the greater the guarantee of immutability.

Third, anonymity. Blockchain users can remain anonymous; that is, the identity need not be revealed.

Fourth, availability. The blocks of the chain are stored within various nodes. This provides high availability of access to information because the transactions are not within a single node.

Regarding the blockchain structure. It contains several blocks linked sequentially according to a chronological order. Each block has a single parent block, except the first block called genesis. A block is a structure that contains headers and transactions. The header is unique, immutable, and contains the following metadata to verify block integrity. (i) Version. It indicates the protocol version of the consensus mechanism (e.g., mining). (ii) Previous hash block. Except for the genesis block, each block contains information from the previous block within its own header. (iv) Merkle tree root. It is based on a procedure that dually groups transactions using hashes. For this, a timestamp is used to certify the cryptographic proof and reject any manipulation attempt within the chain. (iv) Timestamp. It is a field that stores the seconds elapsed since January 1, 1970 (UNIX time) until the exact moment of the block creation. (v) Difficulty target. It specifies a threshold that determines the complexity to find a new block. In mining, the estimated time to discovery is ten minutes. (vi) Nonce. It is a counter that starts at zero and is incremented for each hash. The node that finds the number can generate and validate the block. Currently, this technology is also recognized for its ability to issue, safeguard, and tokenize any type of information or digital asset. In this context, blockchain has the capacity to host (on top of its structure) smart contracts.

Regarding smart contracts. This term was invented by Szabo[2] in the 1990s. It was defined as a stand-alone protocol for transactional operations. A smart contract is a set of instructions based on a programming condition; Its data model is made up of three main fields, namely: (a) code based on Turing complete language, (b) an account balance for sending and receiving monetary tokens, and (c) storage.

Currently, a smart contract is implemented according to the registration of a transaction within the blockchain. The validation of a contract is carried out by all the network nodes using decentralized consensus mechanisms. Thus, the transparency and immutability are guaranteed because the transactions cannot be modified for a particular benefit. Consequently, a self-executing contract prevents the breach of agreements and interprets the contractual terms. In this way, recruitment costs, malicious actions and human errors are minimized. Figure 1 shows how smart contracts interact with the blockchain.

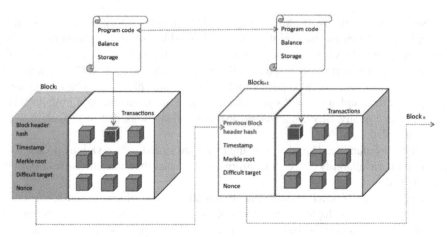

Fig. 1. How do smart contracts interact with blockchain?

3.2 Hardware and Software

A computer with the following characteristics was used: 24 GB RAM, 10th generation Intel Core i7 processor, 1 GB graphic card, 1 TB HDD, and Windows 10 OS. In this line, the following software was using, namely.

- IPFS (Interplanetary File System). It is a protocol that implements P2P methods to access, store and share hypermedia in a distributed system.
- Ant Design. It is a React UI Library for enterprise level graphic design.
- Truffle. It is a development framework for Ethereum Virtual Machine. It offers a set of tools to create, test and deploy smart contracts on the ethereum blockchain.
- MetaMask. It is a virtual wallet installed as a web browser extension. It is a cryptocurrency software to interact with ethereum blockchain.
- Express.js. Es un framework de código abierto basado en JavaScript y disponible en el entorno de ejecución Node.js
- React. It is an JavaScript open source library designed by Facebook and used to build user interfaces. It is a library focused on single-page application development.
- MongoDB. It is an open-source non-relational document database developed using C + + to improve query performance. It uses a data model based on collections and documents.
- Web3.js. It is a collection of JavaScript libraries that allow interaction with ethereum nodes (remotely or locally) using HTTP, IPC or WebSocket.
- Bootstrap. It is an open-source framework for developing frontend and web applications based on HTML, CSS and JavaScript.
- Solidity. It is an object-oriented language used to code and implement smart contracts on blockchain platforms (including ethereum).

3.3 Related Works

The internet promotes the exchange and transparency of information, but it does not protect digital rights. Creators can earn money by uploading digital content to some platform, but due to online availability, the digital asset can be downloaded and copied without authorization; this causes a loss of value. Thus,[3] defines a blockchain to digitally sign the copyright and detect the traceability of the content. Similarly, [4] stored copyright information within the blockchain to test a code plagiarism detection and verification model. The results determined that the blockchain is the ideal technology to store the copyright identifiers of the source code. In this way, traceability, encryption, and immutability provide reliable code management.

Copyright management is also applicable to the educational field. Currently, there are several platforms that offer knowledge through a repository of educational resources, which represents a challenge for the management of digital rights. In this context, [5] develops blockchain-based smart contracts to share and protect multimedia resources in online learning environments. Similarly, [6] develops a decentralized scheme for the protection of multimedia content using blockchain-based authentication. The process of creating digital books contains various participants who help create and sell them. At this point, [7] proposes a framework based on smart contracts to manage the remuneration of all the members of the process (authors and publishers). With this challenge, [8] proposes a reward mechanism for the distribution of music files. Thus, a platform was developed to manage the exchange of multimedia content between composers and consumers. In addition, a set of penalties is coded (within smart contracts) to penalize users who try to upload corrupted files to the network.

Contrary to entities that seek benefits from copyright management, there are non-profit organizations (CMOs), which manage licenses to collect economic benefits for composers. From this perspective, [9] proposes an application based on blockchain and smart contracts to regulate copyright through the domain of a CMO. In this line, [10] seeks to mitigate the copyright problem through the creation of content using artificial intelligence. In turn, a deep learning neural network was proposed to generate musical patterns according to a certain musical style. Similarly, [11] proposes the development of a learning model to generate a more complex composition from a sample. With this model, the code is implemented within a smart contract. In this way, unique works can be created for profit while copyright protection is guaranteed.

Unlike these previous works, our research defines a musical composition acquisition model, whereby content creators upload a musical composition to a platform, and consumers are free to purchase the pre-uploaded content and pay a value to the content owner. In this way, a direct communication between these two actors was created without the need for intermediaries.

4 Results: Functional Requirements and Model Development

A model was designed using 3 layers, namely: storage, business logic, and user. In this sense, Figure x shows the software development activities addressed within each of these components. Consequently, Fig. 2 shows a layered overview for managing music tokens. In addition, Fig. 3 shows a layered overview to manage musical tokens.

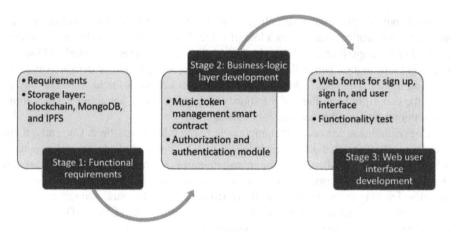

Fig. 2. Stages to develop the model.

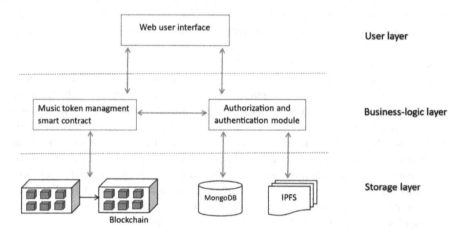

Fig. 3. A layered model to manage musical tokens.

4.1 Storage Layer

In this layer, three data sets are used, namely:

- User credentials, which are stored in MongoDB. The user can play two roles: (i) content creator and (ii) content consumer.
- Digital files of musical compositions, which are stored using IPFS (InterPlanetary File Systems)
- Musical tokens, which are stored within the blockchain and allow listening to a musical composition upon payment.

4.2 Business-Logic Layer

In this layer, three main functionalities were identified in our research, namely: (i) authentication and authorization, (ii) music content management, and (iii) music content consumption.

First, authentication and authorization. This functionality represents the gateway to the application. In addition, it allows user registration, access to the web application, password recovery and activation of privileges according to the user profile. To do so, the user accesses the platform and chooses to log in or register. In both cases, the user must enter the information in the required fields. Also, a password reset option is provided by the platform. Consequently, forms were designed using Express.js and a MongoDB-based schema was created to manage user credentials.

Second, music content management. Basically, music content management consists of four functions, namely:

- Storage of songs within the platform,
- Creation of albums (custom library of songs),
- Editing of musical information (updates of musical composition informational details),
- Visualization of monetary benefits for authors. Figure 4 describes an activity diagram for this functionality.

Third, consumption of musical tokens. Essentially, this functionality allows viewing, selecting, and listening to musical compositions. For this, before listening to a musical composition, the user must pay an access token for it. In this context, the platform requests access to the user's wallet to withdraw funds and makes the payment for listening to a piece of music. In this sense, the musical piece is associated to an access token. Figure 5 describes an activity diagram for this functionality.

With these requirements, the management and consumption functions of music tokens were codified within a smart contract. Thus, a smart contract was designed to carry out the administration transactions and purchases of musical tokens. In this context, the contract design essentially has four sets of elements: (i) structure, (ii) mappings, (iii) function modifier, and (iv) functions.

(i) Structure of the smart contract. A structure was coded to organize the various attributes within the smart contract. Each attribute has a data type. In our case study, a structure to organize music token attributes was developed. Table 1 shows a brief description of this structure.

(ii) Mappings. A mapping is a hash table of key-value pairs, which allow linking a unique ethereum address with its respective value. In this case, a mapping is equivalent to a data dictionary. Table 2 shows a brief description of the mapping used within the smart contract.

(iii) Function modifier. It allows to alter the behavior of the functions of a smart contract. Table 3 shows a description of these modifiers.

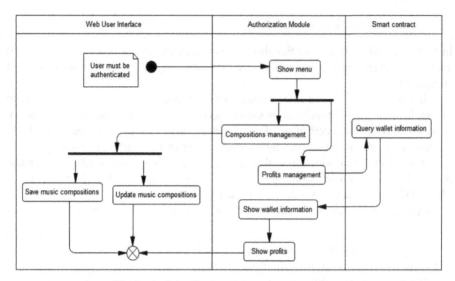

Fig. 4. Activity diagram for content management

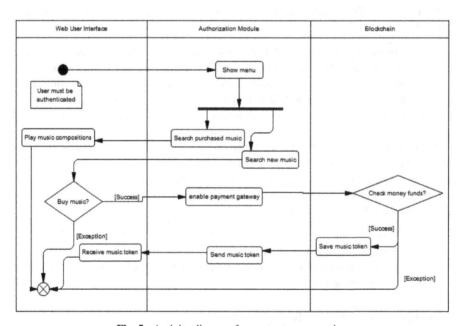

Fig. 5. Activity diagram for content consumption

Table 1. Structure attributes

Attribute	Data type	Description
id	uintd256	Music composition identifier
owner	address	User address who purchases a music token
artistName	string	Artist name who creates or produces the musical composition
title	string	Name for musical composition
description	string	Brief textual description of the musical composition
musicGenre	string	Genre of musical composition
price	uint64	Price for listening to the musical composition
musicCover	string	Hash of the music cover assigned in the IPFS system
musicHashFile	bytes1[120][]	Hash of the music file assigned in the IPFS system

Table 2. Smart contract mappings

Mapping	Key type	Value type	Description
balance	address	uint256[]	It links account balances to blockchain account addresses
userPurchase	address	unint256[]	It links an array with the identifiers of the music tokens purchased by the user
artistMusic	address	unit256[]	It links an array with the identifiers of the musical compositions

Table 3. Function modifier

Modifier	Arguments	Data type	Description
verifyMusicOwnership()	_id	uintd256	Ownership of a musical composition is verified by the music token id
verifyPayment()	_id	uintd256	Using the music token id, the price is transformed from ethers to wei (solidity currency)

(iv) Functions. It interacts with the blockchain and performs specific operations according to user and system requirements. Table 4 shows the functions coded within the smart contract. With these design considerations, the smart contract code is presented in Annex A.

Table 4. Functions

Function	Description
createComposition ()	The artist saves the music composition data
purchaseComposition ()	It purchases the right to hear a musical composition
getBalance ()	It gets the balance of the profits generated by the sale of a musical composition
getProfit ()	It transfers the earnings to the artist's wallet
getArtistMusic ()	It searches musical compositions by artist
getUserPurchase ()	It searches for purchases made by a user
getCompositionInfo ()	It searches for information about the musical compositions registered within the blockchain
countComposition ()	It searches the number of compositions registered within the blockchain
changePrice ()	It searches the price for listening to a musical composition

4.3 User Layer

According to the functional requirements described in the business-logic layer, two user interfaces were designed, namely.

First, interfaces for user authentication. A dialog box was designed to collect user information, such as: first name, last name, email, and password. Then, the user can authenticate in a new dialog. In this sense, the credentials are stored and validated using the MongoDB database. Figure 6 show a description of the interfaces used to test this functionality.

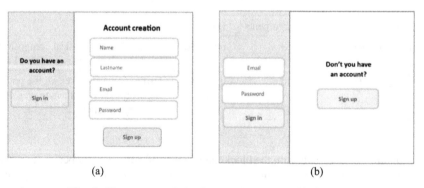

(a)   (b)

Fig. 6. Sign up (a) and sign in (b) using MongoDB database

Second, user interfaces for content management and consumption. An options menu was designed through a navigation bar which allows access to the following functionalities, namely. (i) Item for account management. The user can add compositions and display the profits obtained by selling the musical tokens (Fig. 7). These monetary values are transferred to the user's wallet. (ii) item for new compositions. The user can see information about the recent songs that were uploaded by the content creators. In this sense, the frame shows the details of each musical composition, artist data and the monetary value of the musical token (Fig. 8). (iii) item for shopping. User can view information of all previously acquired compositions using music token (Fig. 9).

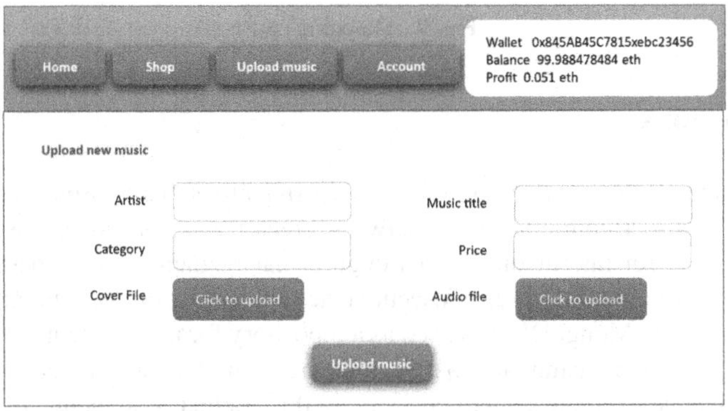

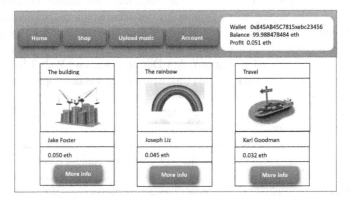

Fig. 7. Upload music compositions

Fig. 8. List of music compositions

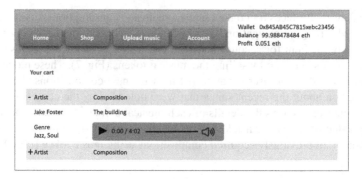

Fig. 9. Shopping cart

5 Conclusions

A model to support the music streaming service using blockchain-based smart contracts. In this way, a direct communication between creator and consumer was established without the need for intermediaries. Through a management scheme based on smart contracts and java modules, three consecutive activities were carried out, namely. First, user authentication. MongoDB was used as a repository for user credentials; in turn, the code was implemented using Node.js. Second, creation of smart contract. Solidity was used as a language to create a smart contract; in this context, statements, functions, and procedures were coded to automate the management and consumption of music tokens. Next, this code was compiled using the Ethereum Truffle environment. Consequently, a JSON file was generated to interact with the web user interface. In addition, a test network was installed for the deployment of the smart contract, which allows communication between the web interface and the blockchain. Third, web user interface development. Interfaces for authentication, management and content consumption were designed using two frameworks (React and Bootstrap), Ant Design class, and Web 3.Js (TypeScript implementation of the Ethereum). In this way, a prototype was developed to demonstrate our proposal.

As future work, this proposal can be expanded with visual content (such as movies, series, documentaries, among others). In this context, blockchain technology in the future may change the way media content is consumed; this will increase the development of decentralized applications to monetize the work done by content creators (in this case, musicians). However, it is necessary to implement legal regulations that regulate the use of technology in the field of digital consumption; so that copyright is protected, and benefits are maximized for both the creator and the consumer of content.

Appendix 1. Smart Contract to Manage Music Tokens

```solidity
pragma solidity ^0.8

contract musicTokenManagement {
  address owner;

constructor() public { owner = msg.sender; }
struct Composition {
  uint256 id;
  address owner;
  string artistName;
  string title;
  string description;
  string musicGenre;
  uint64 price;
  string musicCover;
  bytes1[120][] musicHashFile;

}
Composition[] public compositions;
mapping(address => unit256)balance;
mapping(address => unit256[])userPurchase;
mapping(address => uint256[])artistMusic;
event newComposition(address ownerAddress, string title, string artistName);

modifier verifyMusicOwnership(uint256 _id ){
  require (compositions[_id].owner == msg.sender);
  _; }

modifier verifyPayment(uint256 _id ){
  uint256 weiPrice = compositions[_id].price * 1000000000000000000;
  require (msg.value >= weiPrice);
  _; }

  function createComposition(
    string memory _artistName,
    string memory _title,
    string memory _description,
    string memory _musicGenre,
    uint64 _price,
    string memory _musicCover,
    bytes1[120][] memory _musicHashFile)

  public { uint256 id = compositions.length;
   compositions.push (
```

```
Composition (id,
msg.sender,
_artistName,
_title,
_description,
_musicGenre,
_price,
_musicCover,
_musicHashfile)
                    );
artistMusic[msg.sender].push(id);
emit newComposition(msg.sender,_title, _artistName); }

function userPurchase(unit256 _id) public payable verifyMusicOwnership(_id )    {
balance[compositions[_id].owner] = balance[compositions[_id].owner]+ msg.value; }

function getBalance()public view returns (uint256){
return balance[msg.sender]; }

function getProfit() public {
msg.sender.transfer(balance[msg.sender]);
balance[msg.sender]=0; }

function getArtistMusic () public view returns (uint256[] memory){
return artistMusic[msg.sender];}

function getArtistMusic () public view returns (uint256[] memory){
return artistMusic[msg.sender]; }

function getUserPurchase () public view returns (uint256[] memory){
return userPurchase[msg.sender]; }

function getComposicionInfo (uint256 _id) public view returns ( address, string
memory, string memory, string memory, string memory, uint64, string memory,
bytes1[120][]memory){
return (
  compositions[_id].owner;
  compositions[_id].artistName;
  compositions[_id].title;
  compositions[_id].description;
  compositions[_id].musicGenre;
  compositions[_id].price;
  compositions[_id].musicCover;
  compositions[_id].musicHashFile
);
}
```

```
function compositionCount()public view returns (uint 256) {
  return compositions.lenght;
  }
function changePrice(uint256 _id, uint64 _newPrice)
  public compositionOwner (_id) {
  compositions[_id].price = _newPrice;
  }
```

References

1. Mendoza-Tello, J.C., Mora, H., Mendoza-Tello, T.: The role of blockchain for introducing resilience in insurance domain: a systematic review. Springer Proc. Complex, 587–596(2023). https://doi.org/10.1007/978-3-031-19560-0_50

2. Szabo, N.: Formalizing and securing relationships on public networks. First Monday **2** (1997). https://doi.org/10.5210/fm.v2i9.548

3. Garba, A., Dwivedi, A.D., Kamal, M., et al.: A digital rights management system based on a scalable blockchain. Peer-to-Peer Netw Appl **14**, 2665–2680 (2021). https://doi.org/10.1007/s12083-020-01023-z

4. Jing, N., Liu, Q., Sugumaran, V.: A blockchain-based code copyright management system. Inf. Process. Manag. **58**, 102518 (2021). https://doi.org/10.1016/j.ipm.2021.102518

5. Guo, J., Li, C., Zhang, G., et al.: Blockchain-enabled digital rights management for multimedia resources of online education. Multimed Tools Appl/ **79**, 9735–9755 (2020). https://doi.org/10.1007/s11042-019-08059-1

6. Liu, J., Fan, K., Li, H., Yang, Y.: A blockchain-based privacy preservation scheme in multimedia network. Multimed Tools Appl. **80**, 30691–30705 (2021). https://doi.org/10.1007/s11042-021-10513-y

7. Nizamuddin, N., Hasan, H., Salah, K., Iqbal, R.: Blockchain-based framework for protecting author royalty of digital assets. Arab. J. Sci. Eng. **44**, 3849–3866 (2019). https://doi.org/10.1007/s13369-018-03715-4

8. Halgamuge, M.N., Guruge, D.: Fair rewarding mechanism in music industry using smart contracts on public-permissionless blockchain. Multimed Tools Appl. **81**, 1523–1544 (2022). https://doi.org/10.1007/s11042-021-11078-6

9. Kapsoulis, N., Psychas, A., Palaiokrassas, G., et al.: Consortium blockchain smart contracts for musical rights governance in a collective management organizations (CMOs) use case. Futur Internet **12** (2020). https://doi.org/10.3390/FI12080134

10. Wang, N., Xu, H., Xu, F., Cheng, L.: The algorithmic composition for music copyright protection under deep learning and blockchain. Appl. Soft Comput. **112**, 107763 (2021). https://doi.org/10.1016/j.asoc.2021.107763

11. Cai, Z.: Usage of deep learning and blockchain in compilation and copyright protection of digital music. IEEE Access **8**, 164144–164154 (2020). https://doi.org/10.1109/ACCESS.2020.3021523

Security

Self-adaptive Internet of Things Systems: A Systematic Literature Review

Lenin Erazo-Garzón[1]([✉]), Bayron Gutiérrez[1], Lourdes Illescas-Peña[2], and Alexandra Bermeo[1]

[1] Universidad del Azuay, Av. 24 de Mayo 7-77, Cuenca, Ecuador
{lerazo,alexbermeo}@uazuay.edu.ec, bgutierrez@es.uazuay.edu.ec
[2] Universidad de Cuenca, Av. 12 de Abril, Cuenca, Ecuador
lourdes.illescasp@ucuenca.edu.ec

Abstract. The dynamic and uncertain nature in which IoT systems operate has led to the exploration of new emerging Software Engineering approaches, such as self-adaptation, to provide these systems with autonomous capabilities to adjust their behavior at runtime to environmental changes. There are numerous primary studies on self-adaptation in IoT; however, it is necessary to deepen and update the state of technological knowledge in this area, especially in aspects that have not been addressed in previous reviews. Therefore, this paper presents a systematic review of the literature on self-adaptation in IoT systems, according to the guidelines proposed by Kitchenham et al. and the self-adapting topology created by Krupitzer et al. This review aims to answer the following research questions: i) In what context has self-adaptation been used in the IoT domain? ii) How is self-adaptation performed in IoT platforms? and iii) What is the research approach in studies related to self-adaptive systems in IoT? First, 1136 primary studies were obtained through automatic and manual searches. Then, inclusion and exclusion criteria were applied to select 84 relevant studies on self-adaptation in IoT. Finally, quantitative and qualitative methods based on extraction criteria were used to synthesize the strengths and weaknesses of the studies concerning the research questions as well as to identify research gaps and opportunities.

Keywords: Cyber-physical Systems · Internet of Things (IoT) · Self-adaptation · Software Engineering · Systematic Literature Review

1 Introduction

The complexity of modern systems like the Internet of Things (IoT), characterized by the dynamic and uncertain environments in which they operate, demands significant effort in developing and maintaining these systems [1]. Hence, to address these challenges beyond traditional Software Engineering tools, it is necessary to build self-adaptive IoT systems capable of modifying themselves at runtime in response to changes in the environment, technical resources, and user requirements to ensure a certain level of quality [2, 3].

In the literature, numerous primary studies address theoretical and practical aspects of self-adaptation in IoT systems in different subdomains (e.g., smart environments,

M. Botto-Tobar et al. (Eds.): ICAT 2023, CCIS 2051, pp. 137–157, 2024.
https://doi.org/10.1007/978-3-031-58950-8_11

transportation, healthcare, smart cities). However, it is vitally important to organize and systematize the results obtained in these studies to provide broad, structured, and updated knowledge on self-adaptation in IoT that guide future research. Even more so when the few existing systematic reviews are oriented solely to the self-adaptation of IoT systems at the architectural level [4, 5], neglecting other important aspects (e.g., reasons for self-adaptation, application subdomains, types of solution developed, the moment at which self-adaptation occurs, at what system level the self-adaptation takes place, the approaches, techniques, and decision criteria of self-adaptation used, the empirical evaluation methods applied) [6].

Therefore, this paper presents a systematic literature review to understand the state of technological knowledge on self-adaptation in IoT systems. In particular, this review aims to answer the following research questions: i) In what context has self-adaptation been used in the IoT domain? ii) How is self-adaptation performed in IoT platforms? and iii) What is the research approach in studies related to self-adaptive systems in IoT? In turn, the methodology proposed by Kitchenham et al. [7] and the self-adaptation taxonomy created by Krupitzer et al. [6] have been used for the conduct of the systematic review.

As a result, in the first instance, 1136 primary studies were obtained through automatic and manual searches. Subsequently, inclusion and exclusion criteria were applied to select 84 relevant studies on self-adaptation in IoT systems. Quality criteria were used to prioritize and order the studies according to their relevance, which served as a basis for presenting the research results. Additionally, quantitative and qualitative analysis methods based on extraction criteria were used to address the research questions proposal.

The structure of this paper is as follows: Sect. 2 presents the related work to the topic, Sect. 3 describes the proposed protocol for the systematic review, Sect. 4 discusses the results obtained, and finally, Sect. 5 includes conclusions and future work.

2 Related Work

This research aims to expand previous systematic reviews to obtain an updated, precise, and exhaustive understanding of the progress in the field of self-adaptation in IoT systems. In the literature, there are few systematic reviews on self-adaptation in IoT, which are analyzed below:

Alfonso et al. [4] present a systematic review of self-adaptive architectures in IoT systems. Firstly, the authors identify which dynamic events in the edge/fog and physical layers are the leading causes for triggering adaptations in an IoT system. Then, they identify and analyze how existing solutions in the literature adapt their internal behavior and architecture in response to different dynamic events and determine the consequences of these adaptations on the quality of service (QoS). Finally, the study defines a research agenda based on the findings and weaknesses identified in the literature.

For their part, Muccini et al. [5] propose a systematic review to evaluate the state-of-the-art approaches to manage self-adaptation in cyber-physical systems (CPS) at the architectural level. In the review, the authors collected 1103 candidate studies. After applying the inclusion and exclusion criteria, 42 studies were selected as relevant. The authors conclude that adaptation in CPS is a concern throughout all layers of its architecture, where existing solutions combine different adaptation mechanisms (MAPE, agents, self-organization) within and between layers.

As can be seen, existing research focuses on the self-adaptation of IoT systems at the architectural level, considering that the most current is the one proposed by Alfonso et al. [4]. Therefore, these reviews do not address the self-adaptation of IoT systems from a more general perspective, ignoring essential questions about the proposed solutions in this area, such as: i) When self-adaptation is performed (reactive, proactive); ii) For what reasons the self-adaptation is carried out (changes in context, technical resources, requirements); iii) At what level self-adaptation takes place (application, system software, communication, technical resources, context); iv) what techniques are used for self-adaptation (parameter, structure, context); v) what is the focus of self-adaptation (internal/external); vi) with what criteria (metrics) self-adaptation is carried out (models, rules, objectives, others); and, vi) what is the degree of decentralization of self-adaptation (decentralized, centralized). An aspect to highlight about the present research that marks an advantage over existing reviews is that the questions raised will be addressed through the self-adaptation taxonomy proposed by Krupitzer et al. [6]. Finally, this review seeks to identify findings regarding the aspects mentioned earlier to guide future research in this area better.

3   Research Methods

The guidelines proposed by Kitchenham et al. [7, 8] have been used in this systematic review to ensure a reliable, rigorous, replicable, and auditable process, which is decomposed into three stages: i) planning the review, ii) conducting the review, and iii) reporting the review.

3.1   Planning the Review

Research Question. This systematic review aims to understand the state of technological knowledge about self-adaptation in IoT systems. Therefore, three research questions were defined to achieve this goal:

RQ1. In what context has self-adaptation been used in the IoT domain?
RQ2. How is self-adaptation performed in IoT platforms?
RQ3. What is the research approach in studies related to self-adaptive systems in IoT?

Data Sources and Search Strategy. The digital libraries used in the automatic search of primary studies were: IEEE Xplore, ACM Digital Library, Science Direct and Springer Link. On the other hand, the most representative conferences, magazines, and books on self-adaptation were used in the manual search, combined with the snowball technique. The research was performed starting in 2009, since although Kevin Ashton coined the term "IoT" in 1999, the current understanding of the IoT as a network of smart objects began to evolve around 2009 [9]. Table 1 presents the search string used, the same one that was applied to the article metadata: title, abstract, and keywords.

Table 1. Automatic search string.

Concept	Connector	Synonyms and Acronyms
Self-adaptation	AND	Self-Adaptive
Internet of Things	OR	IoT
Cyber-physical systems		cyber-physical system*
Search string:		*(self-adaptation OR self-adaptive) AND (internet of things OR IoT OR cyber-physical system*)*

Selection of Primary Studies. First, the collected primary studies were evaluated and selected based on title, abstract, and keywords. Then, those discrepancies in the selection of studies were resolved by consensus once the full paper was reviewed. Primary studies meeting any of the following inclusion criteria were included:

IC1. Studies describing theoretical research on self-adaptation for IoT systems.
IC2. Studies that address self-adaptation paradigms, approaches, methods, or techniques for IoT systems.
IC3. Studies that propose self-adaptation tools or applications for IoT systems.

Primary studies that met at least one of the following exclusion criteria were excluded:

EC1. Editorials, prologues, opinions, interviews, news, or posters.
EC2. Duplicate studies in different sources.
EC3. Short articles with less than four pages.
EC4. Articles written in a language other than English.

Quality Assessment of Primary Studies. A checklist composed of three questions was used to evaluate the quality of the primary studies (see Table 2). Each question was evaluated using a scale between 0 and 1. The total score for each article was calculated by adding the scores recorded in the three questions. This quality assessment served only to prioritize the studies according to their scientific rigor and synthesize the presentation of the review results.

Table 2. Quality checklist.

No.	Question	Answer and score
QAQ1	How many citations does the primary study have?	More than 5 citations, very relevant (1) Between 1 and 5 citations, relevant (0.5) No cited, irrelevant (0)
QAQ2	Has the primary study been published in relevant journals or conferences?	Very relevant (1), Relevant (0.5), Irrelevant (0)
QAQ3	Does the study present an empirical evaluation of the proposed solution?	Yes (1), No (0)

Data Extraction Strategy. Table 3 presents the form used to standardize the extraction of information from the studies. This form contains a set of extraction criteria based on the self-adaptation taxonomy proposed by Krupitzer et al. [6] in order to adequately answer the research questions of the review.

Methods of Analysis and Synthesis. Two types of methods were used during the review: i) quantitative, using graphs and tables to represent the frequency of responses for each extraction criterion, and ii) qualitative, description of the research strengths, weaknesses (gaps), and opportunities in the area of self-adaptation of IoT systems.

Table 3. Data extraction form.

RQ1.	In what context has self-adaptation been used in the IoT domain?	
EC1.	Reason for self-adaptation.	[Change in the context, Changes in technical resources, Changes caused by the user]
EC2.	Application subdomain.	[Transport, Education, Government, Health, Finance and banking, Public security - emergency, Monitoring and environmental control, Farming, Logistics and retail, Industrial control, Entertainment and sport, Smart environmental, Smart animal control, Other]
EC3.	Type of solution developed.	[Conceptual, Methodology, Architecture, Middleware, Framework, Model, Application]
RQ2.	How is self-adaptation performed in IoT platforms?	
EC4.	Time.	[Proactive, Reactive]
EC5.	System level at which self-adaptation is performed.	[Application, System Software, Communication, Hardware resources, Context]
EC6.	Self-adaptation technique.	[Parameter, Structure, Context]
EC7.	Self-adaptation approach.	[Internal, External]
EC8.	Self-adaptation decision criteria (metrics).	[Models, Rules/Policies, Goals, Utility]
EC9.	Degree of decentralization of self-adaptation.	[Decentralized, Centralized]
RQ3.	What is the research approach in studies related to self-adaptive systems in IoT?	
EC10.	Type of validation.	[Proof of Concept, Survey, Case Study, Experiment, None]
EC11.	Type of study.	[New, Extension]
EC12.	Scope of the approach.	[Industry, Academy]

3.2 Conducting the Review

In this stage, the activities of collection, selection, and evaluation of the quality of the primary studies were carried out, following the guidelines defined in the review protocol (see Fig. 1):

1. *Automatic search.* The search string was adapted for each library (IEEE Xplore, ACM Digital Library, Springer Link, and Science Direct), collecting 1136 primary studies. Then, 22 duplicate studies were eliminated, leaving 1114 studies for further analysis.
2. *First selection.* The titles, abstracts, and keywords of the studies were evaluated according to the inclusion and exclusion criteria, to determine their relevance. As a result, 116 studies were selected.

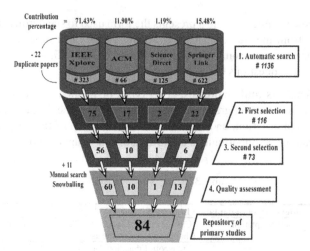

Fig. 1. Conducting the systematic review.

3. *Second selection.* Discrepancies about the selection of certain articles were resolved once the complete article had been reviewed. As a result, the repository was reduced to 73 studies. Also, the snowball technique was also applied to the selected articles, including 11 additional studies. Finally, a repository of 84 primary studies was obtained.
4. *Quality Assessment.* Finally, the selected primary studies were prioritized according to their scientific rigor and relevance level.

4 Results and Discussion

As a result of the execution of the systematic review protocol, the 84 primary studies on self-adaptive IoT systems were selected. Figure 2 presents the number of studies published per year, finding the highest number of studies in the year 2022 with 18 articles, followed by the years 2018 and 2019 with 15 publications, and the years 2020 and 2021 with 9 studies each. These results show that from 2018 onwards, this field of research has had significant growth, finding a greater number of contributions.

Figure 3 presents the quality assessment results of the primary studies, evidencing a fairly mature research area with important contributions that demonstrate high scientific rigor. For question QAQ1, 53 studies were found to be considered highly relevant (with more than 5 citations), 24 relevant (between 1 and 5 citations), and 7 irrelevant (no citations). Regarding question QAQ2, 42, 36, and 6 studies have been published in very relevant, relevant, and irrelevant conferences or journals, respectively. Finally, concerning question QAQ3, 60 studies include an empirical evaluation of the proposed solution.

RQ1. In what context has self-adaptation been used in the IoT domain?

EC1: Reason for Self-adaptation. This extraction criterion aims to recognize the reasons that have led researchers to promote self-adaptation in IoT systems (see Table 4).

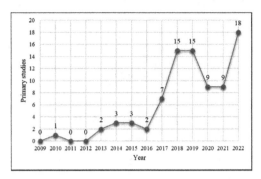

Fig. 2. Distribution of primary studies by year.

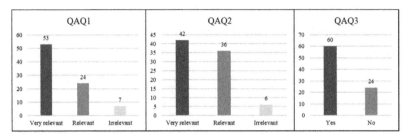

Fig. 3. Quality assessment of the primary studies.

In this sense, an important group of studies, 44.05% have proposed self-adaptation solutions to respond to changes in the context. For their part, 28.57% have oriented their self-adaptation proposals due to the changes caused by users. Finally, 27.38% have addressed self-adaptation as a response to changes in the technical resources of IoT systems (incorporate, eliminate, or modify components).

EC2: Application Subdomain. This extraction criterion identifies the main IoT subdomains in which the self-adaptation proposals have been applied (see Table 5). It should be noted that there are studies that address more than one subdomain. Among the most used subdomains are: environmental monitoring and control (44.05%), industrial control (30.95%), and smart environment (27.38%). At an intermediate level are the subdomains of transportation and public safety - emergency, with 14.29% each. Finally, the remaining subdomains have little or no attention from researchers.

EC3: Type of Solution Developed. Most studies focus on practical solutions, unlike the few conceptual studies (see Table 6). Hence, self-adaptive architectures and models represent the types of solutions that are mainly included in the studies, with 29.76% and 26.19% each. In a smaller proportion, there are self-adaptive proposals on applications (13.10%), middleware (10.71%), methodologies (8.33%), and frameworks (8.33%).

RQ2. How is self-adaptation performed in IoT platforms?

EC4: Time. This extraction criterion analyzes the moment in which the solutions presented in the studies carry out self-adaptation. In this sense, 83.33% of the studies

Table 4. Frequency of studies by reason for self-adaptation.

Options	Relevant studies	Frequency
Change in the context	[10, 12, 15, 16, 18, 19, 22, 23, 28–30, 34, 35, 38–40, 45, 46, 51, 52, 55, 56, 58, 63, 64, 67, 69, 73, 74, 77, 80, 84–86, 89, 90, 92]	37
Changes in technical resources	[14, 17, 21, 25–27, 32, 36, 37, 42, 44, 47, 53, 54, 60, 66, 71, 75, 76, 82, 83, 88, 93]	23
Changes caused by the user	[11, 13, 20, 24, 31, 33, 41, 43, 48–50, 57, 59, 61, 62, 65, 68–70, 72, 78, 79, 81, 87, 91]	24

Table 5. Frequency of studies by application subdomain.

Options	Relevant studies	Frequency
Transport	[11, 26, 27, 32, 36, 37, 51, 54, 55, 70, 77, 80]	12
Education	[14, 21, 33, 39, 66, 93]	6
Government		0
Health	[20, 44, 46, 68, 80]	5
Finance and banking		0
Public security - emergency	[25, 27, 37, 41, 42, 46, 47, 55, 56, 62, 67, 80]	12
Monitoring and environmental control	[10, 13, 15, 17, 18, 22, 23, 30, 37, 40, 41, 43, 46, 47, 49, 50, 52, 53, 55, 56, 59–64, 67, 72, 73, 76, 79, 82, 84, 87, 88, 90, 92]	37
Farming	[80, 85]	2
Logistics and retail	[19, 35]	2
Industrial control	[10, 11, 21, 24, 25, 29, 31, 38, 41, 49, 52, 53, 57, 58, 61, 62, 66, 67, 71 74, 75, 81, 83, 89, 91, 93]	26
Entertainment and sport	[33, 55, 78]	3
Smart environmental	[12, 13, 16, 22, 25, 28, 34, 39, 45, 48, 53, 56, 57, 65–69, 75, 81–83, 86]	23
Smart animal control	[46, 88]	2

Table 6. Frequency of studies by type of solution developed.

Options	Relevant studies	Frequency
Conceptual	[17, 77, 78]	3
Methodology	[29, 52, 58, 60, 67, 70, 85]	7
Architecture	[10, 12, 14, 15, 19, 21, 22, 24, 26, 31, 40–43, 45, 46, 51, 59, 64, 80, 81, 83, 87, 91, 93]	25
Framework	[16, 20, 66, 68, 73, 86, 89]	7
Middleware	[13, 34, 37, 38, 47, 49, 53–55]	9
Model	[11, 28, 30, 32, 35, 36, 39, 48, 50, 61–63, 65, 69, 71, 72, 74, 76, 82, 88, 90, 92]	22
Application	[18, 23, 25, 27, 33, 44, 56, 57, 75, 79, 84]	11

propose proactive self-adaptation, allowing IoT systems to adapt in order to anticipate and prevent future failures or problems, which is a strength of this research area [10–16, 18–21, 23–34, 37–39, 41–50, 53–55, 57–68, 71–76, 78, 79, 81–85, 87–89, 91–93]. On the contrary, the remaining studies propose a reactive self-adaptation approach, which occurs once a specific problem has arisen [17, 22, 35, 36, 40, 51, 52, 56, 69, 70, 77, 80, 86, 90].

EC5: System level at which Self-adaptation is Performed. This criterion identifies at what level of the IoT system the studies prefer the adaptation to be carried out. Hence, in order of frequency of use (see Table 7): i) 44.05% adapt at the context level of the IoT system through actuators; ii) 22.62% adapt at the level of infrastructure (active equipment) and patterns (protocols) of the communications network; iii) 15.48% adapt at the base software level of the IoT system (e.g., operating system, middleware), iv) 11.90% adapt at the level of behavior, functionality, and user interface of the IoT software applications themselves, and iv) 5.95% adapt at the level of hardware resources (e.g., sensors, computers, smartphones, robots).

EC6: Self-adaptation Technique. The method (type of change) that studies prefer to adapt IoT systems is identified at this point (see Table 8). Firstly, 44.05% opted for the context technique, which focuses on modifying the state of the context variables using actuators. Secondly, 33.33% chose the parameter technique, which involves adjusting the values of the system parameters at runtime. Finally, 22.62% used the structure technique, which contemplates modifying the architecture or composition of the components of the IoT system.

EC7: Self-adaptation Approach. The internal approach predominates in this criterion, representing 61.90% of the studies. This approach incorporates adaptation mechanisms into the business logic of the IoT system [10–12, 14, 16–19, 22–26, 29–31, 34, 35, 38, 39, 43, 48, 51, 53, 54, 56–61, 63, 64, 66, 67, 69, 71, 72, 74–76, 79, 80, 82, 84, 85, 87, 89–93]. For its part, the remaining 38.10% of the studies use an external approach, whose adaptation mechanisms are in components independent of the business logic of the IoT system [13, 15, 20, 21, 27, 28, 32, 33, 36, 37, 40–42, 44–47, 49, 50, 52, 55, 62, 65, 68, 70, 73, 77, 78, 81, 83, 86, 88]. Based on these results, future self-adaptation proposals should focus on the second approach, since it will allow the resulting self-adaptation

Table 7. Frequency of studies by system level.

Options	Relevant studies	Frequency
Application	[14, 24, 47, 49, 54, 62, 65, 75, 82, 88]	10
System software	[11, 25, 26, 31, 33, 36, 43, 50, 53, 59, 66, 78, 91]	13
Communication	[13, 20, 21, 27, 37, 41, 42, 48, 57, 68, 70–72, 76, 79, 81, 83, 87, 93]	19
Hardware resources	[17, 32, 44, 60, 61]	5
Context	[10, 12, 15, 16, 18, 19, 22, 23, 28–30, 34, 35, 38–40, 45, 46, 51, 52, 55, 56, 58, 63, 64, 67, 69, 73, 74, 77, 80, 84–86, 89, 90, 92]	37

Table 8. Frequency of studies by self-adaptation technique.

Options	Relevant studies	Frequency
Parameter	[13, 20, 26, 27, 33, 36, 47–50, 53, 54, 57, 61, 62, 65, 66, 68, 70, 71, 75, 76, 78, 81, 82, 87, 88, 91]	28
Structure	[11, 14, 17, 21, 24, 25, 31, 32, 37, 41–44, 59, 60, 72, 79, 83, 93]	19
Context	[10, 12, 15, 16, 18, 19, 22, 23, 28–30, 34, 35, 38–40, 45, 46, 51, 52, 55, 56, 58, 63, 64, 67, 69, 73, 74, 77, 80, 84–86, 89, 90, 92]	37

solutions to be modular (with high cohesion and low coupling), facilitating their reuse in new scenarios or applications.

EC8: Self-adaptation Decision Criteria (Metrics). This criterion shows the approaches used by the studies to obtain metrics that justify the need for adaptation and allow for choosing the most appropriate adaptation plans for the IoT system (see Table 9). According to the frequency: i) 38.10% use approaches based on the objectives to be achieved by the IoT system (e.g., performance, reliability); ii) 34.52% use approaches based on predefined rules or policies that establish how adaptation decisions should be made; iii) 26.19% use approaches based on system models, in order to analyze them and develop adaptation plans; and iv) 1.19% contemplate the evaluation and comparison of different adaptation actions based on their usefulness or expected benefit.

EC9: Degree of Decentralization of Self-adaptation. It was evidenced that 69.05% of the studies use a centralized approach, in which a single component makes adaptation decisions for the IoT system [10–15, 17–19, 21, 25–28, 30, 33, 35, 36, 38–40, 42–45, 47–49, 52, 54, 55, 58, 60, 63–66, 69–73, 75–80, 82–88, 90, 92, 93]. In contrast, the remaining 30.95% of studies use a decentralized approach, in which adaptation decisions are made in a distributed and autonomous manner by multiple components of the IoT system [16, 20, 22–24, 29, 31, 32, 34, 37, 41, 46, 50, 51, 53, 56, 57, 59, 61, 62, 67, 68, 74, 81, 89, 91]. This decentralization strategy can improve the system's responsiveness and fault tolerance, as each component can independently adapt to its local environment and conditions; hence, it constitutes a research opportunity that should be further explored in the future.

RQ3. What is the research approach in studies related to self-adaptive systems in IoT?

EC10: Type of Validation. This extraction criterion allows knowing the type of empirical evaluation used by the studies (see Table 10). Of the 84 proposals, only 28.57% do not contemplate some evaluation. Unlike studies that include an empirical evaluation, 34.52% and 30.95% use proofs of concept and experiments, respectively. While, to a lesser extent, 5.95% apply case studies. Although due to the significant number of studies evaluated, this criterion represents a strength, it is recommended that those proposals that include proofs of concept take a step further, applying evaluations through experiments or case studies in the industry.

EC11: Type of Study. It was found 80.95% are new studies [11–14, 16–20, 22–26, 28, 30, 31, 33–40, 42–44, 46–48, 50, 52–54, 56–61, 63–69, 71–81, 83–88, 90–92], leaving only 19.05% as extensions of previous proposals [10, 15, 21, 27, 29, 32, 41, 45, 49, 51, 55, 62, 70, 82, 89, 93].

EC12: Scope of the Approach. The results show that, 79.76% of the studies were developed in the context of academia [10–20, 22, 23, 25, 27–42, 44–56, 60–63, 65, 66, 68, 70, 72–79, 81, 83–86, 89, 90, 92], while the remaining 20.24% were developed with the participation of industry [21, 24, 26, 43, 57–59, 64, 67, 69, 71, 80, 82, 87, 88, 91, 93].

Table 9. Frequency of studies by self-adaptation decision criteria.

Options	Relevant studies	Frequency
Models	[11, 28, 30, 32, 35, 36, 39, 48, 50, 61–63, 65, 69, 71, 72, 74, 76, 82, 88, 90, 92]	22
Rules/Policies	[20, 22, 26, 27, 33, 34, 38, 44, 46, 51, 54, 55, 59, 60, 64, 68, 70, 73, 75, 77–79, 81, 83, 84, 86, 89, 91, 93]	29
Goals	[10, 12–17, 19, 21, 23–25, 29, 31, 37, 40–43, 45, 47, 49, 52, 53, 56–58, 66, 67, 80, 85, 87]	32
Utility	[18]	1

Table 10. Frequency of studies by type of validation.

Options	Relevant studies	Frequency
Proof of Concept	[11, 13, 14, 16, 19, 21, 22, 24–26, 28, 33, 35, 37, 39, 40, 48, 51, 55, 56, 60, 62, 68, 71, 72, 79, 81, 86, 93]	29
Survey		0
Case Study	[10, 27, 46, 52, 82]	5
Experiments	[12, 20, 30, 32, 34, 38, 42, 44, 45, 47, 49, 54, 57, 58, 61, 63–65, 69, 70, 73, 75, 83, 85, 87, 91]	26
None	[15, 17, 18, 23, 29, 31, 36, 41, 43, 50, 53, 59, 66, 67, 74, 76–78, 80, 84, 88–90, 92]	24

5   Conclusions and Future Work

This systematic review contributed to deepening and updating the state of technological knowledge on self-adaptation in IoT systems, answering a set of questions that have not been addressed in previous reviews. Additionally, the objective of this review has been to provide a roadmap for future research in this area. The main findings and conclusions of the review's research questions are presented below:

RQ1. The main driver for self-adaptation in IoT systems is context switching, which is justifiable due to the ubiquitous, dynamic, and uncertain scenarios in which these systems operate. Concerning the application subdomains, self-adaptation has mainly focused on the areas of environmental monitoring and control, industrial control, and intelligent environments, making it necessary to diversify its application through case studies in other subdomains. Regarding the types of solutions developed, proposals for architectures and models stand out to support adaptive decision-making. On the contrary, self-adaptive solutions such as applications, middleware, methodologies, and frameworks are found in a smaller proportion, constituting an important research opportunity.

RQ2. Most proposed solutions are correctly oriented towards proactive self-adaptation, allowing IoT systems to anticipate and prevent possible failures and problems. Regarding the system level in which self-adaptation occurs, studies focus primarily on the context level with the support of actuators; however, researchers are concerned about managing adaptation at all levels of an IoT system. In turn, the self-adaptation techniques, according to their frequency of use, are: context, parameter, and structure. At the same time, the internal approach is the most used in self-adaptation, which implies that the adaptation logic is incorporated into the internal algorithms of the IoT system; however, an opportunity opens up to explore the external approach, which will contribute to making self-adaptation solutions modular and reusable. On the other hand, the preferred self-adaptation decision criteria are based on objective, rule/policy, and model analysis approaches, with several studies using them in combination. Finally, studies of centralized self-adaptation prevail over decentralized ones, making it necessary to enhance the latter in new research.

RQ3. A strength of this research area is the large number of studies that include an empirical evaluation of their proposals, with proof of concept and experiment techniques being the most used; however, it is indisputable that these proposals are validated through case studies with the participation of the industry, in order to determine their level of adoption in real scenarios.

As future work, it is planned to particularize this review to delve into research subareas such as self-organization, self-configuration, self-healing, and self-protection in IoT system. Furthermore, a self-adaptation approach for IoT systems based on MAPE and runtime models will be built from the results of this study.

Acknowledgment. This work is part of the research project: "Methodology and infrastructure based on models at runtime for the construction and operation of self-aware Internet of Things systems." Hence, we thank the Vice-Chancellor for Research and the Computer Science Research & Development Laboratory (LIDI) of the Universidad del Azuay for their continued support.

References

1. Weyns, D.: Software engineering of self-adaptive systems. In: Handbook of Software Engineering, pp 399–443. Springer, Cham (2019).
2. De Lemos, R. et al.: Software engineering for self-adaptive systems: a Second Research Roadmap. In: Software engineering for self-adaptive systems II, vol. 7475, pp. 1–32. Springer, Berlin, Heidelberg (2013). https://doi.org/10.1007/978-3-642-35813-5_1
3. Kephart, J.O., Chess, D.M.: The vision of autonomic computing. IEEE Comput. **36**(1), 41–50 (2003)
4. Alfonso, I., Garcés, K., Castro, H.: Self-adaptive architectures in IoT systems: a systematic literature review. J. Internet. Serv. Appl. **12**(1), 1–28 (2021)
5. Muccini, H., Mohammad, S., Danny, W.: Self-adaptation for cyber-physical systems: a systematic literature review. In: 1th International Symposium on Software Engineering for Adaptive and Self-managing Systems, pp. 75–81 (2016)
6. Krupitzer, C., et al.: A survey on engineering approaches for self-adaptive systems. Pervasive Mob. Comput. **17**, 184–206 (2015)
7. Kitchenham, B., Charters, S.: Guidelines for performing systematic literature reviews in software engineering, vol. 5. Ver. 2.3 EBSE Technical Report (2007)
8. Erazo-Garzón, L., Erraez, J., Cedillo, P., Illescas-Peña, L.: Quality assessment approaches for ambient assisted living systems: a systematic review. In: International Conference on Applied Technologies, vol. 1193, pp. 421–439 (2019)
9. Cisco: How the next evolution of the internet is changing everything. White paper (2011)
10. Qiu, T., et al.: A 3-D topology evolution scheme with self-adaption for industrial Internet of Things. IEEE Internet Things J. **8**(12), 9473–9483 (2020)
11. Parri, J., et al.: A framework for model-driven engineering of resilient software-controlled systems. Computing **103**, 589–612 (2021)
12. Alkhabbas, F. et al.: A goal-driven approach for deploying self-adaptive IoT systems. In: International Conference on Software and Architecture, pp. 146–156 (2020)
13. Cao, J., Wang, X., Huang, M., Zhou, X.: A mobility-supported routing mechanism in industrial IoT networks. IEEE Access **7**, 25603–25615 (2019)
14. Alfonso, I., et al.: A model-based infrastructure for the specification and runtime execution of self-adaptive IoT architectures. Computing **105**, 1883–1906 (2023)
15. Moin, A., et al.: A model-driven approach to machine learning and software modeling for the IoT. Softw. Syst. Model. **21**, 987–1014 (2022)
16. Souza, A. M., Amazonas, J. R.: A novel smart home application using an Internet of Things middleware. In: European Conference on Smart Objects, Systems and Technology, pp. 1–7 (2013)
17. Tavčar, J., Horvath, I.: A review of the principles of designing smart cyber-physical systems for run-time adaptation. learned lessons and open issues. IEEE Trans. Sys., Man Cyber: Syst. **49**(1) 145–158 (2018)
18. Dehraj, P., Sharma, A.: A review on architecture and models for autonomic software systems. J Supercomputing **77**, 388–417 (2021)
19. Li, Z. et al.: A self-adaptive bluetooth indoor localization system using LSTM-based distance estimator. In: 29th International Conference on Computing Communication and Network, pp. 1–9 (2020)
20. Saduova, A., Al-Masri, E.: A self-adaptive IoT-based approach for improving the decision making of act. surgical robots in hospitals. In: 3rd Eurasia Conference on Biomedical Engineering Healthcare and Sustainability, pp. 270–273 (2021)
21. Bassene, A., Gueye, B.: A Self-adaptive QoS-management framework for highly dynamic IoT networks. In: Multi-conference on Natural and Engineering Science for Sahel's Sustainable Development, pp 1–8 (2022)

22. Cabrera, C., Clarke, S.: A self-adaptive service discovery model for smart cities. IEEE Trans. Serv. Comput. **15**(1), 386–399 (2019)
23. Iftikhar, M. U., Weyns, D.: Activforms: a runtime environment for architecture-based adaptation with guarantees. In: Conference on Software Architecture, pp. 278–28 (2017)
24. Zhang, Y., Qian, C., Lv, J., Liu, Y.: Agent and cyber-physical system based self-organizing and self-adaptive intelligent shopfloor. IEEE Trans. Ind. Inform **13**(2), 737–747 (2016)
25. Brahmia, M. -e. -A. et al.: An adaptive attack prediction framework in cyber-physical systems. In: 9th International Conference on Software Defined Systems, pp. 1–7 (2022)
26. Kit, M. et al: An architecture framework for experimentations with self-adaptive cyber-physical systems. In: 10th International Symposium on Software Engineering for Adaptive and Self-Managing Systems, pp. 93–96 (2015)
27. El Zouka, H.A.: An efficient and secure vehicular networks based on IoT and cloud computing. Sn Comput. Sci. **3**, 240 (2022)
28. Zhang, W., Chen, L., Liu, X., et al.: An OSGi-based flexible and adaptive pervasive cloud infrastructure. Science China Inf. Sci. **57**, 1–11 (2014)
29. Krupitzer, T., et al.: An overview of design patterns for self-adaptive systems in the context of the Internet of Things. IEEE Access **8**, 187384–187399 (2020)
30. Cho, G. et al: Anomaly-aware adaptation approach for self-adaptive cyber-physical system of systems using reinforcement learning. In: 17th Annual System of Systems Engineering Conf. pp. 7–12 (2022)
31. Al Ali, R. et al.: Architecture adaptation based on belief inaccuracy estimation. In: International Conference on Software Architecture, pp. 87–90 (2014)
32. Anda, A. Amyot, D.: Arithmetic semantics of feature and goal models for adaptive cyber-physical systems. In: 27th International Requirements Engineering Conference, pp. 245–256 (2019)
33. Petrovska, A., Weick, J.: Bayesian optimization-based analysis and planning approach for self-adaptive cyber-physical systems. In: International Conference on Autonomic Computing and Self-Organizing System Companion, pp. 293–294 (2021)
34. Liu, S., et al.: Toward context-aware and self-adaptive deep model computation for AIoT applications. IEEE Internet Things J. **9**(21), 20801–20814 (2022)
35. Van Der Donckt, M. et al.: Cost-benefit analysis at runtime for self-adaptive systems applied to an Internet of Things application. IENASE, pp. 478–490 (2018)
36. D'Angelo, M. et al.: CyPhEF: A model-driven engineering framework for self-adaptive cyber-physical systems. In: 40th International Conference on Software Engineer, pp. 101–104 (2018)
37. Moreno, G. et al.: DARTSim: An exemplar for evaluation and comparison of self-adaptation approaches for smart cyber-physical systems. In: 14th International Symposium on Software Engineering for Adaptive and Self-Managing Systems, pp. 181–187 (2019)
38. Lee, E. et al.: Deep learning based self-adaptive framework for environmental interoperability in internet of things. In: 37th Symposium on Applied Computing, pp. 32–35 (2022)
39. Liu, Q., Cheng, L., Jia, A.L., Liu, C.: Deep reinforcement learning for communication flow control in wireless mesh networks. IEEE Netw. **35**(2), 112–119 (2021)
40. Petrovska, A., et al.: Defining adaptivity and logical architecture for engineering (smart) self-adaptive cyber–physical systems. Inf. Softw. Technol. **147**, 106866 (2022)
41. Iftikhar, M. U. et al.: A self-adaptive internet of things exemplar. In: 12th International Symposium on Software Engineering for Adaptive and Self-Managing Systems, pp. 76–82 (2017)
42. Qin, X., Ying, W.: Design of explosive production information and managing system based on Internet of Things. In: International Conference on Automation, Control, and Robots, pp. 173–176. (2015)
43. Horváth, I., Tavčar, J.: Designing cyber-physical systems for runtime self-adaptation: knowing more about what we miss. J. Integr. Des. Process Sci. **25**(2), 1–26 (2021)

44. Junior, E. C. et al.: Development process for self-adaptive applications of the Internet of health things based on movement patterns. In: 9th International Conference on Healthcare Informatics, pp. 437–438 (2021)

45. Provoost, M. et al: A self-adaptive internet-of-things exemplar. In: 14th International Symposium on Software Engineering for Adaptive and Self-Managing Systems, pp. 195–201 (2019)

46. Suciu, A. et al: Disaster early warning using time-critical IoT on elastic cloud workbench. In: International Conference on Communication Systems and Network, pp. 1–5 (2017)

47. Yachir, A. et al.: Event-aware framework for dynamic services discovery and selection in the context of ambient intelligence and Internet of Things. IEEE Trans. Automat. Sci. Eng. **13**(1), 85–102 (2015)

48. Seetanadi, G. N. et al.: Event-driven bandwidth allocation with formal guarantees for camera networks. In: Real-Time Systems Symposium, pp. 243–254 (2017)

49. Stadler, M. et al.: Flexible model-driven runtime monitoring support for cyber-physical systems. In: 44th International Conference on Software Engineering, pp. 350–351 (2022)

50. Wright, T. et al.: Formally verified self-adaptation of an incubator digital twin. In: International Symposium On Leveraging Applications of Formal Methods, pp. 89–109 (2022)

51. Portaluri, M. et al.: From sensors to the cloud: a real-time use-case on vertical integration. In: 23rd International Symposium on Distributed Simulation and Real Time Applications, pp. 1–2 (2019)

52. Anda, A. A., Amyot, D.: Goal and feature model optimization for the design and self-adaptation of socio-cyber-physical systems. J. Integr. Des. Process Sci. **25**(2), 141–177 (2021)

53. Lee, J., et al.: Goal-based automated code generation in self-adaptive system. J. Comput. Sci. Technol. **25**, 1118–1129 (2010)

54. Gong, Y., et al.: Grid-based coverage path planning with NFZ avoidance for UAV using parallel self-adaptive ant colony optimization algorithm in cloud IoT. J. Cloud Comput. **11**, 29 (2022)

55. Saelens, M. et al.: Healthy cycling in a city using self-adaptive internet-of-things. In: International Conference on Autonomic Computing and Self-Organizing Systems Companion, pp. 226–227. (2020)

56. Han, D. et al.: Integrating goal models and problem frames for requirements analysis of self-adaptive CPS. In: 41st Annual Computer Software and Applications Conference, vol. 2, pp. 529–535 (2017)

57. Cogliati, D. et al: Intelligent cyber-physical systems for industry 4.0. In: International Conference on Artificial Intelligence for Industries, pp. 19–22 (2018)

58. Jamshidi, P. et al.: Machine learning meets quantitative planning: enabling self-adaptation in autonomous robots. In: 14th International Symposium on Software Engineering for Adaptive and Self-Managing Systems, pp. 39–50 (2019)

59. Halima, R., Hachicha, M., Jemal, A., et al.: MAPE-K patterns for self-adaptation in cyber-physical systems. J. Supercomputing **79**, 4917–4943 (2023)

60. Bosse, S., Lehmhus, D.: Material-integrated cluster computing in self-adaptive robotic materials using mobile multi-agent systems. Clust. Comput. **22**, 1017–1037 (2019)

61. Song, H., Raj, A., Hajebi, S., et al.: Model-based cross-layer monitoring and adaptation of multilayer systems. Science China Inf. Sci. **56**, 1–15 (2013)

62. D'Angelo, M., Caporuscio, M., Napolitano, A.: Model-driven engineering of decentralized control in cyber-physical systems. In: 2nd International Workshops on Foundations and Applications of Self* Systems, pp. 7–12 (2017)

63. Anda A. A.: Modeling adaptive socio-cyber-physical systems with goals and SysML. In: 26th International Requirements Engineering Conference, pp. 442–447 (2018)

64. Bennaceur, A. et al.: Modelling and analysing resilient cyber-physical systems. In: 14th International Symposium on Software Engineering for Adaptive and Self-Managing Systems, pp. 70–76 (2019)
65. Sylla, A. N. et al.: Modular and hierarchical discrete control for applications and middleware deployment in iot and smart buildings. In: Conference on Control Technology and Applications, pp. 1472–1479 (2018)
66. Gascon-Samson, K. et al: Poster: Towards a distributed and self-adaptable cloud-edge middleware. Symposium on Edge Computing, pp. 338–340 (2018)
67. Settanni, G. et al.: Protecting cyber physical production systems using anomaly detection to enable self-adaptation. In: Industrial Cyber-Physical System, pp. 173–180 (2018)
68. Banouar, Y. et al.: QoS management mechanisms for enhanced living environments in IoT. In: Symposium on Integrated Network and Service Management, pp. 1155–1161 (2017)
69. Romero-Garcés, A., et al.: QoS metrics-in-the-loop for endowing runtime self-adaptation to robotic software architectures. Multimedia Tools Appli. **81**, 3603–3628 (2022)
70. Sodhro, A.H., et al.: Quality of service optimization in an IoT-driven intelligent transportation system. IEEE Wirel. Commun. **26**(6), 10–17 (2019)
71. Cámara, J., Muccini, H., & Vaidhyanathan, K.: Quantitative verification-aided machine learning: A tandem approach for architecting self-adaptive IoT systems. In: International Conference on Softw. Architecture, pp. 11–22 (2020)
72. Bellini, E. et al: Resilience learning through self adaptation in digital twins of human-cyber-physical systems. In: International Conference on Cyber Security and Resilience, pp. 168–173 (2021)
73. Rafique, A., et al.: SCOPE: Self-adaptive and policy-based data management middleware for federated clouds. J. Internet Serv. Appl. **10**, 2 (2019)
74. Gerostathopoulos, I., et al.: Self-adaptation in software-intensive cyber–physical systems: from system goals to architecture configurations. J. Syst. Softw. **122**, 378–397 (2016)
75. Zeadally, S., Sanislav, T., Mois, G.D.: Self-adaptation techniques in cyber-physical systems (CPSs). IEEE Access **7**, 171126–171139 (2019)
76. Narayanankutty, H.: Self-adapting model-based SDSEC for IOT networks using machine learning. In: 18th International Conference on Software Architecture Companion, pp. 92–93 (2021)
77. Svae, A. et al.: Self-adaptive control in cyber-physical systems: the autonomous train experiment. In: Symposium on Applied Computing, pp. 1436–1443 (2017)
78. Lee, E. et al.: Self-adaptive framework with game theoretic decision making for Internet of things. In: TENCON, pp. 2092–2097 (2018)
79. Lee, E., Seo, Y.D., Kim, Y.G.: Self-adaptive framework with master–slave architecture for Internet of Things. IEEE Internet of Things J. **9**(17), 16472–16493 (2022)
80. Muccini, H. et al.: Self-adaptive IoT architectures: An emergency handling case study. In: European Conference on Software Architecture: Companion, pp. 1–6 (2018)
81. Pilgerstorfer, P., Pournaras, E.: Self-adaptive learning in decentralized combinatorial optimization-a design paradigm for sharing economies. In: 2th International Symposium on Software Engineer for Adaptive and Self-Managing System, pp. 54–64 (2017)
82. Islam, C., et al.: SmartValidator: A framework for automatic identification and classification of cyber threat data. J. Netw. Comput. Appli. **202**, 103370 (2022)
83. Rahimi, H. et al.: SMASH: A semantic-enabled multi-agent approach for self-adaptation of human-centered IoT. in Advances in Practical Applications of Agents, Multi-Agent Systems, and Social Good. In: 19th International Conference on PAAMS, pp. 201–213 (2021)
84. Memarian, S. et al.: Social Internet of Things: Interoperability and autonomous computing challenges. In: International Conference on Omni-layer Intelligent Systems, pp. 1–7 (2020)

85. Antonino, P. O., Morgenstern, A., Kallweit, B.: Straightforward specification of adaptation-architecture-significant requirements of IoT-enabled cyber-physical systems. In: International Conference on Softw. Architecture Companion, pp. 19–26 (2018)
86. Junior, B. R. et al.: Succeed: Support mechanism for creating and executing workflows for decoupled SAS in IoT. In: 42nd Annual Computer Software and Applications Conference, pp. 738–743 (2018)
87. Li, W., et al.: The way to apply machine learning to IoT driven wireless network from channel perspective. China Commun. **16**(1), 148–164 (2019)
88. Sun, X., et al.: Toward self-adaptive selection of kernel functions for support vector regression in IoT-based marine data prediction. IEEE IoT J. **7**(10), 9943–9952 (2020)
89. Ouechtati, H. et al.: Towards a self-adaptive access control middleware for the Internet of Things. In: International Conference on Information Networking, pp. 545–550 (2018)
90. Azeri, N. et al.: Towards an approach for modeling and architecting of self-adaptive cyber-physical systems. In: 4th Int. Conf. on Pattern Anal. and Intell. Syst., pp. 1–7 (2022)
91. Afanasov, M., Mottola, L., Ghezzi, C.: Towards context-oriented self-adaptation in resource-constrained cyberphysical systems. In: 38th International Computer Software and Applications Conferences, Workshops, pp. 372–377 (2014)
92. Weiss, G. et al.: Towards integrating undependable self-adaptive systems in safety-critical environments. In: 13th International Conference on Software Engineering for Adaptive and Self-Managing Systems, pp. 26–32 (2018)
93. Bedhief, M. et al: Self-adaptive management of SDN distributed controllers for highly dynamic IoT networks. In: 15th International Wireless Communications and Mobile Computing Conference, pp. 2098–2104 (2019)

Virtual IoT Laboratory Through a Hands-on Approach in Educational Environments

Darío Valarezo[1,2(✉)] , Gabriela Mendieta[3] ,
and Manuel Quiñones-Cuenca[4]

[1] Departamento de Redes y Telecomunicaciones, Instituto Superior Tecnológico
Daniel Álvarez Burneo, Loja, Ecuador
[2] Escuela de Ingeniería en Tecnologías de la Información, Universidad Internacional
del Ecuador, Quito, Ecuador
djvalarezo@istdabloja.edu.ec, davalarezole@uide.edu.ec
[3] Departamento de Electricidad, Instituto Superior Tecnológico Loja, Loja, Ecuador
gbmendieta@tecnologicoloja.edu.ec, gvmendieta@utpl.edu.ec
[4] Departamento de Ciencias de la Computación y Electrónica, Universidad Técnica
Particular de Loja, Loja, Ecuador
mfquinonez@utpl.edu.ec

Abstract. Equal opportunities in the learning process must become
a priority in higher education institutions, where a hands-on approach
enhances the training of the students. This research aims to present a
virtual Internet of Things (IoT) sensor network to improve online education through a low-cost virtual IoT laboratory. This modular solution
uses virtualization to replace hardware platforms, enabling the configuration of virtual nodes at the software level. This proposal combines Virtual
Machines (VMs) to create a virtual network infrastructure, configuring
each VM as a network device. Thus, there is no need for a large budget to implement hands-on approach laboratories in undergraduate and
graduate degrees. Undergraduate technological students of the Instituto
Superior Tecnológico Daniel Álvarez Burneo (ISTDAB, abbreviation in
Spanish) validate the modular solution in the Network Security subject
in the Technology Degree in Network and Telecommunications. A laboratory practice establishes the guidelines for mounting the virtual IoT
sensor network. Finally, a satisfaction survey submits the acceptance
of the proposal in the academic period (October 2022 - March 2023).
Furthermore, the information provides evidence of the flexibility of the
modular system in different scenarios.

Keywords: Cybersecurity · Education Technology · Emerging
Technology · Information and Communications Technology

1 Introduction

Educative innovation generates inclusive and equitable learning opportunities at
all levels of instruction (i.e., primary, secondary, and higher education) [9,19].

M. Botto-Tobar et al. (Eds.): ICAT 2023, CCIS 2051, pp. 158–172, 2024.
https://doi.org/10.1007/978-3-031-58950-8_12

Based on study modalities, online education has a problem with the hands-on approach due to the investment cost in infrastructure for higher education institutions [14]. Most of the time, students also do not have money to buy hardware platforms. Therefore, there is a need to develop educational solutions according to the reality of each developing country [21]. This process includes the development of new pedagogical methodologies through Information and Communications Technology (ICT). An attractive proposal is remote or virtual laboratories as accessible solutions for students who do not have access to physical laboratories [4,13,24]. In both cases, the students have access from anywhere and anytime. However, a virtual laboratory does not require investment in hardware platforms.

A higher education institution that does not have laboratories cannot offer an immersive learning experience to students. In the context of developing countries, the economic inversion is considerable due to the growth of different new technologies. Hence, the existing deficiency of specialized laboratories shows the need to implement virtual laboratories, improving the teaching process [4,13]. Therefore, students anywhere in the country (i.e., urban, rural, or marginal sectors) have equal opportunities to learn with a hands-on approach in educational environments [16,24].

The Research, Development, and Innovation (RDI) implements innovative education solutions focusing on the fourth Sustainable Development Goal (SDG) proposed by the United Nations (UN) [23]. Hence, access to new technologies in higher education permits learning new aptitudes and abilities necessary for Industry 4.0 [6]. One of these emerging technology is the IoT [7]. In a few years, IoT will promote the network device massification in various vertical solutions (i.e., agriculture, building, education, industry, logistic, medicine, among others) [11,15]. In developing countries, the financial outlay does not exist in the budget of the higher education institutions [3]. Therefore, a remote IoT laboratory is challenging to implement. However, a virtual IoT laboratory is an acceptable low-cost solution.

In undergraduate technological education, there is a necessity for practical training due to the growing IoT applications [11,21]. A virtual IoT laboratory needs a local workstation that acts as a host [9], sharing its resources with each virtual network device. The virtualization of the Operative System (OS) validates any IoT device available on the market (i.e., Banana Pi, Odroid, Raspberry Pi, Tinker Board, among others) [2,5]. Therefore, there is no need for investment in hardware platforms to implement software-level functionalities [9]. A hypervisor executes a virtual IoT sensor network (i.e., VirtualBox, VMWare, among others), where each VM acts as a unique virtual node. Hence, the budget to implement hands-on approach laboratories comes down [12].

This research presents a virtual IoT sensor network to improve online education through a low-cost virtual IoT laboratory. Hence, this modular solution creates a virtual IoT laboratory through a hands-on approach in educational environments. Furthermore, this work reduces the financial outlay to implement a network infrastructure for higher education institutions and students. This investigation implements a low-cost solution for the Network Security subject in the Technology Degree in Network and Telecommunications at the ISTDAB [8]. A laboratory practice establishes the guidelines for mounting and testing the virtual IoT sensor network. Finally, this study tests the acceptance of the modular solution in the academic period (October 2022 - March 2023).

The remainder of this paper presents the following sections. Section 2 introduces the materials and methods used in the research. Then, Sect. 3 exhibits the results and discussion. Finally, Sect. 4 submits the conclusions and future research works.

2   Materials and Methods

2.1   Related Works

This section delivers a summary of relevant literature. The state-of-the-art shows different proposals focused on remote and virtual IoT laboratories.

In [9], the study provides an IoT solution for learning microprocessor technology in remote education. The authors integrate different teaching resources in a remote IoT laboratory using a practical approach as an effective way to learn. However, this research utilizes various hardware platforms and software applications, increasing the financial outlay. The study demonstrates that the IoT solution is functional in remote and full-time education. On the other hand, [20], the researchers design a virtual IoT laboratory through virtualization and container technologies. The idea is to reduce the cost of implementation using docker containers. Furthermore, the results test the quality system in different scenarios.

Then, in [21], the investigation presents an emulating virtual laboratory for cybersecurity training in distance education. In this case, this uses the Emulated Virtual Environment-Next Generation (EVE-NG) technology. The system proposes a laboratory that includes cybersecurity, cloud computing, and IoT infrastructure. Furthermore, this focuses on the interaction of the students with the system. On the other hand, in [22], the authors provide a remote IoT laboratory through a web page as a learning tool in distance education. The main objective is to increase the interest in IoT and cybersecurity. Furthermore, the modular solution works with different topologies and scenarios. However, both studies measure the level of satisfaction of the students.

In [14], the authors describe a framework that allows students to access a remote laboratory. The solution converts a hands-on laboratory into a remote laboratory through different workstations on the university campus. In this case, the solution focuses on undergraduate university education. Therefore, the proposal describes the architecture, hardware platforms, software applications, and student guidelines. Furthermore, other subjects can replicate the low-cost remote laboratory, bringing new opportunities to the students. However, this proposal focuses on an existing physical laboratory.

Then, in [3], the work proposes an emulator laboratory based on CupCarbon and Raspberry Pi. In this case, CupCarbon permits the simulation of several IoT devices, and Raspberry Pi implements real IoT devices. This idea presents the proof of concept that deploys intelligent environments. Furthermore, the study proposes the use of the Python programming language. On the other hand, in [10], the authors implement a virtual IoT Laboratory through Node-RED on virtual teaching methodologies. The system reduces coding complexity using a visual programming language. This solution focuses on different IoT communication protocols in real time. Both solutions are compatible with hardware platforms available in the market. However, these proposals need investment in hardware platforms for each workstation.

Finally, in [4], the authors present the design and development of a reconfigurable remote learning laboratory based on cloud computing. This study improves the learning process of the students through experimentation. Therefore, the learning laboratory uses hardware platforms and software applications. The results show that this solution has applications in the pandemic and postpandemic periods. On the other hand, in [13], the work presents the design and implementation of a remote laboratory focused on industrial mechanization. Embedded systems compose the hardware part, and the IoT platform is part of the software component. Furthermore, the students can access the remote laboratory through mobile devices anywhere and anytime. However, the system architecture needs the interaction of a physical laboratory.

The state-of-the-art shows the feasibility of implementing a virtual IoT sensor network. Therefore, the approach of this research is on how to design a virtual IoT laboratory, reducing implementation costs. Furthermore, the related works demonstrate the importance of developing innovative solutions focusing on higher education. Hence, this investigation has to focus on the adaptability to different scenarios of online education.

2.2   Virtual IoT Laboratory

This section describes the proposal that implements a virtual IoT sensor network through a hands-on approach in educational environments. The information explains the modular solution background, architecture, and implementation.

Background. In the Republic of Ecuador, Loja City is the main headquarters of the ISTDAB [8], where the Asociación Marista Ecuatoriana (AME, abbreviation in Spanish) promotes the ISTDAB with community outreach [1]. This higher education institution offers various undergraduate degrees. The Technology Degree in Network and Telecommunications is one of them. This undergraduate technological degree provides a dual study modality (presential and online education). The institution uses a Learning Management System (LMS) (powered by Moodle) and virtual rooms (powered by Google) as virtual learning environments to develop the educational process. However, the ISTDAB has a limited budget to implement physical laboratories.

The Technology Degree in Network and Telecommunications has four semesters, where the Network Security subject has an assignment of 96 h. This subject is mandatory in the last academic year. In the scholarly period (October 2022 - March 2023), there are 49 students enrolled. However, only eight students are in the fourth semester, decreasing the sample to test the virtual IoT laboratory. This undergraduate technological degree has only one physical laboratory without specialized physical equipment, especially in emerging technologies such as IoT. Therefore, any local workstation will provide a low-cost virtual IoT laboratory based on virtualization [3,14], maintaining the quality of the learning process in online education [13,21].

This project has three parts of continuous development. The first part contemplates the implementation of a virtual IoT laboratory. The second part considers the proof of various IoT communication protocols, such as Hypertext Transfer Protocol (HTTP) and Message Queuing Telemetry Transport (MQTT). Finally, the third part validates different security mechanisms of virtual nodes. Each one of the phases contemplates a laboratory practice with the establishment of guidelines for the students. Therefore, this study concentrates on the first part, focusing on the first layer of the IoT reference model [7].

Architecture. IoT unites various disruptive technologies into intelligent systems, promoting a connectivity-oriented World. A pile of protocols distributed in different layers creates a network infrastructure [18]. Therefore, the analysis by layers simplifies the study of devices, protocols, and services. The IoT reference model based on three layers conceptually describes the components of this emerging technology [2,7]. The perception layer manages the functionality of IoT devices. The network layer focuses on exchanging information between the perception and the application layers. Finally, the application layer provides services to final users through Cloud Computing.

The virtualization of an IoT sensor network is possible with Open-Source and licensed software applications [9]. Therefore, this modular solution focuses on implementing a low-cost virtual IoT laboratory through Open-Source software applications, reducing the acquisition cost to $0.00. Furthermore, using Science, Technology, Engineering and Mathematics (STEM) IoT platforms (i.e., ThingsBoard, ThingSpeak, Ubidots, among others) based on educational licenses reduces the budget for Cloud Computing to $0.00. Some IoT platforms offer a maximum of three devices with eight variables. On the other hand, the only economic cost to consider is the use of the local workstation.

The virtual IoT sensor network is a small-scale Wireless Local Area Network (WLAN) implemented at the software level, as shown in Fig. 1. The configuration of any computer into a local workstation enforces a virtual network infrastructure, so there is no possibility of damaging genuine network infrastructure. This local workstation can work in online and offline modes. In both methods, the virtual IoT laboratory verifies different security mechanisms of the virtual nodes at the software level [11]. On the other hand, the online mode proves various IoT communication protocols. The local workstation virtualizes different generic VMs that share a pre-configured OS [11]. The generic VMs use GNU/Linux distributions, implementing an IoT device based on an embedded system. Therefore, a student can replace a generic VM at any time, focusing on the programming of the firmware [9].

The modular system implements different scenarios with the same virtual network infrastructure. A hypervisor executes various generic VMs for each virtual network device (i.e., virtual attacker and virtual node) [4,9], as shown in Fig. 2. Students import and configure generic VMs according to their necessities [14]. If a virtual node crashes, another generic VM will replace it with a new backup copy [4]. However, the design of the virtual IoT laboratory is only for personal use [14]. Therefore, each student has a scalable virtual IoT sensor network using VMs as realistic embedded IoT devices in a local workstation [13]. This research does not contemplate the configuration of the IoT platforms. Hence, the setup focuses only on the virtual network infrastructure.

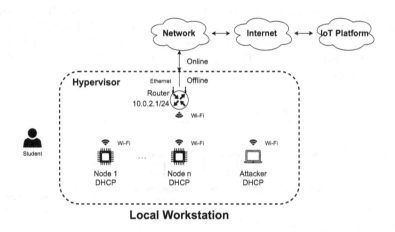

Fig. 1. Virtual IoT laboratory design.

Virtual nodes need to have similar technical specifications to available embedded IoT devices [14]. Therefore, a local workstation has to meet some requirements [5,21], especially the virtualization option enable. There are other technical features related to the processor, Random-access memory (RAM), storage, among others. Hence, this modular solution can run different virtual network devices at the same time. On the other hand, the virtual IoT laboratory does not depend on a specific host OS. The modular solution uses software applications compatible with different OS.

The virtual IoT sensor network has three main components:

- The virtual router implements network services locally.
- Virtual node are responsible for exchanging information with IoT platforms on the Internet.
- And, the virtual attacker validates passive and active attacks.

Virtual Router. A local workstation needs a hypervisor to implement a virtual IoT sensor network. A hypervisor virtualizes stand-alone virtual network devices, as shown in Fig. 2. The hypervisor works as a virtual router, permitting the incoming and outgoing network traffic in the virtual network infrastructure, as shown in Fig. 1. Furthermore, the configuration acts as a virtual switch with a virtual network interface for each VM. The virtual router implements the Network Address Translation (NAT) service based on a Dynamic Host Configuration Protocol (DHCP) server, establishing access to the Internet. On the other hand, the Domain Name System (DNS) server at each VM resolves the public Internet Protocol (IP) address to the Internet.

A virtual network interface has various choices linked to switching the network adapter type, changing the Media Access Control (MAC) address, and establishing the promiscuous mode. The function of the virtual network interface is to provide connectivity to each VM, relating a unique IP address to each virtual network device. The DHCP server supports IPv4 and IPv6. In the online mode, the modular system exchange information with IoT platforms on the Internet. However, in the offline method, the virtual IoT laboratory exchange information locally.

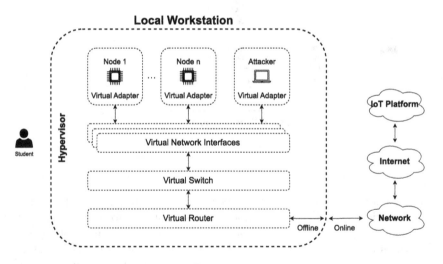

Fig. 2. Hypervisor solution architecture.

Virtual Node. A virtual node acts as an IoT device, as shown in Fig. 1. At the hardware level, the VM configuration has the same technical characteristics as an IoT device available on the market, as shown in Fig. 3. The configuration considers 512 MB of RAM and one core. Nevertheless, the virtual node does not consider external actuators and sensors. Random values between a range simulate the information of the virtual actuators and sensors [7]. At the software level, different embedded OS can create the generic VM (i.e., Raspbian

OS, Ubuntu Server OS, among others). However, the OS needs additional basic configurations. This pre-configured OS serves as a backup copy of the virtual node.

All the IoT devices are configurable through a Command-Line Interface (CLI). However, a node support different programming language to set tasks (i.e., Bash Script, C++, Python, among other) [2,3,5]. This study focuses on Python as a principal programming language. Various Python packages implement IoT communication protocols such as HTTP and MQTT. Hence, a virtual node uses them to exchange information with an IoT platform on the Internet. Furthermore, students learn a new programming language.

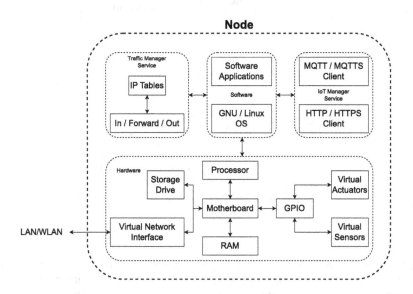

Fig. 3. IoT device architecture.

Virtual Attacker. A virtual attacker functions as a malicious actor, as shown in Fig. 1. At the hardware level, the VM configuration has the exact technical characteristics of a regular computer, as shown in Fig. 4. The configuration considers 1024 MB of RAM and two cores. The virtual network interface is sufficient to implement passive and active attacks on the virtual network infrastructure. At the software level, informatic security OS can create the generic VM (i.e., BlackArch, Kali Linux OS, Parrot OS, among others). Any informatic security distribution has configurations and software applications pre-loaded by default. This pre-configured OS serves as a backup copy of the virtual attacker.

The malicious actor implements active and passive attacks in the virtual network infrastructure. A virtual attacker uses specialized tools associated with network discovery (i.e., arp-scan, netdiscover, among others), network traffic analysis (i.e., TCPdump, tshark, Wireshark, among others), port analysis (i.e., nmap, zenmap, among others), intercepting information (i.e., arpspoof, ettercap, among others), and exploiting vulnerabilities (i.e., exploitdb, metasploit, among others).

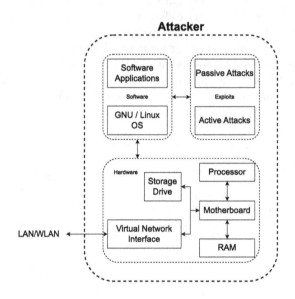

Fig. 4. Attacker architecture.

Implementation. Independent of the OS, the local workstation uses Virtual-Box as a hypervisor, as shown in Fig. 5. In the Network Manager option, the configuration of the NAT network implements the different network services to communicate the virtual network devices between them and the Internet. Then, in the Import Appliance option, each pre-configured OS establishes a generic VM as a virtual network device of the virtual network infrastructure. The number of virtual network devices will depend on the technical features of the local workstation. Finally, in the network configuration of each VM, a network adapter has to be attached to the same NAT Network.

A pre-configured Ubuntu Server OS implements the virtual nodes in the virtual network infrastructure. This generic VM is similar to a Raspberry Pi [5]. The programming languages to set tasks are Bash Script and Python. Both came by default in the OS. However, Python will implement the functions to get and post data to the IoT platforms on the Internet [2,17]. Therefore, each virtual node requires the additional installation of the request library for the HTTP communication protocol and paho-mqtt library for the MQTT communication protocol [5].

On the other hand, a pre-configured Kali Linux OS executes the virtual attacker in the virtual network infrastructure. All the specialized tools came by default in the OS. However, the generic VM has additional disk space to install other software applications.

Fig. 5. Connectivity of the virtual IoT laboratory.

3   Results and Discussion

3.1   Results

This section presents the results of the modular solution in the Network Security subject in the Technology Degree in Network and Telecommunications at the ISTDAB. This study validates the acceptance of the proposal in the academic period (October 2022 - March 2023).

Validation. In the Network Security subject, the IoT topic includes a period of three weeks of dedication. The three laboratory practices fit this time, one for each phase. The laboratory practices work as didactic material where the learners are the main actors in the learning process. Therefore, the first laboratory practice considers tasks for one week. By the end of this laboratory practice, the students have knowledge of hypervisors, VM, OS, network infrastructure, among others. The definition of laboratory practice as a guideline for the learners facilitates the implementation of the virtual IoT sensor network. Step by step, the students configure their local workstations. The laboratory practice requests snapshots of different finished guidelines to have evidence of the advance of the learners [14].

Due to the dual study modality, the validation process needs the continuous participation of the undergraduate technological students and the teacher.

Therefore, the feedback to solve any problem needs to be in real-time. In presential education, the teacher monitors the advance of the learners on-site, resolving any questions. On the other hand, in online education, the teacher uses virtual rooms or remote desktop applications (i.e., AnyDesk, Meets, TeamViewer, Webex, Zoom, among others) to bring remote support [14]. Based on the finished works, 100% of the students completed all the activities of the first laboratory practice in the academic period.

Satisfaction. A satisfaction survey measures the level of acceptance of the modular solution in the Network Security subject [9, 21]. The satisfaction survey contemplates feedback questions and different qualitative aspects (i.e., accessibility, flexibility, inclusion, innovation, replicability, and scalability), where the level of satisfaction is from 1 to 5 (i.e., strongly disagree, disagree, neutral, agree, and strongly agree) [21]:

- Q1. In your experience, What aspects could be improved in the subject?
- Q2. In your experience, What aspects could be improved in the teaching guide?
- Q3. In your experience, What aspects could be improved in laboratory practices?
- Q4. In your experience, laboratory practices are accessible. Where: 1 = strongly disagree, 2 = disagree, 3 = neutral, 4 = agree, and 5 = strongly agree.
- Q5. In your experience, laboratory practices are flexible. Where: 1 = strongly disagree, 2 = disagree, 3 = neutral, 4 = agree, and 5 = strongly agree.
- Q6. In your experience, laboratory practices are inclusive. Where: 1 = strongly disagree, 2 = disagree, 3 = neutral, 4 = agree, and 5 = strongly agree.
- Q7. In your experience, laboratory practices are innovative. Where: 1 = strongly disagree, 2 = disagree, 3 = neutral, 4 = agree, and 5 = strongly agree.
- Q8. In your experience, laboratory practices are replicable. Where: 1 = strongly disagree, 2 = disagree, 3 = neutral, 4 = agree, and 5 = strongly agree.
- Q9. In your experience, laboratory practices are scalable. Where: 1 = strongly disagree, 2 = disagree, 3 = neutral, 4 = agree, and 5 = strongly agree.

The students answered the satisfaction survey when they finished the laboratory practice. This study evaluated the participation of eight students. In this case, the undergraduate technological students answered a survey on the LMS platform of the ISTDAB.

The radar chart presents the Mean (M) for each qualitative aspect, as shown in Fig. 6. The M is from 4.38 to 4.63, and the Standard Deviation (SD) is consistent from 0.48 to 0.71. The accessibility, flexibility, and inclusion are 4.63 out of 5 ($SD = 0.48$). The replicability is 4.50 out of 5 ($SD = 0.71$). And the innovation and scalability are 4.38 out of 5 ($SD = 0.70$). The value in the replicability qualitative aspect is due to problems in the configuration process of the local workstation. Therefore, the students do not perceive any innovation methodology because this first laboratory practice focuses on the virtual network infrastructure setup. On the other hand, scalability is one of the worst because computers have limited technical resources. Depending on the computer, the hypervisor only executes one VM.

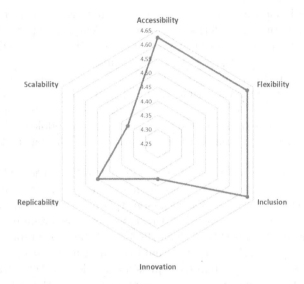

Fig. 6. Level of satisfaction.

Table 1. Results of the survey.

Qualitative Aspects	Strongly Agree	Agree	Neutral	Disagree	Strongly Disagree
Accessibility	62.50%	37.50%	0.00%	0.00%	0.00%
Flexibility	62.50%	37.50%	0.00%	0.00%	0.00%
Inclusion	62.50%	37.50%	0.00%	0.00%	0.00%
Innovation	50.00%	37.50%	12.50%	0.00%	0.00%
Replicability	62.50%	25.00%	12.50%	0.00%	0.00%
Scalability	50.00%	37.50%	12.50%	0.00%	0.00%

A table presents the results of the survey, as shown in Table 1. 100% of the students consider the modular solution as accessible or strongly accessible. 100% of the students perceive the modular solution as flexible or strongly flexible. 100% of the students believe the modular solution as inclusive or strongly inclusive. 87.50% of the students feel the modular solution as innovative or strongly innovative. 87.50% of the students feel the modular solution as replicable or strongly replicable. Finally, 87.50% of the students think the modular solution as scalable or strongly scalable. The rest of the answers are neutral for each qualitative aspects.

3.2 Discussion

This virtual IoT laboratory is a low-cost proposal that brings emerging technologies closer to the students, offering an immersive learning experience through practical training. There is no need for students to invest in hardware platforms. The students in the undergraduate technological degree will learn the secure development of IoT devices at the software level [11]. The pre-configured OS reduces the implementation time of the virtual IoT sensor network in the local workstation [14]. Therefore, this work combines laboratory practice with challenge-based education as an innovative learning methodology. The learners improve their knowledge through experimentation [13], relating the theory with the approach [9].

The virtual IoT laboratory uses the computer of each learner. This modular solution is not valid for students who do not have a computer, have a host with limited technical resources, or use a smartphone as a learning tool. In this case, the physical laboratory at the institution will provide a remote workstation through remote access. Therefore, this solution will be projectable as a Cloud Computing service through different virtual IoT sensor networks on the Internet. Furthermore, the modular system concept is adaptable to other subjects of the Technology Degree in Network and Telecommunications at the ISTDAB [14].

4   Conclusions

The low-cost virtual IoT laboratory presented in this paper provides a hands-on approach in educational environments. This modular solution is adaptable to different IoT devices available on the market. This proposal uses Open-Source software applications compatible with various OS. Therefore, this solution is flexible and scalable.

This type of ICT solution is adaptable to the dual study modality, enhancing the learning process through a hands-on approach. The modular solution is an inclusive and equitable education proposal in higher education, reducing education inequality in rural and marginal urban sectors. There is no need for hardware platforms to validate emerging technologies. Therefore, students have the same learning opportunities. However, the rapid development of emerging technology motivates the continuous improvement of the didactic material, a crucial step to maintaining the educative quality.

The technical specifications of the local workstation limit the functionalities of this proposal. Therefore, providing the service as an infrastructure for Cloud Computing will be a viable upgrade, improving the scalability. On the other hand, this solution can not virtualize embedded IoT devices based on microcontrollers.

In future works, the modular solution will prove the setup of different IoT communication protocols through passive attacks. Besides, the virtual IoT laboratory verifies the configuration of various security mechanisms in IoT devices through active attacks.

Acknowledgment. The Instituto Superior Tecnológico Daniel Álvarez Burneo provides the funds to develop this Work. And the Technology Degree in Network and Telecommunications brings the facilities to implement this research.

References

1. Agrupación Marista Ecuatoriana: Homepage (2023). https://maristasecuador.org/
2. Al Hayajneh, A., Bhuiyan, M.Z.A., McAndrew, I.: Improving internet of things (iot) security with software-defined networking (sdn). Computers **9**(1) (2020). https://doi.org/10.3390/computers9010008, https://www.mdpi.com/2073-431X/9/1/8
3. Bounceur, A., et al.: Cupcarbon-lab: an iot emulator. In: 2018 15th IEEE Annual Consumer Communications Networking Conference (CCNC), pp. 1–2 (2018). https://doi.org/10.1109/CCNC.2018.8319313
4. Chamunorwa, T., Modran, H.A., Ursuțiu, D., Samoilă, C., Hedeiu, H.: Reconfigurable wireless sensor node remote laboratory platform with cloud connectivity. Sensors **21**(19) (2021). https://doi.org/10.3390/s21196405
5. Dinculeană, D., Cheng, X.: Vulnerabilities and limitations of mqtt protocol used between iot devices. Appli. Sci. **9**(5) (2019).https://doi.org/10.3390/app9050848
6. Dobrovská, D., Andres, P.: Digitization and current educational changes in switzerland - inspiration for the Czech Republic? In: Auer, M.E., Hortsch, H., Sethakul, P. (eds.) ICL 2019. AISC, vol. 1135, pp. 402–408. Springer, Cham (2020). https://doi.org/10.1007/978-3-030-40271-6_40
7. Huang, J., Zhang, Z., Li, W., Xin, Y.: Assessment of the impacts of tls vulnerabilities in the https ecosystem of china. Procedia Computer Science **147**, 512–518 (2019).https://doi.org/10.1016/j.procs.2019.01.238, 2018 International Conference on Identification, Information and Knowledge in the Internet of Things
8. Instituto Superior Tecnológico Daniel Álvarez Burneo: Homepage (2023). https://www.istdabloja.edu.ec/
9. Jacko, P., et al.: Remote iot education laboratory for microcontrollers based on the stm32 chips. Sensors **22**(4) (2022).https://doi.org/10.3390/s22041440
10. Kumar, K.V.S.K.R.S., Taparugssanagorn, A., Dumunnage, A.P.S.S.: Virtual internet of things laboratory using node-red. In: Petrillo, A., Felice, F.D., Achim, M.V., Mirza, N. (eds.) Digital Transformation, chap. 14. IntechOpen, Rijeka (2022). https://doi.org/10.5772/intechopen.104127
11. Kwon, S., Son, S.J., Choi, Y., Lee, J.H.: Protocol fuzzing to find security vulnerabilities of rabbitmq. Concurrency Comput. Pract. Experience **33**(23), e6012 (2021). https://doi.org/10.1002/cpe.6012,e6012CPE-20-0718.R1
12. Lim, C.P., Ra, S., Chin, B., Wang, T.: Leveraging information and communication technologies (ict) to enhance education equity, quality, and efficiency: case studies of Bangladesh and Nepal. Educ. Media Internat. **57**(2), 87–111 (2020). https://doi.org/10.1080/09523987.2020.1786774
13. Ramya, M.V., Purushothama, G.K, Ramamurthy, P.: Design and implementation of iot based remote laboratory for sensor experiments. Intern. J. Interact. Mobile Technol. (iJIM) **14**(09), 227–238 (2020).https://doi.org/10.3991/ijim.v14i09.13991

14. McConnell, M., Loparo, K.A., Barendt, N.: A framework for remote hardware lab course delivery: rapidly adjusting to 2020. In: 2021 ASEE Virtual Annual Conference Content Access. ASEE Conferences, Virtual Conference (July 2021).https://doi.org/10.18260/1-2-36581

15. Metongnon, L., Sadre, R.: Beyond telnet: prevalence of iot protocols in telescope and honeypot measurements. In: Proceedings of the 2018 Workshop on Traffic Measurements for Cybersecurity, WTMC 2018, pp. 21–26. Association for Computing Machinery, New York (2018). https://doi.org/10.1145/3229598.3229604, https://doi.org/10.1145/3229598.3229604

16. Mora-Rivera, J., García-Mora, F.: Internet access and poverty reduction: evidence from rural and Urban Mexico. Telecommun. Policy **45**(2), 102076 (2021). https://doi.org/10.1016/j.telpol.2020.102076

17. Naik, N.: Choice of effective messaging protocols for iot systems: Mqtt, coap, amqp and http. In: 2017 IEEE International Systems Engineering Symposium (ISSE), pp. 1–7 (2017). https://doi.org/10.1109/SysEng.2017.8088251

18. Phalaagae, P., Zungeru, A.M., Sigweni, B., Chuma, J.M., Semong, T.: Security challenges in IoT sensor networks. In: Green Internet of Things Sensor Networks, pp. 83–96. Springer, Cham (2020). https://doi.org/10.1007/978-3-030-54983-1_5

19. Rahman, N., Sairi, I., Zizi, N., Khalid, F.: The importance of cybersecurity education in school. Inter. J. Inform. Educ. Technol. **10**(5), 378–382 (2020).https://doi.org/10.18178/ijiet.2020.10.5.1393

20. Ramprasad, B., Fokaefs, M., Mukherjee, J., Litoiu, M.: Emu-iot - a virtual internet of things lab. In: 2019 IEEE International Conference on Autonomic Computing (ICAC), pp. 73–83 (2019). https://doi.org/10.1109/ICAC.2019.00019

21. Robles-Gómez, A., Tobarra, L., Pastor-Vargas, R., Hernández, R., Cano, J.: Emulating and evaluating virtual remote laboratories for cybersecurity. Sensors **20**(11) (2020). https://doi.org/10.3390/s20113011

22. Tobarra, L., Robles-Gómez, A., Pastor, R., Hernández, R., Cano, J., López, D.: Web of things platforms for distance learning scenarios in computer science disciplines: a practical approach. Technologies **7**(1) (2019). https://doi.org/10.3390/technologies7010017

23. United Nations: Final list of proposed sustainable development goal indicators (2016). https://www.sustainabledevelopment.un.org/

24. Yaacoub, E., Alouini, M.: A key 6g challenge and opportunity-connecting the base of the pyramid: a survey on rural connectivity. Proc. IEEE **108**(4), 533–582 (2020). https://doi.org/10.1109/JPROC.2020.2976703

Technology Trends

Enterprise Architecture Model for the Mortgage Loan Lending Process in a Financial Institution Using TOGAF

Oscar Alonso Flores-Chavez[(✉)] [ID], Andrei Alonso Falen-Salazar [ID],
and Emilio Antonio Herrera-Trujillo [ID]

Faculty of Engineering, Universidad Peruana de Ciencias Aplicadas, Santiago de Surco, Lima,
Perú
{u201716787,u201713242,pcsieher}@upc.edu.pe

Abstract. Mortgage loans in financial institutions have evolved thanks to digital transformation, employing emerging technologies to streamline their processes, enhance customer service, and improve the customer experience. This research presents an enterprise architecture considering the development of its three domains: business, applications, and technology, for the financial institution under study. Additionally, we present technological solutions to manage customer verification, pre-qualification, credit assessment, and property evaluation. The proposal and its technological solutions include the enhancement of the mortgage loan lending process in terms of management, reduction of manual tasks, in-person activities at branches, and document submission for credit and property evaluation. In this regard, we use TOGAF and its ADM development methodology. Finally, the model was evaluated based on 5 dimensions with a panel of experts using the Delphi technique, resulting in a 94% acceptance level and a total of 17 items that achieved a high level of consensus. This indicates that the implementation of the model will help optimize the mortgage loan process.

Keywords: Mortgage Loan · Enterprise Architecture · Banking · TOGAF · Credit · Optimization · Business Processes · Delphi

1 Introduction

One of the services provided by financial entities, including banks, savings banks, or cooperatives, is the mortgage loan. This involves a long-term loan granted to a company or individual for the purpose of purchasing, building, or renovating a house, apartment, or property [1]. This service is one of the most common due to people's desire to acquire properties in locations convenient to their work and/or social environment. There is a specific procedure for granting the loan, which involves application, credit assessment of the borrower and property, approval, celebration, and disbursement of the loan [2]. While there have been advances in terms of process digitization in foreign companies, such as in the U.S. [3]. Peruvian financial institutions have not developed digital strategies for this product. In recent years, they have been incorporating digital channels for other products

© The Author(s), under exclusive license to Springer Nature Switzerland AG 2024
M. Botto-Tobar et al. (Eds.): ICAT 2023, CCIS 2051, pp. 175–189, 2024.
https://doi.org/10.1007/978-3-031-58950-8_13

such as mobile banking, personal loans, account opening, or credit cards [4]. However, they do have predictive systems and/or models that determine approval and financial calculations based on variables such as interest rates, down payment, debt capacity, and loan term [5]. Despite this, the mortgage loan process is not fully optimized. Today, many banks still employ traditional methods, involving more effort from staff, infrastructure costs, in-person visits to the bank, and time loss in documentary activities [2]. With the support of trending technologies, the process can take approximately two weeks or less [5].

We address this issue in a Peruvian financial institution that has experienced a noticeable increase in requests for this type of loan, with a growth rate of 39%. However, the procedure used for its management and service is not timely. The company has very old core systems and manual activities that involve the verification of personal documents and the property. Moreover, it requires a lot of face-to-face contact with the client in locations called "Agency Branch" and "Home Loan Center." The approval of the mortgage loan takes approximately a month and a half. The entire process cannot be carried out 100% digitally due to regulations involving the Civil Code, Titles and Securities, and the General Financial Law [3]. While these are limitations for formalizing the loan and carrying out activities with the notary, other procedures can be optimized by applying a thorough analysis of operational processes and technology.

From the research, there are no in-depth studies focused on optimizing processes and enterprise architecture (EA) for the granting of mortgage loans. Studies such as [6–10] are related to bank entities and describe use of EA in financial services. Although, these investigations do not encompass a comprehensive analysis of the issues, motivations for the desired change, business, and technological situations that the process involves. In addition, they focus on the current business situation; for the most part, they do not suggest the necessary improvements to enhance the credit process. The scope of the investigations does not cover all phases of the EA and artifacts.

In this sense, the objective of this research is to provide an enterprise architecture model to a financial institution in Peru, focusing on the mortgage loan process. The key components of our research are formed by The Open Group Architecture Framework (TOGAF) and the Architecture Development Method (ADM) methodology. We cover the feasibility verification, pre-qualification, credit assessment, and property assessment processes.

Contribution. The main contribution lies in the improvements in the three core layers that support the reduction of manual tasks, customer service, and document management. As mentioned, this includes process improvement using Lean Six Sigma, information systems prototypes that leverage Artificial Intelligence (IA) for detecting manual and digital documents that will support both the personnel of the studied entity and the client in the loan application. Additionally, an architecture that supports applications using emerging technologies. On the other hand, as part of the experiment, we calculate the level of acceptance of the model by conducting a Delphi expert judgment. It is our knowledge that there are no systematic review investigations that use the Delphi technique in the evaluation of the motivation, strategy, and core layers of a financial institution. (i.e., Business, Applications, and Technology).

2   Method

The process for designing and validating the model is depicted. Firstly, in Stage 1, a business and IT analysis and diagnosis are conducted. This stage also includes the first two phases of ADM. Subsequently, in Stage 2, the architecture of the baseline and target enterprise is designed across its three layers. Additionally, documentation for the implementation phase and architecture governance (i.e., from phase E to phase H) was carried out integrated with Deming Cycle or PDCA (Plan, Do, Check, and Act). Finally, the model was validated in Stage 3.

2.1   Stage 1: Business and IT Analysis and Diagnosis

Preliminary Phase. Firstly, information was gathered from experts within the financial institution. General information about the company and its objectives was obtained through interviews and virtual meetings. Using the ADM and TOGAF as a reference, the current situation of the studied entity was analyzed to identify internal issues it faces and define a level of maturity. This was done through the analysis of strategic plans, digital transformation documentation, and brainstorming sessions. Subsequently, two quantitative tools, Ishikawa, and Pareto, were employed to identify causes and prioritize them. Afterward, the architecture principles that the proposed model will follow were defined.

Phase A: Architecture Vision. The scope, deliverables, motivations, and stakeholders' drivers were defined. The motivation and strategy layer were elaborated. This layer reflects the goals, objectives, and drivers (motivations) regarding the mortgage loan process. The diagram is segmented into 11 components: stakeholders, internal drivers, external drivers, assessments of the drivers, goals, outcomes to achieve, principles and requirements to be employed (See Fig. 1). On the other hand, strategies, capabilities, and resources necessary to achieve future goals and outcomes were discussed. It's important to design this layer to depict the current situation and outline an architecture that leads to a desired situation. The drivers perceived by stakeholders such as the customer, the planning management, and the IT management should be considered for the creation of the model and to project new changes in the organization's three core layers.

2.2   Stage 2: Enterprise Architecture Design

Once the diagnosis was completed, redundant activities, the absence of systems, and manual tasks were identified in the first four processes at this stage. Applying the phases of the ADM, solution blocks were developed in the three core layers. In Fig. 2, the integrated model by layers is visualized. The suggested improvements and new services are shown in a dark yellow shade for the business layer, light blue for the application layer, and green for the technology layer.

Phase B: Business Architecture. The process consists of 7 processes (See Fig. 2). For the process analysis, Lean Six Sigma methodologies were employed. Initially, the issue was defined and addressed at a general level in the preliminary phase. The bank's

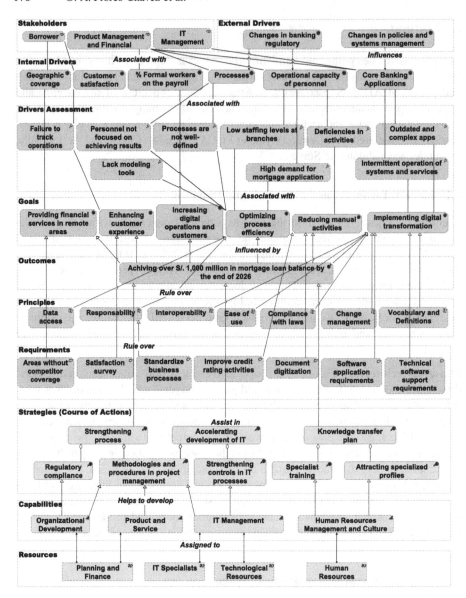

Fig. 1. Motivation and Strategy Layer.

value chain was examined, and SIPOC diagrams were developed to understand the mortgage credit business. Business Process Model and Notation (BPMN) diagrams were also created to model the flow of activities. Subsequently, Key Performance Indicators (KPIs) were defined to measure process performance, and the current performance was identified using data provided by the case study. Following this, causes were analyzed using Ishikawa and Pareto diagrams. A business gap analysis was conducted. Once these activities were completed, the improvement of the first four processes was proposed by incorporating information technologies and enhancing in-person and manual activities. Finally, improvement and control were described with a continuity plan detailed in phase H. Using ArchiMate notation, building blocks were diagrammed in the business layer, identifying actors, services, data obtained in each subprocess, and interfaces connecting the borrower and bank personnel. Subsequently, solution blocks were modeled.

Phase C: Information Systems Architectures. In the application layer, existing applications, modules, functionalities, and services were identified. The core software supporting the process is CRHP-SACH. Its functionalities include conducting credit assessment, recording prequalification information, property evaluation, recording public deeds, contract execution, and loan disbursement. Other supporting applications for the process include Sara Web for checking overdue payments of customers, savings accounts, and debts. There is also the Intranet, where customer credit history and status information can be accessed. Another application is the Web Portal, where customers can simulate and find information and requirements for applying for a mortgage loan. Finally, other supporting software were identified.

Two IT solutions are proposed based on requirements (See Fig. 2). In addition, user interface prototypes were developed to understand the flow of functionalities. These solutions are focused on streamlining activities for both internal actors and borrowers. Firstly, there is a system for online mortgage loan application and tracking called "Mortgage Credit". This platform allows the institution to provide traceability and transparency to the customer. It includes features such as identifying borrower information, conducting loan application and simulation, digitally delivering documentation for both the customer and the property, and tracking the application status until the disbursement phase. The second proposal is a web system called "Real State Title Study", which will assist specialist lawyers in gathering information related to the property to be acquired. This platform will provide a comprehensive profile of the residence in question, including details about the current owner, construction plans, location, photographs of the property. Additionally, it will be interconnected with the "Mortgage Credit" application to allow viewing of documents sent by the customer.

Phase D: Technology Architecture. The current infrastructure supporting the business process was identified, with applications being On Premise. It is suggested to incorporate the RENIEC web service (Citizen Identity Service) into the "Mortgage Credit" application to facilitate customer and/or cohabitant request registration. Additionally, there is a recommendation to contract cloud computing services to host the proposed web applications. Amazon Web Services (AWS) is proposed as Platform as a Service (PaaS) (See Fig. 2) because it promotes cost reduction associated with physical servers and maintenance, improves information security, and ensures greater availability and operability of the applications.

In addition to the above, it is proposed to automate document verification driven by AI, Machine Learning, and Optical Character Recognition (OCR). We suggest using AWS APIs: Amazon Textract and Amazon Comprehend (See Fig. 2). Through pre-trained models, the proposed applications will consume both AI services to validate scanned and handwritten documents requested by the commercial manager of the financial institution in the early stages of the process. Activities such as document verification and validation, which require significant effort and time from agencies and mortgage

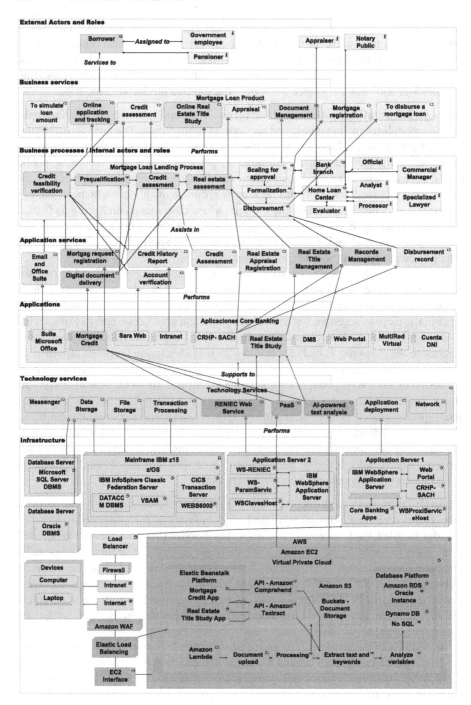

Fig. 2. Integrated Model of Enterprise Architecture in its three core layers.

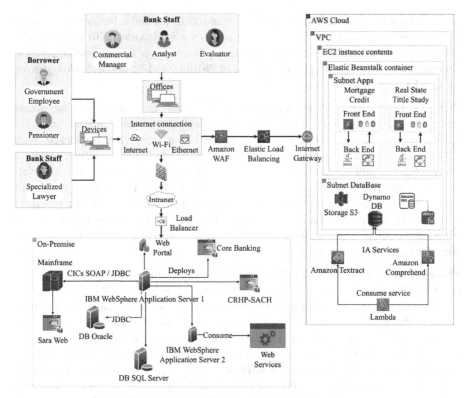

Fig. 3. Physical Architecture of the Technology Layer.

centers, can be streamlined through these technologies. Figure 3 represents the physical architecture of the technological components that will provide support to the business process. It also visualizes the main users of the applications, on-premises components, and the deployment of applications in the cloud.

Phase E: Opportunities and Solutions. In this phase, according to PDCA Cycle, the implementation of the architecture is planned. Documentation is developed to create the project portfolio based on the suggested changes in the three layers. The projects to be executed were defined, involving process redesign, solution development, cost estimation, and a future cloud migration plan. Firstly, key attributes of the desired situation and business constraints for its implementation are identified. Subsequently, we evaluate solution alternatives based on the gaps identified in each core layer of the case study. Lastly, the migration strategy was defined using the PMBOK (Project Manager Book of Knowledge) and Scrum methodology. Finally, candidate projects were defined.

Phase F: Migration Planning. In this phase, according to PDCA Cycle, the implementation of the architecture is done. The scope of this research does not involve implementation. However, for Phase F, a foundational documentation for the architecture migration with the proposed changes was created, evaluating the cost-benefit of the projects. Firstly, the stakeholders involved were identified, and a business case feasibility analysis was developed. Next, a risk analysis was elaborated. To conclude, the projects were prioritized based on cost and time. As a result of this, an implementation roadmap was generated. We propose the use of PMBOK and Scrum methodologies for the development of candidate projects.

Phase G: Implementation Governance. In this phase, procedures were developed for monitoring the implementation of the target architecture, as mentioned in Phase F. According to PDCA Cycle, the implementation of the architecture is checked. With PMBOK, projects can be managed comprehensively from initiation to closure, considering scope, costs, time, and resources as outlined in the guide. Additionally, for the development of applications, Scrum is suggested as an agile method. Through user stories and phases of this methodology, the collection of requirements, interface design, programming, testing, and production deployment will be more flexible among the teams. This allows for feedback, tracking progress of deliverables, reporting issues, and suggesting ideas for increased productivity.

Phase H: Architecture Change Management. In this final phase, procedures were developed for change management, risk management, and decision-making. According to PDCA Cycle, actions are taken in response to changes after implementing improvements in the three core layers. Considering the migrated target architecture with the improvements and implemented IT solutions, a continuity plan is required to ensure the proper functioning of the applications and incident management. First, we defined support roles and the procedure to follow. Then, we proposed the use of Information Technology Infrastructure Library (ITIL) for IT service management. The documented plan covers descriptions and actions to be taken in the management of incidents, problems, changes, service levels, security, and availability.

2.3 Stage 3: Enterprise Architecture Model Validation

According to [11], the Delphi method allows for obtaining a consensus level among experts by evaluating a series of characteristics, criteria, or items using questionnaires or other artifacts. Several rounds are conducted until the proposed level is achieved. Three phases of the experiment were established:

Planning and Preparation. The first phase involves identifying a panel of experts, and the selection should be based on certain requirements [11]. For the panel, professionals with at least 5 years of experience working in the financial institution were prioritized. They should possess knowledge in information technologies and digital media, process optimization, and, most importantly, expertise in the mortgage loan granting process. Therefore, individuals from the Information Technology Department, Planning Department, Product Management and Financial Inclusion Department, and the Mortgage Loans Department were contacted to include the most qualified and involved collaborators in the process. The panel consisted of 10 experts. The study was conducted online, where invitations were sent to the respondents via institutional email, accompanied by a brief introduction to the artifacts that make up the EA model and a questionnaire created with Google Forms. Each participant was assigned a code (i.e., E1

= Expert One, E2 = Expert Two, etc.), and anonymity was maintained among them and their responses. Their opinions were not revealed until the first round was completed, and subsequently in the second round. According to [12] maintaining confidentiality among participants allows for considering the opinions of others and helps mitigate bias or influences.

Table 1. Validation Questionnaire.

Dimension	N°	Item
Architecture's Vision	1	Drivers and assessments identified reflect the current situation
	2	Set goals will allow us to achieve a desired situation
	3	Strategies proposed will allow us to achieve goals
Business Processes	4	The TO BE feasibility verification process is appropriate
	5	The TO BE prequalification process is appropriate
	6	The TO BE credit assessment process is appropriate
	7	The TO BE Real estate assessment process is appropriate
IT Solutions	8	Functionalities of "Mortgage Credit" application provide support to the process
	9	Prototypes of "Mortgage Credit" are user-friendly and reflect the functionalities
	10	Functionalities of the "Real State Title Study" application provide support for the process
	11	"Real State Title Study" prototypes are user-friendly and reflect the functionalities
Emerging Technologies	12	Interoperability of proposed IT solutions with CRHP-SACH
	13	Use of Amazon Textract for the detection of digital texts
	14	Use of Amazon Comprehend API for the detection of handwritten, scanned, and photographed texts
	15	Disposition of the organization to contract cloud services
Intention to Use	16	TOGAF and deliverables are useful for process optimization
	17	The implementation of the model in the bank is feasible
	18	The EA model has a positive impact on the bank and services

Table 1 represents the questionnaire consisting of 18 items and 5 dimensions covering various characteristics of the model. It also includes free-text fields for entering comments and justifying the choice of score for each item [11]. Using the 5-point Likert scale as suggested by [11–13]; participants were required to rate each item (1 =

"Strongly Disagree", 2 = "Disagree", 3 = "Neither Agree nor Disagree", 4 = "Agree" and 5 = "Strongly Agree").

As seen in Table 1, the first dimension (DIM1) is about the architecture vision, encompassing the motivation and strategy layers. DIM2 covers improvements and redesigns to business processes. DIM3 deals with the proposed information systems to support the business. DIM4 details the technologies to be used and changes in the technology layer. Lastly, DIM5 is about the intention to implement the EA model in the case study.

Experts Evaluation. At the start of the first round, the questionnaire was provided to the experts, and they were given a maximum response time of 7 days. Once the deadline was reached, we collected the data and comments. Expert opinions were considered to improve the model and present it in the second round. Additionally, participants were asked to re-evaluate the items from the previous round or maintain their responses if they deemed it appropriate. In the second round, experts were given another 7 days, like the first round.

Data Analysis and Reporting. The last phase aims to analyze the results of each round. A report is prepared, including both quantitative and qualitative analysis related to expert comments using IBM SPSS software. To achieve greater effectiveness in the level of consensus, three statistical measurements were used, as suggested by [13] in their research: (i) Interquartile Range (IQR), (ii) Sample Standard Deviation (SD), and (iii) 51% of expert responses falling within the 4–5-point scale.

"High Consensus" is achieved when the IQR is between 0 and 1, and it complies with the two mentioned measures. "Moderate Consensus" when the IQR is between 1.01 and 1.99, and "No Consensus" when the IQR value is 2.0 or higher [12]. Furthermore, to calculate the standard deviation with a sample of 10 experts, the value should be below 1.5. At the end of each round, the consensus level for each item and the overall acceptance of the model were calculated.

3 Results and Discussion

3.1 Quantitative

The Table 2 presents the calculations made during Round 1 of the Delphi process. It shows the score for each item provided by the participants. Additionally, calculations for the median (Mdn), mean (M), and the three combinatorial measures are included to assess the level of consensus. Each item was assigned a correlational code (I). It was identified that three items did not meet the criteria for the level of consensus. In I11 and I17, both SD and the percentage of responses in the 4–5 Likert range fit within the established limits, but the IQR obtained for both items are 1.25. This indicates that consensus among experts is moderate for these items. On the other hand, there is no consensus at all for item I15. Only the SD value (1.05) is met, but the IQR values (2.00) and the 4–5% (40%) do not surpass the proposed level.

Despite this, most items (15 in total) obtained consensus from the experts in the first round, as seen in Table 2. Items I1 and I12 achieved very high consensus because the IQR is below 0.25, SD is below 1.5, and over 70% of responses fall within the 4–5 Likert scale. Additionally, items I7 and I10 resulted in absolute consensus, meeting all three criteria, with an IQR value of 0.00. This indicates approval of the proposed improvements to the property evaluation process and functionalities for the "Real State Title Study" application. The other items (i.e., from I2 to I6, I8, I9, I13, I14, I16, and I18) also meet all three combinatory measures, with an IQR value at the established limit (1.00).

Table 2. Results of Round N°1 Delphi.

	E1	E2	E3	E4	E5	E6	E7	E8	E9	E10	Mdn	IQR	M	SD	4–5%
I1	4	4	4	5	4	4	4	4	5	4	4.00	**0.25**	4.20	**0.42**	**100%**
I2	4	5	4	5	5	5	4	4	5	4	4.50	**1.00**	4.50	**0.53**	**100%**
I3	4	5	4	4	4	5	5	5	4	4	4.00	**1.00**	4.40	**0.52**	**100%**
I4	3	3	4	4	4	4	3	5	4	2	4.00	**1.00**	3.60	**0.84**	**60%**
I5	4	3	4	4	4	3	4	4	5	3	4.00	**1.00**	3.80	**0.63**	**70%**
I6	4	3	4	4	3	4	4	3	4	3	4.00	**1.00**	3.60	**0.52**	**60%**
I7	4	4	4	5	4	4	4	4	4	3	4.00	**0.00**	4.00	**0.47**	**90%**
I8	4	3	4	5	4	5	5	4	5	4	4.00	**1.00**	4.30	**0.67**	**90%**
I9	4	4	4	4	4	5	5	5	4	3	4.00	**1.00**	4.20	**0.63**	**90%**
I10	4	5	4	4	4	4	4	4	4	4	4.00	**0.00**	4.10	**0.32**	**100%**
I11	4	5	4	4	3	4	4	3	5	2	4.00	1.25	3.80	**0.92**	**70%**
I12	3	3	4	4	4	5	4	4	4	4	4.00	**0.25**	3.90	**0.57**	**80%**
I13	3	5	4	5	4	4	4	4	5	4	4.00	**1.00**	4.20	**0.63**	**90%**
I14	4	5	4	5	4	4	5	4	4	3	4.00	**1.00**	4.20	**0.63**	**90%**
I15	2	3	4	3	4	3	4	2	4	1	3.00	2.00	3.00	**1.05**	40%
I16	4	5	5	4	4	5	5	4	5	4	4.50	**1.00**	4.50	**0.53**	**100%**
I17	3	5	5	4	4	4	4	3	5	4	4.00	1.25	4.10	**0.74**	**80%**
I18	3	5	4	5	5	5	5	4	5	4	5.00	**1.00**	4.50	**0.71**	**90%**

Table 3 presents the results of round 2. Only one item (I15) did not achieve high consensus. Although the IQR is 0.25 and the standard deviation (0.82) falls within the allowed range, the percentage of responses in the 4–5 Likert scale is only 10%. However, there was an improvement in the level of consensus for the other items. These items obtained 100% of responses in the 4–5 scale and an IQR of 0.00, indicating absolute consensus among the experts. These items include: I1 to I6, I9, I11-I14, I16 and I17. It's also worth noting that I11 and I17 shifted to high consensus compared to round 1, where they did not achieve convergence.

Table 3. Results of Round N°2 Delphi.

	E1	E2	E3	E4	E5	E6	E7	E8	E9	E10	Mdn	IQR	M	SD	4–5%
I1	5	5	4	5	5	5	5	5	5	5	5.00	0.00	4.90	0.32	100%
I2	4	5	5	5	5	5	5	5	5	5	5.00	0.00	4.90	0.32	100%
I3	5	5	5	5	5	5	5	5	5	5	5.00	0.00	5.00	0.00	100%
I4	4	5	5	5	5	5	5	5	5	5	5.00	0.00	4.90	0.32	100%
I5	5	5	5	5	5	5	5	5	5	5	5.00	0.00	5.00	0.00	100%
I6	4	5	5	5	5	5	5	5	5	5	5.00	0.00	4.90	0.32	100%
I7	4	5	5	5	5	4	5	5	5	5	5.00	0.25	4.80	0.42	100%
I8	5	5	5	5	4	5	5	5	4	4	5.00	1.00	4.70	0.48	100%
I9	5	5	5	5	5	5	5	5	5	5	5.00	0.00	5.00	0.00	100%
I10	5	4	5	4	4	4	5	5	4	4	4.00	1.00	4.40	0.52	100%
I11	5	5	5	5	5	5	5	5	5	5	5.00	0.00	5.00	0.00	100%
I12	5	5	4	5	5	5	5	5	5	5	5.00	0.00	4.90	0.32	100%
I13	5	5	5	5	5	5	5	5	5	5	5.00	0.00	5.00	0.00	100%
I14	5	5	5	5	5	5	5	5	5	5	5.00	0.00	5.00	0.00	100%
I15	3	5	3	3	2	3	3	3	3	2	3.00	0.25	3.00	0.82	10%
I16	5	5	5	5	5	5	5	5	5	5	5.00	0.00	5.00	0.00	100%
I17	5	5	5	5	5	5	5	5	5	5	5.00	0.00	5.00	0.00	100%
I18	5	4	5	5	5	5	5	5	5	4	5.00	0.25	4.80	0.42	100%

3.2 Qualitative

Some comments regarding the motivation and strategy layer in DIM1 indicate that it does reflect the bank's reality. Concerning DIM2, experts suggest improving the flow of the feasibility verification, prequalification, and property evaluation processes. They recommend specifying the types of tasks in BPMN and which ones will be automated with the applications. For DIM3, they suggest improving the prototypes, making them more interactive like a simulation. In DIM4, experts comment that for interoperability, adjustments to the CRHP-SACH software will be needed. Regarding the use of AWS APIs, they mention that it will expedite the verification process for certain documents, assist in keyword searches, and identify key information. Finally, in DIM5, they believe that the project is viable for the bank, considering management decisions, funding, technology services, and human resources. In the second round, most of the comments were short phrases or words indicating approval of the presented and improved items.

3.3 Discussions

For the selection of the Delphi method as a validation technique, a systematic review was conducted on its application in evaluating enterprise architectures, highlighted in [12], where a proposal for EA in the public sector of Malaysia was made. For this experiment, 13 experts were selected, completing a 42-item questionnaire. However, Delphi was used to determine factors to consider when designing and implementing an enterprise architecture, without validating a TO BE model for the analyzed business process, one that includes optimization improvements. On the other hand, the result of this study was achieved with the consensus of 17 items evaluating every aspect of the proposal, including processes, enterprise architecture terms, applied technologies and IT solutions. It is worth noting that, based on the research conducted, no other EA models validated using the Delphi method have been found.

Some of the suggested comments from the first round were considered to improve the redesigned processes, prototypes, and conducting benchmarking and benefits analysis of cloud computing and AWS. After the second round, which resulted in a higher number of items achieving high consensus, the experiment was concluded. As a result, the overall level of acceptance of the model in Round 1 was 83% with 15 items reaching high consensus. Then, in Round 2, the level increased to 94%, with 17 items obtaining high convergence of opinions. Table 4 provides a summary of the experiment results in both Delphi rounds.

After results, it can be interpreted that most of the evaluated participants agree with the implementation of the proposed architecture, along with the developed applications and the supporting technologies, validating that their use could benefit in performing certain tasks such as title research, document reception, and the traceability of the loan application. However, there is also a concern about the costs of the required technological services to maintain it, as it should be implemented for all offices nationwide, considering the access of certain provinces to the internet, mobile devices, or computers.

Table 4. Summary of results of items grouped by dimension.

Dimension	No. of items	Proportion of items where consensus was achieved (n)	
		Round 1	Round 2
Architecture's Vision	3	100% (3)	100% (3)
Business Processes	4	100% (4)	100% (4)
IT Solutions	4	75% (3)	100% (4)
Emerging Technologies	4	75% (3)	75% (3)
Intention to Use	3	67% (2)	100% (3)
TOTAL	18	83%	94%

4 Conclusions

The deficiencies in the mortgage loan lending processes at the case study institution stem from their lack of digitization, limited personnel, delays in document and signature collection from the client. The implementation of EA model using TOGAF and ADM suggests beneficial changes for the financial institution, which will lead to a desired situation in terms of process automation along with information technologies. Furthermore, this proposal could serve as a reference for other banking institutions.

Using the Delphi method, feedback was obtained from experts in rounds 1 and 2. This achieved a 94% level of acceptance for the enterprise architecture and its 5 dimensions. Positive responses and suggestions for improving the deliverables of each core business layer were also obtained. It is recommended to choose experts with sufficient knowledge in the field, establish response deadlines, request detailed feedback, not short answers and to base their rating choices on the criteria.

Regarding limitations, since it involves a nationally reaching financial institution, the focus is on a proposal for enterprise architecture, as implementing this would require a greater number of resources, time, and funding. On the other hand, there are also some political limitations that do not allow for the complete digitization of the mortgage loan process. Therefore, only the processes were analyzed, and systems were developed to support their automation without affecting or violating any regulations. Future work includes developing the proposed technological solutions and implementing EA. Additionally, when regulations change, other tasks such as property appraisal, contract or document signing that require the presence of notaries could also be automated.

Financing.   Universidad Peruana de Ciencias Aplicadas / UPC-EXPOST-2023–2.

Gratitude.   The authors thank the evaluators for their important suggestions that have allowed a significant improvement of this work. Likewise, to the Research Department of the Universidad Peruana de Ciencias Aplicadas for the support provided to carry out this research work through the UPC-EXPOST-2023–2 incentive.

References

1. Iosifidi, M., Panopoulou, E., Tsoumas, C.: Mortgage loan demand and banks' operational efficiency. J. Financ. Stab. **53**, 100851 (2021). https://doi.org/10.1016/J.JFS.2021.100851
2. Raygada Castillo, M.Á.: Créditos Hipotecarios Digitales en el Perú: estudio y análisis., Lima (2022)
3. Miguel Ángel Raygada Castillo: ¿Es posible celebrar contratos de créditos hipotecarios digitales en el Perú?*. Giuristi: Revista de Derecho Corporativo **3**(6), 4–20 (2022). https://doi.org/10.46631/Giuristi.2022.v3n6.03
4. Miñán, W.: La banca peruana finalmente se digitaliza: adiós a las oficinas, todo será por apps (2023). https://www.america-retail.com/peru/la-banca-peruana-finalmente-se-digitaliza-ahora-todo-sera-por-apps/
5. García, E.: TU DINERO: Ahora se desembolsan créditos hipotecarios hasta en un día (2019). https://gestion.pe/tu-dinero/desembolsan-creditos-hipotecarios-dia-272918-noticia/
6. Gunawan, E., Sutedja, I.: Using enterprise architecture with the open group architecture forum to design information technology plan gap analysis at Bank Pengkreditan Rakyat (BPR). In: Proceedings of 2018 International Conference on Information Management and Technology (ICIMTech), pp. 388–393 (2018). https://doi.org/10.1109/ICIMTECH.2018.8528094
7. Ugarte, D., Santos, B., Mauricio, D.: Enterprise architecture for credits in the microfinance sector in Peru. In: Proceedings of the 2018 IEEE 38th Central America and Panama Convention, CONCAPAN 2018. (2018). https://doi.org/10.1109/CONCAPAN.2018.8596613

8. Saputra, F.B., Rahmania, E.: Banking information system study through enterprise architecture TOGAF. NEWTON: Network. Inform. Technol. **2**(1), 43–50 (2022). https://doi.org/10.32764/newton.v2i1.2597

9. Rachman, F.P., Indrajid, E., Dazki, E.: Enterprise architecture for banking in the industrial revolution era 4.0. JHSS (J. Human. Social Stud.) **6**(2), 142–148 (2022). https://doi.org/10.33751/jhss.v6i2.5394

10. Gunadham, T., Ahmed Mohammed, E.M.: Solving challenges in an electronic banking services company by implementing enterprise architecture. J. Inf. Knowl. Manag. **12**, 252–261 (2022)

11. Richard Skinner, R., Nelson, R., Chin, W.W., Land, L.: The Delphi method research strategy in studies of information systems. Commun. Assoc. Inform. Syst. **37**, 31–63 (2015). https://doi.org/10.17705/1CAIS.03702

12. Sumarni Hussein, S., Maarop, N., Mahrin, M.N., Abu Bakar, N.A.: A Delphi technique as a method to obtain consensus in validation of EA readiness assessment model. Open Int. J. Inform. (OIJI). **6**, 1–13 (2018)

13. Giannarou, L., Zervas, E.: Using Delphi technique to build consensus in practice. Int. J. Business Sci. Appl. Manage. **9**, 65–82 (2014)

Adaptive Learning App for ADHD in Lima Schools

Carlos David Del Pino Herrera[(⊠)] ⓘ, Emilio Adolfo Pinedo Solis ⓘ,
and Emilio Antonio Herrera Trujillo ⓘ

Faculty of Engineering, Universidad Peruana de Ciencias Aplicadas, Lima, Peru
{u201918034,u201513973,pcsieher}@upc.edu.pe

Abstract. Education is fundamental for all children, but those with neurological disorders, such as attention deficit hyperactivity disorder (ADHD), have specific learning needs that are not addressed by traditional educational methods. This project focuses on the creation of a mobile application that employs machine learning algorithms to evaluate the progress of these children through regression methods, focusing on mathematical problem solving in elementary schools in Lima. Results have shown that this initiative has improved the understanding and performance of children with ADHD, highlighting the potential of mobile technology and machine learning to move towards a more inclusive and effective education for this group of students. This project has proven to be a valuable tool in the educational field. The inclusion of technological tools such as the mobile app has allowed personalization in teaching, adapting the content and pace of learning to the individual needs of each student with ADHD. In addition, the use of machine learning has enabled a continuous and accurate monitoring of their progress, identifying areas for improvement early on.

Keywords: ADHD · Educational method · children · student · mindfulness · random forest · machine learning · Lima

1 Introduction

Facing the challenges of attention deficit hyperactivity disorder (ADHD), an innovative approach based on Machine Learning and the cloud has been presented. This solution focuses on the development of a mobile application that uses regression algorithms, such as Random Forest, to personalize the learning experience by estimating the levels of children with ADHD. This method, divided into four key stages, combines Mindfulness strategies, progressive data capture, analysis through Machine Learning, and result projection. The algorithm's implementation takes place in Azure Machine Learning Studio, leveraging a Linux environment, and achieves an accuracy of 94%. This project aims to enhance the mathematical understanding of children with ADHD, positively impacting their academic performance and quality of life.

M. Botto-Tobar et al. (Eds.): ICAT 2023, CCIS 2051, pp. 190–213, 2024.
https://doi.org/10.1007/978-3-031-58950-8_14

1.1 Context

ADHD is a disorder affecting between 5%–7% of the world's population (Demontis et al. 2018) and affecting people's concentration, focus, ability to follow instructions and organizational skills, which impacts their performance in multiple areas of their lives (Steinau 2013).

It should be noted that ADHD is a genuine neurological disorder, not attributable to lack of effort or discipline, and its origin is linked to a combination of genetic and environmental factors, according to research (NIH, 2021). As a result, a Machine Learning-based solution has been proposed to aid the understanding of people with ADHD by solving mathematical equations. The solution is based on cloud computing, through services such as Azure, to save time and economic resources.

To develop the Machine Learning-based solution, several inputs were needed. These inputs will be the questionnaires of children with ADHD, which contain information about their symptoms and the resolutions of mathematical equations of various levels.

For the development of the mobile application, the Android Studio development environment was used, which is an environment for programming applications for mobile devices. This development environment offers a wide variety of tools, which allows to create attractive and entertaining mobile applications for users.

Solutions have been proposed to improve the learning and skills of children with ADHD through mobile applications. One such solution is the application "Mobile application with reinforcement activities for children with ADHD" (Ruiz-Ledesma, Bautista-Rosales, & Garay-Jiménez, 2022), which offers ADHD activities to improve concentration, and assessments for parents. The use of artificial intelligence-driven personalized assistance tools is also being investigated, according to the article "Artificial intelligence-enabled personalized assistance tools to improve the education of children with neurodevelopmental disorders" (Barua et al., 2022). Also, in Peru, the TCT method, created by Dr. Kazuhiro Tajima Pozo, improves cognitive areas through brief 10-min cognitive training sessions (Opticos Optometristas, n.d.).

2 Contribution

This research focuses on developing a mobile application that provides math exercises to children with ADHD, adapting the difficulty according to their progress through the use of machine learning and regression algorithms. The application uses random forest algorithms to vary the difficulty of the proposed exercises, thus personalizing the learning experience for each child based on their performance and individual characteristics.

As can be seen in Fig. 1, the method consists of 4 steps. The four stages encompassed the design of an effective strategy for addressing ADHD in children, opting for Mindfulness. The subsequent focus on data collection / data acquisition involved developing a mobile app for children to progressively solve tailor-made exercises. The third stage employed machine learning, specifically the Random Forest algorithm, to analyze collected data and personalize treatment based on individual performance. The concluding phase seamlessly integrated the proposed elements, merging Mindfulness techniques, tiered continuous resolution, and machine learning. This synthesis holds

Fig. 1. Steps of the implementation

promising implications for positively impacting the enhancement of ADHD treatment and fostering academic performance improvements in children.

3   Material and Method

3.1   Related Works

The field of mobile applications for children with ADHD, specifically in the context of enhancing mathematical equation-solving skills, has seen considerable research. Unlike previous studies that primarily focus on improving attention, our project concentrates on developing equation-solving skills through relaxation and meditation techniques. Paper 01,"UvaMate: a serious game to learn mathematics for children with ADHD: usability evaluation," assesses the usability of a game designed to aid mathematical learning in children with ADHD (Calleros, Guerrero-García, & Navarro-Rangel, 2020). Teachers express satisfaction with its ease of use but suggest improvements. Paper 02 explores the "Effectiveness of web-based play therapy intervention to support the development of children with ADHD," finding web-based play therapy effective for emotional, behavioral, and social development (Budiyarti, Agustini, Hayati, Panjaitan, & Hakim, 2023). However, it centers more on emotional and social aspects than mathematical understanding. Paper 03 discusses a "Mobile application with reinforcement activities for children with ADHD," focusing on detecting ADHD and improving attention levels through modular exercises and assessments (Ruiz-Ledesma et al., 2022). Paper 04, "Artificial Intelligence-Enabled Personalized Assistance Tools to Enhance the Education of Children with Neurodevelopmental Disorders: A Review," explores AI-based tools for students with neurodevelopmental disorders, emphasizing the need for advanced tools to address current limitations and the importance of personalization in education (Barua et al., 2022).

3.2   Method

The choice of Azure provided a scalable cloud environment, complemented by a Linux setup for computational efficiency. The algorithm processed relevant student data, including academic history and demographic information, as input. Multiple tasks were executed in Azure for testing, resulting in the high accuracy observed. This approach demonstrates the effectiveness of combining cloud-based machine learning tools with a well-configured algorithm for improving predictions in ADHD students' academic outcomes.

The data collection was carried out through the prototype application, where students began solving exercises that were arranged in increasing degree of difficulty. These preliminary data were uploaded to the Azure platform, where the Random Forest algorithm was executed. The Random Forest algorithm was used to determine the level at which the student is performing when solving mathematical exercises, as illustrated in Fig. 2:

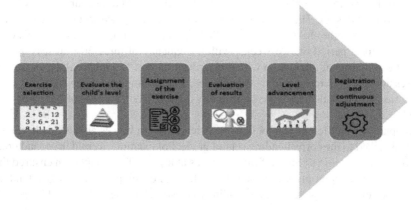

Fig. 2. Process of the random forest algorithm

a. Exercise Selection: When the learner logs into the application, the random forest will be responsible for selecting the next exercise to solve.
b. Evaluate child's level: The random forest will consider the current difficulty level of the student, which was determined based on his/her current grade and previous progress in the application.
c. Assignment of the exercise: Based on the student's level, the application will select a mathematical exercise of equations that is within the expected difficulty.
d. Evaluation of results: The evaluation of results in the application is based on the accuracy of students' answers. If an exercise is solved correctly, a point is added to their progress at that level.
e. Level Advancement: Student progress is based on their performance; solving enough exercises correctly takes them to the next level with higher challenges, while poor performance brings them easier exercises to provide support.
f. Registration and continuous adjustment: The random forest tracks learner performance across exercises and levels, enabling regular adjustments in exercise difficulty and adaptation, ensuring a personalized and effective learning experience.

4   Results

In this section, the results obtained through the experiment designed for improving comprehension and resolution of mathematical problems in children diagnosed with ADHD are discussed. The results show significant advances in the development of mathematical skills, evidencing the effectiveness of personalized approaches in the education of this population.

Experiment Overview: Over a three-week period, 20 children diagnosed with ADHD participated in the experiment. These children aged between 6 to 10 years old, ranging from first through fifth grade of elementary school. This diverse range allowed peda-gogical strategies and learning techniques to be adjusted to the individual needs of each child. A crucial approach was to adapt the difficulty of the exercises according to each child's ability to solve mathematical problems. If a child showed progress at a certain level of difficulty, more challenging exercises were presented to encourage growth.

Experiment design: The experiment was conducted in a face-to-face manner, with the participation of the children in a controlled environment. Each child used the mobile application for a period of two weeks, with a frequency of three 30-min sessions per week, the total time of interaction with the application was 120 min each week. During each session, the children solved math exercises, mainly simple addition and subtraction operations, with a gradual increase in difficulty after a certain number of exercises were solved.

Adaptation to Different School Grades: A level system was established, where each level was linked to the corresponding school grade. For example, a child in second grade started at level 0, while a child in fifth grade was at level 3. This adaptation ensured that the exercises were appropriate for each child's level of development and understanding, encouraging consistent progress and avoiding excessive challenges (Rincon-Flores et al., 2023).

Incorporation of Mindfulness Meditation: In the experiment, mindfulness meditation exercises were introduced and performed daily for 10 min at the beginning of each session. These exercises improved the concentration and focus of the ADHD children, as well as maintained them interested in the learning process.

Motivation and Reinforcement: Reward systems were implemented to maintain the children's motivation. After having completed a level of exercises, teachers or parents delivered motivational and congratulatory messages, additionally, upon the successful completion of each session, treats were offered which acted as incentives.

Measurement Variables: The primary variable assessed in the experiment was the math-learning progress of children with ADHD. Pre- and post-experiment tests, along with observations and performance records during the interaction sessions with the app were used to assess this progress.

Privacy Policy: Anonymous information about the use of the app, including system data, was collected. This information was used only to personalize the user experience and improve the functionality of the application. To conduct this experiment, during the process parents were informed about the use of the data and reassured that these would not be shared with third parties to protect security and prevent the unauthorized use of the data. Data collection was conducted solely for academic purposes and not for commercial or production purposes. This transparency and ethical commitment are fundamental in the project's approach, ensuring respect for the privacy and confidentiality of the collected information.

Detailed Results: The results obtained from the experiment are explained below:

a. Experimental protocol: To carry out the experiment, three-level-difficulty adaptive mathematical exercises were designed specifically for children aged 6 to 8 years with ADHD. In the experiment, 20 children participated using a mobile application for a week, solving a total of 12 exercises per day they had an option of using hints and tips in case help was needed. In addition, meditation breaks and surveys using the Likert scale were implemented to prevent fatigue.

Table 1. Summary of results obtained from 20 students. See Appendix 1 for more details

No	Stage	Iteration	Correct	Incorrect	Current level
1	1	2	24	12	H
2	0	2	26	10	M
3	1	2	20	16	H
4	1	3	19	20	M
5	0	1	22	14	E
6	0	1	19	14	M
7	0	2	21	15	H
8	1	2	20	15	H
9	1	2	22	14	M
10	1	1	24	12	H
11	1	1	24	12	H
12	0	3	22	15	H
13	0	2	19	13	M
14	0	2	21	15	M
15	1	2	23	13	H
16	1	2	22	14	H
17	0	3	24	12	M
18	0	2	21	15	M
19	0	1	18	15	M
20	0	1	24	12	M

b. Results: Despite facing significant challenges while tackling the exercises of greater difficulty, a significant progress in solving medium-difficulty problems was noticed. In the results of the satisfaction surveys, it is important to highlight that the strategy of promoting a positive environment and the inclusion of mindfulness exercises was well-received by the participants (for more details, see Appendix). The project utilized Azure Machine Learning Studio for developing and deploying a Random Forest algorithm, achieving a remarkable 94% accuracy in predicting academic performance for students with ADHD.

Table 1 shows the results in the solution of algebraic problems of a 20-student sample. Some fields included are: stage in which they are, iteration with the highest number of correct answers, number of correct and incorrect answers and the level in which they are in the last iteration (easy, medium or difficult). Overall, the results of the experiment emphasize the importance of customizing educational strategies to the individual needs of children with ADHD.

The physical and logical architecture of the research project is shown below (Figs. 3 and 4):

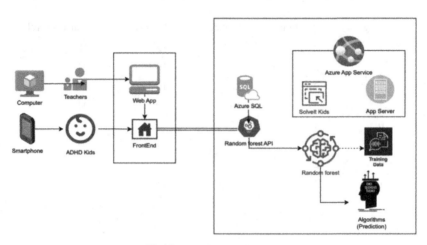

Fig. 3. Physical architecture

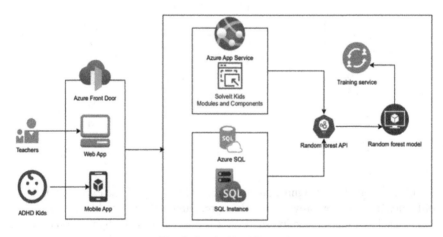

Fig. 4. Logical architecture

In the presented logical and physical architectures, users gain access to the targeted platform via an Android device. This device initiates the front-end interface of the application, prompting children to log in and engage with the exercises. User profiles are managed through a database, while services and the algorithm operate in the Azure cloud, utilizing the Azure database to store student outcomes. Subsequently, the data undergoes processing through the Random Forest algorithm. Caregivers or educators can review the results by connecting through a data analysis program, such as Power BI, equipped with tools to visualize this data through a dedicated web application associated with the program.

5   Conclusions

The method used in the experiment, which involved a mobile application with personalized math exercises for children with ADHD, demonstrated significant progress in the development of mathematical skills. The use of machine-learning and regression algorithms to adapt the difficulty of the exercises according to each child's progress was a key component of the method. Additionally, the incorporation of mindfulness meditation exercises and the implementation of a reward system contributed to maintaining the children's motivation and engagement.

However, it is important to note that the small sample size of 20 children and the short trial duration of two weeks may have limited the generalizability of the results. A larger sample and a longer trial period would possibly provide a more comprehensive understanding of the effectiveness of the method in the long term. Additionally, a longer trial period would allow the observation of sustained progress as well as to identify any potential challenges or limitations that may arise over time.

In conclusion, while the method applied ensures the improvement mathematical skills of children with ADHD, the limitations of the small sample size and short trial duration should be taken into consideration when interpreting the results. Future research with a larger and more random sample, as well as a longer trial period, would provide a more in-depth assessment of the method's effectiveness in the education of children with ADHD.

Financing.   Universidad Peruana de Ciencias Aplicadas / UPC-EXPOST-2023-2.

Gratitude.   The authors thank the evaluators for their important suggestions that have allowed a significant improvement of this work. Likewise, to the Research Department of the Universidad Peruana de Ciencias Aplicadas for the support provided to carry out this research work through the UPC-EXPOST-2023-2 incentive.

Appendix

	Student 1			Student 2			Student 3			Student 4		
Etapa	1			0			1			1		
Iterations	Iteration 1	Iteration 2	Iteration 3	Iteration 1	Iteration 2	Iteration 3	Iteration 1	Iteration 2	Iteration 3	Iteration 1	Iteration 2	Iteration 3
Level	Easy	Easy	Hard	Easy	Easy	Hard	Easy	Easy	Hard	Easy	Hard	Easy
Resolution 1	True	True	True	True	True	False	True	True	True	True	True	True
Resolution 2	True	True	False	True	True	False	True	True	True	True	False	True
Resolution 3	True	True	True	True	False	False	True	True	False	True	False	True
Level	Medium	Medium	Hard	Medium	Medium	Medium	Medium	Medium	Hard	Medium	Medium	Medium
Resolution 4	False	True	False	True	True	True	True	False	False	True	True	True
Resolution 5	True	True	True	False	False	False	False	True	False	True	False	True
Resolution 6	True	True	False	False	False	True	True	True	False	False	True	False
Likert Survey	4	5	3	2	1	4	4	4	3	3	4	5
Level	Hard	Hard	Medium	Easy	Easy	Hard	Hard	Hard	Medium	Hard	Hard	Hard
Resolution 7	False	False	True	True	True	False	False	True	True	False	False	True
Resolution 8	False	False	True	False	True	False	False	False	False	False	False	False

(continued)

(continued)

	Student 1			Student 2			Student 3			Student 4		
Etapa	1			0			1			1		
Iterations	Iteration 1	Iteration 2	Iteration 3	Iteration 1	Iteration 2	Iteration 3	Iteration 1	Iteration 2	Iteration 3	Iteration 1	Iteration 2	Iteration 3
Resolution 9	False	True	True	True	True	True	False	False	True	False	False	False
Level	Medium	Medium	Hard	Medium	Medium	Medium	Medium	Medium	Hard	Medium	Medium	Medium
Resolution 10	False	True	True	True	True	True	True	True	False	True	False	True
Resolution 11	False	True	True	False	True	True	False	True	True	False	False	True
Resolution 12	True	False	False	False	True	True	False	True	False	False	True	False
Likert Survey	3	4	3	4	3	5	3	4	5	4	5	3
Current Level	Medium	Medium	Hard	Medium	Medium	Medium	Medium	Medium	Hard	Medium	Medium	Medium
Total Easy Exercises Solved Correctly	3	3	0	5	5	0	3	3	0	3	0	3
Total Easy Exercises Solved Incorrectly	0	0	0	1	1	0	0	0	0	0	0	0

(continued)

(continued)

	Student 1			Student 2			Student 3			Student 4		
Etapa	1			0			1			1		
Iterations	Iteration 1	Iteration 2	Iteration 3	Iteration 1	Iteration 2	Iteration 3	Iteration 1	Iteration 2	Iteration 3	Iteration 1	Iteration 2	Iteration 3
Total Medium Exercises Solved Correctly	3	5	3	2	4	5	3	5	2	3	3	4
Total Medium Exercises Solved Incorrectly	3	1	0	4	2	1	3	1	1	3	3	2
Total Hard Exercises Solved Correctly	0	2	5	0	0	5	0	1	3	0	2	1
Total Hard Exercises Solved Incorrectly	3	1	4	0	0	1	3	2	6	3	7	2

	Student 1			Student 2			Student 3			Student 4		
Etapa	1			0			1			1		
Iterations	Iteration 1	Iteration 2	Iteration 3	Iteration 1	Iteration 2	Iteration 3	Iteration 1	Iteration 2	Iteration 3	Iteration 1	Iteration 2	Iteration 3
Level	Easy	Easy	Hard	Easy	Easy	Hard	Easy	Easy	Hard	Easy	Hard	Easy
Resolution 1	True	True	True	True	True	False	True	True	True	True	True	True
Resolution 2	True	True	False	True	True	False	True	True	True	True	False	True
Resolution 3	True	True	True	True	False	False	True	True	False	True	False	True
Level	Medium	Medium	Hard	Medium	Medium	Medium	Medium	Medium	Hard	Medium	Medium	Medium
Resolution 4	False	True	False	True	True	True	True	False	False	True	False	True
Resolution 5	True	True	True	False	False	False	False	True	False	True	True	True
Resolution 6	True	True	False	False	False	True	True	True	False	False	True	False
Likert Survey	4	5	3	2	1	4	4	4	3	3	4	5
Level	Hard	Hard	Medium	Easy	Easy	Hard	Hard	Hard	Medium	Hard	Hard	Hard
Resolution 7	False	False	True	True	True	False	False	True	True	False	False	True
Resolution 8	False	False	True	False	True	False	False	False	False	False	False	False

(continued)

(continued)

	Student 1			Student 2			Student 3			Student 4		
Etapa	1			0			1			1		
Iterations	Iteration 1	Iteration 2	Iteration 3	Iteration 1	Iteration 2	Iteration 3	Iteration 1	Iteration 2	Iteration 3	Iteration 1	Iteration 2	Iteration 3
Resolution 9	False	True	True	True	True	True	False	False	True	False	False	False
Level	Medium	Medium	Hard	Medium	Medium	Medium	Medium	Medium	Hard	Medium	Medium	Medium
Resolution 10	False	True	True	True	True	True	True	True	False	True	False	True
Resolution 11	False	True	True	False	True	True	False	True	True	False	False	True
Resolution 12	True	False	False	False	True	True	False	True	False	False	True	False
Likert Survey	3	4	3	4	3	5	3	4	5	4	5	3
Current Level	Medium	Medium	Hard	Medium	Medium	Medium	Medium	Medium	Hard	Medium	Medium	Medium
Total Easy Exercises Solved Correctly	3	3	0	5	5	0	3	3	0	3	0	3
Total Easy Exercises Solved Incorrectly	0	0	0	1	1	0	0	0	0	0	0	0

(continued)

(continued)

Etapa	Student 1			Student 2			Student 3			Student 4		
	1			0			1			1		
Iterations	Iteration 1	Iteration 2	Iteration 3	Iteration 1	Iteration 2	Iteration 3	Iteration 1	Iteration 2	Iteration 3	Iteration 1	Iteration 2	Iteration 3
Total Medium Exercises Solved Correctly	3	5	3	2	4	5	3	5	2	3	3	4
Total Medium Exercises Solved Incorrectly	3	1	0	4	2	1	3	1	1	3	3	2
Total Hard Exercises Solved Correctly	0	2	5	0	0	5	0	1	3	0	2	1
Total Hard Exercises Solved Incorrectly	3	1	4	0	0	1	3	2	6	3	7	2

	Student 9			Student 10			Student 11			Student 12		
Etapa	0			0			0			1		
Iterations	Iteration 1	Iteration 2	Iteration 3	Iteration 1	Iteration 2	Iteration 3	Iteration 1	Iteration 2	Iteration 3	Iteration 1	Iteration 2	Iteration 3
Level	Easy	Easy	Hard	Easy	Easy	Hard	Easy	Easy	Hard	Easy	Easy	Easy
Resolution 1	True	True	False	True	True	True	True	True	True	True	True	True
Resolution 2	True	True	True	True	True	True	True	True	True	True	True	True
Resolution 3	True	True	False	True	True	True	True	True	False	True	True	True
Level	Medium	Medium	Medium	Medium	Medium	Hard	Medium	Medium	Hard	Medium	Medium	Medium
Resolution 4	False	True	True	False	True	False	False	True	True	True	True	True
Resolution 5	True	False	True	True	True	True	True	False	False	True	True	False
Resolution 6	True	True	False	True	False	False	True	True	True	False	True	True
Likert Survey	4	5	4	4	5	5	3	5	3	4	3	3
Level	Hard	Hard	Hard	Hard	Hard	Medium	Hard	Hard	Medium	Hard	Hard	Hard
Resolution 7	True	False	False	False	True	True	False	False	True	True	False	True
Resolution 8	False	True	False	True	False	False	False	True	True	False	False	True

(continued)

(continued)

	Student 9			Student 10			Student 11			Student 12		
Etapa	0			0			0			1		
Iterations	Iteration 1	Iteration 2	Iteration 3	Iteration 1	Iteration 2	Iteration 3	Iteration 1	Iteration 2	Iteration 3	Iteration 1	Iteration 2	Iteration 3
Resolution 9	False	False	True	False	False	False	True	False	False	False	False	False
Level	Medium	Medium	Medium	Medium	Medium	Hard	Medium	Medium	Hard	Medium	Medium	Hard
Resolution 10	False	True	False	True	True	True	False	True	True	False	False	True
Resolution 11	False	True	False	True	False	True	False	True	False	True	True	False
Resolution 12	True	True	True	True	True	False	True	False	True	False	False	False
Likert Survey	3	3	4	3	4	5	4	4	3	3	3	4
Current Level	Medium	Medium	Medium	Medium	Medium	Hard	Medium	Medium	Hard	Medium	Medium	Hard
Total Easy Exercises Solved Correctly	3	3	0	3	3	0	3	3	0	3	3	3
Total Easy Exercises Solved Incorrectly	0	0	0	0	0	0	0	0	0	0	0	0

(continued)

(continued)

	Student 9			Student 10			Student 11			Student 12		
Etapa	0			0			0			1		
Iterations	Iteration 1	Iteration 2	Iteration 3	Iteration 1	Iteration 2	Iteration 3	Iteration 1	Iteration 2	Iteration 3	Iteration 1	Iteration 2	Iteration 3
Total Medium Exercises Solved Correctly	3	5	4	4	4	2	3	4	2	3	4	2
Total Medium Exercises Solved Incorrectly	3	1	2	2	2	1	3	2	1	3	2	1
Total Hard Exercises Solved Correctly	1	1	2	1	1	6	2	1	6	1	0	3
Total Hard Exercises Solved Incorrectly	2	2	4	2	2	3	1	2	3	3	3	3

	Student 13			Student 14			Student 15			Student 16		
Etapa	1			1			0			1		
Iterations	Iteration 1	Iteration 2	Iteration 3	Iteration 1	Iteration 2	Iteration 3	Iteration 1	Iteration 2	Iteration 3	Iteration 1	Iteration 2	Iteration 3
Level	Easy	Easy	Hard	Easy	Easy	Hard	Easy	Easy	Medium	Easy	Easy	Hard
Resolution 1	True	True	False	True	True	False	True	True	True	True	True	True
Resolution 2	True	True	False	True	True	True	True	True	False	True	True	True
Resolution 3	True	True	True	True	True	False	True	True	True	True	True	False
Level	Medium	Medium	Medium	Medium	Medium	Medium	Medium	Medium	Hard	Medium	Medium	Hard
Resolution 4	True	True	True	True	True	True	False	True	True	False	False	True
Resolution 5	True	False	True	False	True	True	True	False	False	True	True	False
Resolution 6	False	True	False	True	True	False	True	True	False	True	True	False
Likert Survey	3	3	3	5	5	4	4	5	5	4	5	3
Level	Hard	Hard	Hard	Hard	Hard	Hard	Hard	Hard	Medium	Hard	Hard	Medium
Resolution 7	False	False	True	False	False	False	False	True	True	False	False	True
Resolution 8	True	True	False	True	False	False	False	True	True	False	False	True

(continued)

(continued)

Etapa	Student 13			Student 14			Student 15			Student 16		
	1			1			0			1		
Iterations	Iteration 1	Iteration 2	Iteration 3	Iteration 1	Iteration 2	Iteration 3	Iteration 1	Iteration 2	Iteration 3	Iteration 1	Iteration 2	Iteration 3
Resolution 9	False	False	False	False	False	True	True	False	False	False	True	True
Level	Medium	Medium	Medium	Medium	Medium	Medium	Medium	Hard	Hard	Medium	Medium	Hard
Resolution 10	True	True	False	False	True	True	False	False	True	True	True	True
Resolution 11	False	True	True	True	False	True	True	False	True	False	False	True
Resolution 12	False	False	False	False	True	False	False	True	True	False	True	False
Likert Survey	3	3	5	3	5	3	3	5	5	4	4	4
Current Level	Medium	Medium	Medium	Medium	Medium	Medium	Medium	Hard	Hard	Medium	Medium	Hard
Total Easy Exercises Solved Correctly	3	3	0	3	3	0	3	3	0	3	3	0
Total Easy Exercises Solved Incorrectly	0	0	0	0	0	0	0	0	0	0	0	0

(continued)

(continued)

Etapa	Student 13			Student 14			Student 15			Student 16		
	1			1			0			1		
Iterations	Iteration 1	Iteration 2	Iteration 3	Iteration 1	Iteration 2	Iteration 3	Iteration 1	Iteration 2	Iteration 3	Iteration 1	Iteration 2	Iteration 3
Total Medium Exercises Solved Correctly	3	4	3	3	5	4	3	2	4	3	4	3
Total Medium Exercises Solved Incorrectly	3	2	2	3	1	2	3	1	2	3	2	0
Total Hard Exercises Solved Correctly	1	1	1	1	0	2	1	3	4	0	1	5
Total Hard Exercises Solved Incorrectly	2	2	2	2	3	4	2	3	2	3	2	4

	Student 17			Student 18			Student 19			Student 20		
Etapa	0			1			1			1		
Iterations	Iteration 1	Iteration 2	Iteration 3	Iteration 1	Iteration 2	Iteration 3	Iteration 1	Iteration 2	Iteration 3	Iteration 1	Iteration 2	Iteration 3
Level	Easy	Easy	Easy	Easy	Easy	Hard	Easy	Hard	Hard	Easy	Easy	Easy
Resolution 1	True	True	True	True	True	False	True	True	False	True	True	True
Resolution 2	True	True	True	True	True	True	True	False	True	True	True	True
Resolution 3	True	True	True	True	True	False	True	False	False	True	True	True
Level	Medium	Medium	Medium	Medium	Medium	Medium	Medium	Medium	Medium	Medium	Medium	Medium
Resolution 4	True	True	True	True	True	True	True	True	True	True	True	True
Resolution 5	False	True	True	True	True	False	True	True	True	True	True	True
Resolution 6	True	False	False	False	False	True	False	False	False	False	True	True
Likert Survey	3	4	4	3	3	3	3	5	4	5	5	3
Level	Hard	Hard	Hard	Hard	Hard	Hard	Hard	Hard	Hard	Hard	Hard	Hard
Resolution 7	False	False	True	False	False	False	False	False	True	False	True	True
Resolution 8	True	True	False	False	True	False	False	False	False	True	False	False

(continued)

(continued)

	Student 17			Student 18			Student 19			Student 20		
Etapa	0			1			1			1		
Iterations	Iteration 1	Iteration 2	Iteration 3	Iteration 1	Iteration 2	Iteration 3	Iteration 1	Iteration 2	Iteration 3	Iteration 1	Iteration 2	Iteration 3
Resolution 9	False	False	False	True	False	True	False	True	False	False	False	False
Level	Medium	Medium	Medium	Medium	Medium	Medium	Medium	Medium	Medium	Medium	Medium	Medium
Resolution 10	False	False	True	False	True	False	True	True	True	False	True	False
Resolution 11	False	True	True	True	False	True	False	False	False	True	False	True
Resolution 12	True	False	True	False	True	True	True	True	True	False	False	False
Likert Survey	3	3	4	3	4	4	5	5	3	3	4	5
Current Level	Medium	Medium	Medium	Medium	Medium	Medium	Medium	Medium	Medium	Medium	Medium	Medium
Total Easy Exercises Solved Correctly	3	3	3	3	3	0	3	0	0	3	3	3
Total Easy Exercises Solved Incorrectly	0	0	0	0	0	0	0	0	0	0	0	0

(continued)

(continued)

	Student 17			Student 18			Student 19			Student 20		
Etapa	0			1			1			1		
Iterations	Iteration 1	Iteration 2	Iteration 3	Iteration 1	Iteration 2	Iteration 3	Iteration 1	Iteration 2	Iteration 3	Iteration 1	Iteration 2	Iteration 3
Total Medium Exercises Solved Correctly	3	4	5	3	4	4	4	4	4	3	4	4
Total Medium Exercises Solved Incorrectly	3	2	1	3	2	2	2	2	2	3	2	2
Total Hard Exercises Solved Correctly	1	1	1	1	1	2	0	1	2	2	1	1
Total Hard Exercises Solved Incorrectly	2	2	2	2	2	4	3	2	4	1	2	2

References

Barua, P.D., et al.: Artificial intelligence enabled personalised assistive tools to enhance education of children with neurodevelopmental disorders—a review. Int. J. Environ. Res. Public Health **19**(3), 1192 (2022). https://doi.org/10.3390/ijerph19031192

Budiyarti, L., Agustini, N., Hayati, H., Panjaitan, R.U., Hakim, N.: Effectiveness of web-based play therapy intervention in supporting the development of children with attention deficit/hyperactivity disorder. La Pediatria Medica e Chirurgica, 45 (s1) (2023). https://doi.org/10.4081/pmc.2023.316

Calleros, C.B.G., Guerrero-García, J., Navarro-Rangel, Y.: UvaMate: a serious game for learning mathematics for children with ADHD: Usability evaluation. Revista Colombiana de Computación **21**(1), 20–34 (2020). https://doi.org/10.29375/25392115.3896

Demontis, D., et al.: Discovery of the first genome-wide significant risk loci for attention deficit/hyperactivity disorder. Nature Genetics **51**(1), 63–75 (2018). https://doi.org/10.1038/s41588-018-0269-7

NIH. El trastorno de déficit de atención con hiperactividad en los niños y los adolescentes: Lo que usted necesita saber. nimh.nih.gov

Rincon-Flores, E.G., Santos-Guevara, B.N., Martinez-Cardiel, L., RodriguezRodriguez, N.K., Quintana-Cruz, H.A., Matsuura-Sonoda, A.: Gamit! icing on the cake for mathematics gamification. Sustainability **15**(3), 2334 (2023). https://doi.org/10.3390/su15032334

Ruiz-Ledesma, E.F., Bautista-Rosales, S., Garay-Jiménez, L.: Mobile app with reinforcement activities for children with ADHD. Revista Internacional de Investigación e Innovación Tecnológica (43), 18 (2022). https://riiit.com.mx

Steinau, S.: Diagnostic criteria in attention deficit hyperactivity disorder – changes in DSM 5. Front. Psychiatry **4** (2013). https://doi.org/10.3389/fpsyt.2013.00049

Opticos Optometristas, C. G. (n.d.). TDAH Trainer. https://www.cgcoo.es/apps/tdah-trainer

MANTRA: Enhancing Worker Safety Through an Integrated BIM-IoT Mobile Application

Francisco Pérez Carrasco[1,2(✉)] [iD], Alberto García García[1] [iD],
Victor Garrido Peñalver[1] [iD], and Piotr Sowiński[3,4] [iD]

[1] FAV Innovation and Technologies COOP.V, 46006 Valencia, Spain
{agarcia,vgarrido,fperez}@favit.es
[2] Universitat Politècnica de València, 46022 Valencia, Spain
frapecar@upvnet.upv.es
[3] Systems Research Institute, Polish Academy of Sciences, Warsaw, Poland
piotr.sowinski@ibspan.waw.pl
[4] Warsaw University of Technology, Warsaw, Poland
https://favit.es

Abstract. In the evolving landscape of construction safety management, the integration of Internet of Things (IoT) and Building Information Modeling (BIM) technologies [1] presents a novel approach to addressing the dynamic challenges of workplace safety. The MANTRA project, developed under the ASSIST-IoT H2020 (Horizon 2020) project [2], introduces an innovative hybrid mobile application designed to enhance the safety of construction workers by providing real-time, interactive visualization and management of temporary danger zones on construction sites.

This paper outlines the development and implementation of MANTRA, focusing on its integration of BIM for detailed site representation and ASSIST-IoT platform for real-time data exchange and alerts management. The application enables workers to identify and mark danger zones directly on digital site models, significantly improving the timeliness and accuracy of safety warnings. By leveraging cross-platform compatibility through Progressive Web App (PWA) Framework [3], MANTRA ensures widespread accessibility and usability.

Preliminary results from field tests and lab evaluations demonstrate MANTRA's effectiveness in improving situational awareness and reducing the risk of accidents. The application not only streamlines the process of marking and communicating hazards but also promotes a proactive safety culture.

MANTRA's contribution to construction safety represents a significant advancement in digital technology application, highlighting the potential for IoT and BIM integration in risk management and worker safety enhancement in dynamic work environments.

Keywords: Internet of Things (IoT) · Building Information Modeling (BIM) · Hybrid Mobile Application · Construction Safety · Real-Time Data Exchange · Situational Awareness

M. Botto-Tobar et al. (Eds.): ICAT 2023, CCIS 2051, pp. 214–225, 2024.
https://doi.org/10.1007/978-3-031-58950-8_15

1 Introduction

1.1 Context

The construction industry, characterized by its dynamic and hazardous environments, has long faced challenges in ensuring the safety and well-being of its workforce. Traditional safety management practices, while foundational, often fall short in addressing the rapidly changing conditions on construction sites [4]. The advent of digital technologies, specifically the IoT and BIM, presents a transformative opportunity to enhance safety protocols and practices in this sector.

IoT, with its network of interconnected sensors and devices, offers unparalleled capabilities in monitoring and communicating real-time data. This technology is crucial in construction sites where conditions can change rapidly, and the timely dissemination of information can be the difference between safety and hazard [5]. BIM, on the other hand, provides a detailed digital representation of physical and functional characteristics of construction projects. When integrated with IoT, BIM can serve not just as a planning and management tool but also as an interactive platform for site safety and risk management [6].

Despite these technological advancements, the construction industry faces challenges in effectively integrating these technologies to address specific safety concerns. Temporary danger zones, which are areas that become hazardous due to ongoing activities or sudden environmental changes, are particularly challenging to manage. Traditional methods of marking and communicating these zones are often manual, reactive, and prone to human error [7]. Furthermore, the diverse and transient nature of construction workforces, including language barriers and varying levels of familiarity with the site, exacerbates the challenge of ensuring that every worker is aware of current dangers.

The MANTRA project emerges in this context as an innovative solution, leveraging the strengths of IoT and BIM to enhance construction site safety. The project's cornerstone is the development of a hybrid mobile application that aims to revolutionize how information about temporary danger zones is communicated and managed. By integrating real-time data from IoT devices with the interactive BIM models, MANTRA enables workers to visualize and understand the dynamic nature of their working environment accurately. This approach not only enhances the timeliness and reliability of safety warnings but also empowers workers to be proactive participants in their safety management.

1.2 The Problem

Construction sites are inherently complex and fluid environments, presenting unique safety challenges. One of the most significant and persistent issues in this sector is the management of temporary danger zones. These zones represent areas that intermittently become hazardous due to various factors such as ongoing construction activities, machinery movement, structural changes, or environmental conditions.

Dynamic Nature of Construction Sites. Unlike static industrial settings, construction sites are continuously evolving. This constant change means that areas previously deemed safe can rapidly become hazardous, necessitating an agile and responsive safety management system. Traditional safety protocols, reliant on manual processes and static signage, are often unable to keep pace with these changes, leading to gaps in safety coverage [8].

Communication Barriers. Effective communication of hazards is crucial in construction sites, where a diverse workforce, including contractors, temporary workers, and those with varying language proficiencies, converge. The conventional methods of communicating dangers, such as verbal briefings or physical signs, are not only slow to disseminate but also prone to misunderstandings and overlooks, especially in a multilingual workforce [9].

Reliance on Human Vigilance. Current practices heavily rely on the vigilance of workers and supervisors to identify and communicate hazards. This reliance introduces human error into safety management, as workers may fail to recognize a newly emerging danger or may not communicate it effectively to all parties [10].

Inadequate Real-Time Response. The lack of real-time monitoring and alert systems in traditional safety approaches means that information about emerging hazards often reaches workers with a delay [11]. This delay is critical in an environment where timely information can prevent accidents and injuries.

Limitations of Current Technology Integration. While there have been advances in incorporating technology into construction safety, these have often been piecemeal and not fully integrated. Solutions like standalone safety apps or basic IoT implementations provide limited functionality and fail to offer a comprehensive and interactive overview of the entire site, crucial for understanding and navigating temporary danger zones [11].

In this context, the construction industry faces the challenge of devising a safety management system that is dynamic, responsive, and comprehensive, addressing the unique nature of temporary danger zones. This system must not only provide real-time updates on site conditions but also be accessible and understandable to a diverse and transient workforce.

1.3 Proposed Solution

In response to the multifaceted challenges of managing temporary danger zones in construction sites, the MANTRA project proposes a groundbreaking solution that synergizes the capabilities of IoT and BIM technologies through a hybrid mobile application. This innovative approach aims to revolutionize safety management in construction environments by providing a dynamic, interactive, and

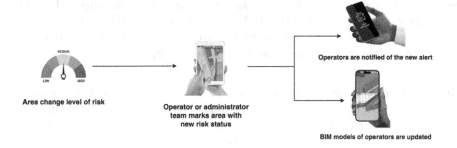

Fig. 1. MANTRA Concept

accessible platform for real-time hazard identification and communication as it is shown in Fig. 1.

Integration of IoT for Real-Time Monitoring. At the core of MANTRA's functionality is the integration of IoT technology. By harnessing the power of a network of sensors and interconnected devices, MANTRA facilitates real-time monitoring of the construction site. This setup enables the immediate detection of changes in the environment that may give rise to new hazards. The real-time data provided by IoT devices ensures that information about temporary danger zones is current, accurate, and instantly available.

Leveraging BIM for Interactive Visualization. MANTRA elevates the use of BIM from a planning and design tool to an active participant in safety management. By integrating BIM models into the application, MANTRA offers detailed 3D visualizations of the construction site, allowing workers to interact with a digital twin of their physical environment. This feature not only enhances the understanding of the site layout but also enables users to pinpoint and visualize the exact locations of potential hazards.

Progressive Web App for Enhanced Accessibility. Developed as a PWA, MANTRA is inherently accessible across a wide range of devices and platforms. This approach ensures that the application can be used on any device with a web browser, without the need for downloading a dedicated app. The PWA framework offers the advantage of a seamless, app-like experience combined with the accessibility and ease of a web application, ensuring that all workers, regardless of their device type, can access critical safety information.

Proactive Safety Communication. A key innovation of MANTRA is its proactive approach to safety communication. Instead of relying on traditional reactive methods, the application allows for the immediate marking and broad-casting of danger zones within the BIM model. Workers can receive instant noti-fications on their mobile devices about emerging hazards, significantly reducing the response time and enhancing the overall safety response.

Empowering Workers with Interactive Features. MANTRA empowers workers by giving them the ability to interact directly with the safety manage-ment system. Users can report hazards, view updates, and even contribute to the safety monitoring process. This interactive participation fosters a proactive safety culture, where each worker becomes an active stakeholder in maintaining a safe working environment.

In summary, the MANTRA project addresses the pressing need for an advanced, integrated safety management system in construction sites. By com-bining real-time data from IoT with interactive BIM visualizations in a user-friendly mobile application, MANTRA offers a comprehensive solution to the challenges of temporary danger zones. This approach not only enhances imme-diate safety responses but also contributes to a long-term culture of safety and awareness in the construction industry.

2   Methodology

2.1   App Development

During MANTRA development activities, the approach was centered around creating a tool that was not only technologically advanced but also user-centric and universally accessible. The decision to utilize a PWA framework was pivotal in achieving these goals. This choice allowed us to develop an application that seamlessly operates across different devices and operating systems, effectively addressing the diverse technological landscape of construction site personnel.

The development process of the MANTRA app was guided by a commitment to simplicity and ease of use. Recognizing that our users range from tech-savvy individuals to those less accustomed to digital tools, we prioritized an intuitive user interface by circulating to our end-users a set of screens mockups like the ones shown in Fig. 2.

The web-based nature of PWAs played a significant role in this aspect. By allowing access through a web browser without the need for downloading a sepa-rate app, we significantly lowered the barrier to entry. This ease of access ensures that every worker, regardless of their level of comfort with technology, can inter-act with the application.

A critical part of the development was the integration of the app with ASSIST-IoT platform for real-time data transmission and BIM for interactive visualizations. This phase required a synergistic effort between the MANTRA app developers team and ASSIST-IoT partners. The goal was to ensure a smooth and effective synergy of these technologies, allowing for a dynamic representation of the construction site and timely updates on potential hazards.

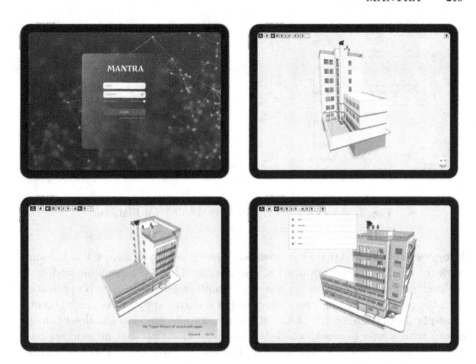

Fig. 2. MANTRA first mockups

Testing and iterative improvement were integral to MANTRA methodology. The application underwent various phases of testing, starting from basic functionality and user interface to more complex aspects like integration with IoT and BIM. This rigorous testing framework enabled us to gather valuable feedback, which was then incorporated into successive iterations of the app. This process of continuous refinement was essential in creating a robust and reliable tool for construction site safety.

Finally, understanding the ever-evolving nature of construction projects and digital technologies, we designed the MANTRA app with scalability and adaptability in mind. The architecture of the app allows for easy updates and the addition of new functionalities as required, ensuring the tool remains relevant and effective in the dynamic landscape of construction site safety management.

2.2 Technologies

For the development of MANTRA application and its integration in the ASSIST-IoT ecosystem, a strategic blend of PWA technology and ASSIST-IoT enablers was employed, creating a platform that is both technologically sophisticated and highly adaptable to the needs of construction site safety management as it is shown in Fig. 3.

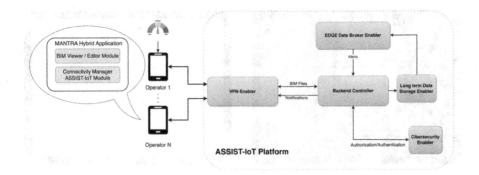

Fig. 3. MANTRA integration with ASSIST-Iot Platform

Progressive Web App Framework. The choice to utilize a PWA framework for the MANTRA application was pivotal. This technology allowed us to build a platform that combines the accessibility and ease of a web application with the performance and user experience of a native app. PWAs are inherently cross-platform, enabling the MANTRA application to function seamlessly on any device with a web browser, which is crucial for ensuring that all workers have unrestricted access to the application. The offline capabilities and fast loading times of PWAs also enhance the app's usability in various on-site conditions, where connectivity can be inconsistent.

Semantic Repository Enabler. [12] The Semantic Repository Enabler from ASSIST-IoT is integral to the app, enabling intelligent data management and interpretation. This enabler allows the application to effectively process and contextualize the data from IoT devices and BIM models, turning it into actionable insights for hazard identification and management.

VPN Enabler. [13] Given the sensitivity of construction site data, security is paramount. The VPN Enabler ensures that all data communication within the MANTRA app is secure, maintaining the confidentiality and integrity of the information transmitted.

Edge Data Broker Enabler. [14] This enabler is crucial for the real-time functionality of the app, allowing for prompt data processing and communication. It ensures that the data from the site is processed efficiently, enabling the MANTRA app to deliver timely and accurate notifications about potential dangers.

Cybersecurity Enabler. [15] To safeguard against cyber threats, the Cybersecurity Enabler provides additional security layers, protecting not only the data but also the integrity of the app's communication channels.

Long Term Data Storage Enabler. [16] This enabler addresses the need for efficient storage and retrieval of historical data, which is essential for risk assessment and the development of long-term safety strategies.

The combination of PWA technology with these ASSIST-IoT enablers results in the MANTRA application being a highly effective tool for safety management in construction sites. The app not only responds to immediate safety needs but also adapts to the evolving demands of construction site environments, ensuring long-term relevance and effectiveness.

3   Results

3.1   App Implementation

The implementation of the MANTRA project, involving the deployment of its PWA in construction environments, was a pivotal phase of the project. This phase was marked by strategic integration within a robust technological ecosystem to ensure effective operation in a live setting.

The rollout at construction sites was carefully planned to minimize disruption, with comprehensive orientation sessions demonstrating the PWA's functionalities and ease of access. The web-based nature of the app facilitated its adoption across various devices.

A key aspect of the implementation was the encapsulation of the PWA and its backend within a Docker container [17], deployed on a Kubernetes infrastructure [18]. This approach ensured high availability and scalability of the application, while Kubernetes provided a stable and adaptable environment, facilitating integration with ASSIST-IoT enablers.

The application was integrated with real-time data sources, including IoT sensors and BIM models, essential for real-time monitoring and processing of site conditions and hazards. User engagement and the app's effectiveness were monitored closely, with feedback collected to identify enhancement areas and ensure the app met user needs.

Continuous performance monitoring and technical support were provided throughout this phase, crucial in fostering user confidence and integrating the app into daily site safety practices. The data analysis conducted offered insights into identified hazards and user responsiveness, informing ongoing safety management strategies.

The successful implementation of MANTRA in a real-world construction setting demonstrated its utility in enhancing digital safety management, setting the stage for its ongoing development and refinement.

3.2   Tests and Validation

The MANTRA project's phase of testing and validation was a crucial part of our efforts, undertaken within the challenging and dynamic environment of the Marshal's Office construction site in Szczecin, Poland. Specifically, the application was evaluated under the ambit of Business Scenario P2-3: Safe Navigation, part of the Smart Safety of Workers Pilot. This scenario offered an ideal opportunity to test the app's capabilities in real-time navigation and emergency response in a complex construction setting as it is shown in Fig. 4.

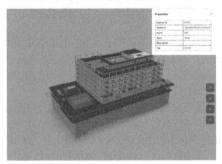
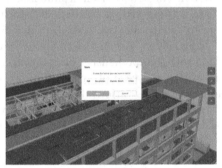

Fig. 4. MANTRA Scenario Demonstration

In implementing the Safe Navigation scenario, the primary objective was to assess MANTRA's effectiveness in guiding construction workers during emergency evacuations. The application, leveraging its integration with IoT and BIM technologies, provided real-time, updated evacuation routes tailored to the constantly changing landscape of the construction site. This feature was particularly significant given the unpredictability of the site conditions, where safety hazards could emerge rapidly due to various factors, including weather changes, ongoing construction activities, and the movement of heavy machinery.

The real-world testing environment of the Marshal's Office site presented a comprehensive range of challenges typical to construction settings. It was crucial for MANTRA to demonstrate its adaptability and accuracy in this dynamic environment. Simulated emergency drills were conducted to evaluate how effectively the application could guide workers to safety, considering both the evolving physical layout of the site and the environmental factors monitored through IoT sensors.

User feedback was an integral component of the validation process at it is reflected in Table 1. The insights gathered from the construction workers and site

Table 1. User Feedback and Satisfaction Ratings for MANTRA App

User Role	Feedback	Rating
Site Manager	MANTRA significantly improved our safety response times	5/5
Construction Worker	The navigation and hazard alerts are very helpful	4.5/5
Safety Officer	This app has made monitoring site safety more efficient	4.8/5
Project Supervisor	The integration of real-time data has been a key point	4.7/5

safety managers were invaluable in assessing the app's usability and its impact on enhancing safety practices on the site. Their experiences and suggestions contributed significantly to iterative improvements, ensuring the application was finely tuned to meet the needs of its end-users effectively.

Additionally, data analysis played a vital role in understanding the application's performance during emergency scenarios. By examining response times, evacuation routes taken by workers, and overall adherence to safety protocols, we were able to gauge the efficiency of MANTRA's navigation guidance. This analysis not only validated the app's functionality in a live setting but also provided essential learnings for future enhancements.

Through this validation process in the Safe Navigation scenario, the MANTRA application proved its potential as a transformative tool in construction safety management. It demonstrated a significant capacity to enhance worker safety by providing informed, real-time navigation solutions, thereby validating the practical application and efficacy of integrating IoT and BIM technologies in managing the complexities of construction site environments.

4   Conclusions and Future Directions

4.1   Conclusions

The MANTRA project has significantly advanced the field of construction safety management. Integrating a Progressive Web App (PWA) with IoT and BIM technologies, the project has successfully tackled the challenge of real-time hazard identification and navigation in dynamic construction environments. The positive feedback from users and the effective implementation of the app underscore its potential to markedly improve safety response times and situational awareness.

Key achievements of the project include:

- Successful deployment of the PWA in a real-world construction environment, demonstrating its practicality and effectiveness.
- Effective integration with IoT sensors and BIM models, enabling real-time data access and site visualizations.
- Positive reception and feedback from users, highlighting improved safety management and operational efficiency.

4.2   Future Directions

Building upon the success of the MANTRA project, the following future directions are proposed:

1. **Enhanced Data Analytics:** Utilizing advanced data analytics and machine learning to predict potential hazards, transitioning from reactive to proactive safety management.
2. **Augmented Reality Integration:** Incorporating AR features for more immersive user experiences, further improving navigation and hazard identification.
3. **Expansion to Other Industries:** Adapting the MANTRA framework for use in industries with similar safety challenges, like mining or manufacturing.
4. **User Experience Optimization:** Continuously refining the app based on user feedback to enhance usability and engagement.
5. **Scalability and Interoperability:** Focusing on scalability for larger projects and enhancing interoperability with other construction industry tools and platforms.

In conclusion, the MANTRA project represents a significant step forward in the use of digital technologies for construction safety. Its future development promises not only to further enhance workplace safety but also to lead the way for smarter, technology-driven practices in the construction industry and beyond.

Acknowledgement. This work has been performed under the H2020 957258 project ASSIST-IoT, which has received funding from the European Union's Horizon 2020 Programme. This paper reflects only the authors' view, and the European Commission is not liable to any use that may be made of the information contained therein.

References

1. Maia, L., Mêda, P., Freitas, J.G.: BIM methodology, a new approach - case study of structural elements creation. Procedia Eng. **114**, 816–823 (2015). ICSI 2015 The 1st International Conference on Structural Integrity, Funchal, Madeira, Portugal
2. ASSIST-IOT Project. https://assist-iot.eu/
3. PWAs. https://web.dev/articles/what-are-pwas?hl=en
4. Bhattacharjee, S., Ghosh, S., Young-Corbett, D.: Safety improvement approaches in construction industry : a review and future directions. In: 47th ASC Annual International Conference (2011)
5. Häikiö, J., Kallio, J., Mäkelä, S., Keränen, J.: IoT-based safety monitoring from the perspective of construction site workers. Int. J. Occup. Environ. Saf. **4**(1), 1–14 (2020)
6. Sooyoung, C., Fernanda, L.: Construction safety planning: site-specific temporal and spatial information integration. Autom. Constr. **84**, 335–344 (2017)
7. Albert, A., Hallowell, M.R., Kleiner, B.M.: Experimental field testing of a real-time construction hazard identification and transmission technique. Constr. Manag. Econ. **32**, 1000–1016 (2014)
8. Dupin, C.: In the zone. Traffic Technology International (2010)

9. Junnor, G., Khan, A.S., Aurini, S.J.: Improving work zone safety through enhanced temporary conditions. In: Today's Transportation Challenge: Meeting Our Customer's ExpectationsInstitute of Transportation Engineers (ITE) (2002)
10. Adebiyi, R.T., Rasheed, A.S.: Strategies for communicating health and safety information on construction. J. Eng. Project. Prod. Manage. **11**, 1–8 (2020)
11. Tsai, M.: Streamlining information representation during construction accidents. KSCE J. Civ. Eng. **18**, 1945–1954 (2014)
12. Semantic Repository enabler - ASSIST-IoT documentation. https://assist-iot-enablers-documentation.readthedocs.io/en/latest/horizontal_planes/datamanagement/semantic_repository_enabler.html
13. VPN Enabler - ASSIST-IoT documentation. https://assist-iot-enablers-documentation.readthedocs.io/en/latest/horizontal_planes/smart/vpn_enabler.html
14. Edge Data Broker Enabler - ASSIST-IoT documentation. https://assist-iot-enablers-documentation.readthedocs.io/en/latest/horizontal_planes/datamanagement/edge_data_broker_enabler.html
15. Cybersecurity Enabler - ASSIST-IoT documentation. https://assist-iot-enablers-documentation.readthedocs.io/en/latest/verticals/cybersecurity/index.html
16. Long-Term Data Storage Enabler - ASSIST-IoT documentation. https://assist-iot-enablers-documentation.readthedocs.io/en/latest/horizontal_planes/datamanagement/long_term_data_storage_enabler.html
17. Docker Technology. https://www.docker.com/
18. Kubernetes. https://kubernetes.io/es/docs/concepts/overview/what-is-kubernetes/

Design and Implementation of an Open Daylight Event Management System Through the Integration of a Business Process Management

Luis E. Benavides Castillo[✉] and Christian X. Castro González

Universidad Espíritu Santo, Km 2 1/2 vía Samborondón, Guayaquil, Ecuador
lebenavides@uees.edu.ec

Abstract. The present research conducts an experimental study with a qualitative approach to the event management of an SDN network. To this end, a conceptual model of event monitoring in SDN networks is proposed that tests the usefulness of Camunda in the handling of multiple events in a network. Also, different scenarios are proposed where the event-driven architecture (EDA) intervenes through services to obtain information from the network and create instances of decision flows in the BPM. The results obtained show a dynamic, robust, and scalable solution for event handling. Camunda's tools make it easy to condition the flow, implement new processes in which different BPM instances are involved, and define the execution time of each event, among others. In addition, BPM scenarios allow you to add an integration layer that contains HTTP libraries for execution and XSLT Saxon API libraries for request and response transformations from external APIs. Finally, an integration interface is implemented capable of formatting the message according to an XSLT template that is then sent to another platform via API-Rest. This interface opens the possibility of new studies related to the definition and execution of multiple services through dynamic criteria, according to the information from an SDN event.

Keywords: SDN · Open Daylight · BPM · Camunda · DMN

1 Introduction

Software Defined Network (SDN) emerged approximately twenty years ago, when the success of the Internet brought with it new challenges for the management and development of network infrastructure. SDN is the product of the need to create a programmable network infrastructure to support programmable packet processing at high speeds. According to history, there are three fundamental stages of networks: (i) active networks, which introduced programmable functions into the network, which led to greater innovation; (ii) the separation of control and data planes, which developed open interfaces; (iii) the OpenFlow API and network operating systems, which represented the first widespread adoption of an open interface and developed ways to make the separation of the control plane and data scalable and practical. Finally, network virtualization

M. Botto-Tobar et al. (Eds.): ICAT 2023, CCIS 2051, pp. 226–238, 2024.
https://doi.org/10.1007/978-3-031-58950-8_16

played an important role throughout the historical evolution of SDN, establishing itself as one of the first significant use cases for SDN. That is why [6] Software-Defined Network (SDN) is an emerging networking paradigm that offers the ability to change the limitations of today's network infrastructure. According to [12, 17], SDN reduces the complexity of network configuration and management. It also facilitates the introduction of innovation into network operations. Therefore, SDN presents an opportunity to automate the verification of the correct behavior of a network.

Although SDN offered a new architecture that provided programmers with the opportunity to work with open interfaces, it also made it possible to simplify network configuration by replacing different configuration commands. There were still limitations in the efficiency of the program that increased the chances of making mistakes since programmers were forced to use assembly language. Therefore, it was very necessary to implement an SDN programming language that would allow network programmers to solve common mistakes when developing a program. As a result, numerous high-level languages for SDN appeared. Among them are: Frenetic, Pyretic, Net Core, and Procera. However, SDN programming languages are not yet capable of incorporating new instruction sets into the data plane for packet processing. In addition, network programmers are forced to write basic applications, as SDN languages are not yet able to provide open interfaces that allow the programmer to incorporate new modules. On the other hand, high-level languages whose purpose is event-driven are impractical, as they are close to the lower-level layer, which makes it easier to translate OpenFlow rules. Using this type of language provides a restricted level of expressive power. In addition, as the size of the network increases, the sheer number of hosts, flows, network events, and policies can cause a state explosion. Likewise, SDN networks specify the behavior of the network through centralized programs. The use of these programs allows SDN networks to: (i) react to events, topology changes, traffic statistics, and packet reception, among others; (ii) integrate network functions, fine-grained access control functions, network virtualization, and traffic engineering. However, deploying the SDN network is a basic process; creating specialized programs for event handling and implementing functions comes with a challenge. SDN users are forced to keep track of coding configurations into prioritized forwarding rules, processing concurrent events, handling asynchronous events, handling unexpected failures, and more. While a few high-level languages have been proposed, these languages do not have the features needed to implement dynamic, event-driven applications. Implementing systems based on an event-driven architecture for SDN networks is still a necessity for users [9, 14, 19].

Business process management (BPM) is a tool generally used for the management of information technology projects. Using BPM for event management gives users the opportunity to model, manage, and optimize these processes to make more profits, prevent errors, and optimize time. BPM tools allow you to decompose processes into reusable process modules. That is why implementing BPM allows users to define the logic of each process and execute it in different ways. Likewise, different templates can be integrated into the processes and make all processes reusable, changeable, and continuously improved. In addition, rule engines can be defined so that the results of each process can be changed in a controlled manner [1, 16].

There are different BPM platforms that allow you to automate the workflow through a series of procedural rules. These include Microsoft Power Automate, Nintex, Joget Workflow, Pipeliner CRM, and Oracle Business Process Management Suite, among others. However, Camunda is an emerging platform that allows you to define BPMN and DMN specifications for process automation. Processes managed by Camunda can integrate APIs, bots, microservices, IoT devices, machine learning, and AI. In addition, Camunda allows its users to work on an intuitive, scalable platform with the ability to integrate multiple technologies for process management [3].

For the reasons previously written, it is important to conduct this research to allow Camunda to be used as an SDN event management tool. Camunda will be used to assist in process management and handling actions for setting easy-to-configure conditions for network programmers. This decision flow will be designed through a Business Process Model and Notation (BPMN).

The objective of this research is to implement BPM software for the monitoring and management of events in an SDN network. To this end, a conceptual monitoring model is designed in which scenarios are simulated where an event can be managed by different Camunda tools that allow conditioning the flow, integrating different instances of events (different BPM), integrating decision tables (DMN), among others. To do this, the following components need to be taken into consideration: (i) Create a virtualized Mininet network; (ii) install Open Daylight; (iii) Connect the controller to the network; (iv) Deploy the Camunda service on the northbound side; (v) Create a process management service that will sense (measure) Open Daylight events and trigger it in Camunda so that it can go through a decision flow.

2 Software-Defined Networking

2.1 Literature Review

Business Process Management (BPM) was implemented by [15] in BINUS Online Learning exam preparation process. For this task, a BPM implementation framework was developed based on model tools, process notation, selection matrices, and costing of activities that allowed a cost and time savings of 85.85%. On the other hand, [45] proposes a study where they try to integrate BPM into the field of symptomatic biology. To do this, they carry out different laboratory experiments where they integrate BPM to capture information about the activities of the users of the system, data from the monitoring of the system, and error reports. Similarly, [24] proposes the integration of BPM with SWS to create a new technological system, which they call semantic business process management (SBPM). All this is with the aim of improving the use of BPM in IT support processes. From the same perspective, [11] implemented an improvement in the BPM processes for use in the Hutchison 3G (H3G) project. Improvements to BPM processes include Web 2.0 features and wiki integration. On the other hand, [2] presents a literature review on the use of BPM in software solutions. In addition, they talk about the use of BPM to optimize, automate, and control business processes. Finally, they talk about the importance of implementing BPM to reduce the rate of failed projects.

2.2 Software-Defined Network (SDN)

A software-defined network (SDN) is an architecture that is characterized by allowing separation of the control plane, in charge of sending and receiving information, and of the data plane, intended to perform routing functions. It also enables rapid reaction to security threats, traffic filtering, and dynamic security policy deployment. In addition, its architecture provides a programming interface within the controller. It also allows network control operations such as running on top of one or multiple servers with higher performance and the ability to communicate with other operating systems or control platforms using standard protocols. [13, 17]. Hence, one of the advantages of SDN is that it brings numerous benefits to the networking scheme. SDN allows you to write high-level software applications for network management that do not require the underlying physical configuration. Likewise, the SDN controller allows for a global network view, giving it a greater security advantage over traditional networks. The global network view is due to centralization, and the network elements are collecting and reporting traffic statistics [4].

On the other hand, [15] says that SDN is also considered an important method that facilitates good networking practices. Since it supports the decoupling of the control layer and data interacting through an open interface between them, in addition, one of the features of SDN is centralized control through a view of the entire network. Therefore, it can be considered that SDN allows programmability in the control plane and support for network applications. In view of this, having a split of planes allows you to reduce the complexity of network configurations by having a complete view of them. Therefore, in this approach, management is carried out by a controller, who is responsible for distributing policies throughout the network. However, this becomes a threat because the control plane becomes a potential bottleneck, and any issue that alters the behavior of the control plane will cause network performance to suffer [10]. Consequently, [18] noticed this drawback and investigated the performance of some Network Operating Systems (NOS). The results obtained in the study showed that an instance of NOS can handle millions of new flows in one second. However, a review of the studies shows that the tests on the NOS used ran very simple network applications, such as Layer 2 switching, but in real networks, administrators will use more complex network applications.

2.3 SDN Architecture

SDN networks are composed of three layers, dividing the responsibilities that are centralized in traditional architectures. SDN is composed of the data, control, and management planes.

The data plane is made up of physical networking equipment such as switches and routers. However, in SDN, the data plane does not make autonomous decisions, as its only function is packet forwarding.

In SDN, the control plane is a separate layer of the data plane consisting of controllers and out-of-band and in-band control channels between controllers and switches. Similarly, control plane performance parameters contain the number of flow requests handled by the controller, configuration latency, and controller availability [8]. On the other hand, languages can provide a wide variety of procedures, such as data plane fault tolerance and a variety of basic building blocks to facilitate the development of applications and software modules [12]. So, Frenetic provides a declarative high-level language that allows you to classify network traffic, and it also has libraries available that allow you to describe high-level packet sending policies [7].

2.4 SDN Controller

The SDN controller is responsible for managing security policies, sending information, and flow tables, among others established by the network administrator. In the same way, it is responsible for collecting all the information related to the network through the control of SDN switches that are managed through the OpenFlow protocol. Therefore, the role of the controller in the SDN network is to become the decision-maker for each traffic flow at all layers of the protocol stack. Although there is a rule for packet forwarding in the required plane, forwarding is done on the interface without the need to involve the controller. A representation of the SDN architecture can be seen in Fig. 1. However, if there is a fault in the flow table, the forwarding plane generates an input packet event and sends it to the controller. On the other hand, if the switch has enough memory to buffer, all packets are sent to the controller [12, 20].

3 Methodology

The present research is based on an experimental study with a qualitative approach that uses a BPM (Camunda) for the management of N events within an SDN network. To this end, a conceptual model of event monitoring was created in which an SDN network is virtualized through Mininet and will have the Open Daylight middleware integrated. Consequently, the Camunda service will be integrated into the northbound interface (Control Panel), and a process management service will be created in charge of monitoring Open Daylight events and triggering them in Camunda so that it can go through a decision flow. Finally, the decision flow will be displayed through a Business Process Model and Notation. The architecture of the conceptual model for event handling in SDN is shown in Fig. 1.

To carry out the research, the methodologist was divided into 4 phases linked to each other and focused on showing a conceptual model of event management in SDN. First is the virtualization phase of the network. For the virtualization of an SDN network, Mininet was used, which is a network emulator that allows the creation of virtual hosts, switches, controllers, and links. The SDN controller is the one that has all the network configuration and is the one that handles the data and events of the network. Likewise, it is the one that communicates with the southbound, which is the network virtualized by the Mininet. An outline of this is shown in Fig. 2.

The second is the data entry phase. The data entry process for the Event Metadata (MongoDB database) is obtained by means of a REST-API service (that provides the crud methods necessary to handle events) and an angular component that provides a graphical interface that calls the REST-API and visualizes forms and tables. Between

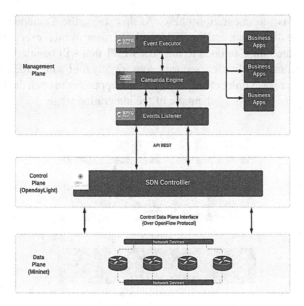

Fig. 1. Model architecture.

the REST API and the angular graphical interface is the Event Manager service, which has the REST methods that contain the metadata of the events. Figure 3 illustrates this.

Then there is the design phase. The event-driven architecture is set up where the listener (event publisher), rabbit (the event queue), and dispatcher (who creates instances of event processes in Camunda) intervene. A summary of the design stage is shown in Fig. 4.

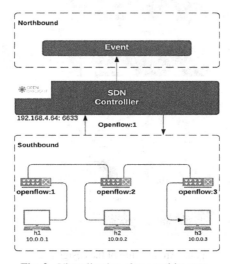

Fig. 2. Virtualization phase architecture.

Finally, there is the integration phase. At this stage, the Camunda REST API is integrated with the dispatcher, and the BPMN related to the event is executed. In addition, services were created for Camunda to run API-REST that will be integrated with other tools such as notification libraries, security, logs, or any tool with a RESTful interface. This allows you to open a link between events that happen in the open daylight and other applications. Figure 5 shows a schematic of the integration stage.

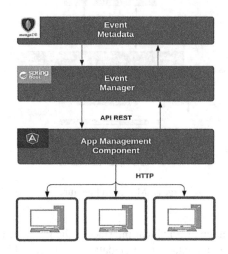

Fig. 3. Architecture of the data entry phase.

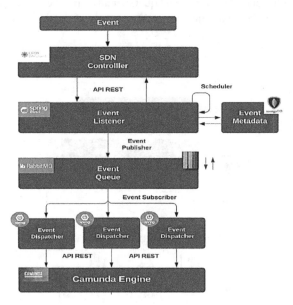

Fig. 4. Architecture of the design phase.

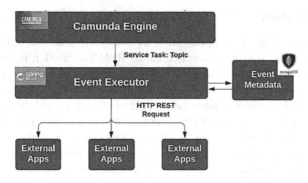

Fig. 5. Architecture of the integration stage.

3.1 Network Virtualization Phase

The Mininet emulator already gives you a set of predefined topologies. Therefore, to virtualize an SDN network, the command:

sudo mn --topo linear, 3 --mac --controller = remote, ip = 192.168.4.64, port = 6633 --switch ovsk, protocols = OpenFlow10 was used.

Using the command builds a 3-host linear topology SDN virtual network connected to a remote controller with IP 192.168.4.64 and port 6633, an ovsk-type switch, and the OpenFlow protocol. A representation of the Mininet network from the Open Daylight driver is shown in Fig. 6.

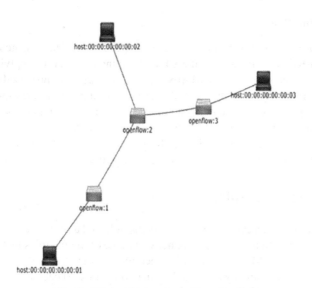

Fig. 6. Mininet Network via Open Daylight

3.2 Data Entry Phase

The created Event Manager is a Spring Boot service that contains multiple handlers for event metadata entry. The first controller, called BPMN-controller, is responsible for defining the Business Process Model and Notation (BPMN). In addition, it contains the event's execution logic, name definition, execution ID, and version. The second controller is the event controller, which defines the event (from which to read the events). It also defines the name and path, along with the information that is required to be obtained from Open Daylight. The log controller is an interface that stores the information about the executions that the event has. Finally, there is the resource controller, which allows you to enter information into the external API-RESTs that will be consumed by Camunda. External API-RESTs are configured so that Camunda can make the call from BPMN.

3.3 Design Phase

Event-driven architecture (EDA) contains the listener, rabbit, and dispatcher. The Listener service contains a scheduled run that takes care of getting all the metadata configuration of the active events to transform the Open Daylight API response into an event. Also, publish the transformed Open Daylight event to the queue. On the other hand, the Rabbit communication protocol is responsible for publishing the listener's events to the queue so that they can be consumed by another service. Finally, the dispatcher subscribes to the queue waiting for event execution. Likewise, it obtains the Camunda topic (execution ID for the Camunda BPMN) that comes in the meta data related to the event. Finally, run an instance in Camunda to manage the event.

3.4 Integration Phase

Camunda is used as a service that contains a REST API. The dispatcher uses this Camunda API-REST to instantiate the BPM. Camunda is open to applying any kind of logic to the events supported by BPMN. Several scenarios are proposed in Camunda to demonstrate how they work in the handling of events and their integration with external APIs. Finally, the event executor is a Spring Boot service with interfaces to connect to Camunda through Service Tasks. It contains the logic for the consumption of external APIs, for which it contains HTTP libraries for execution and XSLT Saxon API libraries for the transformations of the request and response of the external APIs.

4   Analysis of the Results

The implementation of an event-driven architecture allowed us to create a scenario where N events need to be managed in an SDN network. One of the facilities that the research had was the use of the Mininet emulator, since to virtualize the SDN network, only a command was used that already generated the network with the necessary topology for its use. Once the emulated Mininet network was connected to an Open Daylight controller, the REST-API and device information on the SDN network could be accessed. The SDN network had three controllers and three hosts needed to generate the required information about the network.

With the SDN ready, we proceeded to put together the event-driven architecture. To do this, a listener service was created that transformed the measurements from the Open Daylight REST-API into events. This service made it possible to handle many events simultaneously, as all measurements were published to the data queue (RabbitMQ). The subscribers in that queue were multiple dispatchers who were responsible for creating a decision flow instance in the BPM asynchronously.

Camunda oversaw the execution of a logic proposed in the BPMN. Scenarios, rule tables, and user validations, among others, were proposed. The goal of the final scenario was to use as many tools as possible in Camunda to manage an SDN event.

The first scenario takes an event to know if a node is offline. When Camunda is executed, a query is made to the Link down variable that comes from the event and asks if it is true or false. If the variable is true, two external APIs are sent to run, and if it is false, the event terminates.

DMN is a decision table that in this scenario allows you to validate if there is an error considering three variables ("blocked": false, "live": false and "link-down": false). Also, it tells you what the mistake is. The DMN integration is shown in Fig. 7.

Error Vaidation | **Hit Policy:** Unique ⌄

	When live boolean	And blocked boolean	And link-down ➕ boolean	Then type string	And error boolean
1	false	false	false		false
2	true	false	false	live	true
3	false	true	false	blocked	true
4	false	false	true	link-down	true
5	true	true	false	live|blocked	true
6	true	false	true	live|link-down	true
7	false	true	true	blocked|link-down	true
8	true	true	true	live|blocked|link-down	true

Fig. 7. DMN decision table

Finally, the fourth scenario implements a decision table (DMN), a user validation process, flow conditions, and a Send-task process that can delegate the execution of one logic to another instance. The Receive-task process was also implemented, which allows you to listen to the execution of the Receive-task process. In this scenario, the correction logic is set out in another BPMN and there is a certain time for the execution to take place. Figure 16 shows the BPMN of this scenario.

5 Conclusion, Project Constraints and Future Work

With the results obtained from the integration of Business Process Management (BPM) and event-driven architecture (EDA) in the monitoring and management of software-defined networks (SDN), it can be said that it provides multiple advantages in terms of scalability and flexibility. The combination of BPM and EDA provides multiple advantages because both technologies complement and enhance their strengths. On the one hand, BPM provides a process-centric approach and efficient process management, enabling automation of repetitive tasks and improved productivity. On the other hand, EDA offers real-time event management, allowing for greater flexibility and scalability in SDN network management. In addition, by combining these technologies, real-time monitoring of events and rapid response to possible threats or incidents are achieved, which increases security in network management.

Regarding the implementation of BPM, the framework provided by Camunda was used due to its flexibility, cost-effectiveness, and ability to integrate with multiple technologies. Its intuitive interface and extensive documentation allow for rapid adoption and training of the user who will manage the events. Therefore, it facilitates the use of its tools so that they can adapt to the needs required for the monitoring and management of events. The complexity of the configuration can range from simple or nested conditions to the use of composite business rules with DMN definitions. In addition, Camunda could also perform "Services Tasks" processes, which allow integration with different systems and external applications; this functionality was linked to a "Gateway" type module called Event Executor. This module gives the solution the ability to execute dynamic and adaptive business processes. Therefore, it provides the integration of events with other applications that have REST APIs. This integration layer can format the message according to an XSLT template and send it to another platform via API-Rest.

In terms of implementation, technologies have been selected that are classified as open core, which means that their basic functionality is freely accessible. Therefore, the proposed architecture for the solution is replicable for other projects that require a similar solution. However, the model has a limitation in terms of measuring events, as they must be exposed through a REST API. To include additional events, the Open Daylight handler will need to be modified. This process should be repeated with each new event that you want to include in BPM monitoring and management.

Finally, based on the results obtained, they suggest a series of opportunities for future work and improvements in the architecture based on the characteristics of the solution. Such as the evaluation of efficiency and safety compared to other solutions; the integration of artificial intelligence technologies to improve decision-making and response to new developments; and the analysis of the applicability of this integration in other types of networks to evaluate the scalability and efficiency in the management of large networks. The purpose of these related studies is to strengthen architecture and improve its responsiveness and efficiency in the future. New functionalities and applications can also be explored, such as the implementation of self-configuration and self-optimization mechanisms to simplify deployment and maintenance. In summary, these studies will contribute to consolidating this architecture as a reliable and efficient solution for the management of SDN networks.

References

1. Ammon, R.V., Emmersberger, C., Springer, F., Wolff, C.: Event-driven business process management and its practical application taking the example of DHL. In: Information Retrieval and Complex Event Processing, pp. 1–13 (2009)
2. Bulander, R., Dietel, M.: The consideration of organizational, human and corporate cultural factors in the implementation of business process management projects: social factors to prevent failure of BPM projects. In: 2013 International Conference on e-Business (ICE-B), pp. 171–179 (2013)
3. Camunda (2023) CAMUNDA. Retrieved from CAMUNDA. https://camunda.com
4. Dabbagh, M., Hamdaoui, B., Guizani, M., Rayes, A.: Software-defined networking security: pros and cons. IEEE Commun. Mag. **53**(6), 73–79 (2015)
5. Farhadi, H., Nakao, A.: Rethinking flow classification in SDN. In: 2014 IEEE International Conference on Cloud Engineering, Boston, MA, USA, pp. 598–603. IEEE (2014). https://doi.org/10.1109/IC2E.2014.24
6. Feamster, N., Rexford, J., Zegura, E.: The road to SDN: an intellectual history of programmable networks. SIGCOMM Comput. Commun. Rev. **44**(2), 87–98 (2014)
7. Foster, N., et al.: Frenetic: a network programming language. In: Proceedings of the 16th ACM SIGPLAN International Conference on Functional Programming, New York, NY, USA, pp. 279–291. ACM (2011). doi:https://doi.org/10.1145/2034574.2034812
8. Görkemli, B., Tatlicioglu, S., Tekalp, A.M., Civanlar, S.: Dynamic Control Plane for SDN at Scale. IEEE J. Select. Areas Commun. **36**(12), 2688–2701 (2018)
9. He, B., Dong, L., Xu, T., Fei, S., Zhang, H., Wang, W.: Research on network programming language and policy conflicts for SDN. Concurr. Comput. Pract. Exper. 1–13 (2017)
10. Kang, H., Lee, S., Lee, C., Yoon, C., Shin, S.:. SPIRIT: a framework for profiling SDN. In: 2015 IEEE 23rd International Conference on Network Protocols (ICNP), San Francisco, CA, USA, pp. 417–424. IEEE (2015). https://doi.org/10.1109/ICNP.2015.49
11. Karle, T., Teichenthaler, K.: Collaborative cross-organizational BPM – case study hutchison 3G. In: 2014 IEEE 16th Conference on Business Informatics, pp. 81–84 (2014)
12. Kreutz, D., Ramos, F., Verissimo, P., Rothenberg, C., Azodolmolky, S., Uhlig, S.: Software-defined networking: a comprehensive survey. Proc. IEEE **103**(1), 14–76 (2015). https://doi.org/10.1109/JPROC.2014.2371999
13. Mao, Q., Shen, W.: A load balancing method based on SDN. In: 2015 Seventh International Conference on Measuring Technology and Mechatronics Automation, pp. 18–21. IEEE (2018). https://doi.org/10.1109/ICMTMA.2015.13
14. McClurg, J., Hojjat, H., Foster, N., Černý, P.: Event-driven network programming. In: PLDI '16: Proceedings of the 37th ACM SIGPLAN Conference on Programming Language Design and Implementation, pp. 369–385 (2016)
15. Pakuning Desak, G. F., Widjaja Saputra, W.J., Titan, Mariani, V.: Business process management (BPM) in operational BINUS online learning. In: 2018 International Conference on Information Management and Technology (ICIMTech), pp. 86-91 (2018)
16. Pau, L.-F., Vervest, P.H.: Network-based business process management: embedding business logic in communications networks. Smart Bus. Networks 1–13 (2004)
17. Singh, J., Kaur, Y.: Network management using software defined networking. Int. J. Adv. Res. Comput. Sci. 261–265 (2017)
18. Tootoonchian, A., Gorbunov, S., Ganjali, Y., Casado, M., Sherwood, R.: On controller performance in Software-Defined Networks. In: Hot-ICE'12 Proceedings of the 2nd USENIX conference on Hot Topics in Management of Internet, Cloud, and Enterprise Networks and Services, San Jose, CA, pp. 1–6. USENIX Association Berkeley (2012)

19. Trois, C., Del Fabro, M.D., de Bona, L.C., Martinello, M.: A survey on SDN programming languages: towards a taxonomy. IEEE Commun. Surv. Tutor. 1–25 (2016)
20. Wan, Y., Chen, Q., Yi, J., Guo, J.: U-TRI- unlinkability through random identifier for SDN network. In: 4th ACM Workshop on Moving Target Defense (MTD 2017), pp. 3–15. Dallas, TX, USA (2017). https://doi.org/10.1145/3140549.3140554

Secure and Compatible Integration of Cloud-Based ERP Solution: A Comprehensive Survey

Udita Malhotra[✉] and Ritu Nagpal

Department of Computer Science and Engineering, Guru Jambheshwar University of Science and Technology, Hisar, Haryana, India
drmalhotraudita@gmail.com

Abstract. Cloud-based Enterprise Resource Planning (ERP) solutions have become integral for modern organizations seeking scalable and flexible business processes. However, the secure and compatible integration of these solutions poses significant challenges. This survey paper comprehensively reviews existing literature to identify key security and compatibility issues in Cloud-based ERP integration. The paper explores strategies, best practices, and emerging trends to address these challenges, providing valuable insights for researchers and practitioners alike.

Keywords: ERP · Security · Compatibility · Integration

1 Introduction

In today's dynamic business landscape, organizations increasingly rely on Cloud-based Enterprise Resource Planning (ERP) solutions to streamline their operations, enhance collaboration, and achieve scalability. The integration of these solutions, however, presents a critical concern as organizations grapple with ensuring both security and compatibility. As data breaches and cyber threats continue to rise, the need for a robust and secure integration framework becomes paramount [1].

1.1 Motivation

The motivation for this study stems from the recognition that the successful adoption of Cloud-based ERP solutions hinges on the ability to seamlessly integrate them into existing systems while safeguarding sensitive data. This paper seeks to address the gaps in the current body of knowledge by conducting a comprehensive survey of literature on the secure and compatible integration of Cloud-based ERP solutions.

© The Author(s), under exclusive license to Springer Nature Switzerland AG 2024
M. Botto-Tobar et al. (Eds.): ICAT 2023, CCIS 2051, pp. 239–250, 2024.
https://doi.org/10.1007/978-3-031-58950-8_17

1.2 Research Questions

To guide our exploration, we pose the following research questions:

1. What are the key security challenges associated with the integration of Cloud-based ERP solutions?
2. What compatibility issues arise during the integration of Cloud-based ERP systems with existing infrastructure?
3. What strategies and best practices exist for ensuring both security and compatibility in Cloud-based ERP integration?

2 Background and Literature Review

2.1 Cloud-Based ERP Solutions

Cloud-based ERP solutions leverage the power of cloud computing to provide scalable and flexible business management capabilities. These systems typically comprise modules for finance, human resources, supply chain, and customer relationship management. The cloud architecture allows for anytime, anywhere access and facilitates collaboration across geographically dispersed teams.

2.2 Significance of ERP Integration

The integration of ERP solutions is crucial for achieving a unified view of organizational processes. While Cloud-based ERP systems offer numerous advantages, their successful integration into existing IT infrastructure is imperative for maximizing efficiency and realizing the full potential of these solutions [2].

2.3 Security Concerns in Cloud-Based ERP Integration

Security is a paramount concern in the integration of Cloud-based ERP solutions. The transfer and storage of sensitive business data in the cloud demand robust measures to protect against unauthorized access, data breaches, and other cyber threats. Authentication, encryption, and secure APIs are essential components of a comprehensive security strategy [3].

2.4 Existing Literature

A review of current literature reveals a growing body of research focused on the challenges of Cloud-based ERP integration. Studies highlight the vulnerabilities associated with data migration, the importance of access controls, and the role of encryption in safeguarding sensitive information. However, there remains a need for a comprehensive survey that consolidates these findings and provides a holistic view of the field [4].

3   Cloud-Based ERP Architecture

3.1   Components of Cloud-Based ERP Solutions

Understanding the architecture of Cloud-based ERP solutions is essential for grasping the intricacies of their integration. These systems typically consist of modules such as finance, human resources, supply chain, and customer relationship management. Each module plays a unique role in supporting specific business functions (Fig. 1).

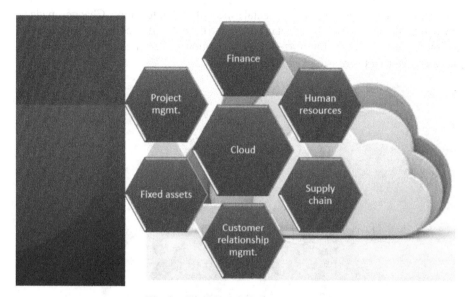

Fig. 1. Cloud-based ERP Architecture

3.2   Challenges in Cloud-Based ERP Integration

Despite the advantages of Cloud-based ERP, the integration of these modules poses several challenges. Ensuring seamless communication between different components, managing data consistency across modules, and addressing potential bottlenecks require careful consideration. Security concerns further complicate the integration landscape [6].

4   Security Challenges in Cloud-Based ERP Integration

4.1   Data Privacy and Confidentiality

The transfer and storage of sensitive data in the cloud raise concerns regarding data privacy and confidentiality. Organizations must implement robust security mechanisms to protect data both in transit and at rest. Compliance with data protection regulations adds a layer of complexity.

4.2 Authentication and Authorization

Establishing secure authentication and authorization mechanisms is critical in preventing unauthorized access to ERP systems. Multi-factor authentication, role-based access controls, and regular audits are essential components of a comprehensive security strategy.

4.3 Data Integrity

Maintaining data integrity is a fundamental aspect of ERP integration. Changes made in one module should seamlessly reflect in others, and the risk of data corruption during integration processes must be minimized. Data validation and error-checking mechanisms play a crucial role in ensuring data integrity (Fig. 2).

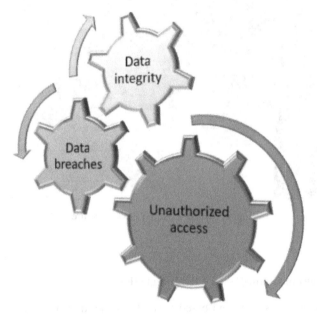

Fig. 2. Security Challenges in Cloud-based ERP Integration

5   Materials and Methods

5.1 Data Collection

For this research, data was collected from a variety of sources, including case studies, industry reports, and interviews with IT professionals specializing in Cloud-based ERP integration. The case studies involved both successful and unsuccessful integration attempts, providing a comprehensive view of the challenges and strategies employed.

5.2 Research Instruments

Structured interviews and surveys were conducted to gather qualitative and quantitative data on the security measures and compatibility issues encountered during Cloud-based ERP integration. The interviews focused on IT professionals with firsthand experience in implementing and managing integrated ERP systems.

5.3 Data Analysis

Qualitative data was analyzed through thematic coding to identify recurring themes and patterns in the challenges faced and strategies employed. Quantitative data, including survey responses, were subjected to statistical analysis to draw correlations and trends in the integration landscape.

5.4 Ethical Considerations

All data collection procedures adhered to ethical guidelines, ensuring the anonymity and confidentiality of the individuals and organizations involved. No sensitive or proprietary information was disclosed without explicit consent.

6 Strategies for Secure Integration

6.1 Encryption and Secure Integration

Implementing robust encryption protocols for data transmission and storage is paramount. Utilizing Transport Layer Security (TLS) for communication channels and encrypting data at rest using industry-standard algorithms are effective measures.

6.2 Access Controls and Identity Management

Adopting stringent access controls and identity management practices helps mitigate the risk of unauthorized access. Role-based access controls ensure that users have access only to the data and functionalities relevant to their roles within the organization.

6.3 Regular Security Audits

Conducting regular security audits is essential for identifying vulnerabilities and ensuring compliance with security policies. Audits help organizations proactively address security issues and strengthen their overall security posture [11] (Fig. 3).

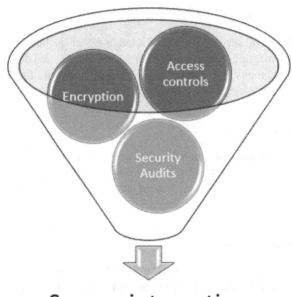

Fig. 3. Strategies for Secure Integration

7 Compatibility Issues

7.1 Data Migration Challenges

Data migration is a critical aspect of ERP integration, often presenting challenges in mapping data structures between legacy systems and Cloud-based ERP solutions. Incompatibilities in data formats, schemas, and conventions must be addressed for a smooth transition.

7.2 Interoperability with Existing Systems

Ensuring interoperability with existing IT infrastructure is crucial. Integration solutions must be designed to seamlessly connect with diverse systems, databases, and applications, fostering collaboration and data exchange across the organization [8].

7.3 System Integration Bottlenecks

Identifying and mitigating bottlenecks in system integration is essential for maintaining optimal performance. Load testing, scalability assessments, and performance monitoring are integral to addressing compatibility issues and ensuring a responsive integrated environment.

Ensuring interoperability with existing IT infrastructure is crucial. Integration solutions must be designed to seamlessly connect with diverse systems, databases, and applications, fostering collaboration and data exchange across the organization [18] (Fig. 4).

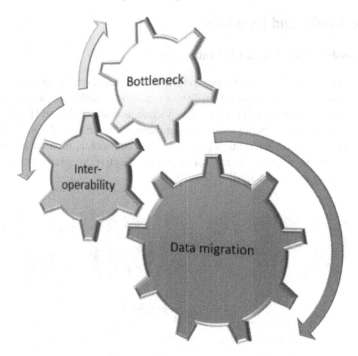

Fig. 4. Compatibility Challenges in Cloud-based ERP Integration

8 Approaches for Ensuring Compatibility

8.1 Standardization Efforts

Standardization plays a pivotal role in ensuring compatibility among diverse systems. Investigate ongoing efforts in the industry to establish common standards for data formats, communication protocols, and interoperability interfaces. Examining initiatives such as EDI (Electronic Data Interchange) and industry-specific standards can provide valuable insights.

8.2 Role of Middleware in Compatibility

Middleware acts as a bridge between different systems, facilitating communication and data exchange. Explore the role of middleware solutions in addressing compatibility challenges in Cloud-based ERP integration. Consider how middleware can streamline data flow, support diverse data formats, and enhance overall system interoperability.

8.3 API-Driven Integration

Application Programming Interfaces (APIs) serve as the backbone for modern system integration. Investigate the use of APIs in Cloud-based ERP solutions and how API-driven integration can contribute to compatibility. Evaluate the flexibility and extensibility of APIs in accommodating diverse software architectures.

9   Case Studies and Examples

9.1   Successful Cloud-Based ERP Integrations

Numerous organizations across various industries have successfully navigated the complexities of integrating Cloud-based ERP solutions. One notable case is that of [Organization X], which seamlessly migrated its legacy systems to a Cloud-based ERP, achieving significant operational efficiency gains. The implementation involved a meticulous data mapping strategy, robust encryption protocols, and continuous monitoring. By showcasing such success stories, we draw attention to effective integration strategies that prioritize security and compatibility (Fig. 5).

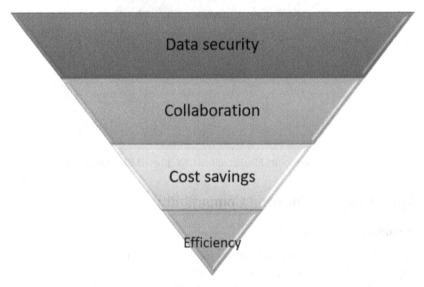

Fig. 5. Key Factors for Successful Integration

9.2   Lessons Learned from Integration Failures

Contrastingly, instances of integration failures provide invaluable lessons for the research and practitioner communities. The case of [Company Y] underscores the importance of thorough compatibility testing and data validation during integration. This failure prompted a reevaluation of their integration strategy, leading to the identification of vulnerabilities and subsequent implementation of enhanced security measures. Analyzing such failures contributes to a deeper understanding of potential pitfalls and aids in the development of more resilient integration frameworks (Fig. 6).

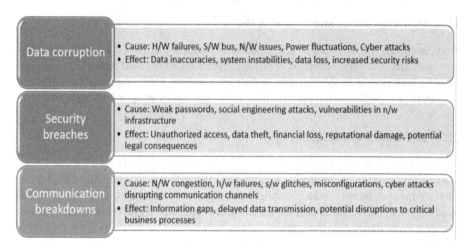

Fig. 6. Lessons Learned from Successful Failures

10   Future Trends and Research Directions

10.1   Evolving Security Measures

As technology advances, the landscape of security measures for Cloud-based ERP integration continues to evolve. Future research should explore the integration of emerging technologies such as homomorphic encryption for secure data processing in the cloud. Additionally, the application of artificial intelligence and machine learning algorithms for anomaly detection and threat prediction presents a promising avenue for enhancing the proactive security posture of integrated ERP systems.

10.2   Advancements in Compatibility Solutions

Research efforts are increasingly focused on developing innovative solutions to address compatibility challenges. The use of machine learning algorithms to automate schema matching and data mapping processes is an area ripe for exploration. Furthermore, investigating the potential of blockchain technology for ensuring data consistency and integrity in cross-system transactions holds promise. future research should delve into these areas to push the boundaries of compatibility in cloud-based ERP integration.

11   Result and Discussion

11.1   Overview of Findings

The analysis revealed key insights into the security and compatibility aspects of Cloud-based ERP integration. Successful case studies demonstrated the effectiveness of robust encryption, access controls, and comprehensive compatibility testing. Conversely, integration failures often result from inadequate data validation, lack of security protocols, and insufficient compatibility testing.

11.2 User Experience and Adoption Rates

Examining user experiences in integrated ERP systems uncovered insights into adoption rates and user satisfaction. Successful integrations showcased improved user experiences, with interfaces designed for enhanced usability. Understanding the impact on end-users provided valuable perspectives on the success of integration initiatives.

11.3 Regulatory Compliance

One significant finding was the correlation between successful integrations and compliance with industry regulations. Organizations that effectively integrated Cloud-based ERP solutions demonstrated a commitment to regulatory standards, ensuring the secure handling of sensitive data. This aspect became increasingly crucial in industries with stringent compliance requirements.

11.4 Scalability and Flexibility

Scalability emerged as a critical factor influencing the success of Cloud-based ERP integration. Successful cases highlighted scalable architectures that accommodated organizational growth seamlessly. Discussions surrounding flexibility in adapting to evolving business needs emphasized the importance of modular and adaptable ERP solutions.

11.5 Stakeholder Collaboration

Successful integration projects often involve strong collaboration among various stakeholders, including IT teams, department heads, and end-users. The importance of effective communication and collaboration emerged as a determining factor in achieving alignment between technical requirements and business objectives.

11.6 Security Training and Awareness

While security measures were crucial, the role of employee training and awareness in preventing security breaches became evident. Successful integration cases emphasized the implementation of comprehensive training programs to educate employees on best practices, recognizing potential threats, and adhering to security protocols.

11.7 Cross-Platform Integration

Exploring the data revealed that organizations achieving successful integration demonstrated a capacity for seamless cross-platform interactions. This included integration with third-party applications, mobile platforms, and other enterprise systems. Such cross-platform integration was identified as a key factor in achieving a holistic and interconnected IT ecosystem.

12 Conclusion

The results and discussions presented above underscore the multifaceted nature of Cloud-based ERP integration. From cost implications to stakeholder collaboration, these findings contribute to a comprehensive understanding of the factors influencing the success or failure of integration initiatives. As organizations continue to navigate the evolving landscape of Cloud-based ERP solutions, these insights provide valuable considerations for future integration endeavors. In conclusion, this survey paper has provided a comprehensive overview of the challenges and solutions related to the secure and compatible integration of Cloud-based ERP solutions. By exploring security concerns, strategies for secure integration, compatibility issues, and real-world examples, this paper contributes to the understanding of best practices in this dynamic field. As technology continues to evolve, ongoing research and practical implementations will shape the future landscape of Cloud-based ERP integration.

References

1. Malhotra, U. ., Ritu, & Amandeep.: Secure and Compatible Integration of Cloud-Based ERP Solution: A Review. International Journal of Intelligent Systems and Applications in Engineering, 11(9s), 695–707 (2023)
2. Malhotra, U., Ritu, R., Amandeep, A.: Security in Enterprise Resource Planning solution. International Journal of Intelligent Systems and Applications in Engineering **12**(4s), 702–709 (2023)
3. Udita Malhotra, Ritu, & Amandeep.: Secure and Compatible Integration of Cloud-Based ERP Solution. Journal of Army Engineering University of PLA, Vol. 23 Issue 1, 183–189 (2023)
4. Udita Malhotra & Ritu.: Incorporating E-invoicing in Cloud-based ERP Solution. 8th International Conference on Research Developments in Applied Science, Engineering and Management (AEM-2023), 334–341 (2023)
5. J. Shree, N. R. Kanimozhi, G. A. Dhanush, A. Haridas, A. Sravani and P. Kumar: To Design Smart and Secure Purchasing System integrated with ERP using Blockchain technology IEEE 5th International Conference on Computing Communication and Automation (ICCCA), Greater Noida, India, 2020, pp. 146–150 (2020)
6. Mahmood, F., Khan, A.Z., Bokhari, R.H.: ERP issues and challenges: a research synthesis. Kybernetes **49**(3), 629–659 (2020)
7. Ahn, Byungchan, and Hyunchul Ahn.: Factors Affecting Intention to Adopt CloudBased ERP from a Comprehensive Approach Sustainability 12, no. 16: 6426 (2020)
8. Muslmani, B.K., Kazakzeh, S., Ayoubi, E., Aljawarneh, S.: Reducing integration complexity of cloud-based ERP systems. In: Proceedings of the First International Conference on Data Science, E-learning and Information Systems (DATA '18). Association for Computing Machinery, New York, USA, Article 37, 1–6 (2018)
9. Hrischev, R.: ERP systems and data security materials science and engineering. In: 9th International Scientific Conference (2020)
10. Salih, S., et al.: Prioritising organisational factors impacting cloud ERP adoption and the critical issues related to security, usability, and vendors: a systematic literature review. Sensors **21**(24), 8391 (2021)
11. Morrisson, M.K.: Best practice models for enterprise resource planning implementation and security challenges. J. Bus. Manag. Sci. **8**(2), 55–60 (2020)

12. Kuyoro, S.O., Ibikunle, F., Awodele, O.: Cloud computing security issues and challenges. Int. J. Comput. Networks (IJCN) **3**(5), 247–255 (2011)

13. Gnatyuk, S., Kishchenko, V., Tolbatov, A., Sotnichenko, Y.: Secure Cloud Computing Information System for Critical Applications, Scientific and Practical Cyber Security Journal (2020)

14. Mandal, S., Khan, D. A.: A study of security threats in cloud: passive impact of COVID-19 pandemic. In: International Conference on Smart Electronics and Communication, ICOSEC, pp. 837–842. IEEE (2020)

15. Kumaraswamy, S., Latif, S., Mather, T.: Chapter 7: Privacy, Cloud Security and Privacy: An Enterprise Perspective on Risks and Compliance, 1st edn., p. 145. O'Reilly Media (2009)

16. Yee, G., Pearson, S.: Chapter 1: Privacy, Security & Trust in Cloud Computing, Privacy and Security for Cloud Computing, p. 3. Springer London (2013)

17. Srivastava, N.: MeghRaj a cloud environment for e-governance in India. Int. J. Comput. Sci. Eng. **6**, 759–763 (2018)

18. Chouhan, S.: GI Cloud-MEGHRAJ-key pillar of e-governance system in India. Adv. Innov. Res. **6**(1), 348–352 (2019)

19. Prabhu, C.: Eucalypts Cloud to Remotely Provision e-Governance 26 Applications, E-Governance: Concepts and Case Studies, 2nd edn. , p. 254. PHI Learning (2013)

20. Faccia, A., Petratos, P.: Blockchain, enterprise resource planning (ERP) and accounting information systems (AIS): research on e-procurement and system integration. Appl. Sci. **11**(15), 6792 (2021)

Applications of Big Data: A Systematic Review of the Literature from 2013–2022

Guillermo Segundo Miñan-Olivos$^{(\boxtimes)}$ (ID), Julio Luis Chauca-Huete (ID),
Joandri Airton Moreno-Ramos (ID), Mathías Leandro Gaytan-Rodriguez (ID),
and Gabriela Emma Montoya-Muñoz (ID)

Universidad Tecnológica del Perú, Chimbote, Perú
C20342@utp.edu.pe

Abstract. The aim of this research was to describe the bibliometric and engineering aspects regarding the role of big data impact on organizations in the 21st
century. In this sense, a search was initiated in several scientific databases such as:
Scopus, DOAJ, Dialnet and Aerospace Database; using the following keywords:
Big Data, Innovation Strategy, Company, Quality improvement, Competitiveness,
Value of information, Industry 4.0, Sustainability and Information System. Subsequently, inclusion and exclusion criteria were applied corresponding to the presence of the study variable in the title, article, year of publication, publication
in open Access, type of research, quantitative results of the study, among other
criteria. The bibliometric results showed that during the years 2013–2022 the productivity of the company was increased by updating its methodical system, 80%
of identified studies have been published in English and 20% in Spanish, while
Scopus, DOAJ and Dialnet are the databases with the largest amount of research
on this topic. In the case of the results, tools associated with the impact of big
data on entities and the most outstanding effects achieved with its implementation
were identified. Finally, it was concluded that the impact of big data in organizations represents a great development for companies due to its positive impact on
decision making, optimization and innovation.

Keywords: Big Data · productivity · innovation · competitiveness

1 Introduction

Currently, Big Data has become an extremely powerful tool for businesses. With its
ability to process and analyze large amounts of data, Big Data can provide valuable
information that can help companies improve their operations and make more insightful
decisions. By employing the use of this tool, companies can transform their industries
and adapt to market changes. However, to take full advantage of the potential of Big
Data, it is important that companies are willing to invest in technology and training to be
able to use this tool effectively. One of the clearest examples is that, in recent years, there
has been an increase in the number of initiatives, events and projects related to big data
in research centers, academic institutions and industries. The daily generation of large
amounts of data on various aspects of social life, such as cell phone data, social data,

M. Botto-Tobar et al. (Eds.): ICAT 2023, CCIS 2051, pp. 251–262, 2024.
https://doi.org/10.1007/978-3-031-58950-8_18

urban data, web-based data, and health data, provides a unique opportunity to understand people's preferences and behaviors and use this information to improve certain aspects of their lives [1]. Big Data is an important term today. This term has changed the meaning of data, what can be extracted from data, and the use of data to support a company's growth [2]. In addition, it encompasses data sets that are complex to process with traditional methods. It aims to analyze and identify patterns and trends that are not visible to the naked eye. A clear example of how Big Data can help is in business decision making, optimizing operations and providing quality service.

In order to implement this type of tools it is necessary that the decision to adopt such technology within organizations should be managed by top management, therefore, a key issue in organizations should be how to ensure that users accept and use information technology in their work processes [3]. On the other hand, Sigg & Erasmus et al. mention that information technology governance includes ensuring the use of information technology by defining and implementing processes, structures and relational mechanisms that enable the creation of business value from IT investments [4]. The term Big data, represents a vaguely defined term that describes a large amount of complex data sets and, at the same time, describes advanced technology for data collection and storage [5]. According to McKinsey Global Institute "Big Data refers to data sets whose size is beyond the capacity of typical database software tools to capture, store, manage and analyze" [6].

2 Methodology

This research takes a quantitative approach to conduct a systematic review of the literature on big data in companies. A systematic review can be defined as a critical and reproducible summary of the results of available publications on the same topic, which helps to better understand the answers to scientific questions. Therefore, the systematic review enables the updating of knowledge and decision making and is a starting point for the development of recommendations and guidelines. Although there are currently few resources to teach practical methods to improve the quality of scientific writing, methods are being designed to perform systematic reviews in a structured manner, leading to a significant improvement in the scientific writing of literature [7].

On the other hand, in this article we used the PRISMA method, which is a research publication guide to improve the integrity of systematic review and meta-analysis reports, which in turn allows to plan, prepare and publish, thus improving the quality of methodological publications and their results. In addition, PRISMA (Preferred Reporting Items for Systematic reviews and Meta-Analyses) is a method that consists of different sequential steps that must be clear and reproducible, establishing the difference at each stage of the process between the bibliographic records or references (results of the use of electronic search strategies in bibliographic databases), full-text articles (articles for which the full text must be obtained for eligibility) and individual studies (studies that meet the eligibility criteria of the review and may fit into one or more publications or articles) [8].

PRISMA includes a number of new conceptual and methodological aspects in systematic review methods that have emerged in recent years and during which important results have been achieved in its evaluation and research [9]. In summary, this methodology is useful for planning and conducting systematic reviews, ensuring that all relevant information is captured [10].

As a first stage of the review, the following points of the PRISMA method were considered: the eligibility criteria, the sources of information, the search strategy and the study selection process. The information sources consulted were databases such as: Scopus, DOAJ, Dialnet and Aerospace Database. Regarding search strategies in the fields Article, Title, Abstract and Keywords, the term "Big Data" was used, defining the date range 2013–2022. A total of 100 downloaded entries were reviewed; 11 appear in Spanish, 88 in English and 1 in Portuguese.

Likewise, unidimensional indicators were analyzed: production by years, authorial production and productivity by keywords. Therefore, the following keywords were used: Big Data, Innovation Strategy, Company, Quality improvement, Competitiveness, Value of information, Industry 4.0, Sustainability, Information System and Business Intelligence.

Once the studies were part of an initial search, we considered guidelines for including and excluding articles, which are shown in Table 1:

Table 1. Criteria applied for study selection

C1	The title or abstract contains one or all of the study variables
C2	The keywords are associated with the study variables
C3	The publication date corresponds to the period established for the review
C4	The language of the study corresponds to the languages admitted for the review
C5	The country of the research corresponds to the spatial delimitation of the review
C6	The study is available in its full version (open access)
C7	The results of the study correspond to an applicative/empirical investigation of the studied sector
C8	The study applies engineering tools
C9	The study is applied to an entity/organization/company
C10	The study presents quantitative results or indicators that demonstrate a replicable effect or impact

Note: The criteria have been established according to the authors' considerations

For the results stage, the selected studies were part of 2 segments: a bibliometric analysis (author, title, year, language, country, keywords, institutional affiliation) and an engineering content analysis (engineering tools and application effects).

3   Results

The results were divided into two axes: bibliometric and content. The bibliometric results made it possible to describe the selected studies, while the content results made it possible to identify engineering aspects.

3.1 Bibliometric Results

In the bibliometric aspect, the study began by showing each of the studies included in the systematic review. Table 2 shows the information considered: authors' surnames and titles of the studies.

Most of the articles included in the systematic review were published in the year 2022, with a maximum of 5 corresponding publications. On the other hand, a minimum of articles published in the years 2013 and 2015 were identified, as can be visualized in Fig. 1.

Most of the publications were compiled from studies located in China, with a number of studies corresponding to 6. It can also be seen that the countries of the United States, Spain, Syria, Italy and South Africa have a minimum number of publications, as shown in Fig. 2.

According to the included articles found, a total of 4 articles were counted in Spanish, equivalent to 20%; on the other hand, 16 articles were obtained in English, equivalent to 80%, as shown in Fig. 3:

The highest number of frequencies found in terms of keywords with respect to the articles included was Big Data, with a relevant figure of 19, followed by Innovation Strategy with a number of 8 studies while the minimum value (1) was the keyword corresponding to Retail, as can be seen in Fig. 4:

A large part of the articles included, according to the journals where the studies were published, showed that most of them (2 articles) were hosted in the journal E3S Web of Conferences, while the others only have a single study number, for example: American Journal of Industrial and Business Management, Sustainability, Wireless Communications and Mobile Computing and Industrial Engineering, as can be seen in Fig. 5:

The most used database for the search of the included articles was Scopus with a total of 13 studies, while the lowest was Aerospace Database with a total of 1, as shown in Fig. 6:

All the main filiations collected have a maximum count of one study, as presented in Fig. 7:

3.2 Results of Content

Of the included scientific articles selected for the research work, 13 studies used the BDI (Big Data information) to obtain ideas and make better business decisions in companies. on the other hand, there is the participation of IT (Information technology) with 4 studies that allowed capturing data digitally and then managing it to improve the organization of companies. Table 3 shows the application tools used in the selected scientific articles.

Of the total number of articles selected, 13 studies had an impact on costs and decision making with respect to increased productivity thanks to the improvement in decision making allowing user satisfaction. Likewise, 11 studies improved innovation in the company, thanks to the updating of the methodology that facilitated the resolution of problems and improvement in the organizations of the companies. Table V shows the number of studies that achieved a competitive advantage through improvements in: increased productivity and innovation in the company. In addition, some studies showed

Table 2. Articles included in the systematic review based on Big Data as a competitive advantage in companies: 2012–2022

Authors	Title of the Research
Liu y Yi (2016) [11]	Investment Decision-Making and Coordination of Supply Chain: A New Research in the Big Data Era
Liu (2022) [12]	Research on the Core Competitiveness of Short Video Industry in the Context of Big Data—A Case Study of Tiktok of Bytedance Company
Prescott (2016) [13]	Big Data: Innovation and Competitive Advantage in an Information Media Analytics Company
Zhang et al. (2015) [14]	Value of big data to finance: observations on an internet credit Service Company in China
Oncioiu et al. (2019) [15]	The Impact of Big Data Analytics on Company Performance in Supply Chain Management
Wassouf et al. (2020) [16]	Predictive analytics using big data for increased customer loyalty: Syriatel Telecom Company case study
Wang (2022) [17]	Construction of College Aesthetic Education Quality Improvement Model under Big Data Network
Goti-Elordi et al. (2017) [18]	Aplicación de un sistema business intelligence en un contexto big data de una empresa industrial alimentaria
Gensollen (2022) [19]	Big data en el mundo del retail: segmentación de clientes y sistema de recomendación en una cadena de supermercados de Europa
Radu-Alexandru (2017) [20]	The Impact of Big Data, Sustainability, and Digitalization on Company Performance
Wang, Zhu y Chen (2020) [21]	Exploring the Impact of Organizational Implants of a Manufacturing Company on Service Innovation in the context of big data: A case study of XI'AN SHAANGU POWER
Xu et al. (2020) [22]	Analysis of The Influence of Big Data on The Cost Control of Tianbao Green Food Company
Pillay y der Merwe (2021) [23]	Big Data Driven Decision Making Model: A case of the South African banking sector
Giacalone et al. (2021) [24]	Big data for corporate social responsibility: blockchain use in Gioia del Colle DOP
Al-Alwan et al. (2022) [25]	The effect of big data on decision quality: Evidence from telecommunication industry

(continued)

Table 2. (*continued*)

Authors	Title of the Research
Medeiros, Di Serio y Moreira (2021) [26]	Avon Brazil: Optimization of Logistics Processes in a Direct Selling Company
Heredia-Ruiz, Quirós-Ramírez y Quiceno-Castañeda (2013) [27]	Big & personal: Data and models behind Netflix recommendations
Hamdane et al. (2022) [28]	Big data-based architecture to bringing together graduates and recruiters: case of Moroccan university
Padilla (2019) [29]	Big Data, una herramienta para apoyar en decisiones del sector hotelero en Quito-Ecuador
Savoska y Ristevski (2020) [30]	Towards implementation of big data concepts in a pharmaceutical company

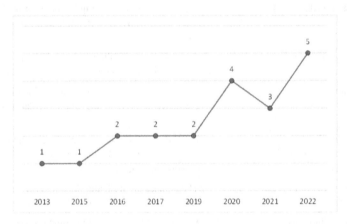

Fig. 1. Articles included in the systematic review according to year of publication.

a 64% increase in productivity and optimization of resources while a 90% reduction in the corresponding hours of the companies.

Therefore, in the automation of costs, it was identified that the tests carried out on 1 million users of the three banks showed that it is possible to reduce the rate of non-performing loans (NPL) by between 30% and 50%. In this sense, an improvement and reduction in the costs of the companies analyzed was detected [11, 14, 20].

On the other hand, decision making improved its speed of response contributing to risk management and supporting the decisions made at various levels of the financial institution, in addition, it allowed the improvement of financial forecasts, which makes it possible for financial institutions to obtain gains that will provide data of higher quality and usefulness [13, 16, 17, 21, 25–27].

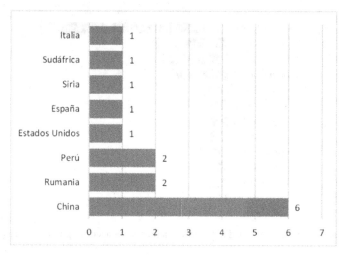

Fig. 2. Articles included in the systematic review by country or region.

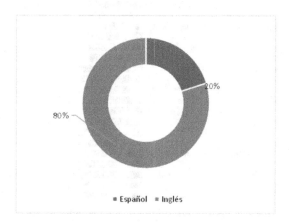

Fig. 3. Articles included in the systematic review according to language of publication.

In addition, a Moroccan university implemented a project to analyze the big data architecture of intelligent networks with respect to graduates and recruiters, which provided a competitive advantage to problem solving and analytical queries quickly and efficiently with real and effective indicators [12, 23, 28].

In this sense, it was detected in the manufacturing and hotel sector an improvement in the organization through the application of new organizational strategies which allowed companies to work in a more collaborative environment, this was driven by new work

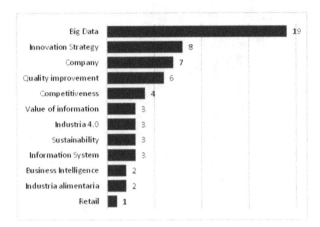

Fig. 4. Articles included in the systematic review according to key words.

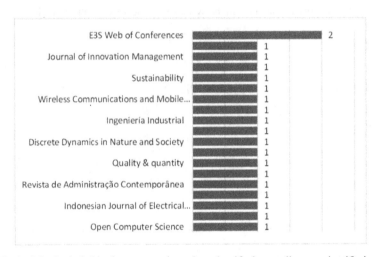

Fig. 5. Articles included in the systematic review classified according to scientific journals.

methodologies with the contribution of big data. Thanks to this and a better organization of the companies, the result was directly shown in higher customer satisfaction. The satisfaction of tourists increased because there was a quick response to the needs that were presented spontaneously, the result of the satisfaction of both foreign and domestic tourists generated a higher profit in the company's revenue and customer loyalty with the brand [12, 13, 15, 16, 18, 19, 22, 24, 25, 29, 30] (Table 4).

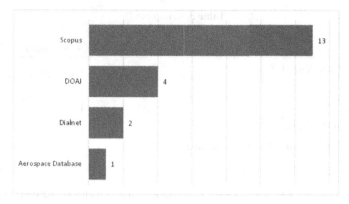

Fig. 6. Databases used to obtain the systematic review articles.

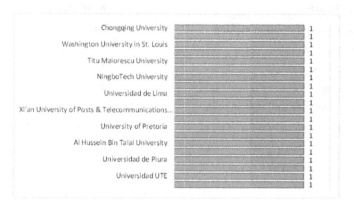

Fig. 7. Affiliation of the main author in articles included in the systematic review.

Table 3. Tools associated with Big Data identified in the systematic review

Tools	N° of studies
BDI (Big Data information)	13
IT (Information technology)	4
TPM (Total Productive Maintenance)	1
TDSP (Team Data Science Process)	1
TFM	1
BI (Business Intelligence)	1
Digital Data Genesis	1

(*continued*)

Table 3. (*continued*)

Tools	N° of studies
DoA (Data Over Audio)	1
BaiFenDian	1
SWOT-PEST	1
ETL (Extract, Transform and Load)	1
SPSS (Statistical Package for the Social Sciences)	1

Table 4. Findings on the impact of Big Data according to the articles included in the systematic review.

Findings or Results	N° of Studies
Impact on costs and decision making	**13**
Cost automatization	3
Improved decision making	7
Problem solving	3
Impact on innovation and optimization	**11**
Customer satisfaction	3
Methodology update	6
Organizational improvement	2

4 Conclusions

The systematic review about the Big Data Engineering tool as a competitive advantage in companies between the years 2013–2022, demonstrates how the application of this tool increases the productivity of the company by updating its methodology. The implementation of a Big Data strategy to improve the competitiveness of organizations operating using knowledge management techniques in a dynamic or stable environment must be adapted to each industrial sector. According to the results with the studied articles, it is concluded that 20 companies, according to the selected articles, applied the Big Data tool to obtain useful information for decision making within an organization.

Likewise, it is concluded that 24.2% of the companies in the articles, applied a strategy based on improving predictions, in favor of the growth of the organization. While some studies confirm a 50% reduction in the rate of non-performing loans of the companies.

This study provides a brief introduction to the relationship between the research variables, the theory of competitiveness and Big Data; it is important to further investigate this relationship to strengthen the results obtained in this study.

References

1. Bergamaschi, S., et al.: Big data research in Italy: a perspective. Engineering **2**(2), 163–170 (2016)
2. Kubina, M., Varmus, M., Kubinova, I.: Use of big data for competitive advantage of company. Procedia Econ. Finan. **26**(1), 561–565 (2015)
3. Sargent, K., Hyland, P., Sawang, S.: Factors influencing the adoption of information technology in a construction business. Constr. Econ. Build. **12**(2), 72–86 (2012)
4. de León, M., Villa, J., Vázquez, S., Rentería, J.: Explicación de la Adopción de Tecnologías de Información en Pequeñas Empresas Usando el Modelo del Usuario Perezoso: un Caso de Estudio. RISTI: Revista Ibérica de Sistemas e Tecnologias de Informação **1**(1), 91–104 (2014)
5. Kubina, M., Koman, G.: Big data technology and its importance for decision-making in enterprises. Commun. Sci. Lett, Univ. Žilina **18**(4), 129–133 (2016)
6. McKinsey Global Institute. Big Data: The next frontier for innovation, competition, and productivity. Mckinsey & company Retrieved February 14, 2015 (2011). http://bigdatawg. nist.gov/MGI_big_data_full_report.pdf
7. Linares-Espinós, E., et al.: Metodología de una revisión sistemática. Actas Urológicas Españolas **42**(8), 499–506 (2018)
8. Hutton, B., Catalá, F., Moher, D.: La extensión de la declaración PRISMA para revisiones sistemáticas que incorporan metaanálisis en red: PRISMA-NMA. Med. Clin. **147**(6), 262–266 (2016)
9. Urrútia, G., Bonfill, X.: Declaración PRISMA: una propuesta para mejorar la publicación de revisiones sistemáticas y metaanálisis. Med. Clin. **135**(11), 507–511 (2010)
10. Page, M., et al.: Declaración PRISMA 2020: una guía actualizada para la publicación de revisiones sistemáticas. Revista Española de Cardiología **74**(9), 790–799 (2021)
11. Liu, P., Yi, S.: Investment decision-making and coordination of supply chain: a new research in the big data era. Discret. Dyn. Nat. Soc. **1–10**, 2016 (2016)
12. Liu, K.: Research on the core competitiveness of short video industry in the context of big data—a case study of Tiktok of Bytedance company. Am. J. Ind. Bus. Manag. **12**(4), 699–730 (2022)
13. Prescott, M.: Big data: innovation and competitive advantage in an information media analytics company. J. Innov. Manag. **4**(1), 92–113 (2016)
14. Zhang, S., Xiong, W., Ni, W., Li, X.: Value of big data to finance: observations on an internet credit Service Company in China. Finan. Innov. **1**(1), 1–18 (2015)
15. Oncioiu, I., et al.: The impact of big data analytics on company performance in supply chain management. Sustainability **11**(18), 1–22 (2019)
16. Wassouf, W., Alkhatib, R., Salloum, K., Balloul, S.: Predictive analytics using big data for increased customer loyalty: Syriatel Telecom Company case study. J. Big Data **7**(1), 1–24 (2020)
17. Wang, X.: Construction of college aesthetic education quality improvement model under big data network. Wirel. Commun. Mob. Comput. 1–10 (2022)
18. Goti-Elordi, A., De-La-Calle-Vicente, A., Gil-Larrea, M., Errasti-Opakua, A., Uradnicek, J.: Aplicación de un sistema business intelligence en un contexto big data de una empresa industrial alimentaria. Dyna (Spain) **92**(3), 347–353 (2017)
19. Gensollen, C.: Big data en el mundo del retail: segmentación de clientes y sistema de recomendación en una cadena de supermercados de Europa. Ingeniería Industrial **1**(1), 189–216 (2022)
20. Radu-Alexandru, Ş: The impact of big data, sustainability, and digitalization on company performance. Stud. Bus. Econ. **12**(3), 181–189 (2017)

21. Wang, R., Zhu, D., Chen, J.: Exploring the impact of organizational implants of a manufacturing company on service innovation in the context of big data: a case study of XI'AN SHAANGU POWER. E3S Web Conf. **214**, 1–6 (2020)

22. Xu, Z., Ji, X., Wang, J., Guo, T.: Analysis of the influence of big data on the cost control of Tianbao green food company. E3S Web Conf. **214**, 1–4 (2020)

23. Pillay, K., van der Merwe, A.: Big data driven decision making model: a case of the South African banking sector. South African Comput. J. **33**(2), 55–71 (2021)

24. Giacalone, M., Santarcangelo, V., Donvito, V., Schiavone, O., Massa, E.: Big data for corporate social responsibility: blockchain use in Gioia del Colle DOP. Qual. Quant. **55**(6), 1945–1971 (2021)

25. Al-Alwan, M., Al-Nawafah, S., Al-Shorman, H., Khrisat, F., Alathamneh, F., Al-Hawary, S.: The effect of big data on decision quality: evidence from telecommunication industry. Int. J. Data Network Sci. **6**(3), 693–702 (2022)

26. Medeiros, F., Serio, L., Moreira, A.: Avon Brazil: optimization of logistics processes in a direct selling company. Revista de Administração Contemporânea **25**(4), 1–16 (2021)

27. Heredia-Ruiz, V., Quirós-Ramírez, A., Quiceno-Castañeda, B.: Big & personal: data and models behind Netflix recommendations. Revista de Comunicación **1**(1), 1–6 (2013)

28. Hamdane, A., Belhaj, N., El Hamdaoui, H., Aissaoui, K., El Bekkali, M., El Houda, N.: Big data based architecture to bringing together graduates and recruiters: case of Moroccan university. Indon. J. Electr. Eng. Comput. Sci. **26**(3), 1701–1709 (2022)

29. Padilla, C.: Big Data, una herramienta para apoyar en decisiones del sector hotelero en Quito-Ecuador. INNOVA Res. J. **4**(3), 80–88 (2019)

30. Savoska, S., Ristevski, B.: Towards implementation of big data concepts in a pharmaceutical company. Open Comput. Sci. **10**(1), 343–356 (2020)

CONTINGENT: Advanced Solution to Enhance Cyber Resilience Through Machine Learning Techniques

Francisco Pérez Carrasco[1,3]([⊠]) [iD], Alberto García García[1] [iD],
Victor Garrido Peñalver[1] [iD], Rafael Company Peris[2] [iD],
and Pablo Gimenez Salazar[2] [iD]

[1] FAV Innovation and Technologies COOP.V, 46006 Valencia, Spain
{agarcia,vgarrido,fperez}@favit.es
[2] Fundación Valencia Port, 46024 Valencia, Spain
{rcompany,pgimenez}@fundacion.valenciaport.com
[3] Universitat Politècnica de València, 46022 Valencia, Spain
frapecar@upvnet.upv.es
https://favit.es

Abstract. The CONTINGENT project, developed under the CYRENE H2020 (Horizon 2020) project [1], is a pioneering initiative by FAVIT [2] to bolster cybersecurity in evolving Information and Communication Technologies (ICT) systems. The project's focus is on enhancing cyber resilience through advanced Machine Learning (ML) techniques, addressing the increasing need for robust cybersecurity solutions in various sectors like transport, healthcare, and energy.

CONTINGENT aims to develop and deploy a suite of cybersecurity services/products for Supply Chain Services, utilizing HoneyPots (HPs) and Digital Twins (DTs) [3] to gather rich, actionable data [4]. These tools simulate vulnerable services, attracting and analyzing potential cyber threats. The collected data feeds into ML algorithms, enabling real-time analysis and identification of unknown attack patterns, ensuring proactive defense against cyber threats.

The proposed solution includes a set of docker containers with configurable HP services and ML models, integrated within the CYRENE platform. This integration will facilitate seamless data sharing and visualization through CYRENE's dashboard, enhancing overall cybersecurity measures.

Through CONTINGENT, FAVIT addresses significant technical challenges, including managing vast log data, ensuring easy integration across environments, and adhering to CYRENE's guidelines. This project represents a significant step forward in securing ICT systems against evolving cyber threats, ensuring the resilience and safety of critical infrastructures and data.

Keywords: Cybersecurity · Mahine Learning · Supply Chain Security · HoneyPots · Data Analysis · ICT Resilience

M. Botto-Tobar et al. (Eds.): ICAT 2023, CCIS 2051, pp. 263–275, 2024.
https://doi.org/10.1007/978-3-031-58950-8_19

1   Introduction

1.1   Context

The evolution of ICT has transformed the global landscape, becoming a pivotal aspect of modern life. This technological advancement, while creating unprecedented opportunities for growth and innovation, has also introduced significant vulnerabilities, making cybersecurity a paramount concern. The rapid digital transformation across various sectors, including healthcare, energy, finance, and transportation, has heightened the dependence on ICT systems, simultaneously increasing the risk of cyber threats [6].

In recent years, the escalation of sophisticated cyber-attacks has revealed the fragility of existing cybersecurity measures. These attacks not only target individual organizations but also exploit the interconnected nature of supply chains, leading to widespread disruptions [7]. The increasing complexity of ICT ecosystems, coupled with the emergence of new technologies like the Internet of Things (IoT) and cloud computing, has expanded the attack surface, challenging traditional security paradigms.

This context underlines the urgent need for innovative and adaptive cybersecurity solutions. The landscape is characterized by a dynamic threat environment where attackers continuously evolve their tactics, techniques, and procedures. As a result, there is a critical requirement for cybersecurity strategies that are not only reactive but also proactive, capable of anticipating and mitigating potential threats before they materialize [8].

The European Union, recognizing the importance of this challenge, has launched initiatives like the Horizon 2020 ICT-02-2020 call [9] to foster the development of robust, resilient, and adaptable cybersecurity solutions. These initiatives aim to enhance the security of ICT systems, safeguard critical infrastructures, and protect sensitive data against the backdrop of a rapidly evolving cyber threat landscape.

In this context, the CONTINGENT project emerges as a timely and essential response, aiming to strengthen the resilience of ICT systems through advanced ML techniques and innovative cybersecurity approaches. The project aligns with the European Union's broader objectives of securing digital infrastructures and ensuring the safe and uninterrupted operation of essential services across various sectors.

1.2   The Problem

In the rapidly advancing digital age, the proliferation of sophisticated cyber threats poses a significant challenge to the integrity and security of ICT systems. The core of the problem lies in the evolving nature of these threats, which are becoming increasingly complex, frequent, and damaging [10]. Traditional cybersecurity measures, primarily focused on reactive defense mechanisms, are proving insufficient against the backdrop of an ever-expanding digital landscape.

One of the primary issues is the vulnerability of supply chains. As cyber-criminals refine their tactics, supply chain attacks have become more prevalent, exploiting the interconnectedness and interdependencies of modern businesses. These attacks target multiple entities simultaneously, causing widespread disruptions, financial losses, and erosion of trust in digital systems. The recent surge in such attacks highlights a critical gap in existing cybersecurity strategies, which often overlook the intricacies of supply chain dynamics [7].

Another significant aspect of the problem is the sheer volume and complexity of data generated by modern ICT systems. The integration of technologies like IoT, cloud computing, and big data has led to an exponential increase in data points, making it challenging to monitor, analyze, and secure vast networks effectively [11]. Traditional security tools struggle to keep pace with the scale and sophistication of modern cyber threats, often resulting in delayed detection and response times.

Furthermore, the constantly evolving landscape of cyber threats necessitates a shift from static, rule-based security systems to more dynamic, adaptive solutions. Cybercriminals are continuously developing new methods to bypass security measures, exploit vulnerabilities and launch attacks. This evolving nature of threats demands a proactive approach to cybersecurity, one that can anticipate, identify, and mitigate emerging threats in real-time [8].

The problem is further compounded by the lack of skilled cybersecurity professionals and the high costs associated with implementing and maintaining robust security infrastructures. Small and medium-sized enterprises (SMEs), in particular, face significant challenges in this regard, often lacking the resources and expertise to effectively protect their digital assets [12].

In summary, the primary problem addressed by the CONTINGENT project is the need for an advanced, adaptive, and scalable cybersecurity solution that can effectively counteract the evolving landscape of cyber threats, particularly in the context of complex supply chains and the vast, intricate networks of modern ICT systems.

1.3   Proposed Solution

The CONTINGENT project proposes a cutting-edge solution to address the multifaceted cybersecurity challenges in modern ICT systems, with a particular focus on supply chain vulnerabilities. Our solution is designed to be proactive, intelligent, and adaptable, leveraging the capabilities of ML to enhance cyber resilience in an evolving digital landscape. Figure 1 shows the proposed architecture for CONTINGENT project and its components.

At the heart of CONTINGENT is the deployment of advanced HPs in a DT to simulate vulnerable services and systems. These HPs serve as decoys to attract cyber threats, allowing for the collection of rich, actionable data on potential attacks. This approach enables the identification of attack patterns and behaviors, providing insights into the latest tactics used by cybercriminals.

The collected data from HPs is then processed through sophisticated ML algorithms, which are designed to analyze and interpret complex data patterns.

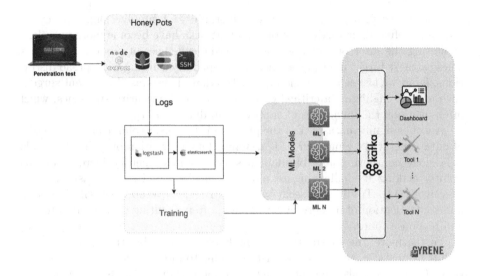

Fig. 1. CONTINGENT Concept

These algorithms can detect anomalies, identify potential threats, and predict attack vectors in real-time, significantly reducing the response time to potential security breaches. By continuously learning from new data, the ML models can adapt to the evolving nature of cyber threats, ensuring that the defense mechanisms remain effective over time.

To ensure seamless integration and ease of deployment, the CONTINGENT solution is containerized using Docker technology. This approach allows for flexibility and scalability, enabling the deployment of the solution across various environments and infrastructures, including on-premises and cloud-based systems. The modular nature of the solution also allows for customization based on specific organizational needs and threat landscapes.

An important part of the solution is its integration with the CYRENE platform. This integration allows for the efficient sharing of threat intelligence and analysis results, enhancing the overall security posture of the ICT systems. The information generated by CONTINGENT is communicated to the CYRENE platform using a standardized data model, ensuring compatibility and facilitating the use of the data across different components and tools within the platform.

As it is shown in Fig. 1, the CONTINGENT project offers an innovative, comprehensive, and scalable cybersecurity solution, uniquely tailored to address the challenges of the modern digital era. By combining the power of ML with the strategic use of HPs and DTs, the project aims to revolutionize the way cybersecurity is approached, providing robust protection against the ever-changing landscape of cyber threats.

2 Methodology

2.1 Solution Development

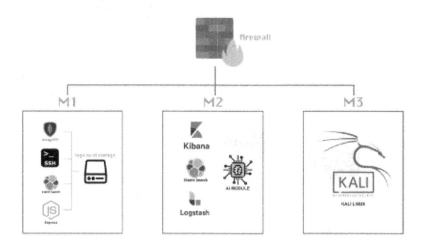

Fig. 2. CONTINGENT Local deployment (Phase 1)

The development of the CONTINGENT solution was a multi-phase, iterative process, integrating advanced cybersecurity technologies with the CYRENE
framework to address evolving ICT system challenges. This subsection outlines
the key stages and methodologies employed in developing the CONTINGENT
solution.

- **Phase 1: Initial Testing and Component Configuration**
  - In the initial phase (Fig. 2, the solution was tested in a controlled, private
    local network environment. This setup involved three main machines:
    * Machine M1 hosting the HPs,
    * Machine M2 running the entire Elastic Stack [13], and ML models
    * Machine M3 equipped with Kali Linux [14] for simulating cyberat-
      tacks.
  - The primary focus was on validating the functionality of HPs, ensuring
    the efficiency of the Elastic Stack in processing and storing logs, and
    testing the initial versions of ML algorithms.
- **Phase 2: Public Deployment and Real-time Attack Simulation**
  - Moving to a more realistic setting (Fig. 3, Machine M1 was placed outside
    the FAVIT Firewall, making it accessible to the internet. This change
    allowed real-time attack simulations, eliminating the need for a dedicated
    attack simulation machine (M3).

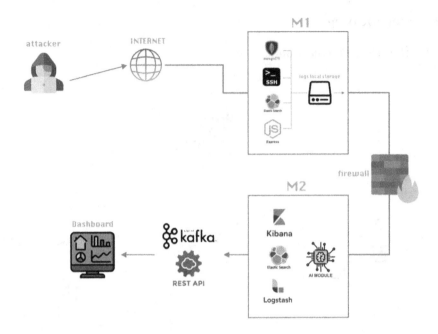

Fig. 3. CONTINGENT Partial Cloud deployment (Phase 2)

- The public exposure of Machine M1 aimed to capture live cyberattack data, enhancing the relevance and accuracy of the datasets used for ML model training.
- **Containerization and Microservices Architecture**
  - CONTINGENT's architecture was designed based on microservices, ensuring modularity, scalability, and ease of deployment. Each component, particularly HPs and ML models, was containerized using Docker technology [15].
  - This approach allowed for flexible deployment across different environments, including on-premises and cloud-based infrastructures, and facilitated easy integration with the CYRENE framework.
- **ML Model Development and Training**
  - A critical aspect of CONTINGENT's development was the creation and continuous training of ML models. These models were designed to analyze incoming log data from HPs in real-time, identifying anomalies, and potential cybersecurity threats.
  - The training phase involved processing extensive datasets to fine-tune the models, ensuring high accuracy and reduced false positives or negatives.
- **CYRENE Framework Integration**
  - Integration with the CYRENE platform was achieved through a Kafka broker [16], ensuring seamless data transfer and communication between CONTINGENT components and CYRENE.

- The development team also established a standardized JSON message structure to facilitate data ingestion and processing within the CYRENE framework.
- **Final Testing and Deployment**
  - The CONTINGENT solution underwent rigorous testing phases, including unit tests, integration tests, and functional tests, to ensure robustness and reliability.
  - The final implementation phase involved deploying CONTINGENT in a real-world environment, initially proposed at the Port of Valencia [17]. Due to network configuration complexities, the deployment was shifted to a cloud-based environment, simulating a real-use case scenario.

Throughout the development process, CONTINGENT maintained a focus on scalability, adaptability, and responsiveness to evolving cyber threats, aligning with the overarching objectives of the CYRENE project. The iterative approach, from controlled testing to real-world application, ensured that the solution was not only technically sound but also practical and effective in diverse operational settings.

2.2   Technologies

The CONTINGENT project integrates a suite of advanced technologies to create a robust cybersecurity solution. This subsection outlines the key technologies employed and their roles in the project's architecture.

- **HoneyPots (HPs):**
  - HPs are critical for simulating vulnerable systems to attract and analyze cyber threats. They provide valuable data on attack patterns and methods, enhancing the training datasets for ML models.
  - Different types of HPs, such as Cowrie, Elastic, and Mongo, are deployed to simulate various vulnerable services and capture a wide range of cyber-attacks.
- **Elastic Stack:**
  - The Elastic Stack, consisting of tools like Elasticsearch and Logstash, is used for efficient log management. It processes and stores large volumes of data generated by HPs.
  - This technology is crucial for indexing and searching through logs, providing a foundation for data analysis and ML model training.
- **ML Algorithms:**
  - Advanced ML algorithms form the core of CONTINGENT's threat detection and analysis capabilities. They process data from HPs to identify patterns, anomalies, and potential threats.
  - Algorithms like Logistic Regression [18], Naïve Bayes [19], K-Nearest Neighbors [20], Decision Trees [21], and Support Vector Machines [22] are used, tailored to specific cybersecurity use cases.

- **Docker Containers:**
  - Docker technology is employed for the containerization of CONTINGENT components. This approach ensures the modularity, scalability, and ease of deployment across various environments.
  - Containerization facilitates the seamless integration of CONTINGENT components with existing infrastructures and the CYRENE platform.
- **Kafka Broker:**
  - The Kafka broker is a central element in the integration with the CYRENE platform. It serves as a message queue system for efficient data transfer and communication.
  - The Kafka broker enables real-time data streaming from CONTINGENT to CYRENE, ensuring that the platform is continually updated with the latest threat intelligence.
- **Advanced Dashboard:**
  - The Advanced Dashboard is a critical component of CONTINGENT, developed using the Angular framework [23]. It provides a user-friendly interface for real-time monitoring and analysis of cybersecurity data.
  - Utilizing the chart libraries from PrimeNG [24], the dashboard offers sophisticated data visualization capabilities. These visualizations aid in the interpretation of complex data patterns and threat intelligence, enhancing decision-making processes.

Each of these technologies has been carefully selected and integrated into CONTINGENT to provide a comprehensive, efficient, and scalable cybersecurity solution. The synergy between these technologies enhances the project's capability to address the dynamic and complex nature of modern cyber threats.

3   Results

3.1   Solution Implementation

The implementation of the CONTINGENT solution was a crucial phase in bringing the project's conceptual framework to a practical, operational state. This subsection details the key steps and methodologies employed in the implementation process.

- **Deployment Strategy:**
  - The CONTINGENT components, including HPs, Elastic Stack, and ML models, were deployed following a strategic plan that prioritized security, scalability, and integration efficiency.
  - The deployment leveraged Docker containerization, ensuring that each component could be seamlessly integrated and operated within diverse IT environments.

- **Integration with CYRENE:**
  - A pivotal aspect of the implementation was the integration of CON-TINGENT with the CYRENE platform. This involved establishing reliable data pipelines using Kafka brokers and ensuring compatibility with CYRENE's data models and communication protocols.
  - The integration allowed for continuous data exchange between CONTIN-GENT's detection mechanisms and the CYRENE platform, enabling real-time threat monitoring and response.
- **Real-World Testing and Validation:**
  - Before full-scale deployment, the solution underwent extensive testing in controlled environments to validate its effectiveness and fine-tune its performance.
  - Real-world testing scenarios were created to simulate typical operational conditions and potential cyberattack patterns, ensuring the solution's preparedness for actual deployment.
- **Dashboard Deployment and User Interface Optimization:**
  - The Advanced Dashboard, developed using Angular and PrimeNG chart libraries, was deployed to provide an intuitive, interactive interface for monitoring and analysis.
  - The dashboard was optimized for user experience, ensuring that data visualizations were both informative and accessible to users of varying technical expertise.
- **Feedback Incorporation and Iterative Improvement:**
  - User feedback and performance metrics were continuously monitored and used to make iterative improvements to the solution.
  - Regular updates were implemented to refine the ML algorithms and enhance the overall security and usability of the system.

The implementation of the CONTINGENT solution marks a significant milestone in the project, demonstrating the practical applicability and effectiveness of the proposed cybersecurity framework. This phase not only solidified the theoretical aspects of the project but also set a foundation for future enhancements and scalability.

3.2   Tests and Validation

The CONTINGENT project's testing and validation phase was pivotal in ensuring the system's effectiveness and reliability within a real-world environment. This phase was predominantly conducted at the Port of Valencia, in collaboration with Fundación Valenciaport, a private non-profit research center with deep expertise in ICT, maritime, intermodal transport, logistics, and transport economics.

Fundación Valenciaport's role was instrumental in providing a real-world context and operational nuances for the Vehicle Transport Service (VTS) and the Supply Chain Services (SCS). The Port of Valencia, with its intricate network of processes and companies involved in various operations, presented an ideal environment for testing. This complex backdrop emphasized the importance of robust cybersecurity across interconnected ICT infrastructures.

During the pilot testing, simulations of critical operational processes, such as stopover requests and the preparation of loading and unloading lists, were carried out. These exercises were crucial in evaluating the system's ability to secure sensitive data exchanges through the Port Community System (PCS). The focus was not only on assessing the security of the service providers but also on evaluating the assets of various business partners within the SCS to identify potential vulnerabilities.

Fig. 4. CONTINGENT Results of Pilot exercise integrated in CYRENE

An essential part of this phase was to examine the integration of CON-TINGENT with the CYRENE platform, ensuring that the provided tools could effectively assess and reinforce the cybersecurity infrastructure at various levels. Feedback from different stakeholders at the Port of Valencia was meticulously gathered and analyzed, offering valuable insights into potential improvements and adjustments needed in the CONTINGENT solution. Figure 4 shows the integration of CONTINGENT project results in the CYRENE Dashboard.

The outcomes of these pilot tests were cruzial in demonstrating the CONTIN-GENT solution's capacity to manage complex data exchanges securely and its efficiency in a dynamic and interconnected environment like the Port of Valencia providing lesson learned for future enhacements.

4 Conclusions and Future Directions

4.1 Conclusions

The CONTINGENT project has successfully demonstrated a significant advancement in the field of cybersecurity for evolving ICT systems, particularly in the context of supply chain services. The project's implementation at the Port of Valencia, in collaboration with Fundación Valenciaport, has provided valuable insights into the practical application and effectiveness of the developed solution.

Key achievements of the project include:

1. The development and deployment of an advanced cybersecurity solution leveraging HPs, Elastic Stack, and ML algorithms, effectively identifying and mitigating cyber threats in real-time.
2. Successful integration with the CYRENE framework, enhancing the platform's capability to assess and respond to cybersecurity challenges across various stakeholders in the supply chain.
3. The deployment of an intuitive and interactive Angular-based Advanced Dashboard, utilizing PrimeNG chart libraries for sophisticated data visualization and analysis.

The project has highlighted the critical importance of proactive and dynamic cybersecurity measures in safeguarding interconnected ICT infrastructures, especially in complex environments like maritime and intermodal transport.

4.2 Future Directions

Looking ahead, the CONTINGENT project sets the stage for several future developments and enhancements:

– **Reinforcement Learning Methodologies:** Plans are underway to incorporate new methodologies based on reinforcement learning. This approach aims to further understand and interpret different attack patterns and response flows, allowing for anticipation and better response to recurrent cyber threats.
– **Expansion to Other Critical Infrastructures:** The successful pilot at the Port of Valencia paves the way for applying the CONTINGENT solution to other critical infrastructure sectors, diversifying its applicability and impact.
– **Continuous Improvement and Adaptation:** The project will continue to evolve, with regular updates and improvements based on ongoing feedback, technological advancements, and changing cyber threat landscapes.
– **Broader Collaborative Efforts:** Building on the collaboration with Fundación Valenciaport, future efforts will focus on forging partnerships with other entities and industries to enhance the scope and efficacy of cybersecurity measures.

In conclusion, the CONTINGENT project has not only achieved its set objectives but also laid a robust foundation for future innovations in the realm of cybersecurity, promising a more secure and resilient digital future.

Acknowledgement. This work has been performed under the H2020 952690 project CYRENE, which has received funding from the European Union's Horizon 2020 Programme. This paper reflects only the authors' view, and the European Commission is not liable to any use that may be made of the information contained therein.

References

1. CYRENE Project. https://www.cyrene.eu
2. FAVIT. https://favit.es
3. Mihai, S., et al.: Digital twins: a survey on enabling technologies, challenges, trends and future prospects. IEEE Commun. Surv. Tutorials **24**(4), 2255–2291 (2022)
4. Cabaj, K., Denis, M., Buda, M.: Management and analytical software for data gathered from honeypot system. Inf. Syst. Manag. **2**, 182–193 (2013)
5. Kamel, N.E., Eddabbah, M., Lmoumen, Y., Touahni, R.: A smart agent design for cyber security based on honeypot and machine learning. Secur. Commun. Netw. **2020**, 8865474:1–8865474:9 (2020)
6. Chhillar, S., Geach, D.: Digital transformation and emerging ICS/OT cyber attacks - imminent threats to our society. In: Proceedings of the 2th Workshop on CPS&IoT Security and Privacy (2021)
7. Davis, A.: Building cyber-resilience into supply chains. Telev. New Media **5**, 19–27 (2015)
8. Colbaugh, R., Glass, K.: Proactive defense for evolving cyber threats. In: Proceedings of 2011 IEEE International Conference on Intelligence and Security Informatics, pp. 125–130 (2011)
9. SU-ICT-02-2020. https://ec.europa.eu/info/funding-tenders/opportunities/portal/screen/opportunities/topic-details/su-ict-02-2020
10. Borrett, M., Carter, R., Wespi, A.: How is cyber threat evolving and what do organisations need to consider? J. Bus. Continuity Emerg. Plann. **7**(2), 163–71 (2013)
11. Díaz, M., Martín, C., Rubio, B.: State-of-the-art, challenges, and open issues in the integration of Internet of things and cloud computing. J. Netw. Comput. Appl. **67**, 99–117 (2016)
12. Emer, A., Unterhofer, M., Rauch, E.: A Cybersecurity Assessment Model for Small and Medium-Sized Enterprises. IEEE Eng. Manage. Rev. **49**, 98–109 (2021)
13. Elastic Stack. https://www.elastic.co/es/elastic-stack
14. Kali Linux. https://www.kali.org
15. Docker. https://www.docker.com
16. Apache Kafka. https://kafka.apache.org/
17. Valencia Port. https://www.valenciaport.com/
18. Scott, A.J.: Review of Applied Logistic Regression., by D. W. Hosmer & S. Lemeshow. Biometrics **47**(4), 1632–1633 (1991)
19. Soms, N., Hariharan, S., Jeeva, K., Karthick, C.: Naive bayes machine learning framework for auto detection of spam mails. Int. J. Health Sci. **6**(S3), 7270–7277 (2022)
20. Archibald, R.K., Doucet, M., Johnston, T., Young, S.R., Yang, E., Heller, W.T.: Classifying and analyzing small-angle scattering data using weighted k nearest neighbors machine learning techniques. J. Appl. Cryst. **53**, 326–334 (2020)

21. Quinlan, J.: Induction of decision trees. Mach. Learn. **1**, 81–106 (1986)
22. Mammone, A., Turchi, M., Cristianini, N.: Support vector machines. WIREs Comp. Stat. **1**, 283–289 (2009)
23. Angular. https://angular.io/
24. PrimeNG. https://primeng.org/

Technological System for Improving Physical Performance in Children from 4 to 8 Years Old with High Obesity Rates of Type 1 and 2 Using IoT-Based Wearables in Private Schools in Metropolitan Lima

Alejandro Espejo-Gonzalez[(✉)], Felix Bancayan-Aranda, and Daniel Burga-Durango

Department of Information Systems, Universidad Peruana de Ciencias Aplicadas, Lima 15023, Peru

{u201815565,u201523627}@upc.com.pe, daniel.burga@upc.pe

Abstract. According to a study conducted by UNICEF, the main causes of childhood obesity are the high consumption of processed foods and the low amount of physical activity performed by children, generating a higher risk of respiratory, metabolic and cardiovascular conditions. Based on research conducted in different studies, we found that there are not many technologies that monitor and improve the physical performance of children. This paper presents a technological system based on IoT and using wearables to improve the physical performance of children with high obesity rates type 1 and 2. This technological system was verified by conducting a study with 30 children between 4 and 8 years old, evaluating their physical activity and collecting the data obtained from the smartwatch. This study showed, according to the conclusions found, that it is a useful tool for the collection of data required by specialists and easy to use for children and their parents. In addition, it is a means to overcome the obesity problem.

Keywords: smartwatch · fitness · obesity · children

1 Introduction

The World Health Organization (WHO) considers that one of the most important public health problems in the world is childhood obesity [1]. This is due to the fact that approximately 13% of children and adolescents in underdeveloped countries and 23% in developed countries are overweight or obese [1]. Based on what is mentioned by [2], overweight children may feel unmotivated, causing them to be less physically active during the day, thus leading them to spend more of their time watching television or on social networks.

Children who are overweight or obese tend to remain with the same problem they get older, thus possessing a greater likelihood of chronic physical problems [4]. According to [5], the continuing advances in wrist-worn activity device technology offer significant potential for applications required by specialists. Likewise, the monitoring of PA with wearables allows the improvement of people's PA levels. However, it is necessary to know the accuracy of these tools in people to know their current PA levels and to evaluate their effectiveness. Thus, according to [6], they evaluate the effectiveness of obesity prevention among children aged 10 to 12 years using an application called HAPPY ME. However, it does not have the participation of specialists to carry out progress monitoring of children.

On the other hand, there are few recent studies of this problem in Peru, of which the one carried out in the regional hospital of Moquegua [3] and in the Central Military Hospital Coronel Luis Arias Schreiber in Lima between 2016 and 2019 [13] stand out.

The first case presents a result of 51% of children with excess weight that shows that there is an increase in the prevalence in this region, compared to previous years [3]; providing accurate information that complements the problem. The second case shows that, out of a total of 127 children between 5 and 15 years of age, 52% suffer from obesity and 18.9% from overweight [13].

Taking these data, and complementing previous works carried out in other countries, we propose a tool to improve the physical performance of children with obesity. Our contributions are as follows:

- Physical performance monitoring by a health specialist.
- It is proposed that the specialist can assign different physical activity goals to the children and validate their constant progress.
- Specialists may assign meal plans according to the case.

This paper is organized as follows. Section 2, related work on implemented solutions that have to use wearables. Section 3 describes the context of the solution and its development. Section 4 explains how the study was conducted and the validation of the application. Section 5, the results obtained from the validation. Section 6, we conclude with the most important results of the research, limitations and future work.

2 Related Work

In [7], the Internet of Things (IoT)-powered Physical Activity Recognition System for higher education was proposed. This system gathers relevant data from the IoT and interacts through the cloud with the mobile and obtains real-time data. In [8] participants wore an activity sensor called "Garmin vivofitjr" over seven days, collecting minutes of moderate to vigorous physical activity (MVPA) and step volume (time outside or inside the school). This study reports 50% compliance with the 13,000 steps per day and 120 min per day of MVPA. In [5, 9] and [10] they use wrist-worn activity device to monitor total step count and total energy expenditure in adolescents in free-living conditions. However, they agree that more studies are needed to test the validity of these devices in different types of physical activities. In [14], they used Fitbit Charge 5 wristbands to monitor children aged 13–17 years for three weeks to collect several digital biomarkers, including moderate to vigorous physical activity (MVPA) and analyze compliance with the recommended step count during school and non-school days. Finally, in [6], an application called "HAPPY ME" was developed, designed to improve healthy behaviors, and prevent childhood obesity. This study aims to facilitate the participation of children, parents and teachers, as it includes the mobile application and a website for the school.

3 Context

The main problem is the need to improve the physical performance of children with obesity. To build the solution, we conducted several analyses of different technologies in order to find the best components for the development of the tool. Based on research conducted and various comparisons between smartwatch brands, it was decided to use the Xiaomi Mi Band 4, because it is more affordable, provides all the necessary physical activity functions (steps, heart rate, distance, calories) and allows it to be configurable by third parties, facilitating the connection with our solution.

In Fig. 1, based on the information extracted in [11] we can determine that the best option to use in our study is a wrist wearable or also known as a smartwatch or smartband. This type of device has a similar score to the ankle wearable, but the difference is seen in the comfort criterion. When it comes to having children as users, a key factor is that they can be comfortable, which means that they do not remove the device.

Evaluation criteria	Weighting	WRIST		WAIST		ANKLE	
		Score	Average	Score	Average	Score	Average
User comfort	25%	4	1	2	0.5	3	0.75
Help functions	38%	4	1.52	3	1.14	4	1.52
Product accessibility	25%	4	1	2	0.5	4	1
Configurable by third parties	12%	3	0.36	2	0.24	3	0.36
TOTAL	100%	15	3.88	9	2.38	14	3.63

Fig. 1. Type of wearable

In Fig. 2, based on the information extracted from the thesis [12], we can determine that the best cloud provider is Azure. This will be used to host the application database.

Evaluation criteria	Weighting	AZURE		AWS		GOOGLE	
		Score	Average	Score	Average	Score	Average
Availability	20%	3	0.6	1	0.2	3	0.6
Reliability	25%	4	1	3	0.75	4	1
Performance	10%	3	0.3	4	0.4	3	0.3
Cost	10%	3	0.3	2	0.2	2	0.2
Security	25%	1	0.25	3	0.75	1	0.25
Interface	5%	4	0.2	4	0.2	2	0.1
Framework	5%	NA	NA	NA	NA	2	0.1
TOTAL	100%	18	2.65	17	2.5	17	2.55

Fig. 2. Cloud providers

In Fig. 3, based on the information extracted in [11] we can affirm that the Xiomi Mi Band 4 smartband is the best choice. Moreover, according to the information provided on the official website of the brand, this device has several useful features, such as heart rate monitoring, step counter, activity log, multisport mode, among others.

Evaluation criteria	Weighting	FITBIT Inspire		Xiomi Mi band 6		Samsung Gear Fit 2	
		Score	Average	Score	Average	Score	Average
User comfort	25%	4	1	4	1	4	1
Help functions	38%	2	0.76	3	1.14	4	1.52
Product accessibility	25%	2	0.5	4	1	3	0.75
Configurable by third parties	12%	4	0.48	1	0.12	2	0.24
TOTAL	100%	12	2.74	12	3.26	13	3.51

Fig. 3. Brands and models of wrist wearables

Based on research conducted and various comparisons between smartwatch brands, it was decided to use the Xiaomi Mi Band 4, because it is more affordable, provides all the necessary physical activity functions (steps, heart rate, distance, calories) and allows it to be configurable by third parties, facilitating the connection with our solution.

Figure 4 shows the physical architecture of the solution, where you can see how the user interacts with the application.

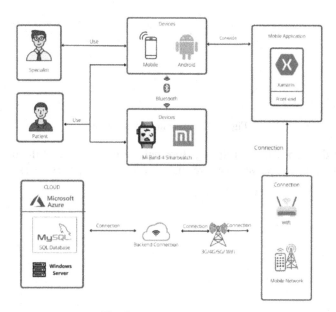

Fig. 4. Physical architecture

Each of the users (patient and specialist) will use a mobile device with Android, where they will have installed the MyHealth application, which is developed with Xamarin language. It was decided to use this language due to compatibility with the SDK that allows the connection with the smartwatch.

Once they are logged in with their account, they will be able to access the modules offered to each role. When the patient logs in, it will be able to connect the Xiaomi Mi Band 4 to the mobile application via Bluetooth. This will allow them to obtain the physical activity data provided by the smartwatch and keep track of their progress.

After this, the application will require an internet connection, either mobile network or wifi, to perform the respective queries to the MySQL database that is deployed in the

Azure cloud. All the data collected from the physical activity will be stored there, in addition to the users' information (Fig. 5).

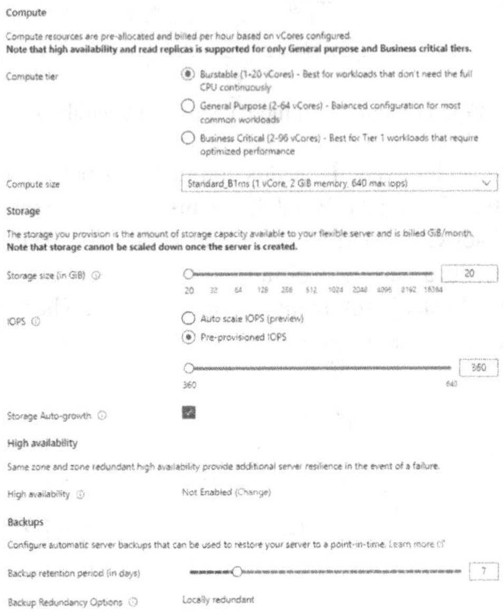

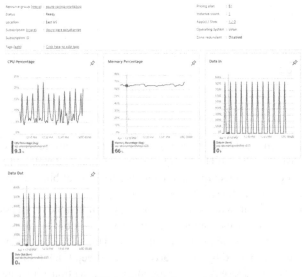

Fig. 5. Database hosted in Azure

An API developed in Java Spring Boot will be used to access the data from the database. This is also deployed in Azure, making use of the App Service resource (Fig. 6).

Fig. 6. API deployed in Azure App Service

By deploying the backend and the database in a cloud provider, it allows high availability of the service. In addition, it offers scalability and elasticity as it is a flexible database. In case there is any inconvenience with the continuity of the service, the provider will be in charge of solving it as soon as possible.

User Stories List	
US01	Create user account
US02	User login
US03	View profile
US04	Update profile data
US05	Update user
US06	List users
US07	Delete user
US08	Delete account
US09	Register user information
US10	Link smartwatch
US11	Delete patients from the list
US12	View patient list
US13	Filter patients by name
US14	Add new patients to the list
US15	Add meal plans to patients
US16	Eliminate meal plans
US17	View meal plans
US18	Record physical activity
US19	View exercise report
US20	Filter report by date or time period
US21	Set daily or weekly objectives
US22	Visualize the achievement of objective
US23	View patient's physical activity summary
US24	View detailed patient data
US25	View patient's physical activity reports
US26	Modify objective
US27	Delete objective
US28	Modify meal plans
US29	View meal plans

Fig. 7. Application User Stories

Once it was defined how the application will be built based on the user stories in Fig. 7 and the components to be used, the mockups and the development of the application began.

This application has 2 views for each type of user as shown in Fig. 8. The first one, the patient view. In this view, the patient will be able to see his physical progress and the goals assigned by his specialist, as well as the fulfillment of these goals. In addition, they will have a view to see the dietary plans that were established for him/her. They can also modify their profile information to provide more detailed information (weight and height) to the specialist. The second one, the view for the specialist. Here, you can add new patients to your list, in order to keep track of their physical progress. On the profile of each of your patients, you will be able to see their detailed information, a summary of their physical activity during the day, a complete report on a date with a set interval, and the option to add new daily and weekly goals and meal plans, as well as to modify or delete them.

Fig. 8. Application view

Due to the way the application is developed, anyone, with an Android phone, can download and install it on their cell phone, having the possibility to follow their progress from anywhere in the world at any time, since the backend and the database are hosted in the cloud. They will only need an internet connection. With this application, My Health, it will be possible to improve the physical performance of children with obesity, being monitored by pediatricians or nutritionists.

4   Method

To collect data related to physical activity improvement, we considered 3 data described in Fig. 9. These data are steps, distance and calories.

Data	Measure
Steps	Number of steps
Distance	Meters
Kilo-calories burned	kcal

Fig. 9. Data and measures

To obtain the data in Fig. 9, we must make use of the SDK (Software Development Kit), which allows us to extract data from the smartwatch such as steps, distance and calories to be displayed in the application.

It is important to verify the accuracy of this data because the SDK libraries only handle the steps data and the other data as formulas in relation to the steps. For this reason, in the case of distance and calories, the formulas provided by the SDK must be readjusted so that their calculation is $\pm10\%$ more accurate according to the smartwatch.

Fig. 10. Data verification

5 Experiment

Data collection was carried out in a school called "D'Pequenitos" located in Lima-Peru over a period of 2 weeks. 30 primary school students between 4 and 8 years old were tested during their school day. Each day, 4 children were given a watch to collect data.

5.1 Use of Wearables

To collect the data, children's accounts had to be created in the app, filling in their personal data and assigning them a watch to be synchronized. Then, the school students had to put the Xiomi Mi Band 4 smartwatch on their wrist. Finally, they were to perform their physical activity as normal in their school day.

5.2 Data Comparison

To verify the accuracy of the data, the smartwatch had to be linked to each child's account via Bluetooth. These data should maintain an accuracy of $\pm 10\%$ compared to the smartwatch. Taking this into account, the AM (Arithmetic Mean) was calculated according to each data, and this can be seen in the following formula:

$$MA = \frac{\sum_{i=1}^{n} X_i}{n}$$

5.3 Usability Validation

A Google Form survey was conducted and sent to the children's parents or guardians. This will allow us to understand the users' experience with the application and their opinion about its usability. The questions asked can be seen in Fig. 11.

ID	Questions
1	How easy was it for you to log in to the application?
2	How easy was it for you to navigate through the application?
3	How easy was it for you to update your child's personal data?
4	How easy was it for you to review your child's physical report?
5	How easy was it for you to review the meal plan assigned by the specialist?
6	How easy was it for you to review the daily and weekly objectives assigned by the specialist?
7	How satisfied are you with the ease of use of the application?
8	How likely would you be to use the application?
9	How likely would you be to recommend the application to a family member or friend?

Fig. 11. Survey to parents or guardians

6 Results

After performing both data accuracy and usability validations, the following results were obtained and presented in the figures.

6.1 Distance Accuracy

In this process, the percentage accuracy indicator of the distance traveled in meters and the formula that allows us to find it were defined, as shown in Fig. 12.

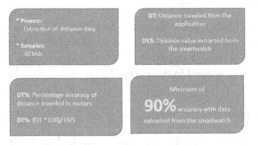

Fig. 12. Distance Traveled Indicator

To obtain more accurate distance data, we had to modify the formula provided by the SDK, which was steps multiplied by 0.7, changing the value to 0.65 to obtain a more accurate result according to what was shown on the clock.

Fig. 13. Accuracy percentage of distance traveled per student compared to smartwatches.

As can be seen in Fig. 13, the data accuracy results are higher than the expected 90% and lower than 110%, presenting almost accurate data in the application compared to those presented in the watch. With the data obtained, the average of these is obtained, resulting in a weighted accuracy value of.

98.3%, which is within the expected range.

6.2 Kilo-Calorie Accuracy

In this process, the percentage accuracy indicator of calories burned and the formula that allows us to find it were defined, as shown in Fig. 14.

Fig. 14. Calories Burned Indicator

To obtain more accurate kilo-calorie data, we had to modify the formula provided by the SDK, which was steps multiplied by 0.04, changing the value to 0.021 to obtain a more accurate result to that shown on the watch.

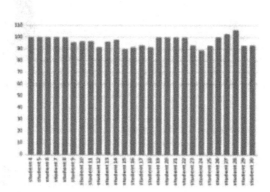

Fig. 15. Accuracy percentage of kilocalories burned per student compared to smartwatch.

As can be seen in Fig. 15, the data accuracy results are higher than the expected 90%, reaching a value of 100%, presenting almost accurate data in the application compared to those shown on the clock. With the data obtained, the average of these is obtained, resulting in a weighted accuracy value of 96.7%, which is within the defined range.

6.3 Application Usability

To measure the level of usability of the application, we conducted surveys to each of the children's parents or guardians, since they were the ones who interacted with the application in order to visualize the progress of the children's physical performance (Figs. 16, 17, 18, 19, 20, 21, 22, 23).

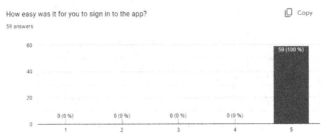

Fig. 16. How easy was it for you to sign into the application

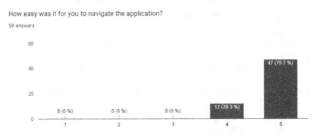

Fig. 17. How easy was it for you to navigate the application

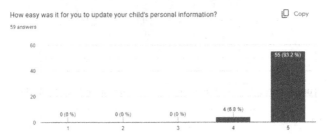

Fig. 18. How easy was it for you to update your child's personal information?

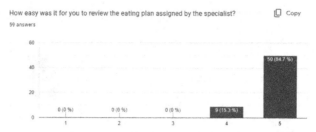

Fig. 19. How easy was it for you to review the eating plan assigned by the specialist?

Fig. 20. How easy was it for you to review the daily and weekly goals assigned by the specialist?

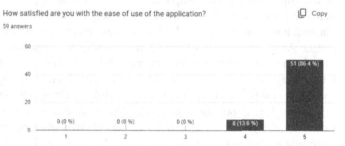

Fig. 21. How satisfied are you with the ease of use of the application?

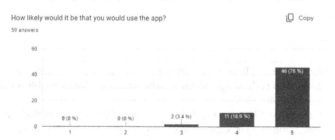

Fig. 22. How likely would it be that you would use the app?

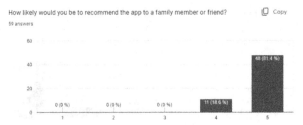

Fig. 23. How likely would you be to recommend the app to a family member or friend?

As can be seen in the answers to one of the questions asked, parents mention that they are very satisfied with the usability of the application, since is easy to navigate on it. This indicates that the implemented solution has a good user experience.

7   Conclusion

One of the limitations of this research was the number of children recruited and, although we collected data for an ideal amount of time, a larger number would yield more accurate insights. The results obtained allow us to standardize the validation of step counts, calories burned and distance traveled provided by the smartwatches. The accuracy of the data extracted from the smartwatch to the app and the usability of the app's functionalities were evaluated. Furthermore, 86.4% of the users were very satisfied with the use of the application. In addition, an accuracy of $\pm 10\%$ was always maintained when comparing the extracted data. As shown in Figs. 10 and 12, it is possible to adequately obtain data on calories and distance traveled by the children, in addition to steps, thus achieving the objective of measuring the children's physical performance. The tool, if implemented, would help to improve the physical performance of the children through the intervention of a health specialist. It is important to highlight that these tests were performed on students between 4 and 8 years of age during their school day. Future research should continue with testing and validation in more schools in Metropolitan Lima to see if our research can be generalized to the population of Peru. Also, as the technology develops, new wearable devices or other devices should be used to test the results.

References

1. Aragon-Martín, R., et al.: Independent and combined association of lifestyle behaviours and physical fitness with body weight status in schoolchildren. Nutrients **14**(6) (2022). https://doi.org/10.3390/nu14061208
2. Nieto, A., Suhrcke, M.: The effect of TV viewing on children's obesity risk and mental well-being: evidence from the UK digital switchover. J. Health Econ. **80** (2021). https://doi.org/10.1016/j.jhealeco.2021.102543
3. Medina-Valdivia, J.L.: Sobrepeso y obesidad infantil en el hospital regional moquegua. Revista de la Facultad de Medicina, 19(2), 11 (2019). https://doi.org/10.25176/RFMH.v19.n2.2069

4. Gadaire, C.B., Armstrong, L.M., Levens, S.M.: Development and validation of the child weight risk questionnaire. Eating Weight Disorders 27(2), 525–534 (2022). https://doi.org/10.1007/s40519-02101181-w
5. Hao, Y., Ma, X.K., Zhu, Z., Cao, Z.B.: Validity of wristwearable activity devices for estimating physical activity in adolescents: comparative study. JMIR Mhealth Uhealth 9(1), 1–13 (2021)
6. Yang, H.J., et al.: Interventions for preventing childhood obesity with smartphones and wearable device: a protocol for a non-randomized controlled trial. Int. J. Environ. Res. Public Health 14(2) (2017). https://doi.org/10.3390/ijerph14020184
7. Wang, Y., Muthu, B.A., Sivaparthipan, C.B.: Internet of things driven physical activity recognition system for physical education. Microprocess. Microsyst. 81, 103723 (2020). https://doi.org/10.1016/j.micpro.2020.103723(2021)
8. Díaz-Quesada, G., Bahamonde-Perez, C., Gim´ enez-Egido, J.M., Torres-Luque, G.: Use of wearable devices to study physical activity in early childhood education. Sustainability (Switzerland) 13(24) (2021). https://doi.org/10.3390/su132413998
9. Gould, Z.R., et al.: A catalog of validity indices for step counting wearable technologies during treadmill walking: the CADENCE-Kids study. Int. J. Behav. Nutrition Phys. Activity 18(1), 1–14 (2021). https://doi.org/10.1186/s12966-021-01167-y
10. Kang, S., Kim, Y., Byun, W., Suk, J., Lee, J.M.: Comparison of a wearable tracker with actigraph for classifying physical activity intensity and heart rate in children. Int. J. Environ. Res. Public Health 16(15) (2019). https://doi.org/10.3390/ijerph16152663
11. Gonzales, A., Samuel, P., Chacón, J., Jaime, E.: Solución tecnológica para alertar la agresión contra la mujer Item Type info:eu-repo/semantics/bachelorThesis, pp. 1–112 (2020). http://hdl.handle.net/10757/652323
12. Ladera, E., Alfredo, J.: Análisis predictivo para el cálculo de la valoración del fondo acumulado del afiliado en el Sistema Privado de Pensiones usando técnicas y herramientas de machine learning Item Type info:eu-repo/semantics/bachelorThesis. 1–96. https://doi.org/10.19083/tesis/652592 (2020)
13. Diaz, J.: El sobrepeso y la obesidad en pacientes pediátricos hospitalizados por crisis asmática en el Hospital Militar Central durante el período 2016–2018 (2019)
14. Arfan, A., et al.: Wearable artificial intelligence for assessing physical activity in high school children. Sustainability 15(1), 638 (2022). https://doi.org/10.3390/su15010638

Process Architecture for the Integration of Outpatient, Hospitalization and Emergency Services in Level III Hospitals in Peru

Miguel Albornoz, Caroline Ranilla[✉], David Mauricio, and Daniel Burga-Durango

Universidad Peruana de Ciencias Aplicadas, Prolongación Primavera 2390, Monterrico,
Santiago de Surco, Lima, Perú
{u201819284,u201819316,pcsidmau}@upc.edu.pe, daniel.burga@upc.pe

Abstract. Peru has a fragmented health system, which limits access to its health services because the people seeking medical services can only be treated in specified health centers that are determined by their health insurance. Additionally, this causes each health provider to count and manage their processes and information in an isolated and independent manner. In the Peruvian case, this generates an overload in public health services, since, of the 83.3% of insured nationwide, 73.1% belong to the public sector. Therefore, a process architecture is presented, based on the Zachman framework, that integrates the processes of health services (outpatient, hospitalization and emergencies), as well as an Information Technology (IT) process that supports them. The architecture aims to ensure that level III hospitals in Peru have standardized processes and information, as well as to guarantee their application regardless of the hospital regime. The processes were designed based on information from two Peruvian level III hospitals, belonging to the Sistema Integrado de Salud (SIS) and Seguro Social de Salud (EsSalud). A time simulation of the current processes and those proposed by the architecture, show an average improvement percentage of 69% in the outpatient process, 27% in emergencies and 7% in hospitalization. In addition, an expert judgment was made obtaining a very high assessment on the usefulness of the architecture.

Keywords: Process Architecture · Healthcare · Zachman Framework · Business Process Management · BPM

1 Introduction

The Peruvian health system is currently fragmented due to the complex division of its healthcare services; and the healthcare providers operate independently from each other. The public health system covers more than half (60%) of the country's population [1]. Within the civil public system there are two main Instituciones Administradoras de Fondos de Aseguramiento (IAFAS): the Seguro Integral de Salud (SIS) and the Seguro Social de Salud (EsSalud), the first for universal health insurance aimed at the entire population, while the second is aimed towards the working class. In other words, in Peru, insurance coverage is fragmented by having two very different public insurance plans,

© The Author(s), under exclusive license to Springer Nature Switzerland AG 2024
M. Botto-Tobar et al. (Eds.): ICAT 2023, CCIS 2051, pp. 290–304, 2024.
https://doi.org/10.1007/978-3-031-58950-8_21

especially their conditions and procedures [2]. In addition, each insurance plan (SIS and EsSalud) has their own healthcare hospitals and are mutually exclusive of each other; this means that people who are insured with one plan can only seek medical services in the healthcare centers of their own insurance. Thus, making the benefits of health services very restrictive and limited. Furthermore, according to statistics presented by the Instituto Nacional de Estadística e Informática in the last quarter of 2021, 83.3% of the population had some type of insurance, where 55% belongs to the SIS, while 23.1% to EsSalud, generating an overload of attention for the Instituciones Prestadoras de Servicios de Salud (IPRESS) designated by the first [3].

The overload of patients in the public health sector greatly affects the delivery of its services. For example, the health services provided to SIS insured people by Peruvian hospitals belonging to the Ministerio de Salud (MINSA) present several complaints due to the increasing number of affiliates each year, as well as the low development of the healthcare centers of this institution [4]. In this regard, in a study carried out in 2018, where 366 people with managerial positions in 184 IPRESS of different levels of care, both public and private, were interviewed, the shortage or lack of human resources (54.92%), poor infrastructure (36.89%) and the budget deficit (28.42%) were identified as the main problems in health facilities; the interviewees mentioned the frequent complaints by users or patients of their healthcare centers were the lack of attention by specialist medical doctors (34.97%), lack of appointments (34.70%), delay in care (28.14%), non-compliance with schedules (14.21%), among others [5]. Another example is a study conducted on the quality of outpatient services in two level III hospitals in the city of Lima (Peru), the result reveals that the patients of this service are not satisfied with it, where 28.7% rated it as terrible, 70.6% as average and 0.6% as good, the main reasons were: difficulty in finding appointments, waiting times for medical appointments, problems on the part of staff to find medical records, non-compliance with office hours and poor care by doctors [6].

Fragmentation in health systems leads to complex delivery in health services [7]. A study discovered 32 factors that should be prioritized to promote health integration projects, where, among the most important, was the optimization and reorganization of business processes [8]. Business Process Management (BPM) represents a novelty in the field of healthcare, having a positive impact on the management and optimization of clinical processes by standardizing and redesigning them more efficiently; however, due to the limitations and singularities of the health field, there is a difficulty in its application [9]. Despite this, different process architectures have been developed in hospitals: to improve the quality of outpatient services [10], to redesign surgical and perioperative activities adding value to them and eliminating unnecessary tasks [11] and improving the use of resources in emergency services [12]. However, no architectures have been identified that seek to integrate hospital processes with different health providers, since they are generally oriented to a single specific hospital and service.

This article proposes the development of a process architecture to articulate the public offer of health services through the integration and standardization of processes for MINSA and EsSalud hospitals, which allows to have a single health care process for the different IPRESS, serving as a model or guide for the respective Peruvian institutions and authorities. In this way, the solution will allow these services to be modeled as independent processes to the hospital that is applied to them and, thus, will contemplate the necessary scenarios to provide health benefits for all types of patients: payers, SIS or EsSalud insured. In this way, the main contributions of this work consist of an architecture of processes for outpatient, hospitalization and emergency, which integrates the processes of MINSA and EsSalud; and conduct a case study to show the benefits of the proposed architecture.

2 Related Work

This section provides an overview of studies related to solving the problem.

2.1 Process Architecture in the Health Sector

The work on process architectures for health services focuses on the analysis of a single service and process. For example, Torres-Salgado [10] designed a process architecture to improve the quality of medical care by reducing the time to schedule medical appointments for outpatient services in two highly specialized hospitals in Mexico. Likewise, the same author designed another process architecture for surgical activities and the perioperative medicine service, in this way, after making a diagnosis of the processes, it was identified which stages add value, which do not and which are considered wasted, and, hence, improve and redesign the processes eliminating all wasted activities [11]. On the other hand, Barros [12] proposes a process architecture for the emergency department, through a case study of a hospital in Chile, to improve the use of resources for the emergency service, resulting in a 26% reduction in the delay of patient care thanks to the new workflows. In this way, process architectures can be used for different objectives, whether it is redesigning processes by eliminating unnecessary or irrelevant tasks [10], improving and reducing service times [9], or improving the allocation and use of resources [12].

2.2 Health System Integration

As for works related to the integration of health systems, these serve to better understand the necessary aspects that must be considered for the effective integration of this process architecture. For example, a study in Tanzania concluded that ensuring universal health coverage requires a functional and interoperable health information system [13]. Moreover, another study in China discovered the key factors that affect integration in medical consortiums, discovering a total of 32 factors, of which 17 were key, so they should be prioritized to promote health integration projects, among which is the optimization and reorganization of business processes [8]. In contrast, a study of health system processes in Namibia showed that fragmented health systems face distinct challenges, such as different standards of healthcare interoperability and the absence of unclear policies, functions and structures, which are necessary to promote and drive health systems integration initiatives [14]. Finally, a study shows that fragmentation in health systems leads to complex service delivery, making them not patient-centered, so that, in order to reverse this situation, it is necessary to integrate health services with patients and their needs at the center [7].

3   Methodology

This section defines the selected methodology, what a process architecture is, describes in a general way the current architectures of two hospitals, as well as the proposed solution.

The BPM methodology consists of a structured approach to managing an organization's processes to optimize them to ensure their efficiency, effectiveness, and alignment with the organization's strategy [15]. It has a five-phase life cycle: Design, Model, Execute, Monitor, and Optimize [16]. These phases are developed in the following way: first the processes are currently analyzed, then a visual representation of them is developed both as they are now (as-is) and the new ones as you want them (to-be), the third step consists of testing the new processes to see them in action, and then, as a fourth step, analyze the data based on the established KPIs, finally, in the optimize phase, the processes are refined and improved based on the results previously obtained [16].

A process architecture has been developed to represent the solution. In other words, this consists of the design of the processes and components of an organization in a structured way, in order to be able to use it to show the components of these processes, that is, it consists of a visual map of the hierarchy and process flows of an organization and how they interact with each other [17]. Thus, for the present research work, only the second phase of the BPM life cycle (Model) has been reached, developing a process architecture, which consists mainly of the redesigned process diagrams of the organization, this is due to the difficulty of actually applying the process architecture in Government-owned hospitals, mainly due to the bureaucratic nature of politics in the Peruvian Republic, however, simulations were carried out based on the experience of the health personnel of the hospitals subject to study in order to be able to carry out the execute and monitor phases.

3.1   Current Architecture

Currently, level III hospitals in Peru are the IPRESS with greater specialization and resource capacity to meet the health needs of the population, among its main services are: outpatient consultation, hospitalization and emergencies; however, each of them handles the processes differently and according to their own institutional guidelines. Therefore, two case studies of two level III hospitals in Peru were reviewed, taking into consideration our three study processes and how these are currently implemented, considering the respective differences of each process.

3.1.1   MINSA Hospital

The processes of the outpatient and hospitalization services are in a single process called "Health Recovery and Rehabilitation Process", where a patient goes for outpatient care and, if necessary, will be hospitalized according to their evaluation. Additionally, these processes are divided by types of patients: insured and paying, so there are two processes for each of these services. In the case of the emergency service process, this is called the "Emergency Patient Care Process," and includes the two hospitalization service processes mentioned above.

3.1.2 EsSalud Hospital

Outpatient, hospitalization and emergency services are in the process called "Health Care Process", which is composed of four processes: The first manages the acceptance of the patient for care, the second provides outpatient care and, if necessary, the patient is referred to the emergency so that he can be treated. Finally, if necessary, the patient is treated in the last hospitalization process.

3.2 Proposed Process Architecture

The proposed process architecture is proposed under the Zachman framework and the BPM methodology, through which the use of Business Process Management Notation (BPMN) was applied to perform the modeling of each diagram through the Bizagi Modeler tool.

After having analyzed both hospitals, a process architecture was developed that has the three standardized health processes: outpatient, hospitalization and emergencies, as well as an additional IT process, which have been integrated so that they can be applied in both MINSA and EsSalud level III hospitals. In this way, each process diagram has subprocesses, tasks (activities), defined instances (milestones) and internal roles of stakeholders (collaborators within each institution) at a general level. Additionally, a functional decomposition diagram was designed for each of the processes, which allows the architecture to be broken down into less complex modules that facilitate the understanding of each one and serve as a model for the future development of a system, since it includes the possible functionalities that an Integrated Health System must have.

3.2.1 Outpatient Process

The "Outpatient Care Process" was divided into two subprocesses: "Outpatient Admission" and "Medical Care" (See Fig. 1). In the first subprocess, you perform all the tasks related to managing the patient's appointment, for example, registering the patient in the system if you are new or getting a medical appointment, whether you have insurance or not (See Fig. 2). In the second subprocess, the patient will be attended to and depending on his diagnosis: (i) he will be able to start or continue with his treatment, either in the same specialty or another; (ii) be referred to emergencies discharged (See Fig. 3).

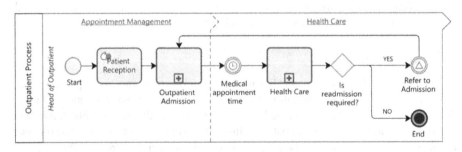

Fig. 1. Outpatient Process

The novelty of this process is to ensure that the information is in real time, in order to accelerate the patient's attention time from the time they request a medical appointment until the end of the care with the registration of their diagnosis, which is evidenced in the orange tasks and subprocesses, which have managed to be automated compared to the processes of the current architectures as shown in the Fig. 2 and Fig. 3. It also seeks to ensure proper management of medical records, by eliminating tasks that are currently performed manually, such as searching for and returning medical records, filling out reports and generating massive orders. Finally, it allows the process to be applied regardless of the type of patient, since this is only considered a data to be registered, that is, the type of patient will only be decisive for the management of the payment or exoneration of this according to their insurance.

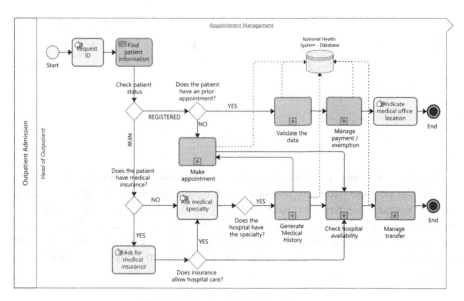

Fig. 2. Outpatient Admission Process

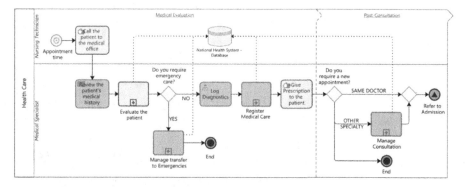

Fig. 3. Health Care Process

3.2.2 Emergency Process

According to Fig. 4, the "Emergency Care Process" begins with the "Admission and Triage Care" subprocess, where the patient is received to perform the respective triage and, subsequently, be attended according to the degree of emergency. In the case of the first subprocess, the necessary orders are issued depending on the patient's condition, where the priority can be low, medium, or high (See Fig. 5). Subsequently, according to the orders issued, the respective actions are taken, and the patient's health status is observed constantly, until determining whether he should be discharged or hospitalized (See Fig. 6).

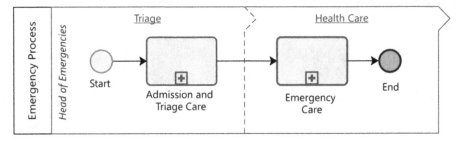

Fig. 4. Emergency Process

The novelty is that it allows the transfer of patients with high priority between hospitals in case the initial hospital does not have the necessary specialty to care for them. Likewise, by having the medical history in the system, it is ensured that the attention time is more efficient, since it keeps the information updated in real time allowing communication between areas, for example, when recording the results of the patient's medical exams, the delay in the transfer of these in a physical-manual way is avoided.

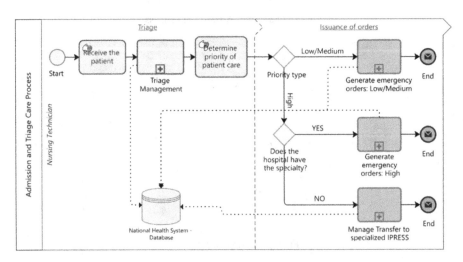

Fig. 5. Admission and Triage Care Process

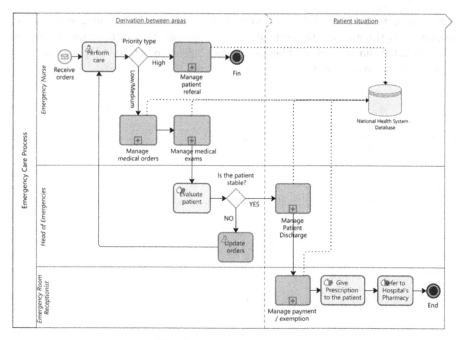

Fig. 6. Emergency Care Process

3.2.3 Hospitalization Process

The "Hospitalization Process" has the "Inpatient Treatment" subprocess (See Fig. 7). The latter begins with the admission of the patient, where the personnel in charge are designated, the patient's bed, the medicines that must be administered regularly and the tests that must be performed, according to the constant monitoring of their health status so that the patient can be treated correctly during their stay in the hospital until they are discharged (See Fig. 8).

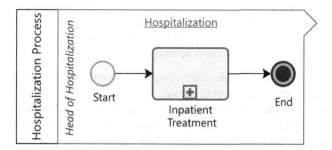

Fig. 7. Hospitalization Process

The novelty of the process is that it considers the transfer of patients between hospitals regardless of the insurance to which they correspond, so that they can access the healthcare service they need (be it an emergency surgery or other), as long as they are in an emergency situation and the hospital of origin does not have the necessary resources, which is in the sub-process of "Manage Surgery". Also, as shown in Fig. 8, threads in orange consider system usage.

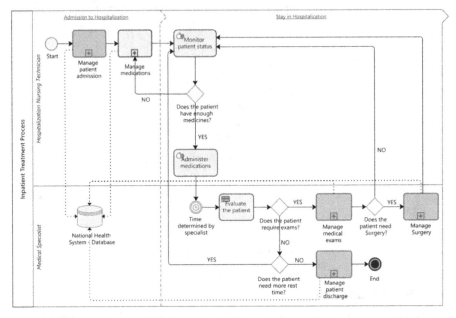

Fig. 8. Inpatient Treatment Process

3.2.4 Information Technology Process

Although the proposed process architecture covers three healthcare processes, in order to correctly implement this proposal, we needed an IT process called "Information Technology Process" which will provide the necessary support for the application of information technologies and will contribute to the creation of an integrated health system. Thus, the following threads were designed:

- User Management: Establishes the management for the creation, elimination and modification of registered users in the system.
- Security Management: Establishes that information security plans should be considered to protect and ensure the privacy of hospital and patient information.
- Management of Technological Resources: Establishes the procedures to be followed to manage the technological resources of the hospital that store information, establishing corrective and preventive maintenance.
- System Management: Establishes how the management and maintenance of the hospital system should be carried out. As well as giving support to the diagrammed databases in the processes; related to medical record, surgery, test, and lab.

- Data Governance: Establishes that plans, guidelines and policies must be considered for data management, since it will allow standardizing the different codes of services, diseases, among other data, in order to ensure the integration of processes.

3.2.5 Functional Decomposition

Additionally, having used the Zachman Framework, the development of a Functional Decomposition of the integrated processes was considered to know which modules would be necessary when implementing the integrated health system. In this way, the modules, or functions, presented will allow the optimization of the processes, by serving as a model for their subsequent development, since, as next steps, a business architecture must be designed based on this decomposition, where the layers of applications, data and technology are defined, thus allowing that, as a last step, user stories can be raised to develop the system (See Fig. 9).

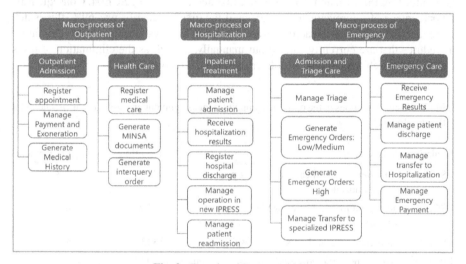

Fig. 9. Functional Decomposition

4 Results

This section details the results obtained through the validations of the time simulations carried out on the processes, as well as the judgment of experts for the assessment of the usefulness of the solution proposal, according to a Likert Scale.

4.1 Time Indicator

For the time indicator, it was considered to quantify the attention times with the Bizagi Modeler tool for the outpatient, emergency, and hospitalization processes, in order to compare the times of the current processes (AS IS) and the proposed architecture (TO

BE). To this end, the hospital staff was asked for the average time of attention of the processes, who managed to provide it for the case of the first process; However, for the others they mentioned that the analysis of these is complex, since it depends on the health situation of the patient, so, for these last two cases, specific scenarios were considered.

4.1.1 Outpatient Simulation

In the case of outpatient consultation, for the simulation of the current processes of the hospitals, their staff was used to provide their subjective assessment of the average time of attention, who mentioned that this was approximately 15 min. Based on this, the admission of 200 patients was considered for the analysis.

Table 1 shows the results of the 4 scenarios ESCE01 and ESCE02 for the MINSA hospital, ESCE03 for the EsSalud hospital and ESCE04 for the proposed process architecture. Thus, per patient had an approximate time of 1 h and 13 min for ESCE01, 1 h and 22 min for ESCE02, 1 h and 7 min for ESCE03 and 23 min for ESCE04. Consequently, the percentage of improvement on average of the first 3 scenarios was 69%, this is due to the fact that several of the activities are supported by a system capable of automating procedures that are currently carried out manually, as well as the elimination of tasks such as the search, reception and delivery of medical records.

Table 1. Simulation times in the outpatient appointment assignment processes of the first hospital in Bizagi Modeler

Scenarios	Process Name	Total time (m)	% improvement
ESCE01	Outpatient medical care for paying patients at the MINSA hospital	14662	67.93%
ESCE02	Outpatient medical care for SIS patients at MINSA hospital	16560	71.61%
ESCE03	Outpatient care of the EsSalud hospital	13431	64.99%
ESCE04	Healthcare of the proposed process architecture	4702	-

4.1.2 Emergency Simulation

In the case of emergency, the simulation of a specific case was performed, where a patient presents for a mild anaphylactic picture, requiring sample examinations, application of antihistamine medications and an observation time of 5 h. Table 2 shows the results obtained from the time of attention per patient and the percentages of improvement of the current processes according to the time of the solution proposal. Thus, the average percentage improvement of the first two scenarios was 27%, this is because they eliminate tasks related to revenue management and add results recording tasks in a system.

Table 2. Simulation times of mild anaphylaxis in emergency in Bizagi Modeler

Scenarios	Process Name	Total time (m)	% improvement
ESEA01	Initial care of the patient in emergency situation of the MINSA hospital	498.5	26.04%
ESEA02	Emergency and Critical Care of the EsSalud hospital	470	28.03%
ESEA03	Emergency Response of the proposed process architecture	368.71	-

4.1.3 Hospitalization Simulation

In the case of hospitalization, the simulation of a specific case was performed, where a patient is hospitalized for a picture of acute appendicitis, requiring sample and imaging tests, operation, postoperative treatment, which includes the application of antibiotics and analgesics, and a hospitalization time of 3 days (72 h).

Table 3 shows the results obtained: The approximate total time in hours for the MINSA hospital was 81.12 for patients insured to the SIS (ESH01) and 80.87 for paying patients (ESH02), while, for the EsSalud hospital (ESH03), the total time was 80.58. In the case of the proposed architecture (ESH04), the time was approximately 75.34 h. In this way, an average improvement percentage of 7% was obtained, reducing the time by 6 h, since tasks related to the transfer of exams in a physical way are eliminated.

Table 3. Times of the simulation of the case of appendicitis in hospitalization in Bizagi Mode-ler

Scenarios	Process Name	Total time (h)	% improvement
ESH01	Hospitalization of SIS patients from the MINSA hospital	80.87	7.12%
ESH02	Hospitalization of paying patients of the MINSA hospital	81.12	6.83%
ESH03	Hospitalization care at the EsSalud hospital	80.58	6.51%
ESH04	Treatment in Hospitalization of the proposed process architecture	75.34	-

4.2 Expert Judgement

In addition to the time simulations, we opted for the validation of the usefulness of the process architecture through the judgment of experts, with knowledge in process management and / or in the Peruvian health sector. Being a total of five experts: three health experts with 16, 23 and 25 years of experience in the sector, an expert in process management with 16 years of experience and an expert in process management and the health sector with 24 years of experience.

In this way, they were presented with the architecture with all its artifacts, along with a series of questions (See Table 4) whose answers were rated according to the Likert scale (1: Strongly disagree, 2: Disagree, 3: Neither agree nor disagree, 4: Agree, 5: Strongly agree). The questions were answered through a form in Google Forms, which was sent to the experts after the presentation of the architecture.

Table 4. Questions for experts

ID	Questions	Averages
On the problem identified:		
P1	The architecture solves the current problem of limited health services	4.6
P2	The architecture integration proposal helps to counteract the problem of fragmentation of the health system	4.4
On the process architecture approach:		
P3	The process diagrams are correctly laid out	4
P4	The diagrams of the health processes (Outpatient, Hospitalization and Emergency) cover all the activities necessary to provide a good service to patients	3.8
P5	The IT process provides proper support to health processes	3.8
P6	IT processes efficiently address information security and privacy	4
On its possible application in level III hospitals		
P7	The architecture would improve patients' care times for the assignment of their outpatient appointments (without considering the waiting days between assignment and the date of consultation)	4.4
P8	The architecture could be applied in the future in level III hospitals of EsSalud and SIS	4.6
P9	The functions identified in the functional decomposition are useful for a future system that supports the proposed processes	4.4
P10	Based on what has been developed, more health processes could continue to be developed, in addition to the initial 3	4.4

In this way, according to experts, the architecture is well planned, and they consider it a good contribution to the integration of the Peruvian health system, obtaining a total average of 4.24 and demonstrating that it has a very high utility.

5   Conclusions and Future Work

In the present work, a proposal for process architecture has been presented to integrate three health services: outpatient, hospitalization and emergencies, considering a situation where there is a fragmented health system with different health providers, as well as an IT process and a functional decomposition, which indicates the necessary functions that the future system that supports the processes must have as a minimum. Thus, demonstrating that the integration of the two different health providers is possible in terms of processes. In this way, the difference with the current processes of the hospitals consists in the elimination or replacement of several manual tasks that make patient care processes cumbersome, so the proposed solution improves care times by having an integrated system, as well as standardized processes, data and services, which allow to manage the information in a more complete way.

In addition, based on the results obtained from the simulations of time analysis of the processes, an average percentage of improvement was obtained: 69% for outpatient consultation, 27% for the case of mild anaphylaxis in emergency and 7% for the case of appendicitis in hospitalization. However, it should be noted that it was a simulation based on the information provided by the hospital's health personnel and not an application in a real-life scenario. Even so, the simulation shows that, by having automated tasks supported by a system, care times for patients can be improved. Also, the judgment of experts on architecture demonstrates a very high utility according to the Likert scale, so it would serve to solve or mitigate the identified problem.

The limitations of the research consisted in not being able to carry out rigorous quantitative validations, due to the fact that there is currently no system or application that supports the process architecture, nor a test environment where it can be tested and executed, in other words, in order to carry out further tests it is necessary to create an interconnected information system between several hospitals and adapt their environment so that they can be applied processes. In addition, given the nature of the numerous and complex bureaucratic procedures, the research work could be delayed by having to apply for permits from different state entities.

For future work, it is proposed to carry out an enterprise architecture under the TOGAF (The Open Group Architecture Framework) framework, which would establish the guidelines for the organization, propose the functional modules for a future integrated health system and define the necessary guidelines of the software for its deployment, and, finally, determine the hardware required to support the system for its execution, as well as the server connectivity guidelines.

References

1. Schwalb, A., Seas, C.: The COVID-19 pandemic in Peru: what went wrong? Am. J. Trop. Med. Hyg. **104**(4), 1176–1178 (2021)
2. Gianella, C., Gideon, J., Romero, M.J.: What does COVID-19 tell us about the Peruvian health system? Canadian Journal of Development Studies/Revue canadienne d'études du développement **42**(1–2), 55–67 (2021)
3. El 83,3% de la población del país accedió a un seguro de salud en el IV trimestre del 2021. https://www.gob.pe/institucion/inei/noticias/594991-el-83-3-de-la-poblacion-del-pais-accedio-a-un-seguro-de-salud-en-el-iv-trimestre-del-2021. Accessed 03 Aug 2023

4. Ponce de León, Z.: Sistema de Salud en el Perú y el COVID-19. Políticas y Debates Públicos **2**, 1–8 (2021)
5. Espinoza-Portilla, E., Gil-Quevedo, W., Agurto-Távara, E.: Principales problemas en la gestión de establecimientos de salud en el Perú. Revista Cubana de Salud Pública **46**(4), e2146 (2020)
6. Carhuancho-Mendoza, I.M., Nolazco-Labajos, F.A., Bejarano, G.: Calidad de servicio en hospitales de nivel III de la ciudad de Lima. Perú. Revista Venezolana de Gerencia: RVG **26**(5), 693–707 (2021)
7. Siersbaek, R., Ford, J., Ní Cheallaigh, C., Thomas, S., Burke, S.: How do health system factors (funding and performance) impact on access to healthcare for populations experiencing homelessness: a realist evaluation. Int. J. Equity Health **22**(1), 1–15 (2023)
8. Tian, S.H., Chen, Y., Bai, T.Z.: Key influencing factors of vertical integration of electronic health records in medical consortiums. Int. J. Med. Informatics **170**, 104959 (2023)
9. De Ramón Fernández, A., Ruiz Fernández, D., Sabuco García, Y.: Business Process Management for optimizing clinical processes: a systematic literature review. Health Informatics J. **26**(2), 1305–1320 (2020)
10. Torres-Salgado, M.K.: Arquitectura de procesos con indicadores estratégicos en los servicios médicos de consulta externa en hospitales de alta especialidad. Gac. Med. Mex. **155**(6), 576–584 (2019)
11. Torres-Salgado, M.K.: Arquitectura de procesos para hospitales: construcción de modelado estratégico de indicadores. Revista del Hospital de Juárez de México **89**(3), 136–144 (2022)
12. Barros, O.: A process architecture pattern and its application to designing health services: emergency case. Bus. Process. Manag. J. **26**(2), 513–527 (2020)
13. Nsaghurwe, A., et al.: One country's journey to interoperability: Tanzania's experience developing and implementing a national health information exchange. BMC Med. Inform. Decis. Mak. **21**(1), 1–16 (2021)
14. Kapepo, M.I., Yashik, S.: A process analysis of the Namibian Health System: an exploratory case study. Ethiopian J. Health Dev. **32**(4), 200–209 (2018)
15. What is BPM Methodology in Process Management? https://www.cflowapps.com/bpm-methodology/. Accessed 15 Nov 2023
16. Malak, H.A.: BPM Lifecycle: 5 Stages to Business Process Excellence. https://theecmconsultant.com/what-is-bpm-lifecycle/. Accessed 15 Nov 2023
17. Process Architecture: Definition, Benefits and Examples. https://www.indeed.com/career-advice/career-development/process-architecture. Accessed 03 Aug 2023

Z AT for Engineering Applications

Assessing Burnout Syndrome Among Medical Staff at a Tertiary Hospital in Guayaquil

Carlos Campos-Rivera[1], Lester Veliz-Franco[1], Kenny Escobar-Segovia[2]([⊠]) [iD],
and Daniela Paz-Barzola[2] [iD]

[1] Universidad Espíritu Santo, Samborondón, Ecuador
{carloscamposr,lveliz}@uees.edu.ec
[2] Escuela Superior Politecnica del Litoral, Guayaquil, Ecuador
{kescobar,dpaz}@espol.edu.ec

Abstract. Burnout is a professional mental health syndrome marked by exhaustion, growing detachment from work, and decreased work efficiency. It can lead to serious consequences for physicians, including medical errors, legal disputes, substance abuse, and suicidal thoughts. This study aimed to assess the prevalence of Burnout Syndrome among doctors in a tertiary hospital in Guayaquil. Utilizing the Maslach Burnout Inventory (MBI-HSS) assessment tool, it was found that 21.8% of the 78 doctors surveyed met all criteria for Burnout Syndrome. Notably, male physicians exhibited more pronounced signs of burnout than their female counterparts. This underscores the importance of personalized interventions and a holistic understanding of workplace challenges, especially in high-pressure environments like healthcare. Future policies and workplace reforms should address these issues to ensure both the well-being of medical professionals and the quality of patient care.

Keywords: Mental health · Burnout · physicians · Guayaquil · interventions

1 Introduction

The World Health Organization (WHO) defines Burnout as an Occupational Mental Health syndrome, characterized by "feelings of energy depletion and exhaustion, increased mental distance from one's job, cynicism, or negative feelings about one's work, and reduced professional efficacy" [1]. The International Classification of Diseases describes burnout as a syndrome conceptualized as a result of chronic workplace stress that has not been successfully managed [2].

Burnout was first described in healthcare providers in 1974 by Herbert J. Freudenberger. While working intensively as a psychiatrist in the free clinic movement, he observed and personally experienced a series of psychological findings: exhaustion, overcommitment to bodily functions, and poor emotional control. Borrowing a term from the drug-addict slang of his patients in New York's East Village, he described "staff burnout": a syndrome defined as failure or exhaustion due to excessive demands on energy, strength, or resources.

"Physician Burnout" is defined as a work-related syndrome of emotional exhaustion, feelings of depersonalization, detachment from patients, and a low sense of personal accomplishment. Physician burnout has been linked with higher rates of medical errors, involvement in malpractice lawsuits, substance use, and suicidal ideation [3]. Burnout can lead to decreased effectiveness and productivity, reduced job engagement, negative impacts on home life, adverse effects on personal health, and compromises in patient safety [4]. Burnout occurs when job demands exceed work resources.

Among the psychosocial risks and job demands that are significant factors for the presence of Burnout, according to the job demands-resources theory from psychology and organizational behavior, are role ambiguity, role conflict, job insecurity, and work overload. Meanwhile, job resources include autonomy, social support from colleagues, performance feedback, and supervisory coaching [5].

In addition to exhaustion, the syndrome is characterized with physical findings such as frequent headaches, gastrointestinal disorders, insomnia, and difficulty breathing; and behavioral symptoms like frustration, anger, paranoia, overconfidence, cynicism, depression, and the use of sedatives [6].

Burnout is a topic of significant public and research interest, reflecting its severe consequences, with costs to the global economy estimated at over $300 billion annually and a "pandemic" of exhaustion predicted by the World Health Organization (WHO) in the coming decade [7].

Christina Maslach, a psychologist from the University of Berkeley, found that nurses faced a higher risk of post-traumatic stress disorder factors, characterized by negative behavior towards patients, increased workload, excessive role ambiguity, and role conflict. Maslach categorized burnout into three dimensions: emotional exhaustion, depersonalization (i.e., cynicism), and a diminished sense of personal accomplishment. She also developed the first survey to measure the incidence and severity of the syndrome.

In 2019, the WHO added Burnout to its International Classification of Diseases as a syndrome resulting from unmanaged chronic workplace stress. WHO characterized burnout in three dimensions: (1) feelings of energy depletion or exhaustion, (2) increased mental distance from one's job, or feelings of negativism or cynicism related to one's job, and (3) decreased professional efficacy. According to WHO, burnout refers specifically to phenomena in the occupational context and shouldn't be used to describe experiences in other areas of life [6].

Burnout is a major health concern that has been intensified by the added stressors stemming from the 2019 novel coronavirus (COVID-19) pandemic. Emergency Department (ED) healthcare workers (HCWs) had one of the highest burnout incidences even before the pandemic [4, 8–10]. Being on the frontlines, directly interacting with suspected or confirmed COVID-19 patients, exacerbates this issue [11].

The global COVID-19 pandemic is dramatically impacting social norms, causing widespread disruption across all health disciplines and consequent delays in healthcare delivery systems [12].

This surge in burnout has been amplified by the ongoing COVID-19 pandemic. The current level of staff burnout is believed to be directly tied to a loss of meaning and purpose in daily work [13].

Since burnout hampers cognitive performance by intensifying negative emotions, it also leads to biased decision-making, exacerbating issues like disparities in care. Ultimately, burnout is contributing to a shortage of medical staff and may be causing a decline in the quality and equity of emergency care [6].

The onset of the COVID-19 pandemic brought about a swift transition to remote work for a large portion of the workforce. While there are potential benefits, such as reduced commuting time and more family time, there are also downsides like reduced human interaction and no physical boundary between work and home [14]. There's a significant risk that remote work may contribute to employee burnout as the lines blur between professional and personal life. This remote work shift can be especially stressful during the COVID-19 pandemic, when schools have closed, and individuals ramp up caregiving activities with little warning to set up optimal home IT resources [15].

It's unsurprising that physician burnout is much higher than in the general working population and remains elevated despite growing recognition of its effects [16]. There's a pressing need to understand burnout causes and develop preventive interventions to ensure the healthcare workforce's health and well-being [6].

Given the significance and growing relevance of this condition among professionals, especially healthcare providers, this study aims to determine the occurrence of Burnout Syndrome among medical staff at a tertiary-level hospital in Guayaquil. The study employs the assessment and identification instrument for burnout known as the Maslach Burnout Inventory (MBI-HSS).

2 Literature Review

Health is humanity's most valued asset, defined as a state of complete physical, mental, and social well-being, not merely the absence of disease or infirmity [17]. Occupational health, as outlined by the WHO [18], promotes and maintains the highest degree of physical, mental, and social well-being for workers in all occupations. This is achieved by preventing health deviations, controlling risks, and adapting the job to the person and vice versa.

Work is a source of health [19]. Through it, individuals can access various benefits for maintaining good health. However, work can also be detrimental, with its impacts closely tied to an individual's adaptability to specific workplace conditions. The work environment encompasses the organization where one works and how one interacts with the elements of the physical or natural setting involved in the work process. Within this environment, harmful and dangerous risk factors can jeopardize health, leading to accidents and work-related diseases [20].

Healthcare systems comprise organizations, institutions, individuals, and resources dedicated to providing health services to people [21]. Lately, they have been under scrutiny due to the high job demands placed on healthcare workers during the Covid-19 pandemic. These professionals are exposed to significant psychological, emotional, and physical stress, making them particularly susceptible to burnout [22].

Burnout, also termed as work-related exhaustion syndrome, is nowadays regarded as one of the most significant psychosocial occupational hazards, as outlined by the National Institute for Occupational Safety and Health [23]. As defined by the International Classification of Diseases-11, Burnout arises from chronic workplace stress and is characterized by feelings of emotional exhaustion, depersonalization, and diminished professional accomplishment [24].

Emotional exhaustion denotes the draining of emotional resources and the sensation that one cannot provide any more to another person, forming a central aspect of this syndrome. It represents fatigue and a steady energy decline [25]. Depersonalization encompasses cynical, negative attitudes about one's clients, manifesting as irritability and impersonal reactions to service recipients [26]. Meanwhile, decreased personal accomplishment pertains to negative self-responses and work-related perceptions. It embodies deteriorated self-worth accompanied by feelings of inadequacy, insufficiency, and distrust in one's abilities [26].

According to the National Institute for Occupational Safety and Health [23], burnout primarily arises from the worker's interaction with their working environment or from interpersonal relationships between the worker and those they serve. This syndrome essentially hinges on three variable types:

Individual Variables: Gender appears to be a significant factor in burnout scores, particularly in the dimensions of exhaustion and professional inefficacy.

Social Variables: This relates to the tangible or perceived support a worker receives from close social circles. Social support allows one to feel cherished, esteemed, and appreciated in their job and organization.

Organizational Variables: These relate to job performance and job content, including the lack of reciprocity, organizational climate, and more.

3   Methodology

The study focused on the medical staff of a tertiary-level hospital in Guayaquil. It adopted a quantitative, non-experimental descriptive approach, as data was directly collected from the medical personnel without any alteration. The study's design was cross-sectional, as data was gathered at one specific point in time, with a correlational scope to measure the relationships or degree of association between two or more variables [27].

Using the hospital's total medical staff population of 93 individuals and factoring in a 95% confidence level and a 5% margin of error, a representative sample of 76 individuals was derived for the study. The sample was determined through a calculation based on simple random sampling to ensure a comprehensive and unbiased representation.

The assessment instrument for identifying Burnout Syndrome among the medical staff consisted of three parts: sociodemographic variables, occupational variables, and the Maslach Burnout Inventory - Human Services Survey (MBI-HSS), formulated by Christina Maslach and Susan Jackson in 1981 [28].

The instrument's first two sections, pertaining to sociodemographic and occupational variables, covered areas such as gender, age, marital status, number of children, type of contract, work experience, daily working hours, and relationship dynamics with coworkers.

The third section utilized the Maslach Burnout Inventory (MBI-HSS), which remains the preferred assessment tool within the scientific community for evaluating burnout in care settings [29]. Its global acceptance stems from its high reliability, validity, and ease of application and interpretation [22]. Designed to evaluate the three burnout components: Emotional Exhaustion (EE), Depersonalization (DP), and Personal Accomplishment (PA), the inventory contains 22 items on a 7-point Likert scale, ranging from 0 (never) to 6 (every day).

MBI scores for each component are obtained by summing numerical responses from items linked to each dimension. High scores in the first two dimensions (EE and DP) and low scores in the third dimension (PA) indicate burnout [28]. MBI scores categorize EE as low ($\leq$18 points), moderate ($\geq$19 and $\leq$26 points), or high ($\geq$27 points); DP as low ($\leq$5 points), moderate ($\geq$6 and $\leq$9 points), or high ($\geq$10 points); and PA as low ($\leq$33 points), moderate ($\geq$34 and $\leq$39 points), or high ($\geq$40 points).

The assessment was conducted online in September 2021. To secure a favorable margin of completed surveys, the sampling was expanded by 5, yielding 81 filled surveys. During data processing, 3 surveys were discarded due to incomplete information, leaving a total of 78 valid surveys for analysis. Data organization, processing, and analysis including correlations, were conducted using SPSS and Excel, producing tables of measurements, standard deviation, and p-values for the sociodemographic and occupational variables. Graphs were generated for each individual burnout indicator and an overarching graph representing the total individuals meeting all the burnout syndrome criteria.

4 Results

Table 1 displays the sociodemographic characteristics of the respondents. It shows that 75.6% are female, while 24.4% are male. The most represented age groups are 31–40 years (30.8%) and 41–50 years (29.4%). Regarding marital status, 32% are single, and 44.9% are married. In terms of the number of children, 38.5% have none, while 61.5% have children.

The association between the MBI-HSS scores and sociodemographic variables, as presented in Table 2, showed that the average scores of men are closer to the required scores for the Burnout Syndrome classification than those of women. For the PA dimension, there was a significant dependency between the variables ($p = 0.004$). Regarding marital status, no statistical significance was found between the variables in any of the three dimensions. In contrast, age showed significance in EE ($p = 0.008$) and PA ($p = 0.001$), and the number of children demonstrated dependency across all three dimensions: EE ($p = 0.02$), DP ($p = 0.009$), and PA ($p = 0.003$).

When analyzing the association of job-related variables with the MBI-HSS as shown in Table 3, it is evident that the variables of professional experience were statistically significant in all three dimensions: EE ($p = 0.003$), DP ($p = 0.024$), and PA ($p = < 0.001$). In contrast, the type of contract and the number of work hours per day were significant in only one dimension, specifically in EE ($p = 0.001$) and PA ($p = 0.021$), respectively.

Furthermore, it was observed that in the variable "type of relationship with colleagues", the average scores of individuals with regular and poor relationships were closer to the scores required for the diagnosis of Burnout Syndrome compared to the average scores of those with good and very good relationships. Dependency between variables was evident in the EE ($p = 0.005$) and PA ($p = 0.003$) dimensions.

Table 1. Sociodemographic variables of the study population.

Variable	Category	n	%
Sex	Male	19	24.4
	Female	59	75.6
	20–30 years	13	16.7
	31 - 40 years	24	30.8
Age	41 – 50 years	23	29.5
	51 - 60 years	14	17.9
	>60 years	4	5.1
Marital Status	Single	25	32.0
	Married	35	44.9
	Common-law	10	12.8
	Divorced	7	9.0
	Widowed	1	1.3
Number of children	0	30	38.5
	1	17	21.8
	2	19	24.4
	3	9	11.5
	>3	3	3.8

In Fig. 1, the scores of the 78 study participants are displayed across the three MBI-HSS dimensions. High EE were seen in 29.5% (23 individuals), medium in 14.1% (11 individuals), and low in 56.4% (44 individuals); High DP were recorded for 42.3% (33 individuals), medium for 11.5% (9 individuals), and low for 46.2% (36 individuals); and high PA were noted in 39.7% (31 individuals), medium in 19.2% (15 individuals), and low in 41.1% (32 individuals).

This data underscores the varying degrees to which medical professionals at the hospital are experiencing symptoms related to Burnout. Notably, nearly a third are reporting high levels of EE, a critical dimension of the Burnout syndrome.

The results displayed in Fig. 2 allow us to observe that, out of the 78 individuals who were part of the study's sample population (medical staff), 21.8% (17 individuals) were diagnosed with Burnout Syndrome. This contrasts with the 78.2% (61 individuals) who were not diagnosed with the syndrome. This data indicates that approximately one in five medical professionals from the study's sample are currently experiencing Burnout Syndrome.

Table 2. Association of sociodemographic variables with Burnout Syndrome dimensions.

Variable	n (%) n = 78	Emotional Exhaustion			Despersonalization			Personal Achievement		
		Mean	SD	P Value	Mean	SD	P Value	Mean	SD	P Value
Sex										
Male	19 (24.4)	25.7	17.1	0.110	12	9.7	0.250	29.4	9.7	0.040*
Female	59 (75.6)	17.2	14.8		8	8.1		36.4	9.3	
Age										
20–30 years	13 (16.7)	32.2	12.1	0.008*	15.2	7.3	0.060	31	6	0.001*
31–40 years	24 (30.8)	21.8	16.6		9.8	8.2		29.4	10.9	
41–50 years	23 (29.5)	17.2	15.5		7.8	8.9		38.7	8.6	
51–60 years	14 (17.9)	9.2	10		5.8	8.2		38.6	8.7	
>60 years	4 (5.1)	9.3	6.9		2.3	3.9		41.8	3.9	
Marital Status										
Single	25 (32)	22.7	15.2	0.380	11.3	8.2	0.151	30.8	10	0.156
Married	35 (44.9)	16.1	15.2		6.9	7.9		37.1	8.9	
Common-law	10 (12.8)	24.6	17.3		12.4	9.7		34.2	9.9	
Divorced	7 (9)	16.3	18		7.7	10.3		36.7	11.7	
Widowed	1 (1.3)	12	-		0	-		38	-	
Number of children										
0	30 (38.5)	26.6	14.8	0.020*	13.1	8.1	0.009*	26.6	14.8	0.003*
1	17 (21.8)	15.1	14.9		5.4	7.5		15.1	14.9	
2	19 (24.4)	15.6	15.2		7.9	8.2		15.6	15.2	

(continued)

Table 2. (*continued*)

Variable	n (%)	Emotional Exhaustion			Despersonalization			Personal Achievement		
	n = 78	Mean	SD	P Value	Mean	SD	P Value	Mean	SD	P Value
3	9 (11.5)	11.7	13.7		4.6	6.7		11.7	13.7	
>3	3 (3.8)	15.3	19.7		8.7	14.2		15.3	19.7	

* Statistically significant values indicate a dependency between the variables (P Value < 0.05).

Table 3. Association of job-related variables with Burnout Syndrome dimensions.

Variable	n (%)	Emotional Exhaustion			Despersonalization			Personal Achievement		
	n = 78	Mean	SD	P Value	Mean	SD	P Value	Mean	SD	P Value
Contract Type										
Temporary	6 (7.7)	17	11.3	0.001*	6.2	8	0.170	32.5	12.7	0.370
Permanent	24 (30.7)	12.8	12.4		5.6	6		33.9	11.3	
Fixed Term	41 (52.6)	21.3	17.1		10.2	9.3		36.2	9	
Substitute/Replacement	7 (9.0)	31.4	12.6		15.9	8.3		30.6	5.4	
Experience										
<1 year	2 (2.6)	30	17	0.003*	17	9.9	0.024*	25.5	13.4	<0.001*
1–5 year	28 (35.9)	28.1	15		12.5	8.3		31.2	7.6	
6–10 year	13 (16.7)	17.3	13.2		8.2	7.8		28.9	11.3	
>10 year	35 (44.9)	12.3	13.7		6.1	8.2		40.2	8	
Working Hours per Day										
<8 h	27 (34.6)	13.9	13.2	0.161	7.1	7.8	0.440	36.6	8.8	0.021*
8–12 h	47 (60.3)	21.9	16.3		9.8	8.7		33.7	10	

(*continued*)

Table 3. (*continued*)

Variable	n (%)	Emotional Exhaustion			Despersonalization			Personal Achievement		
	n = 78	Mean	SD	P Value	Mean	SD	P Value	Mean	SD	P Value
Shift Work	4 (5.1)	24.5	19.1		12.5	12.8		33	15.2	
Relationship with Colleagues										
Very Good	41 (52.6)	13.4	12.6	0.005*	6.3	7.2	0.140	39.2	7.9	0.003*
Good	29 (37.2)	22.3	16.3		9.9	8.7		31.1	9.7	
Regular	7 (9.0)	35.9	8.9		18.7	5.3		25	7.3	
Poor	1 (1.3)	54	-		28	-		23	-	

* Statistically significant values indicate a dependency between the variables (P value < 0.05).

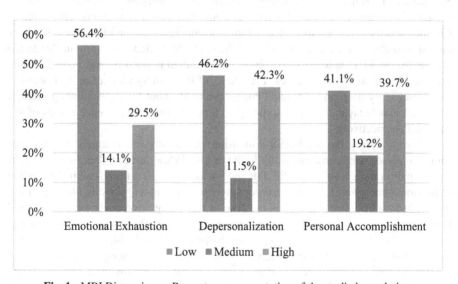

Fig. 1. MBI Dimensions – Percentage representation of the studied population.

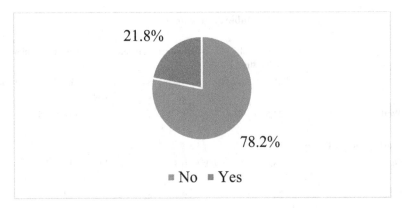

Fig. 2. Burnout Syndrome – Percentage representation of the studied population.

5 Discussion

The current research revealed that less than a quarter of the medical staff at the analyzed hospital suffers from Burnout Syndrome. This result is consistent with other studies conducted in the country on medical personnel from other health institutions. These studies have not greatly exceeded the value obtained in this research, and in some cases have even shown lower values. For instance, in the study "Prevalence of Burnout Syndrome among doctors in a Quito hospital", 26% of the studied population was identified with Burnout [30]. Similarly, the studies "Prevalence of Burnout Syndrome among doctors in a Latacunga city hospital" [31] and "Prevalence of Burnout Syndrome among medical personnel in a Guayaquil city hospital" [32] reported Burnout presence values of 9% and 2.6%, respectively.

When analyzing the MBI-HSS dimensions separately and comparing them with similar analyses, we found variability in the results. While some studies showed higher representation at the high level in EE, DP, and PA, as happened in the research "Evaluation of Burnout syndrome in the medical personnel working in a Quito city hospital" [33], others showed the opposite, as was the case in this study. Moreover, some had mixed representations across different dimensions, as occurred in the research "Prevalence of burnout syndrome in San Francisco general hospital in Quito" [34].

The distinct outcomes across each of these studies, despite using the same Burnout assessment tool and applying it to similar professional groups (medical personnel) and work settings (hospitals), suggest that consistent results cannot be expected. Rather, it can be asserted that outcomes depend heavily on the physical and mental characteristics of everyone in the studied population and their capacity to adapt to the social and work pressures of their environment.

The 29.5% of medical staff showing symptoms of Burnout in the emotional exhaustion dimension might be attributed to facing extended work hours and the inability to spend time with their families. The results are similar to the findings of Puli [34], where the population with high incidence in the emotional exhaustion dimension was also linked to high work demands. As for the 42.3% presenting a high level in depersonalization, it could be related to prolonged professional experience leading to monotony in work tasks and, similarly to emotional exhaustion, extended working hours and distance from their family nucleus.

Concerning the third dimension, personal accomplishment, 39.7% of the medical staff were found at a low level. Such an indication of Burnout may be due to a lack of job stability, insufficient income, limited work experience, negative experiences with patients, among other factors, as asserted by Gallardo [30].

The information and correlation presented by the authors in the study have been developed based on statistical analyses and estimates calculated from the data obtained through surveys. Being conducted online, these surveys might carry potential biases and might not necessarily express the reality.

6 Conclusions

In this study, it was determined that the occurrence of Burnout Syndrome among doctors in a tertiary hospital in the city of Guayaquil, who met all the diagnostic criteria for Burnout Syndrome, was 21.8%.

Within the MBI-HSS study, it can be observed that even though most of the population fell within the low levels in each of the burnout dimensions, there are significant values placed at a high level in EE and DP, which clearly indicates Burnout symptoms. While it's true that to diagnose Burnout Syndrome one must meet high values in the first two dimensions (EE and DP) and low scores in the third dimension (PA), the results are a clear sign of a probable positive diagnosis in the near future.

Additionally, it was determined that even though females dominated the study with two-thirds representation compared to males, it was the men who showed higher signs of Burnout than women across all three MBI-HSS dimensions.

References

1. Hoffman, K.E., Garner, D., Koong, A.C., Woodward, W.A.: Understanding the intersection of working from home and burnout to optimize post-COVID19 work arrangements in radiation oncology. Int. J. Radiat. Oncol. Biol. Phys. **108**, 370–373 (2020)
2. Bakken, B.K., Winn, A.N.: Clinician burnout during the COVID-19 pandemic before vaccine administration. J. Am. Pharm. Assoc. **61**, e71–e77 (2021)
3. Khalafallah, A.M., et al.: Burnout and career satisfaction among attending neurosurgeons during the COVID-19 pandemic. Clin. Neurol. Neurosurg. **198**, 106193 (2020)
4. Adanaqué-Bravo, I., et al.: Relationship between psychological distress, burnout and work engagement in workers during the COVID-19 pandemic: a systematic review. Int. J. Public Health **67** (2023)
5. Guenette, J.P., Smith, S.E.: Burnout: job resources and job demands associated with low personal accomplishment in United States radiology residents. Acad. Radiol. **25**, 739–743 (2018)
6. Sanchez, L.D., Wolfe, R.E.: Physician well-being. Emerg. Med. Clin. North Am. **38**, 297–310 (2020)
7. Tavella, G., Hadzi-Pavlovic, D., Parker, G.: Burnout: redefining its key symptoms. Psychiatry Res. **302**, 114023 (2021)

8. Gómez-Salgado, J., et al.: Sense of coherence in healthcare workers during the COVID-19 pandemic in Ecuador: association with work engagement, work environment and psychological distress factors. Int. J. Public Health **67** (2022)
9. Ruiz-Frutos, C., et al.: Work engagement, work environment, and psychological distress during the COVID-19 pandemic: a cross-sectional study in Ecuador. Healthcare (Switzerland) **10** (2022)
10. Ruiz-Frutos, C., et al.: Factors associated to psychological distress during the COVID-19 pandemic among healthcare workers in Ecuador. Int. J. Public Health **67** (2022)
11. Chor, W.P.D., et al.: Burnout amongst emergency healthcare workers during the COVID-19 pandemic: a multi-center study. Am. J. Emerg. Med. **46**, 700–702 (2021)
12. Peck, J.L., Sonney, J.: Exhausted and burned out: COVID-19 emerging impacts threaten the health of the pediatric advanced practice registered nursing workforce. J. Pediatr. Health Care **35**, 414–424 (2021)
13. Southwick, S., Wisneski, L., Starck, P.: Rediscovering meaning and purpose: an approach to burnout in the time of COVID-19 and beyond. Am. J. Med. **134**, 1065–1067 (2021)
14. Izquierdo-Yanez, D., Crespo-Verdugo, C., Duque-Cordova, L., Escobar-Segovia, K., Carrozzini-Villagrán, A.: Mental Health Conditions Under the Home Office Modality Due to Covid-19 in Employees of a Bottling Company in Ecuador. in 338–350 (2022). https://doi.org/10.1007/978-3-030-96046-9_25
15. Gold, K.J.: Combating burnout: back to medicine as a calling. Ann. Fam. Med. **17**, 485–486 (2019)
16. Tawfik, D.S., Profit, J.: Provider burnout: Implications for our perinatal patients. Semin. Perinatol. **44**, 151243 (2020)
17. PAHO. Salud en las Américas+, edición del 2017. Resumen: panorama regional y perfiles de país (2017)
18. WHO. Documentos Básicos (2014)
19. Parra, M.: Conceptos básicos en salud laboral : eje para la acción sindical (2003)
20. Guerrero Pupo, J., et al.: Calidad de vida y trabajo: algunas consideraciones útiles para el profesional de la información. ACIMED 14 (2006)
21. WHO. Informe sobre la salud en el mundo: 2000: mejorar el desempeño de los sistemas de salud (2000)
22. Elghazally, S.A., Alkarn, A.F., Elkhayat, H., Ibrahim, A. K., Elkhayat, M.R.: Burnout impact of COVID-19 pandemic on health-care professionals at Assiut University Hospitals, 2020. Int J Environ Res Public Health 18, (2021)
23. Instituto Nacional de Seguridad e Higiene en el Trabajo. NTP 732: Síndrome de estar quemado por el trabajo 'Burnout' (III): Instrumento de medición (2004)
24. AlJhani, S., et al.: Burnout and coping among healthcare providers working in Saudi Arabia during the COVID-19 pandemic. Middle East Current Psychiatry **28**, 29 (2021)
25. Castillo Ramírez, S.: El síndrome de 'Burn Out' o síndrome de agotamiento profesional. Medicina Legal de Costa Rica 17 (2001)
26. Martínez Pérez, A.: El síndrome de Burnout, evolución conceptual y estado actual de la cuestión. VivatAcademia **112**, 42–80 (2010)
27. Hernández, R., Fernández, C., Baptista, M. del P.: Metodología de la investigación
28. Maslach, C., Jackson, S., Leiter, M.: Maslach burnout inventory manual (1996)
29. Rostami, Z., Abedi, M., Schaufeli, W., Ahmadi, A., Sadeghi, A.: The psychometric characteristics of maslach burnout inventory student survey: a study students of isfahan university. Zahedan J. Res. Med. Sci. **16**, 55–58 (2013)
30. Gallardo, T.: Prevalencia del síndrome de burnout y factores asociados a los médicos residentes de un hospital en Quit. (Universidad Internacional SEK, 2017)

31. Castañeda, C., Medina, D., Gómez, J.: Prevalencia del síndrome de burnout en el personal médico del Hospital General de Latacunga. (Universidad Regional Autónoma de los Andes, 2018)

32. Flor Calero, J., Álvarez Plua, P., Honores Calle, M.I.: Estudio del síndrome de burnout. (Escuela Superior Politécnica del Litoral, 2015)

33. Flores Díaz, J., Imbaquito Beltrán, G.: Evaluación del síndrome de Burnout en el personal médico que labora en un hospital de la ciudad de Quito-Ecuador . Revista científica de investigación del mundo de las ciencias 1 (2017)

34. Puli, L.: Prevalencia del síndrome de burnout en la unidad de emergencia del hospital general San Francisco IESS en Quito, durante la contingencia viral por el SARS-CoV-2 (COVID 19). Marzo - septiembre 2020. (Universidad Internacional SEK, 2021)

Maximum Power Extraction Techniques of Grid Connected Wind Turbines

Virendra Kumar Maurya[1](✉), J. P. Pandey[2], Chitranjan Gaur[3], and Shweta Singh[4]

[1] Department of Electrical Engineering, Maharishi University of Information Technology, Lucknow, Uttar Pradesh, India
virendrakmaurya123@gmail.com
[2] Kamla Nehru Institute of Technology, Sultanpur, Uttar Pradesh, India
[3] Suyash Institute of Information Technology, Gorakhpur, Uttar Pradesh, India
[4] Department of Electrical Engineering, Maharishi University of Information Technology, Lucknow, Uttar Pradesh, India

Abstract. In this paper, we give the main focus on the continuous advancement in the field of wind energy. Public make great attention towards the renewable energy because of rapid increase in energy demand, cost increase in electric power, limited reserves of energy, and adverse environmental impact by fossil fuels etc. At the same time on the other hand, latest technology, available low cost materials, and governmental incentives. Wind energy is one of the ultimate clean and sustainable source of energy on the Earth. By above reasons, wind become a fastest growing renewable energy resource. Here maximum power technique of wind turbines with the help of generator are used to generate electric power from wind. Here thirty three publications are given on the same topic for the quick reference to researchers.

Keywords: WECT · Wind Energy Conversion Technique · FRT · Fault Ride Through · SCIG · Squirrel Cage type Induction Generator · WRIG · Wound Rotor type Induction Generator · WRSG · Wound Rotor type Synchronous Generator · PMSG · Permanent Magnet type Synchronous Generator & DFIG · Doubly-fed Induction Generator

1 Introduction

Wind energy is going to become one ultimate source of energy out of renewable sources day by day. It is playing very important role in different fields from hundreds of years as milling, pumping, and sailing etc. the seas. A twelve kW DC generator has been developed with the help of wind mill in late nineteenth century. This was the first step to generate electricity by windmills. Over the past two decades this technology has been matured enough to produce electricity. Now, several technologies have been developed in the field of wind power, It means that conversion efficiency increases and production cost reduces [1–3]. Wind turbines are developed as per the requirement i.e. from few kilowatts to Megawatts. These are installed at offshore and onshore [4–6].

© The Author(s), under exclusive license to Springer Nature Switzerland AG 2024
M. Botto-Tobar et al. (Eds.): ICAT 2023, CCIS 2051, pp. 320–330, 2024.
https://doi.org/10.1007/978-3-031-58950-8_23

1.1 Independent Type Grid Connected WECT

This type of system is also known as stand alone type WECT. Here, wind turbines can be used as independent, low-power units to power farms, islands, and settlements in areas with difficult or expensive access to the utility grid. In stand-alone systems, additional energy sources are typically needed because wind power is not a steady source. In order to create a more dependable distributed generation (DG) system, standalone wind energy systems frequently work in tandem with energy storage units, diesel generators, or solar energy systems. Due to its restricted applications, These are rarely installed [7–10].

1.2 WECT as Per Installation [On Land/Offshore]

In this application large capacity wind farms placed on land area. These turbines have following characteristics.

- Easy construction
- Low maintenance cost

These turbines have following characteristics.

- Appropriated wind resources
- Low maintenance cost

This is especially true in places with high population densities, like parts of Europe. The fact that offshore wind speeds are frequently both much greater and more consistent than on land is another crucial factor. Wind turbines can capture more energy while they are running offshore since their energy output is proportional to the third power of wind speed.

2 Wind Turbine and Technology

Here, types & Technology of wind turbine are given.

- Horizontal axis Wind Turbines
- Vertical axis Wind Turbines
- Turbine with Fixed or variable speed [11, 12].

2.1 Horizontal Axis Wind Turbines

HAWT: As per the orientation, it is named. It is technically installed so that sufficient space is given to rotor blade to rotate in good conditions of wind. In highly populated regions like several European countries, this is especially true. The fact that offshore winds are frequently both considerably stronger and more consistent than onshore winds is another crucial factor. In light of the fact that wind turbine energy is directly related to the third power of wind speed, offshore operations allow the turbines to harness more energy.

2.2 Vertical Axis Wind Turbines

VAWT: As per the orientation, it is named. This is especially true in places with high population densities, like some European nations [13–15]. The fact that offshore wind speeds are frequently much greater and more consistent than on land is another crucial factor. Because wind turbines' energy output is directly related to the third power of wind speed, By offshore location more energy can be generated.

2.3 Turbine with Fixed or Variable Speed

As per speed concerned WECT are classified as:

- Fixed-speed WECT (constant speed turbine).
- Variable-speed WECT

Only at a specific wind speed (3 to 15 m/s) can the optimum conversion efficiency be reached; at other wind speeds, the system efficiency decreases [16]. Aerodynamic shape of blades shields the turbine from potential harm from strong gusts of wind [17–20].

3   Wind Turbine Components

Wind turbine components are given below:

- Turbine Blade (aerodynamically)
- Rotor Mechanical Brake
- Tower and Foundation
- Rotors and other parts
- Singe-blade turbines
- Pitch Mechanism
- Yaw Drive
- Generator
- Gearbox
- Sensors

According to the Bernoulli's principle, the sum of pressure energy, kinetic energy and potential energy is constant. In wind turbine as speed of a moving fluid increases, it means K.E. increases hence, as per equation the pressure decreases. [21, 22] (Fig. 1).

Vw1: speed of wind above the blade.

Vw2: speed of wind below the blade.

$$V_{w1} > V_{w2}$$
$$P_{w2} > P_{w1}$$

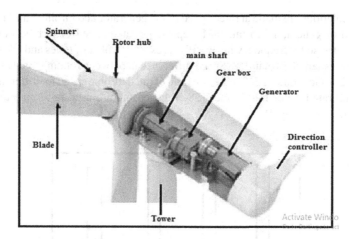

Fig. 1. Component of wind turbine

Due to the pressure difference a F_w is created on blades. F_w has a certain distance from the pivot point hence torque τ_w is developed, which creates the rotational movement of the wind turbine [24–27]. The power which is generated due to wind speed V_w can be calculated by the following formula.

$$P_w = 0.5\rho . A. (V_w)^3$$

where, 'ρ' represents air density in kg.m^{-3}. Its value is approx 1.25 kg.m^{-3}. 'A' represents sweep area by wind in m^2 and V_w represents wind speed in ms^{-1}. Speed has three power in formula so we say that speed the prominent component in all. 'C_p' represents Power coefficient of the blade, generally its value is 0.59 according to the Betz limit [23–25].

So, for mechanical power:

$$P_w = 0.5\rho . A. (Vw)^3 . C_p$$

The gearbox plays a very important role in wind turbine as per speed concerned.

$$R_{gb} = n_m/n_M = (1-s)60f_s/P.n_M$$

All calculations are made at rated speed of the generator and turbine. 'nm' represents rated speed of generator in rpm, 'nM' represents rated speed of turbine in rpm, 'fs' represents rated stator frequency in Hz, 'P' represents number of Poles and 's' represents slip which is usually less than 1% (Speed difference in between rotating magnetic field & rotor) [26–28]. Gear ratio is defined as the ratio of rated turbine speed for different number of poles and rated stator frequencies [28–30]. Sensors are used in turbine to increase efficiency [29, 30] (Fig. 2).

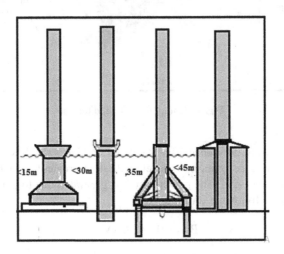

Fig. 2. Foundations for off shore wind turbines

4   Wind Energy Conversion System Configuration

Configuration of WECS are given below:

Fixed Speed SCIG: **Advantages** Initial cost is low, simple in construction &reliable. **Disadvantages** Variable wind speed effect the grid, Lowconversion efficiency.	
Semi Variable Speed type WRIG: **Advantages** High efficiency, Low mechanical stress, Lowmaintenance & Long life. **Disadvantages** High rotor loss, Low efficiency.	
Semi Variable Speed DFIG: **Advantages** Robust in operation, Good dynamic performance **Disadvantages** Fixed rated power converters, Regular maintenance of brushes.	
Full Variable Speed SCIG: **Advantages** High speed operated turbine, high efficiency, FRTcompliance good, Robust in nature. **Disadvantages** Complex in construction, High converterlosses.	
Full Varible Speed WRSG: Advantages High efficiency, Low cost**Disadvantages** High mechanical loss.	

5 Mathematical Form for Wind and Wind Turbine Power

Mathematical expression, Pwind $= 0.5 \times 3.14$. Pair. $R^2.V^3$ for wind power & wind turbine power is given here, Electric power is generated by slow speed of wind. Wind strikes the blades, creating force which will rotate the blade. By this rotation the generator generate electricity. Speed is maintained by the gear box system. WECS extracts the kinetic energy by the formula [31–33].

$$Pwind = 0.5 \times 3.14.Pair.R^2.V^3$$

Cp(coefficient called power) = Wind turbine power/wind power

$$Cp(\lambda, \beta) = C1.[C2/\lambda 1 - C3\beta - C4].e^{-(C5/\lambda 1)} + C6$$

$$1/\lambda 1 = [1/(\lambda + 0.08.\beta)] - \left[0.035/\left(\beta^3 + 1\right)\right]$$

λ	Ratio of tip speed
β	Angle between the plane of rotation and the blade
C6	0.0068
C3	0.40
C1	0.52
C4	5.00
C5	21.00
C2	116.00

The mechanical power of wind turbine produces torque, hence rotational speed [33] (Fig. 3).

$$T_m = P_m/\omega turb$$

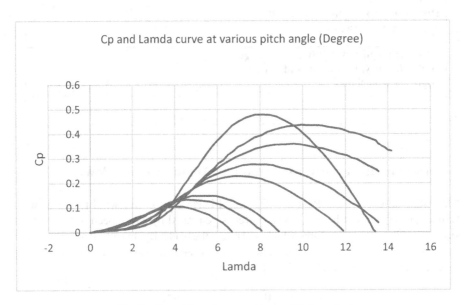

Fig. 3. Cp and Lamda curve (Acc. to Pitch angles)

6 Power Speed Characteristic of a WECT

The power-speed characteristic curve, also known as the power curve or power-wind speed curve, is a graphical representation that illustrates the relationship between the mechanical power output of a wind turbine and the wind speed at a particular location. This curve is crucial for understanding how a wind turbine performs under varying wind conditions. The wind power characteristics data for further calculation is provided by the manufacturers. Which is directly used by researchers. A prototype model of wind turbine as shown figure, which is confederate at MPPT (Fig. 4).

$$w = \lambda \; v_{wind}/R$$

$$wm = N \; x \; w \; turb$$

Power characteristic (3MW)		
1	Power speed (0–5 m/s)characteristic **Region-1**	**Cut-in wind speed:** The wind speed at which the turbine starts generating power. Below this speed, the turbine may not be producing significant power
2	Turbine power Speed (5–10 m/s)characteristic **Region-2**	**Rated wind speed:** The wind speed at which the turbine reaches its rated power output. At this point, the turbine is operating at its optimal efficiency
3	Turbine power Speed (10–20 m/s) characteristic **Region-3**	**Cut-out wind speed:** The cut-out wind speed is the maximum wind speed at which a wind turbine is designed to operate safely. Beyond this speed, the turbine goes into a shutdown or braking mode to prevent damage to the turbine components and ensure the safety of the system. This is crucial because extremely high wind speeds can put excessive stress on the turbine's structure and components, potentially leading to mechanical failure or other issues

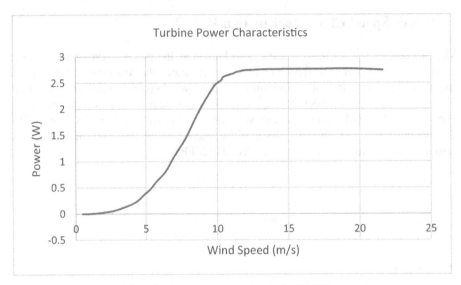

Fig. 4. Power speed characteristic (3 MW)

7 Result and Conclusion

These control strategies are designed to enhance the efficiency of wind turbine by ensuring they operate at or near their maximum power points under varying wind conditions. The specific approach chosen may depend on factors such as the turbine design, environmental conditions, and the desired balance between efficiency and stability. Power extraction of 3MW is shown in graph. Each technique aims to extract the maximum possible power from the available wind resource.

References

1. Dwivedi, R., et al.: Indian Wind Energy – A Brief Outlook, Global Wind Energy Council (2016)
2. Herbert, G.M.J., Iniyan, S., Amutha, D.: A review of technical issues on the development of wind farms. Renew. Sustain. Energy Rev. **32**, 619–641 (2014)
3. Swaminathan, C., Nagarathinam, G.: A perspective observation of power generation using wind energy and its benefits. SSRG Int. J. Ind. Eng. **3**(3), 7–11 (2016)
4. Li, K., Shi, L., McLaren, P.G.: Neural-network-based sensorless maximum wind energy capture with compensated power coefficient. IEEE Trans. Ind. Appl. **41**(6), 1548–1556 (2005)
5. Wang, W., Huang, X., Tan, L., Guo, J., Liu, H.: Optimization design of an inductive energy harvesting device for wireless power supply system overhead high-voltage power lines. Energies **9**, 242 (2016)
6. Wiggelinkhuizen, E., Verbruggen, T., Braam, H., Rademakers, L., Xiang, J., Watson, S.: Assessment of condition monitoring techniques for offshore wind farms. J. Solar Energy Eng. **130**, 031004.1–031004.9 (2008)
7. Das, D., Pan, J., Bala, S.: HVDC light for offshore wind farm integration. In: Proc. IEEE, Symp. Electron. Mech. Wind Appl. (PEMWA) pp. 1–7, July 2012

8. Flourentzou, N., Agelidis, V.G., Demetriades, G.D.: VSC-based HVDC power transmission systems: an overview. IEEE Trans. Power Electron. **24**(3), 592–602 (2009)
9. Williams, J.H., et al.: The Technology path to deep greenhouse gas emissions cuts by 2050: the pivotal role of electricity. Science **335**(6064), 53–59 (2012)
10. Flourentzou, N., Agelidis, V., Demetriades, G.: VSC-based HVDC power transmission system: an overview. IEEE Trans. Power Electron. **24**(3), 592–602 (2009)
11. Gaillard, A., Poure, P., Saadate, S.: Active filtering capability of WECS with DFIG for grid power quality improvement. In: Proc. IEEE Int. Symp. Ind. Electron., Jun. 30, 2008, pp. 2365–2370
12. Mohamed, B., Mokrani, L., Machmoum, M.: Full capability of harmonic current mitigation for a wind energy system, II Elect. Power Comp. Syst. **42**(15), 1743–1753 (2009)
13. Wang, L., Chai, S., Yoo, D., Gan, L., Ng, K.: PID and predictive control of electrical drives and power converters using Matlab/Simulink. Wiley-IEEE Press, Singapore (2015)
14. Jimichi, T., Fujita, H., Akagi, H.: A dynamic voltage restorer equipped with a highfrequency isolated DC–DC converter. IEEE Trans. Ind. Appl. **47**(1), 169–175 (2011)
15. Gee, A.M., Robinson, F., Yuan, W.: A superconducting magnetic energy storageemulator/battery supported dynamic voltage restorer. IEEE Trans. Energy Convers. **32**(1), 55–64 (2017); Yaramasu, V., Wu, B., Sen, P.C., Kouro, S., Narimani, M.: High power wind energy conversion systems: State-of-the-Art and emerging technologies. Proc. IEEE, pp. 1–49 (2015)
16. Mohseni, M., Islam, S.M., Masoum, M.A.S.: Impacts of symmetrical and asymmetrical voltage sags on DFIG–based wind Turbines considering phase–angle jump, voltage recovery, and sag parameters. IEEE Trans. Power Electron. **26**(5), 1587–1598 (2011)
17. Singh, B., Al-Haddad, K., Chandra, A.: A review of active filters for power quality improvement. IEEE Trans. Industr. Electron. **46**(5), 960–971 (1999)
18. El Ouanjli, N., Taoussi, M., Derouich, A., Chebabhi, A., El Ghzizal, A., Boussoufi, B.: High performance direct torque control of doubly fed induction motor using fuzzy logic. Gazi Univ. J. Sci. **31**(2) (2018)
19. Zheng, X., Xiao, L., Lei, Y., et al.: Optimisation of LCL filter based on closed-loop total harmonic distortion calculation model of the grid-connected inverter. IET Power Electron. **8**(6), 860–868 (2015)
20. Bao, C., Ruan, X., Wang, X., et al.: Step-by-step controller design for LCL-type grid-connected inverter with capacitor-current-feedback active-damping. IEEE Trans. Power Electron. **29**(3), 1239–1253 (2014)
21. Poddar, G., Ranganathan, V.T.: Sensorless double-inverter-fed wound-rotor induction-machine drive. IEEE Trans. Ind. Electron. **53**(1), 86–95 (2006)
22. Bossoufi, B., Karim, M., Lagrioui, A., Taoussi, M., El Hafyani, M.L.: Backstepping control of DFIG Generators for Wide-Range Variable-Speed Wind Turbines. IJAAC Int. J. Automation Control **8**(2), 22–140 (2014)
23. Mensou, S., Essadki, A., Nasser, T., Idrissi, B.B.: An efficient nonlinear backstepping controller approch of a wind power generation system based on a DFIG. Int. J. Renewable Energy Res. **7**(4), 1520–1528 (2017)
24. Zhou, D., Blaabjerg, F., Franke, T., Tonnes, M., Lau, M.: Reduced cost of reactive power in doubly fed induction generator wind turbine system with optimized grid filter. IEEE Trans. Power Electron. **30**(10), 5581–5590 (2015)
25. Rockhill, A.A., Liserre, M., Teodorescu, R., Rodriguez, P.: Gridfilter design for a multi-megawatt medium-voltage voltage-source inverter. IEEE Trans. Ind. Electron. **58**(4), 1205–1217 (2011)
26. Wu, W., He, Y., Tang, T., Blaabjerg, F.: A new design method for the passive damped LCL and LLCL Filter-based single-phase grid-tied inverter. IEEE Trans. Ind. Electron. **60**(10), 4339–4350 (2013)

27. Taoussi, M., Karim, M., Hammoumi, D., Elbakkali, C., Bossoufi, B., El Ouanjli, N.: Comparative study between Backstepping adaptive and Field-oriented control of the DFIG applied to wind turbines. In: 3rd IEEE International Conference on Advanced Technologies for Signal and Image Processing, May 2017
28. Takahashi, R., et al.: Efficiency calculation of wind turbine generation system with doubly-fed induction generator. In: Proc. Int. Conf. Electr. Mach., pp. 1–4 (2010)
29. Liserre, M., Cardenas, R., Molinas, M., Rodriguez, J.: Overview of multi-MW wind turbines and wind parks. IEEE Trans. Ind. Electron. **58**(4), 1081–1095 (2011)
30. Chehaidia, S.E., Abderezzak, A., Kherfane, H., Boukhezzar, B., Cherif, H.: An improved machine learning techniques fusion algorithm for controls advanced research Turbine (Cart) power coefficient estimation. UPB Sci. Bull. C **82**, 279–292 (2020a)
31. Fayssal, A., Chaiba, A., Mekhilef, S.: High performances of Grid- connected DFIG based on direct power control with fixed switching frequency via MPPT strategy using MRAC and Neuro-Fuzzy Control. J. Power Technol. **96**, 27–39 (2016)
32. Jiefeng, H., Zhu, J., Dorrell, D.G.: Model-predictive direct power control of doubly fed induction generators under unbalanced grid voltage conditions in wind energy applications. IET Renew. Power Gener. **8**, 687–695 (2015)
33. Vargas, R., Rodriguez, J., Rojas, C.A., Rivera, M.: Predictive control of an induction machine fed by a matrix converter with increased efficiency and reduced common mode voltage. IEEE Trans. Energy Conversion **29**(2), 473–485 (2014)

Identification of the Main Adverse Effects of Covid-19 Vaccination Among Workers in a Construction Company in the City of Guayaquil

Giannella Muriel-Granda[1], Jorge Aguirre-Iñiguez[1] , Kenny Escobar-Segovia[2(✉)] ,
Daniela Paz-Barzola[2] , and Luis Duque-Cordova[3]

[1] Universidad Espíritu Santo, Samborondón, Ecuador
{giannellamuriel,jaguirreiniguez}@uees.edu.ec
[2] Escuela Superior Politécnica del Litoral, Guayaquil, Ecuador
{kescobar,dpaz}@espol.edu.ec
[3] Universidad del Pacífico, Guayaquil, Ecuador
luis.duque@upacifico.edu.ec

Abstract. The COVID-19 disease is caused by SARS-CoV-2, which has caused an unprecedented health, economic and social crisis, globally and regionally. The objective is to identify the main adverse effects of the Covid-19 vaccination in the workers of a construction company in the city of Guayaquil-Ecuador, through Google drive forms where a questionnaire was applied that was answered individually by a sample of 215 workers of a construction company in Guayaquil. The results indicated that the symptom that predominated in this dose or booster dose was the third pain in the injection area with 14.4% and fatigue with 12.6%. 61.4% do not present any symptoms. During this year and a half since vaccination for Covid-19 began, the vaccines used to reduce serious illness have proven to be safe and effective regardless of the name of the vaccine.

Keywords: Covid-19 · vaccination · immunization · adverse events and sequelae

1 Introduction

The Covid-19 disease causes an unprecedented global and regional health, economic and social crisis [1, 2]. On March 11, 2020, the World Health Organization (WHO) declared the Covid-19 virus a global pandemic, emphasizing the need to activate and enhance emergency response mechanisms at the national level for its prevention [3]. Consequently, the Ministry of Public Health issued Ministerial Agreement No. 00126-2020, establishing a State of Health Emergency. Then, on March 13, President Moreno decreed a State of Emergency [4].

A vaccine is a biological product used as a primary prevention strategy [5]. Over the years, vaccines have become essential tool to reduce the incidence, morbidity and mortality of various infectious diseases [6]. SARS-CoV-2 is the specific virus, while

M. Botto-Tobar et al. (Eds.): ICAT 2023, CCIS 2051, pp. 331–342, 2024.
https://doi.org/10.1007/978-3-031-58950-8_24

COVID-19 is the disease that results from infection with this virus. The vaccines against SARS-CoV-2, developed in record time, considering the extensive research and development of previous vaccines over five, ten, or even more years [7] Currently, several classes of vaccines are under development for COVID-19, including nucleic acid-based vaccines, viral vector vaccines, protein subunit or peptide vaccines, and live attenuated vaccines [8, 9].

Janssen, AstraZeneca, Sputnik-V and CanSino vaccines use human and primate adenovirus vectors. Pfizer-BioNTech, Moderna and CureVac utilize mRNA technology [10]. Bharat Biotech, Sinopharm and Sinovac develop a third type of vaccine using inactivated SARS-CoV-2 complexes. All available Covid-19 vaccines, including Comirnaty (BioNTech/Pfizer), Moderna mRNA-based vaccines, Vaxrevia (AstraZeneca), and Janssen vector vaccines, provide beneficial immunity against SARS-CoV-2 infection. However, these vaccines may also cause adverse effects [11].

Symptoms associated with Pfizer vaccines include headache, vomiting, diarrhea, myalgia, arthralgia and injection site bruising. Less frequent symptoms include lymphadenopathy, anaphyllaxia or hypersensitivity (angioedema, urticaria, pruritus or exanthema), facial paralysis, insomnia, limb pain. For the Moderna vaccine, symptoms include lymphadenopathy, cephalic, rash, vomiting, diarrhea, myalgia, arthralgia, pain, and erythema at the injection site. Less frequent symptoms are facial paralysis, myocarditis, pericarditis, facial swelling, and pruritus. AstraZeneca vaccine is associated with mild transient thrombocytopenia, headache, nausea, myalgia, arthralgia, fatigue, chills, pain, hematoma, and pruritus at the injection site. Less frequent symptoms reported are hyperhidrosis, dizziness, anaphylaxis, decreased appetite, somnolence, and thrombosis syndrome with thrombocytopenia. The Johnson and Johnson vaccine reports frequent symptoms such as headache, nausea, myalgia, asthenia, fever, cough, tenderness, swelling, and pain at the injection site. Rare symptoms include sneezing, odynophagia, tremors, thrombosis syndrome with thrombocytopenia, hyperhidrosis, exanthema, and arthralgia [11].

These effects may occur in the short, medium, or long term. However, despite these adverse events, the benefits of vaccines are not solely related to interrupting virus transmission or preventing the disease altogether, but rather to reducing the likelihood of experiencing moderate or severe forms of coronavirus illness.

Health authorities in each country should report and maintain a record of adverse events associated with different vaccines [12]. This is essential for conducting a rigorous analysis to implement preventive measures, provide treatment for adverse events, and assess the safety of the vaccines used in the country. The frontline sector, comprising medical personnel, was one of the most affected groups and responsible for the distribution of vaccines [13, 14].

A year after the outbreak, the global effort has resulted in developing and distributing safe and effective vaccines endorsed by relevant health authorities. However, achieving immunization of a critical mass of the world's population, which is crucial to control the pandemic, faces a new set of challenges. These challenges include the emergence of dangerous new strains of the virus, global competition for a limited supply of doses, and public skepticism about vaccines [11]. In this scenario, only some states in the region have made rapid progress in immunizing their populations, while others face limitations in accessing doses or have not yet begun [1].

The aim of this study is to identify the main adverse effects of COVID-19 vaccination in the workers of a construction company in the city of Guayaquil, Ecuador. Through a comprehensive analysis, we aim to contribute valuable insights into the vaccine's impact on this specific workforce, shedding light on potential symptoms and experiences related to vaccination. By focusing on a localized context, this research endeavors to enhance our understanding of how COVID-19 vaccination manifests among individuals in the construction industry in Guayaquil, thereby facilitating more targeted and effective public health measures.

2 Methodology

This is a quantitative, descriptive, cross-sectional study conducted on the workers of a construction company in Ecuador during the period from February to March 2022.

The study included 215 employees of a construction company who met the inclusion criteria of having completed the full vaccination schedule for COVID-19. The inclusion criteria ensured that participants had received the entire recommended course of vaccinations. The questionnaire was distributed to all eligible workers at the company, and participation was voluntary, emphasizing the confidentiality of their responses. Data was collected using a questionnaire developed in an electronic application and shared through a digital link.

The questionnaire served as our primary data collection tool, consisting of three main sections. The first section gathered demographic information, including age, gender, occupation, and pre-existing health conditions. The second section delved into participants' vaccination history, covering the type of vaccine received, the number of doses administered, and the dates of vaccination. The third section focused on the assessment of adverse effects, encompassing the presence or absence of symptoms, specific adverse effects experienced, and the duration of these effects (short-term, medium-term, or long-term).

The questionnaire results were entered into an Excel database and analyzed using SPSS version 22.0. Descriptive statistics were employed to summarize the collected data, providing an overview of the demographic characteristics, vaccination history, and adverse effects experienced by the participants. The prevalence of adverse effects was calculated as percentages, offering insights into the most reported symptoms.

3 Results

A total of 215 workers participated in the survey. Among them, males constituted the majority with 74.9%, while females accounted for 25.1%. The age of the workers was divided into age groups, with 40% represented by workers aged 31 to 40 years. This was followed by workers aged 18 to 30 years at 31.6%, the age group between 41 to 50 years represented 19.1%, and those over 50 years old accounted for 9.3% (see Table 1).

Table 1. Sex and Age Group Distribution of Covid-19 Vaccinated Personnel.

Sex	Frequency	%
Male	161	74.9
Female	54	25.1
Total	215	100
Age group		
18–30 years	68	31.6
31–40 years	86	40.0
41–50 years	41	19.1
Over 50 years old	20	9.3
Total	215	100

Note: Personnel vaccinated with at least one Covid-19 vaccine

Table 2 shows the distribution of Personal Medical History among Vaccinated Personnel. 84.7% did not present any preexisting medical conditions, 6.5% had hypertension, while 2.8% had asthma, and 1.4% each accounting, hypothyroidism, and allergies. Other described diseases accounted for 0.5% each, included cancer, type II diabetes mellitus, lupus, gout, migraines, chronic gastritis, and polycystic ovary syndrome.

Table 2. Distribution of Personal Medical History among Vaccinated Personnel.

Personal Medical History	Frequency	%
Allegy	3	1.4
Asthma	6	2.8
Cancer	1	0.5
Hypertension	14	6.5
Type II Diabetes mellitus	1	0.5
Hypothyroidism	3	1.4
Lupus	1	0.5
Gout	1	0.5
Chronic Gastritis	1	0.5
Polycystic Ovary Syndrome	1	0.5
Migraine	1	0.5
None	182	84.7
Total	215	100

All the population under study received at least one dose of the Covid-19 vaccine. The Sinovac vaccine was the most administered, accounting for 73%, followed by the

Pfizer vaccine with 18.6%, and the AstraZeneca vaccine with 7%. The less frequently used vaccines were CanSino, Johnson & Johnson, and Moderna, each representing 0.5% of the population, as shown in Table 3.

Table 3. Distribution of the First Dose of Covid-19 Vaccines among the Population.

First Dose of Covid-19 vaccine	Frequency	%
Pfizer	40	18.6
Sinovac	157	73.0
AstraZeneca	15	7.0
CanSino	1	0.5
Jhonson y Johnson	1	0.5
Moderna	1	0.5
Total	215	100

Table 4 displays the most frequently reported symptoms. Injection site pain accounted for 25.8%, followed by fever with 13.4%. The least commonly reported symptoms were drowsiness and myalgia, each with 0.6%

Table 4. Distribution of Post-First Dose Covid-19 Vaccine Symptoms.

Post-symptoms	Frequency	%
Headache	18	5.3
Injection site pain	87	25.8
General discomfort	41	12.2
Fatigue	16	4.7
Dizziness	8	2.4
Redness at the injection site	5	1.5
Fever	45	13.4
Chills	7	2.1
Myalgia	2	0.6
Arthralgia	3	0.9
Nausea	3	0.9
Drowsiness	2	0.6
None	100	29.7
Total	337	100

Note: Each worker may experience multiple symptoms as described

The symptoms described in Table 4 were reported by the population with varying durations, with the majority experiencing symptoms for only 1 day (20.9%), while only 0.9% reported symptoms lasting for 5 or 7 days (see Table 5).

Table 5. Distribution of the number of days on which symptoms occurred following the first dose of vaccination.

Number of days with post-vaccination symptoms after the first dose	Frequency	%
None	100	46.5
1	45	20.9
2	41	19.1
3	21	9.8
4	4	1.9
5	2	0.9
7	2	0.9
Total	215	100

Table 6 shows a total of 211 individuals received the second dose of the Covid-19 vaccine, with only 4 individuals yet to receive the second dose. The Sinovac vaccine was the most commonly administered, accounting for 71.6% of the population, followed by the Pfizer vaccine with at 18.1%.

Table 6. Distribution of the Second Dose of Covid-19 Vaccines among the Population.

Second Dose of Covid-19 vaccine	Frequency	%
Pfizer	39	18.1
Sinovac	154	71.6
AstraZeneca	17	7.9
Moderna	1	0.5
None	4	1.9
Total	215	100

Table 7 exhibits the most frequently reported symptoms, with injection site pain at 23.6% and fever at 11.3%.

Regarding the duration of symptoms, 23.7% experienced symptoms for one day, and only two workers reported persistent symptoms for 7 or 9 days (see Table 8).

Table 7. Distribution of Post-Second Dose Covid-19 Vaccine Symptoms.

Post-symptoms	Frequency	%
Headache	9	3.3
Injection site pain	65	23.6
General discomfort	26	9.5
Fatigue	9	3.3
Dizziness	4	1.5
Redness at the injection site	4	1.5
Fever	31	11.3
Chills	4	1.5
Myalgia	2	0.7
Arthralgia	1	0.4
Nausea	3	1.1
None	117	42.5
Total	275	100

Table 8. Distribution of the number of days on which symptoms occurred following the second dose of vaccination.

Number of days with post-vaccination symptoms after the second dose	Frequency	%
None	111	51.6
1	51	23.7
2	24	11.2
3	22	10.2
4	3	1.4
5	2	0.9
7	1	0.5
9	1	0.5
Total	215	100

A total of 66.5% of the workers received the third dose or booster dose for Covid-19, while 33.5% still needed to receive the booster dose, as shown in Table 9. The predominant vaccine was AstraZeneca with 33.5%.

The predominant symptom in this COVID-19 booster vaccine was injection site pain with 14.4%, followed by fatigue with 12.6%. 61.4% did not experience any symptoms after receiving the vaccine, as described in Table 10.

Table 9. Distribution of patients with Covid-19 booster doses.

Booster dose for Covid-19	Frequency	%
Yes	143	66.5
No	72	33.5
Total	215	100
COVID-19 booster vaccine		
Pfizer	52	24.2
Sinovac	18	8.4
AstraZeneca	72	33.5
Moderna	1	0.5
None	72	33.5
Total	215	100

Table 10. Distribution of Post-Booster Dose Covid-19 Vaccine Symptoms.

Post-symptoms	Frequency	%
Headache	11	5.1
Injection site pain	31	14.4
General discomfort	12	5.6
Fatigue	27	12.6
Chills	1	0.5
Nausea	1	0.5
None	132	61.4
Total	215	100

The symptoms of the workers predominantly lasted for one to two days, and only 0.9% experienced symptoms for seven days, as observed in Table 11.

Table 12 shows that a group of workers still experience symptoms that vary in intensity and frequency. 0.6% persist with pain at the injection site. 0.3% each persist with fatigue, arthralgia, phlegm cough, cough, dyspnea, chest pain, and recurrent cold symptoms.

Table 11. Distribution of the number of days on which symptoms occurred following the booster dose of vaccination.

Number of days with post-vaccination symptoms after the booster dose	Frequency	%
None	131	60.9
1	36	16.7
2	27	12.6
3	16	7.4
4	3	1.4
7	2	0.9
Total	215	100

Table 12. Distribution of persisting symptoms following Covid-19 vaccination.

Persistent symptom	Frequency	%
Fatigue	1	0.3
Arthralgia	1	0.3
Recurrent cold	1	0.3
Phlegm cough	1	0.3
Cough	1	0.3
Shortness of breath	1	0.3
Chest pain	1	0.3
Injection site pain	2	0.6
Ninguno	206	95.8

4 Discussion

The findings of our study align with broader observations on the safety and effectiveness of COVID-19 vaccines globally [15, 16]. However, it's crucial to note that vaccine protection against severe illness might decrease over time, particularly in older populations, and the emergence of new variants poses challenges to vaccine efficacy.

The average age of the confirmed cases to date is 42.28 years, and the median age is 40 years. The age range of individuals who received the Covid-19 vaccine in the study was between 31 and 40 years, accounting for 40% of the population, followed by the age range of 18 to 30 years with 31.6% [17].

In general, the frequency of adverse effects is lower in individuals over 55 years old compared to younger age groups. Also, the frequency of systemic adverse effects is slightly higher with the second dose. Unlike the study, where there is a lower number of adverse events in the age group over 50 years old compared to the group under 40 years old, which has a higher concentration of workers and therefore a higher number of adverse events.

In phase 2 clinical trials, the incidence of adverse reactions was 35% for the 0.14-day regimen and 19% for the 0.28-day regimen. The most common adverse reaction was pain at the injection site, with an incidence of 26% [18].

Our study shares similarities with the study of Vanegas et Al. [19], which focused on adverse reactions among healthcare workers in Guayaquil. Both studies identified pain at the injection site as the most reported adverse effect, with a comparable incidence rate. The duration of symptoms, especially after the third dose, showed consistency between the studies. However, our study includes a broader demographic, encompassing various occupations within a construction company, providing a more comprehensive perspective on vaccine effects across different work environments.

In comparison with another study, Pérez-Tasigchana [20], which evaluated vaccine effectiveness in preventing severe outcomes, our focus on adverse effects complements the broader understanding of vaccine outcomes. While this study emphasizes the positive impact of vaccines on hospitalizations, ICU admissions, and deaths, our findings shed light on the symptomatic experiences of a specific occupational group. Together, these studies contribute to a holistic view of COVID-19 vaccination in Ecuador.

Despite the valuable insights gained, our study has limitations, including a relatively small sample size and a focus on a specific industry. Future research could expand the scope to include diverse occupational sectors and larger populations. Collaborative efforts between studies can enhance the overall comprehension of COVID-19 vaccination, addressing both safety and effectiveness.

5   Conclusions

The exploration of adverse effects stemming from Covid-19 vaccination among workers in a Guayaquil-based construction company has provided valuable insights into the safety and impact of vaccination in this specific population.

The study, encompassing 215 participants, revealed a predominantly male workforce (74.9%), with 40% falling within the 31 to 40 years age group. The comprehensive examination of the participants' personal medical history underscored that the majority (84.7%) had no preexisting medical conditions.

Vaccination patterns showcased widespread coverage, with all participants receiving at least one dose of the Covid-19 vaccine. The Sinovac vaccine emerged as the most administered (73%), followed by Pfizer (18.6%) and AstraZeneca (7%).

The meticulous analysis of reported symptoms post-vaccination unraveled injection site pain as the most prevalent (25.8%), followed by fever (13.4%). Notably, a considerable portion of the workforce (61.4%) reported no symptoms after receiving the booster dose. Symptoms, when present, typically exhibited a short duration, with the majority lasting one to two days. The persistency of symptoms beyond this timeframe was notably rare, with only 0.9% reporting symptoms lasting for seven days.

Concerning the booster dose, 66.5% of workers received it, predominantly with the AstraZeneca vaccine (33.5%). Common symptoms post-booster included injection site pain (14.4%) and fatigue (12.6%). Interestingly, the majority (61.4%) did not report any symptoms after this additional dose. A minor subset of the workforce continued to experience varied symptoms post-vaccination, underscoring the importance of ongoing monitoring.

This study contributes to the growing body of knowledge regarding Covid-19 vaccination outcomes in the construction industry. The findings underscore the safety and efficacy of the vaccines used, particularly in mitigating severe adverse effects. However, acknowledging the study's limitations, including a focused participant pool and potential technology access disparities, future research endeavors should aim for a more diverse and representative sample.

As vaccination efforts persist, continuous monitoring and research remain crucial to refining public health strategies. Future studies should delve deeper into the long-term effects and explore factors influencing ongoing symptoms, ensuring a comprehensive understanding of Covid-19 vaccination dynamics.

In essence, this study, along with concurrent research, contributes vital information to guide informed decisions in the ongoing battle against the pandemic, emphasizing the importance of tailored public health measures in diverse occupational settings like the construction industry.

References

1. Comisión Interamericana de Derechos Humanos. Las vacunas contra el COVID-19 en el marco de las obligaciones interamericanas de derechos humanos, pp. 1–13 (2021)
2. Paz-Barzola, D., et al.: The impact of COVID-19 for the Ecuadorian mining industry in 2020: risks and opportunities. Miner. Econ. (2023). https://doi.org/10.1007/s13563-023-00369-z
3. WHO. WHO Coronavirus Disease (COVID-19) Dashboard. https://covid19.who.int/ (2021)
4. UNICEF-Ecuador. Plan De Respuesta humanitaria covid-19. Naciones Unidas 1–77 (2020)
5. Asociación Colombiana de Infectología ACIN. Consenso colombiano de atención, diagnóstico y manejo de la infección por SARS-CoV-2/COVID-19 en establecimientos de atención de la salud 20 de febrero de 2021. Recomendaciones sobre vacunación contra SARS-CoV-2 (2021)
6. Villar-Álvarez, F., Martínez-García, M., Jiménez, D., Fariñas-Guerrero, F., Lejarazu-Leonardo, R.: Recomendaciones SEPAR sobre la vacuna COVID-19 en las enfermedades resiratorias. 1–32 Preprint at (2021)
7. Hann Ng, W., Liu, X., Mahalingam, S.: Development of vaccines for SARS-CoV-2. F1000Res **9**, 991 (2020)
8. Soldevilla, P., et al.: Revisión sobre las vacunas frente a SARS-CoV-2. Actualización a 31 de enero de 2021. Enf. Emerg **20**, 7–19 (2021)
9. Logunov, D.Y., et al.: Safety and efficacy of an rAd26 and rAd5 vector-based heterologous prime-boost COVID-19 vaccine: an interim analysis of a randomised controlled phase 3 trial in Russia. The Lancet **397**, 671–681 (2021)
10. Polack, F.P., et al.: Safety and efficacy of the BNT162b2 mRNA Covid-19 Vaccine. N. Engl. J. Med. **383**, 2603–2615 (2020)
11. Gómez-Marco, J.J., Álvarez-Pasquín, M.J., Martín-Martín, S.: Efectividad y seguridad de las vacunas para el SARS-CoV-2 actualmente disponibles. FMC **28**, 442–451 (2021)
12. Lozada-Requena, I., Núñez Ponce, C.: COVID-19: respuesta inmune y perspectivas terapéuticas. Rev. Peru Med. Exp. Salud Publica **37**, 312–9 (2020)

13. Gómez-Salgado, J., et al.: Sense of coherence in healthcare workers during the COVID-19 pandemic in Ecuador: association with work engagement, work environment and psychological distress factors. Int. J. Public Health **67** (2022)
14. Adanaqué-Bravo, I., et al.: Relationship between psychological distress, burnout and work engagement in workers during the COVID-19 pandemic: a systematic review. Int. J. Public Health **67** (2023)
15. Urbiztondo, L., Borràs, E., Mirada, G.: Vacunas contra el coronavirus. Vacunas **21**, 69–72 (2020)
16. Zerón, A.: Vacuna y vacunación. Revista de la Asociación Dental Mexicana **77**, 282–286 (2020)
17. Luzuriaga, J., et al.: Impact of vaccines against COVID-19 on the incidence of new SARS-COV2 infections in health care workers of the Province of Buenos Aires. Scielo5 Preprints (2021)
18. Santander, S., González, C.: FICHA VACUNA CONTRA SARS-COV-2 (2021)
19. Vanegas, E., et al.: Adverse reactions following COVID-19 vaccination: an ecuadorian experience. Annal. Med. Surg. **72**, 103044 (2021)
20. Pérez-Tasigchana, F., et al.: Effectiveness of COVID-19 vaccines in Ecuador: a test-negative design. Vaccine X **15**, 100404 (2023)

Mathematical Modeling of Anaerobic Treatment of Urban Wastewater Using Multivariate Regression

Jonathan Bravo-Moreno[1]([⊠]), Alberto León-Batallas[2], and Lohana Lema-Moreta[1]

[1] Universidad de Especialidades Espíritu Santo, Km 2.5 via Samboróndon, Guayaquil, Ecuador
jbravomoreno@uees.edu.ec

[2] Universidad Estatal de Milagro (UNEMI), Km 1.5 via Km 26, Ciudadela Universitaria, Milagro 09150, Ecuador

Abstract. This study is based on the proposal of a mathematical model that allows to know the amount of Biochemical Oxygen Demand (BOD) at the outlet of a wastewater treatment plant, to achieve this multivariate regression will be used as a strategy to obtain the parameters of the mathematical model. For this, a subjective characterization of the main variables involved in the treatment process of the wastewater plant was carried out, taking into account the information provided by the company, discriminating between the variables that do not add value and those that are derived from others. The type of method used is quantitative and the technique used to collect the information was primary. Then we proceeded to formulate the mathematical model using multivariate regression and for this the SPSS software was used, then we continued with the validation of the model, to achieve this we used the criterion of the assumptions of multivariate regression which are: assumption of normality, assumption of correlation of variables, assumption of multicollinearity, assumption of independence of errors, assumption of homoscedasticity, assumption of normality of waste. As a result and analysis of the present research, it was concluded that the mathematical model obtained is acceptable since it complies with the regression assumptions, the value of R-squared is acceptable.

Keywords: Mathematical model · Forecasts · Multivariate regression · Wastewater treatment

1 Introduction

The resulting composition of urban wastewater is highly variable, largely due to the factors that influence it, where the average consumption of water per inhabitant per day affects the concentration (quantity) and eating habits of the population that characterizes its chemical composition (quality). [2] Urban wastewater is collected by the sewer network to be transported to a treatment plant [3]. The flow rate of this wastewater usually varies during the day. When this drainage system is designed to collect wastewater and stormwater together, the input of rainwater can often far exceed the average flow rate of wastewater, resulting in high levels of wastewater dissolution and the resulting treatment difficulties [4].

© The Author(s), under exclusive license to Springer Nature Switzerland AG 2024
M. Botto-Tobar et al. (Eds.): ICAT 2023, CCIS 2051, pp. 343–355, 2024.
https://doi.org/10.1007/978-3-031-58950-8_25

The design and management of wastewater treatment plants require the assessment of wastewater quality. The main parameters evaluated were: Total Suspended Solids (TSS), Chemical Oxygen Demand (COD), Biochemical Oxygen Demand in five days (BOD5), Nutrient Content (nitrogen [N] and phosphorus [P]), Germ Content, Heavy metals [5, 6].

The models used to design and simulate wastewater treatment plants are a mathematical description of a wide range of chemical, physical, and biological processes that occur in a bounded space (reservoir and reactors) [7]. However, the fact that a model fits well with the experimental data and predicts the behavior of the system under study does not mean that the mechanisms of the model are correct from the microbial point of view [8].

In the design of wastewater treatment plants, models are expressed by mass balances taking into account the reaction kinetics and hydrodynamics of the process [9]. The development of these balance equations results in systems of differential equations that are difficult to solve, requiring the use of some program or software. This type of special platform software is called simulators [10].

[11] They present a method that allows to analyze the current state of the manufacturing processes in the company, and also serves to face the problem of variability within the process. The method proposed within his research uses the probability of the multivariate regression model, as well as data analysis.

[12] A mathematical model was developed using multivariate regression applied to the monthly consumption of drinking water in the city of Puno, the population of analysis was 19209 households, using stratified sampling with optimal fixation. For his model, he analyzed 19 independent variables, which were subjected to a selection process. The model underwent a validation process using multivariate regression.

[13] They propose a selection of which ones they consider should be the main intervening variables in the multiple linear regression model, which for this work were: Stock Exchange Capacity, Customers, Sales and Cost of Sales; Finally, he validated the model with the results obtained [14] (Table 1).

2 Material and Method

The objective of this research will be to propose an appropriate mathematical model that allows to predict in an agile way the amount of BOD in the output of a wastewater treatment plant that will be used for irrigation of a farm, in the agricultural sector in the Milagro city, using multivariate regression.

This work is longitudinal, since we are analysing what happens or what is the behaviour at different points of time of the different independent variables that could intervene within the proposal of the mathematical model.

For this research, we will work with all the data, that is 100% of the data collected by the company in the treatment of wastewater. The supplied data is 100 in size.

Variables
The dependent variable to be considered is the Amount of Biochemical Oxygen Demand at the DBO_Sal Outlet (mg/l), this data was obtained from the information provided by

the company, it corresponds to the BOD at the exit of the plant, that is, after the water has been treated, to the samples taken from a volume of 250 ml.

Table 1. Model Variable Summary

Variables	Description	Variable Type
And	DBO_Sal	Numeric – comma
X1	DBO_Ent	Numeric – comma
X2	Phosphate	Numeric – comma
X3	Nitrate	Numeric – comma

As a first approximation, 3 possible independent variables will be analyzed, and with the analysis of excluded variables, it is expected to see the degree, weight or contribution of each one that they have within the mathematical model, so that the variable that contributes very little or does not contribute to the model is not taken into account or eliminated.

a) Amount of Biochemical Oxygen Demand DBO_Ent (mg/l), at inlet.
   It is the Biochemical Amount of Oxygen Demand (BOD) that raw water has, i.e. the water that enters the treatment plant.
b) Nitratos (mg/l).
   This is the nitrate value of raw water when it enters the treatment plant. Typical values for clean water are 0.3 to 5 mg/L.
c) Stillforo P (mg/L).
   It is the value of phosphorus in the raw water at the inlet of the treatment plant. Phosphorus above 5.0 mg/L can cause nutrient deficiencies. The normal value of irrigation water should be less than 2.0 mg/L.

The characterization of the variables was carried out subjectively, taking into account the information provided directly by the microenterprise, which seeks to include the most relevant variables within the Multiple Linear Regression model.

Method, Technique and Use of Data Processing and Analysis Software
The method used is quantitative and the analysis techniques are multivariate regression or multiple linear regression, evaluating the basic assumptions of the regression model, an analysis of excluded variables will be carried out for how much it contributes to the model, that is, if any of the independent variables should be excluded; The goodness of fit is analyzed through the coefficient of determination (R^2) and the analysis of variance (ANOVA), finally the coefficients of the multivariate regression and their degree of significance for the aforementioned variables will be obtained.

The information will be processed by the statistical software IBM SPSS version 24, for the processing and analysis of the data.

Formulation of the Multiple Linear Regression Model
To perform the formulation of the mathematical model using multivariate regression as a first step, the dependent variable (Y) and the independent variables (X) must be selected, then the selection of the variables and the equation are shown.

The dependent or output variable corresponds to the Biochemical Oxygen Demand at the DBO_Sal Output, the independent variables are: Biochemical Demand of Oxygen Input DBO_Ent, Phosphate and Nitrate.

$$Y = \beta_o + \beta_1 X_1 + \beta_2 X_2 + \beta_3 X_3 \tag{1}$$

Diagnosis and Validation of the Multiple Linear Regression Model
To interpret a regression model well, we must always accompany our research with the diagnosis and validation of the model. This diagnosis includes analyzing whether the basic hypotheses of the model are verified:

- Linearity: Parameters and their interpretation are meaningless if the data does not actually come from a linear model, a situation in which predictions can also be completely wrong.
- Normality of errors: The linear regression model assumes that the distribution of the error is Normal.
- Homoscedasticity: The variance of the error is constant.
- Error independence: The random variables that represent the errors independent of each other.
- The explanatory variables X1; X2;...; Xn, are linearly independent

3 Results and Discussions

Assumption of Normal Waste
The Normality assumption aims to demonstrate that both the independent variables, as well as the dependent variable, have to be normally distributed.

Since the sample is larger than 50 data then we must use the Kolmogorov-Smirnoff test (K-S), and this test tells us that the significance has to be greater than 0.05 to say that the data correspond to a sample with normal distribution.

As can be seen in Table 2, the level of significance is 0.066; so the p-value (SIG) > 0.05; Therefore, it is demonstrated that the assumption of normality of the data is met.

As can be seen in Table 3 and Fig. 1, the assumption that the waste has a normal distribution is accepted.

Detection of atypical residues: for the detection of the standard values we use the criterion that these values must be between −3 and 3.

Table 3 presents a table of residue statistics, in which it has been verified that there are no outliers, because the maximum and minimum values of the standardized residues are less than 3 in absolute value.

Normal Distribution of Waste
To verify the assumption of normality of the residues, the normal P-P regression test Standardized Residue was performed, the results are shown below.

Table 2. Kolmogorov-Smirnov test for a sample

		Standardized Residual
N		100
Normal parameters[des,b]	Stocking	0,0000000
	Standard deviation	0,98473193
Maximum Extreme Differences	Absolute	0,066
	Positive	0,043
	Negative	−0,066
Test Statistician		0,066
Asymptotic (bilateral) sig.		, 200[c,d]

to. Test distribution is normal.
b. It is calculated from data.
c. Correction of Lilliefors' significance.
d. This is a lower limit of true significance.

	Hipótesis nula	Prueba	Sig.	Decisión
1	La distribución de Standardized Residual es normal con la media -0,00000 y la desviación estándar 0,985.	Prueba de Kolmogorov-Smirnov para una muestra	,200[1,2]	Retener la hipótesis nula.

Se muestran significaciones asintóticas. El nivel de significación es de ,05.

[1]Lilliefors corregida

[2]Se trata de un límite inferior de la significancia real.

Fig. 1. Hypothesis Testing Summary

Figure 2 shows a P-P diagram comparing the cumulative frequency of the typed residuals with the probability expected under the normality hypothesis.

Residuals do not appear to have a problematic relationship with predictor variables or predicted values. The P-P graph shows that the residuals, although slightly skewed, are distributed roughly like a normal distribution. Consequently, the assumption of normal waste is verified reasonably well. This further suggests that the model is well specified.

Assumption of Independence of Observations
To answer the assumption of error independence, the Durbin-Watson test is used. The criterion for saying that there is independence of observations is that the Durbin-Watson value must be as close as possible to 2 with an oscillation of ±1. Therefore, values between 1 and 3 are fine, to accept that the residuals are independent.

To answer the assumption of error independence, the Durbin-Watson test is used. The criterion for saying that there is independence of observations is that the Durbin-Watson value must be as close as possible to 2 with an oscillation of ±1. Therefore, values between 1 and 3 are fine, to accept that the residuals are independent.

Table 3. Waste statistics[to]

	Minimal	Maximum	Media	Standard deviation	N
Forecasted Value	7,9867	14,4941	11,8400	1,59832	100
Standard Forecasted Value	−2,423	1,648	0,000	1,000	100
Predicted Value Standard Error	0,065	0,249	0,123	0,034	100
Corrected Forecast Value	7,9852	14,5139	11,8600	1,59909	100
Residue	−1,64901	1,71503	0,00000	0,62872	100
Standard Waste	−2,583	2,686	0,000	0,985	100
Studentized waste	−2,645	2,726	0,000	1,004	100
Waste Eliminated	−1,72908	1,76678	0,00003	0,65379	100
Studentized waste suppressed	−2,732	2,824	−0,001	1,016	100
Distance from Mahal	0,044	14,052	2,970	2,246	100
Cook's Distance	0,000	0,085	0,010	0,016	100
Focused Influence Value	0,000	0,142	0,030	0,023	100

a. Dependent variable: DBO_Sal

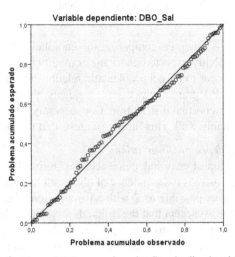

Variable dependiente: DBO_Sal

Fig. 2. Normal P-P regression plot Standardized residual

Table 4. Waste statistics[a]

Model	R	R-squared	Adjusted R-squared	Standard Estimation Error	Durbin-Watson
1	0.931 A	0,866	0,862	0,63846	1,755

a. Predictors: (Constant), Nitrate, Phosphate, DBO_Ent
b. Dependent variable: DBO_Sal

Table 5. Correlations

		DBO_Ent	Phosphate	Nitrate	DBO_Sal
DBO_Ent	Pearson's correlation	1	0,656[**]	0,601[**]	0,819[**]
	Sig. (bilateral)		0,000	0,000	0,000
	N	100	100	100	100
Phosphate	Pearson's correlation	0,656[**]	1	0,445[**]	0,789[**]
	Sig. (bilateral)	0,000		0,000	0,000
	N	100	100	100	100
Nitrate	Pearson's correlation	0,601[**]	0,445[**]	1	0,746[**]
	Sig. (bilateral)	0,000	0,000		0,000
	N	100	100	100	100
DBO_Sal	Pearson's correlation	0,819[**]	0,789[**]	0,746[**]	1
	Sig. (bilateral)	0,000	0,000	0,000	
	N	100	100	100	100

**The correlation is significant at the 0.01 level (two-sided)

Table 4 shows that the Durbin-Watson coefficient has a value of 1.755; which is an acceptable value very close to 2, so the assumption of independence of the observations is satisfied.

Assumption of Homoscedasticity
Homoscedasticity is a feature of a linear regression model that implies that the variance of the error is constant over time. Also, if a variance, in addition to being constant, also smaller, this would lead to a more reliable model prediction.

The assumption of homoscedasticity will be answered graphically; To do this, the residues must be distributed homoscedastically along the predicted scores.

From the scatter plot examination in Fig. 3, it can be seen that there is no systematic relationship between the typified residuals and the typified predicted values of Biochemical Output Oxygen Demand. Therefore, we can consider the assumption regarding the homoscedastity of the data to be fulfilled.

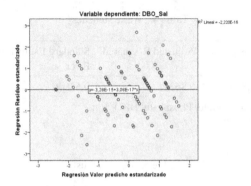

Fig. 3. Scatter Plot

Assumption of Linearity

The assumption of linearity implies that the relationship between the dependent variable and the independent variables must be linear (Table 5).

As can be seen in Table 10 of correlation, there is a positive correlation between the input variables and the output variable. The matrix shows that all correlation values are positive and greater than 0.6; So we can conclude that the independent variables are highly correlated with the dependent variable, and that this correlation is positive.

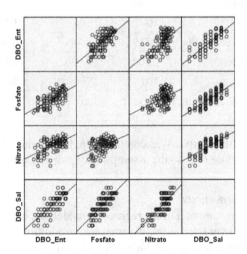

Fig. 4. Correlation of variables

As can be seen in Fig. 4, the assumption of linearity between the dependent variable and the independent variables is fulfilled, and it can be seen in the figure that there is a positive correlation between the variables, some with a correlation closer to 1 than others.

Multicollinearity Assumption

For the diagnosis of collinearity, the FIV (inflated variance factor) will be used, this assumption is to know whether or not there is multicollinearity between the independent variables. No independent variable can be above 10, otherwise there is multicollinearity between the variables.

As can be seen in Table 10, for the present multivariate regression model, no FIV value is greater than 10.

In this case, as we are going to work with the collinearity diagnostics matrix, the following steps must be followed:

1. Identify indices that are above the threshold: 30
2. For the indices identified, identify variables with variance ratios above 90%: There will be multicollinearity if it occurs with two or more coefficients.

Table 6. Collinearity diagnostics[a]

Model	Dimension	Self-Value	Condition Index	Variance ratios			
				(Constant)	DBO_Ent	Phosphate	Nitrate
1	1	3,955	1,000	0,00	0,00	0,00	0,00
	2	0,028	11,925	0,11	0,28	0,09	0,02
	3	0,014	16,700	0,00	0,50	0,90	0,01
	4	0,003	34,421	0,89	0,22	0,01	0,96

to. Dependent variable: DBO_Sal

As can be seen in Table 6, in the condition index there is a single value greater than 30 which is 34.421, and in the Variance Proportions there is also a single value greater than 90% which is Nitrate with 0.96.

It can be concluded that there is no multicollinearity since this with two or more variables.

The Mathematical Model of Multivariate Regression

The R-squared value is the coefficient of determination, which ranges from 0 to 1 is 0 to 100%, this means that with the variables you have you can only predict a % of the linear equation.

It should be remembered that the adjusted R-squared takes into account the number of independent variables that are used to predict the dependent variable.

Model 1.- In this model we worked with three independent variables: the biochemical oxygen demand at the input, phosphate and potassium, as observed in this model the R^2 of 0.866, which means that with these three independent variables we can already explain 86.6% of the variance; and we have an adjusted R^2 of 86.2%

As can be seen, it is supported to work with a Mathematical Model with 3 variables, since it presents a better fit to reality, and the 3 selected variables contribute positively to the prediction of the dependent variable.

Table 7 is an analysis of the test of variance showing whether the variance

Table 7. ANOVA[a]

Model		Sum of squares	Gl	Quadratic mean	F	Say.
1	Regression	252,907	3	84,302	206,807	0,000[b]
	Residue	39,133	96	0,408		
	Total	292,040	99			

a. Dependent variable: DBO_Sal
b. Predictors: (Constant), Nitrate, Phosphate, DBO_Ent

The regression variance is significantly different from the unexplained variance.

The mathematical model used has a value of the test statistic $F = 206,807$ and has a P_ value equal to $0 < 0.05$, so the null hypothesis is rejected and it is concluded that the linear dependence is statistically significant so the model is adequate.

Table 8. Coefficients

Model		Standardized coefficients		Standardized coefficients	t	Say.	Collinearity Statistics	
		B	Standard Error	Beta			Tolerance	BRIGHT
1	(Constant)	−1,003	0,717		−1,399	0,165		
	DBO_Ent	0,040	0,007	0,331	5,951	0,000	0,450	2,222
	Phosphate	0,302	0,037	0,409	8,229	0,000	0,565	1,770
	Nitrate	0,862	0,111	0,365	7,769	0,000	0,634	1,577

a. Dependent variable: DBO_Sal

Taking into account the results in Table 8, it can be deduced that the regression equation is:

$$Y = -1,003 + 0,040X_1 + 0,302X_2 + 0,862X_3 \tag{2}$$

As shown in Eq. (2), it has been possible to construct an equation that allows predicting the amount of DBO_Sal based on three input variables.

Standardized regression Eq. (3) shows the variables in the same dimension as follows:

$$Z = 0,331Z_1 + 0,409Z_2 + 0,365Z_3 \tag{3}$$

Comparing Actuals to Forecasted Data

Next, the actual DBO_Sal data is compared with the data obtained with the mathematical model proposed DBO_Sal_P-RM.

As can be seen in Table 9, the mean of the data obtained with the mathematical model is 11.83, and the mean of the actual data observed is 11.86, these means are very

Table 9. Paired Sample Statistics

		Media	N	Standard deviation	Standard Error Mean
Pair 1	DBO_Sal_P-RM	11,8306	100	1,59306	0,15931
	DBO_Sal	11,8600	100	1,71753	0,17175

Table 10. Testing Paired Samples

		Paired Differences								Sig. (bilateral)
		Media	Standard deviation	Standard Error Mean	95% Difference Confidence Interval					
					Inferior	Superior	t		gl	
Pair 1	DBO_Sal_RM - DBO_Sal	−0,02943	0,62874	0,06287	−0,15418	0,09533	−0,468	99	0,641	

similar or similar, so that as there is a very small difference between them, it can be said that the mathematical model is quite good.

As can be seen in Table 10, the even difference between the means is very low, − 0.02943, which can be said to be the error made with the proposed mathematical model.

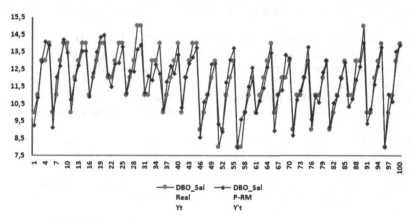

Fig. 5. Comparison Between Real DBO_Sal vs DBO_Sal P-RM

As can be seen in Fig. 5, a visual comparison is made between the real values obtained at the exit of the treatment plant represented by Real DBO_Sal, with the values obtained through the use of the mathematical model proposed by means of multivariate regression DBO_Sal P-RM.

You can see that the model has a very good approximation, a good fit, so it can be said that the model serves to predict.

4 Conclusions

The factors influencing the control of the urban wastewater treatment plant that have been identified for this case study are the following variables: biochemical oxygen demand at the outlet of the wastewater treatment plant DBO_Sal; biochemical oxygen demand at the inlet of the DBO_Ent wastewater treatment plant; phosphates and nitrates.

An analysis of the incidence of each factor that affects the control of an urban wastewater treatment plant was carried out, which is reflected in Table 8, where the mathematical model is later reflected.

The multivariate regression model was formulated taking into account the selected independent variables, then the data were entered into the SPSS program, and the model analysis was carried out using the 5 assumptions of the multivariate regressions.

It is concluded through the validation of the molding that, for the water treatment plant, with the use of the selected variables biochemical demand of oxygen at the inlet, phosphate and nitrate, these allow predicting a model with a significant relationship of 86.69%.

References

1. Bedoya-Urrego, K., Acevedo-Ruíz, J.M., Peláez-Jaramillo, C.A., Agudelo-López, S.d.P.: Characterization of biosolids generated in the San Fernando wastewater treatment plant, Itagüí (Antioquia, Colombia). Revista de Salud Pública 15(5), 778–790 (2013)
2. Rojas, R.: Wastewater treatment systems. Integr. Manag. Wastewater Treatment 1(1), 8–15 (2002)
3. Díaz-Cuenca, E., Alavarado-Granados, A.R., Camacho-Calzada, K.E.: Domestic wastewater treatment for sustainable local development: the case of the technique of the unitary system for the treatment of water, nutrients and energy (SUTRANE) in San Miguel Almaya. Quivera 14(1), 78–97 (2012)
4. Aragonez González, M.P.: Thermogravimetric Analysis of the Pyrolysis of Biosolids from the El Salitre Wastewater Treatment Plant, Department of Chemical and Environmental Engineering (2015)
5. Bejarano Novoa, M.E., Escobar Carvajal, M.: Efficiency of the use of microorganisms for domestic wastewater treatment in a wastewater treatment plant. De La Salle University. Faculty of Engineering. Environmental and Sanitary Engineering (2015)
6. Hernández, D., Sánchez, S.: Design of a wastewater treatment plant for the municipality of San Marcos-department of Sucre. Universidad Católica de Colombia. Faculty of Engineering. Civil Engineering Program, Bogotá (2014)
7. Gaibor Chávez, J.A.: Characterization of the wastewater generated in the El Salirito dairy plant – Salinas Parish – Guaranda Canton for the design of a treatment plant. Revista de Investigación Talentos 1(1), 107–112 (2014)
8. Carreño Sayago, U.F., Méndez Sayago, J.A.: Estimation of the reliability of wastewater treatment plants operating with stabilization lagoons in the upper and middle Bogotá River Basin. Nat. Resour. Environ. Eng. 10, 56–64 (2011)
9. Tchobanoglous, G., Burton, F.L.: Wastewater Engineering: Treatment Disposal Reuse, 3rd edn. McGraw-Hill, Singapore (1991)
10. Sánchez Ramírez, J.E., Mejía Fajardo, A., Amorocho Cruz, C.M.: Engineering software specialized in the design and simulation of wastewater treatment plants: review. Revista Ingeniería y Región 13(1), 57–71 (2015)

11. Limones Lara, J.A.: Method for the control of defective production within the metal form-ing process. ZF Sachs Automotive Mexico Case, Mexican Materials Research Corporation, Saltillo (2012)
12. Montoya Valer, S.K.: Socioeconomic factors that affect domestic consumption of drinking water using multiple regression, Universidad Nacional del Altiplano, Puno (2017)
13. Martínez-López, Y., García, M.M., Bello Pérez, R., Falcón Martínez, R., Cabrera Bermúdez, X.: Expert system for wastewater treatment (SECTRARES). Revista Ingeniería Agrícola **4**(3), 51–55 (2014)
14. Forero Gómez, G., Martínez Lozano, J.A.: Multiple linear regression model for the forecast of sales of ecological bags for the company Boleco S.A., in the city of Bogota D.C., Universidad Cooperativa de Colimbia, Bogotá (2020)

Comparative Study on Modern Techniques for Maximum Power Extraction of Solar and Wind Energy Systems

Itisha Singh[1][(✉)], J. P. Pandey[2], Chitranjan Gaur[3], and Shweta Singh[1]

[1] Department of Electrical Engineering, Maharishi University of Information Technology, Lucknow, Uttar Pradesh, India
vkm629@gmail.com
[2] Kamla Nehru Institute of Technology, Sultanpur, Uttar Pradesh, India
[3] Suyash Institute of Information Technology, Gorakhpur, Uttar Pradesh, India

Abstract. In this paper, we give the main focus on the comparative study on Modern Techniques used for Maximum Power Extraction of Solar and Wind Energy Systems. A prototype model has been made for Solar and Wind, Results are compared with lookup table. We have also discuss regarding advantages, disadvantages and applications of renewable energy. 26 publications on this topic are here for the quick reference.

Keywords: Current-Voltage (I-V) · Maximum Power Point (MPP) · Photovoltaic (PV) · Wind Energy Converters System (WECS)

1 Solar Energy

Solar energy is indeed a clean, cheap, and abundantly available renewable energy source. It is harnessed from the sun's radiation and can be converted into electricity or used directly for heating purposes. While solar energy has numerous advantages, it also presents some challenges, including the cyclic nature of its availability and relatively low power density. Power density varies from 0 to 1 kW/m^2 i.e. in defused form, and affected by the following factors like atmospheric clarity, degree of latitude and location etc. Array is needed due to defusing nature. [1, 2] For designing a solar modal, it is necessary to have the knowledge of following factors.

- Solar Power Variation
- Orientation of the solar panels
- Location of Solar plant
- Tilt angle

M. Botto-Tobar et al. (Eds.): ICAT 2023, CCIS 2051, pp. 356–366, 2024.
https://doi.org/10.1007/978-3-031-58950-8_26

1.1 Photovoltaic Module Array Characteristics

I-V curve is the characteristics of photovoltaic module array. Its performance & characteristics depends on the following:

- Materials
- Manufacturing technology
- Operating conditions etc.

1.2 Maximum Power Point Tracker Technique (MPPTT)

This is a characteristics i.e. I-V curve of the PV module, simulated with the MATLAB tool. In the curve there is a point known as knee point, here maximum power is obtained, this point is known as maximum power extraction point [3, 4].

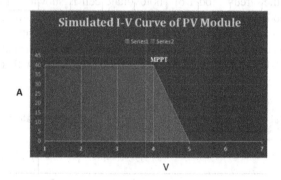

Fig. 1. Simulated I-V Curve of PV Module

Extracted power varies according to the value of solar radiation, At day time, solar radiation increase so output current increases, the horizontal part of the curve moves upward, it means more generation of power on other hand (vice versa) it produces the opposite effect [5]. The I-V curves indicate photovoltaic response for all possible loads. Its characteristics is shown in Fig. 1.

- Absolutely, you've highlighted a crucial concept in solar power systems known as Maximum Power Point Tracking (MPPT). The output power of a photovoltaic (PV) module is highly dependent on its operating conditions, such as sunlight intensity, temperature, and load characteristics. The MPPT is the point at which the PV module operates to produce the maximum possible power for a given set of conditions (Fig. 2).

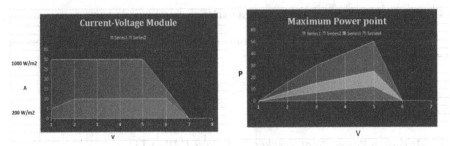

Fig. 2. 200 to 1000 W/m² solar radiation curves at Tf = 25⁰ (0 to 75 ⁰C temperature curves at solar radiation Eo = 1kW/m²)

1.3 Modeling and Simulation

Here in Fig. 3, the circuit model of photovoltaic cell is shown, which is made with the help of a Diode which is connected in parallel with current source [6, 7]. Circuit is simulated as shown in Fig. 4. Corresponding equations are written over here. In the equations, Vpv is considered as input voltage and Ipv is as o/p current. By running the MATLAB model, I-V & P-V characteristics are piloted at MPPT with different isolation levels [8, 9] (Table 1).

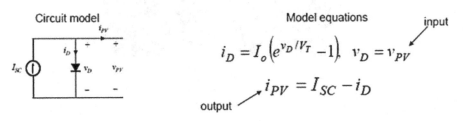

Fig. 3. Model of PV Cell

$$i_{PV} = I_{SC} - i_D$$

where:
   Ipv = Output current
   Isc = Current (Solar radiation)
   ID = Diode current

2 Wind Energy

Wind energy is playing an increasingly important role in meeting this demand. Wind power is a clean and abundant source of renewable energy that harnesses the kinetic energy of moving air to generate electricity. Here are some key points about wind energy [10, 11].

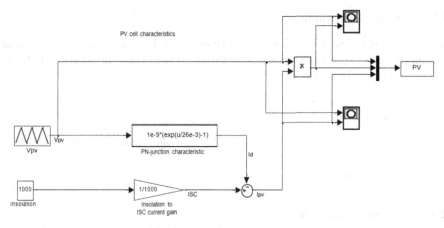

Fig. 4. Modeling of Solar Cell

Table 1. I-V and P-V characteristic plots at the different isolation levels (radiation). i.e. 1.000, 0.800 and 0.600 kW/m^2.

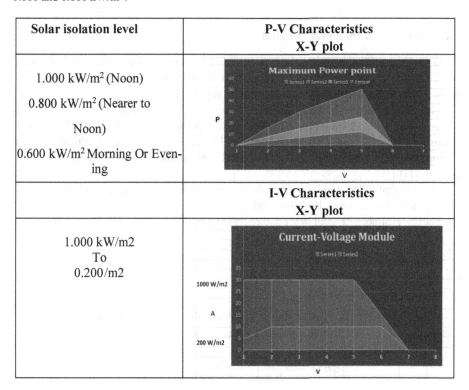

Solar isolation level	P-V Characteristics X-Y plot
1.000 kW/m^2 (Noon) 0.800 kW/m^2 (Nearer to Noon) 0.600 kW/m^2 Morning Or Evening	
	I-V Characteristics X-Y plot
1.000 kW/m2 To 0.200/m2	

2.1 Clean and Renewable

Wind energy is a clean and renewable source of power. It produces electricity without emitting greenhouse gases or other air pollutants, contributing to efforts to mitigate climate change and reduce environmental impact.

2.2 Abundant Resource

Wind is an abundant resource available on Earth. Wind turbines can be deployed in various locations, including onshore and offshore, to take advantage of different wind patterns and intensities [12, 13].

2.3 Wind Speed Variation

The speed of wind varies widely, and the power output of a wind turbine is proportional to the cube of the wind speed. Therefore, higher wind speeds result in significantly more power generation. Wind turbines are designed to capture energy efficiently across a range of wind speeds [14].

2.4 Power Generation and Demand

Wind power contributes to meeting the increasing demand for electricity. Wind farms consist of multiple wind turbines connected to the grid, and their combined output can make a significant impact on a region's power supply [15].

The global electrical energy demand is increasing day by day. Rise in demand as power generation, transmission, distribution and utilization can be meet by wind energy because at MPPT amount of energy that can be extracted from the 0–100 m layer of air has been found to be of the order of 1012 KWh/annum, which is alike hydroelectric potential [16].

Since stopping the wind would prohibit more air from passing through the rotor, it is not practical to harness all of the wind's energy.

Energy available in wind is kinetic energy:

$Pa = \frac{1}{2} \alpha . A . V^3$ (Watts)
V = Wind speed (m/s)
α = Air density (kg/m^3)
A = Swept area by rotor (m^2)

Power coefficient (Cp), describes the fraction of the power in the wind that may be converted by the wind turbine into mechanical work.

$$Cp = \frac{Power\ output\ from\ Wind\ Turbine}{Power\ available\ in\ wind}$$

Wind Speed, Cross-section of wind swept by rotor and Conversion efficiency of the rotor are three factors used for determining the power from wind turbine system [17, 18].

2.5 Technological Advances

Ongoing technological advancements in wind turbine design and materials have led to more efficient and cost-effective systems. Taller towers, larger rotor diameters, and improvements in materials and manufacturing processes have contributed to increased energy capture and reduced costs.

2.6 Grid Integration

The integration of wind power into electricity grids requires careful planning to manage the intermittent nature of wind. Energy storage, smart grid technologies, and advanced forecasting methods help balance supply and demand and ensure a stable grid [19].

2.7 Economic Benefits

Wind energy projects contribute to job creation, economic development, and energy independence. They can stimulate local economies through manufacturing, installation, and maintenance activities associated with wind turbines [20].

2.8 Environmental Considerations

While wind energy is environmentally friendly compared to many conventional energy sources, it's essential to consider potential environmental impacts, such as habitat disruption and effects on bird and bat populations. Proper site selection and impact assessments are crucial in minimizing these concerns. As the demand for power generation continues to rise, wind energy, along with other renewable sources, plays a vital role in diversifying the energy mix and moving towards a more sustainable and low-carbon future. Advances in wind power technology and increased investments in renewable energy infrastructure contribute to the ongoing growth and development of the wind energy sector [21, 22].

2.9 Mathematical Representation of Wind Energy and Turbine Energy

A wind turbine uses the wind to capture kinetic energy from the air by revolving its blades at a low speed, which the machine then converts into energy (WECS) [23, 24] (Fig. 5).

$$P_{wind} = 0.5 \cdot \rho_{air} \cdot \pi \cdot R^2 \cdot V_{wind}^3$$

Where:

P_{wind} = Power of wind
ρ_{air} = Density of air = 1.226 Kgm^{-3} (approx.)
R = Radius of turbine blade (in m)
V_{wind} = speed of wind in ms^{-1}.
ω = Angular speed of wind turbine in rpm
Cp = Value given by the manufacturers

$$T_m = P_m / \omega_{turb}$$

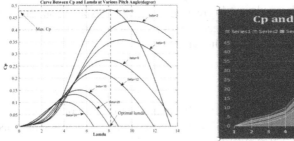 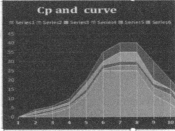

Fig. 5. Cp and λ curve (λ = tip speed ratio for different pitch angles)

2.10 Classification of Wind Energy Conversion Technology

A thorough simulation model is necessary in order to provide a workable and accurate analysis for a system. The type and objectives of the intended study will determine the amount of information needed, therefore some parameters can be omitted to speed up computation and cut down on time. Depending on the kind of wind energy converter that is being simulated, the model varies [25, 26].

There are four types of wind energy converters (WEC), and these are classified according to the capability of controlling the rotational speed as shown in figures (Figs. 6, 7, 8 and 9).

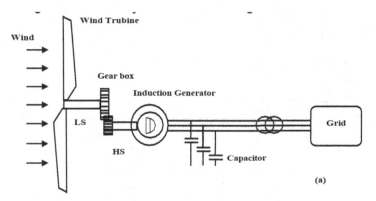

Fig. 6. Type1: Fixed Speed WECs without Power Converter Interface using squirrel cage induction generator.

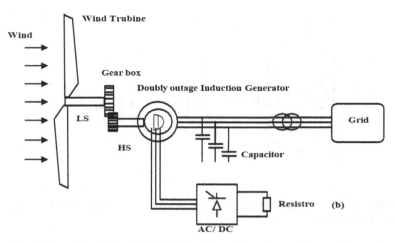

Fig. 7. Type-2: Speed (partial variable) WEC with variable rotor resistance using squirrel cage induction generator.

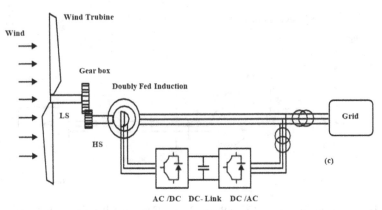

Fig. 8. Type-3: Variable Speed System with reduced capacity converter using Doubly Fed Induction Generator.

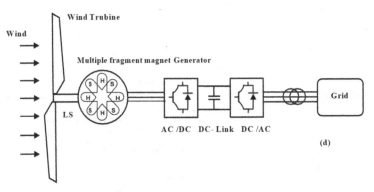

Fig. 9. Type 4: Variable Speed System with full capacity converter using Permanent Magnet Synchronous Generator.

3 Conclusion

Comparative study has been done over here in between solar & wind. Operation points of solar and wind curve are analyzed for maximum power extraction. I-V characteristic and P-V characteristic of solar system are piloted at the different solar radiation i.e. 1000 W/m², 800 W/m², 600 W/m². It has been analyzed and found that 1000 W/m² gives the best response i.e. maximum output, on the other hand several types of WECSs are discussed. In both cases rms value of output voltage is 215 V (Approx.) and this value remains constant in spite of the load fluctuation.

References

1. Elmitwally, A., Abdelkader, S., Elkateb, M.: Performance evaluation of fuzzy controlled three and four wireshunt active power conditioners. In: IEEE Power Engineering Society Winter Meeting, 23–27 January 2000, vol. 3, pp. 1650–1655 (2000)

2. Vinothkumar, V., Kanimozhi, R.: Power quality improvement by PV integrated UPQC using multi-level inverter with resilient back propagation neural network approach. J. Intell. Fuzzy Syst. Preprint, 1–18 (2022)
3. Rastegar, F., Paydar, Z.: Improving the performance of unified power quality conditioner using interval type 2 fuzzy control. In: 2022 30th International Conference on Electrical Engineering (ICEE), pp. 437–441. IEEE (2022)
4. Rechka, S., Ngandui, E., Xu, J., Sicard, P.: A comparative study of harmonic detection algorithms for active filters and hybrid active filters. In: IEEE 33rd Annual Power Electronics Specialists Conference, vol. 1, pp. 357–363 (2002)
5. Shang, Y., Wu, A.: TS-Fuzzy-controlled shunt active- power filter for power quality improvement. In: International Conference on Electrical and Control Engineering, pp. 1869–1872
6. Hamadi, A., Al-Haddad, K., Rahmani, S., Kanaan, H.: Comparison of fuzzy logic and proportional integral controller of voltage source active filter compensating current harmonics and power factor. In: IEEE International Conference on Industrial Technology, pp. 645–650 (2004)
7. Liu, J., Zanchetta, P., Degano, M., Lavopa, E.: Control design and implementation for high performance shunt active filters in aircraft power grids. IEEE Trans. Industr. Electron. **59**(9), 3604–3613 (2012)
8. Jou, H.L., Wu, J.C., Chu, H.Y.: New single-phase active power filter. In: Proceedings of the Institution of Electrical Engineers-Electric Power Applications, vol. 141, no. 3, pp. 129–134, May 1994
9. Mojiri, M., Bakhshai, A.R.: An adaptive notch filter for frequency estimation of a periodic signal. IEEE Trans. Autom. Control **49**(2), 314–318 (2004)
10. Komurcugil, H., Kulkrer, O.: A new control strategy for single phase shunt active power filters using a Lyapunov function. IEEE Trans. Ind. Electron. **53**(1) (2006)
11. Salam, Z., Awang, T.A.: Harmonics mitigation using active power filter: a technological review Faculty of Electrical Engineering Universiti Teknologi Malaysia. Elektrika **8**(2), 17–26 (2006)
12. Peng, F.-Z., Ott, G.W., Adams, D.J.: Harmonic and reactive power compensation based on the generalized instantaneous reactive power theory for three-phase four-wire systems. IEEE Trans. Power Electron. **13**(6), 1174–1181 (1998)
13. Singh, B., Verma, V., Chandra, A., Al-Haddad, K.: "Hybrid filters for power quality improvement" IEE Proceedings-Generation. Transm. Distrib. **152**(3), 365–378 (2005)
14. Balasubramaniam, P., Prabha, S., et al.: Power quality issues, solutions and standards: a technology review. J. Appl. Sci. Eng. **18**(4), 371–380 (2015)
15. Abdel Aziz, M.M., Abou El-Zahab, E.E.-D., Zobaa, A.F., Khorshied, D.M.: Passive harmonic filters design using Fortran feasible sequential quadratic programming. Electric Power Syst. Res. **77**(5–6), 540–547 (2007)
16. Pucci, M., Vitale, M., Miraoui, A.G.: Current harmonic compensation by a single-phase shunt active power filter controlled by adaptive neural filtering. IEEE Trans. Ind. Electron. **56**, 3128–3143 (2009)
17. Singh, K.-H., Chandra, A.: A review of active filters for power quality improvement. IEEE Trans. Industr. Electron. **46**(5), 1–12 (1999)
18. Salam, Z., Tan, P.C., Jusoh, A.: "Harmonics mitigation using active power filter: a technological review", harmonics mitigation using active power filter: a technological review. Elektrika J. Electr. Eng. **8**, 17–26 (2006)
19. Watanabe, E.H., Stephan, R.M., Aredes, M.: New concepts of instantaneous active and reactive powers in electrical systems with generic loads. IEEE Trans. Power Delivery **8**(2), 697–703 (1993)
20. Afonso, J.L., Silva, H.R., Martins, J.S.: Active filters for power quality improvement. In: IEEE Power Technology 2001, Porto, Portugal, 10–13 September 2001

21. Jain, S.K., Agrawal, P., Gupta, H.O.: Design simulation and experimental investigations on a shunt active power filter for harmonics and reactive power compensation. In: Electric Power and Components and Systems, pp. 671–692. Taylor & Francis Inc. (2003)

22. Mattavelli, P., Marafao, F.P.: Repetitive based control for selective harmonic compensation in active power filters. IEEE Trans. Industr. Electron. **51**(5), 1018–1024 (2004)

23. Mahela, O.P., Shaik, A.G.: Topological aspects of power quality improvement techniques: a comprehensive overview. Renew. Sustain. Energy Rev. **58**, 1129–1142 (2016)

24. Matsuo, H., Lin, W., Kurokawa, F., Shigemizu, T., Watanabe, N.: Characteristic of the multiple-input dc-dc converter. IEEE Trans. Ind. Electron. **51**(3), 625–631 (2004)

25. Wang, K., Lin, C., Zhu, L., Qu, D., Lee, F., Lai, J.: Bi-directional DC to DC converters for fuel cell systems. In: Proceedings of the IEEE Workshop Power Electronics in Transportation, Dearborn, MI, USA, October 1998, pp. 47–51 (1998)

26. Su, G.J., Peng, F.Z.: A low cost, triple-voltage bus DC-DC converter for automotive applications. In: Proceedings of the IEEE Applied Power Electronics Conference and Exposition (APEC), March 2005, vol. 2, pp. 1015–1021 (2005)

Author Index

M. Botto-Tobar et al. (Eds.): ICAT 2023, CCIS 2051, pp. 367–369, 2024.
https://doi.org/10.1007/978-3-031-58950-8